EXECUTION FOR DUTY

EXECUTION FOR DUTY

The Life, Trial and Murder of a U-boat Captain

by

Peter C. Hansen

Pen & Sword
MARITIME

First published in Great Britain in 2005 by
Pen & Sword Maritime
an imprint of
Pen & Sword Books Ltd

Copyright © Peter C. Hansen, 2005

ISBN 1 84415 322 3

A CIP catalogue record for this book is
available from the British Library

Typeset in Sabon by
Phoenix Typesetting, Auldgirth, Dumfriesshire

Printed and bound in England by
CPI UK

Pen & Sword Books Ltd incorporates the Imprints of Pen & Sword Aviation, Pen
& Sword Maritime, Pen & Sword Military, Wharncliffe Local History,
Pen & Sword Select, Pen & Sword Military Classics and Leo Cooper.

For a complete list of Pen & Sword titles please contact
PEN & SWORD BOOKS LIMITED
47 Church Street, Barnsley, South Yorkshire, S70 2AS, England
E-mail: enquiries@pen-and-sword.co.uk
Website: www.pen-and-sword.co.uk

Contents

This book is dedicated to the memory of Vice-Admiral Lothar von Arnauld de la Pèriere, the most successful submarine commander of all times in any navy, who, during the First World War, on fifteen war patrols lasting thirty-six months, sank 196 ships, totalling 456,266 tons, and remained a gentleman.

His death in an air crash on 24 February 1941, near Le Bourget airport in Paris, was suspected as having been caused by sabotage. Erich Raeder ordered a full investigation by a professional team of naval investigators. But Hermann Göring successfully prevented this, instructing the Gestapo, whose first Head he had been, to make absolutely sure that there would be no naval examination of this crash.

They have sown the wind and
they shall reap the whirlwind!

Hosea 8:7

Foreword

During the early years of both world wars, speedy airplanes with long-range did not exist and reliable long-distance radio communications between ships at sea were not available. They could only use either signal flags or the semaphore type of signal lamps to do so, using abbreviated Morse code phrases.

Submarines proceeding to their respective operational areas, usually moved on the surface to save time and felt safe doing so. Submarine captains and U-boat commanders had developed a chivalrous attitude towards each other, based upon mutual professional respect, while facing quickly rising losses and sudden chances of awful death. Fast reaction torpedoes to kill other submarines had not yet been invented. Whenever submarines met unexpectedly at sea, generally in the darkness, a courtesy greeting system had soon developed, using a mixed language Morse code.

The Germans signaled the letters: G-M-Y, standing for: Gott Mit You, meaning: 'God (be) With You'. The British responded with: M-Y-T, standing for: Mit You Too, meaning: 'With You Too', while passing each other. At times even waving their hats.

These unofficial greeting signals swiftly became known to submariners all over the world and in all navies and are still used customarily today. I have been greeted in this way verbally in many different places over the years by other submariners, as a member of a friendly international society.

Would it not be a step forward, if such a customary mutual approach became normal between all people who have common interests and traditions?

Peter Hansen 2005

Acknowledgements

In spite of existing regulations regarding secrecy matters, which some governments would like to retain for ever, many witnesses and confidential sources of information have related the facts of their personal experiences and discussed with me operations and occurrences in which they somehow became involved, usually not by their own choice. Most of them have talked only on condition that they could remain anonymous. The reader will understand that I am bound by such a promise.

But a few people have agreed to the use of their names, and I should like to thank them here for their invaluable information, their personal input and the important documents they provided. I am most grateful for their cooperation and assistance and fully appreciate their contributions to this book. Consequently, in deep gratitude for their help with this book, I thank Horst Fröhlich, Hellmuth Kirchammer, Peter Marl and Herbert A. Werner.

Needless to say, all conclusions reached and any assessments made are entirely my own, as are any errors, incorrect assumptions, misunderstandings or specific interpretations of facts and documents.

Over the years there have been many friends, associates and mentors, who have strongly encouraged me on this long journey to ferret out the truth without shielding in any way the personal sensitivity of politicians – or anybody else for that matter.

But fairness and thankfulness dictate that I must express my most sincere appreciation to Peter Padfield, author of numerous books in different areas from history to maritime matters. His always practical advice and many helpful suggestions based upon his extensive professional experience in the publishing field have benefited me greatly and enforced my persistence to stay firmly on course.

Michael L. Denneny I thank deeply for his candid, straightforward recommendations with respect to script structure, clarity and balance of text, which considerably improved this book.

Last, but not least, I have to thank Sandra 'Sandy' Leisengang for her patience, equanimity and consideration in helping to get this script into the right shape and required computerized format, which would have been impossible without her.

Every individual mentioned and each person named in this book was a real person, and their actual names are used. Only a handful of men insisted that their names must not appear in print for personal reasons, which I was obliged to respect.

Peter C. Hansen
North Palm Beach, Florida

Historical Introduction

In order to be able to understand the events you will read about, some advance information is essential. Otherwise, the state of things in Germany and German-occupied Europe during the Second World War is almost incomprehensible to people who were fortunate enough to live elsewhere.

To make it easier for readers to follow matters and understand specific actions, particular decisions and operational occurrences, and especially to obviate lengthy footnotes, confusing cross-references, excessive technical details and inordinate statistics, it is at times necessary to explain beliefs and views prevalent during that period in history.

For many reasons there prevails in most political and military circles a strong tendency towards secrecy, not so much to fool the enemy or confuse particular opponents, but mainly to prevent reliable information and actual facts from reaching their own folk. To inform the people correctly is seen as dangerous by the politicians in charge. Often those in authority prefer to act and proceed on that old Roman motto, *De mortuis nil, nisi bene* (Do not speak ill of the dead).

However, I believe this approach is outdated and quite wrong. I think that this proverb needs to be modified to *De mortuis nil, nisi* VERE, as one ought to stick to the truth and talk about facts, even if they are rather unpleasant ones, whenever dead people are involved.

I believe strongly that the individual is important and that his or her life and personality must not be subjected to the uncontrolled powers of any state, which tends to disregard the individual's rights and interests. This is one of the main reasons why this book was written.

It is a well-known fact that fiction is less twisted and far less incredible than the bare truth, the pure reality of life. Even the wildest imagination will rarely equal the truth. Fiction must remain believable while obvious impossibilities have to be avoided. Therefore, the naked actuality of what really took place is often a lot more interesting or scandalous than any type of fiction could be. Moreover, truth frequently defies the possibilities of logic, common sense, human reasoning and justice.

It has been said that there are two experiences that mould a man more than anything in life, and considerably influence his personality and character. These two things are military service, usually with obligatory conscription rather than voluntarily, and having to spend time in prison. Regardless of the reasons responsible for it, few men survive such periods in their lives and return unchanged to the customary routines of normal living. They have invariably undergone some personal transformation and have grown different in many ways.

There is little doubt that in any war, declared or not, the truth is the very first casualty. The longer any war lasts, the more this is the case. Truth is largely replaced by those terrible twins – censorship and government propaganda.

When you hear and read the war propaganda releases of all countries, it is quite evident that your soldiers are always the shining white knights on even whiter horses, while the enemy forces are nothing but murderers, gangsters, robbers and ugly hostiles with black hats and even blacker hearts. In reality, most soldiers were drafted men, with a sprinkling of volunteers and a handful of long-term professionals, who were in uniform because they did not have much choice in the matter and simply tried to make the best of it, hoping to survive.

During the Second World War submariners were seen as a rather special breed of man in many ways, a kind of élite group of sailors. The American and British were nothing but daring heroes, while the German U-boat men were supposed to be nothing but pirates, killers and murderers. The truth, as so often, is somewhat different and less black and white. A total of 40,800 men undertook U-boat training, but 30,226 did not return from the seas. Another 5,038 became prisoners of war until 5 May 1945.

The U-boat Command was assisted and supported by a further 10,900 men in various shore locations. They worked in administrative offices, as drivers, as guards and watchmen, as kitchen helpers or inventory control clerks. Others were permanently used as training and school instructors, as communications clerks, working in the naval mail and censorship department or in transportation and shipping units. Finally, there were the naval military courts with many clerks and the naval judge advocates. All of these men were considered part of the U-boat Command, but they never undertook U-boat training, and many of them were physically unqualified to serve on U-boats in any position.

If one includes these support soldiers, the entire U-boat Command during the war years had no more than 52,000 men serving in it. Contrary to propaganda claims, only a small number of them were actually volunteers. The majority were simply transferred into the U-boat Command because they were physically qualified and the positions had to be filled. This amounted to only one quarter of one per cent (0.25%) of the men who were inducted into the German armed forces.

But through clever propaganda and a broad-based publicity campaign by special naval units formed for precisely that purpose, many people have somehow gained the impression that the German Navy was rather large and the U-boat force quite immense. In reality, Germany was an army-centred continental power and only a small naval and maritime power. Even the German Air Force, the *Luftwaffe*, was more than twice as large as the Navy, because it included the numerous anti-aircraft gunnery commands.

As in any sizeable group of soldiers there were quite a few different types of men in the U-boat Command. Fanatical Nazis, hot-headed super-patriots, aggressive men and 'eager beavers'. But also toadies, yes-men and big-mouths, as well as conscientious, pleasant and considerate men who were humane individuals, the *Mensch* type. Some of them you will get to know in this book.

During the Second World War, between 1939 and 1945, more than 22,000 German soldiers, sailors and airmen were condemned to death by military courts and actually executed. This number equals two full-strength infantry divisions. Another 29,000 soldiers of all service branches were condemned to death by these same military courts, but their death sentences were commuted to lesser penalties or to probation in one of the numerous penal companies, or to service with one of the special bomb or mine defusing and clearing squads. While they were granted reconsideration of their death sentences, only about twenty per cent of those reprieved men returned alive from their probationary assigments, quite a few as cripples: a questionable kind of mercy.

In comparison, the British executed 317 soldiers during the war, most of them for serious criminal offences like murder, including quite a few men from the various countries of the Empire. The United States of America shot one single soldier in Europe, Private Eddie Slovik. But he was posthumously re-habilitated, while all others condemned to death were pardoned and received commuted prison terms.

In addition to these military courts, the Nazi Party functionaries set up a complete new chain of Party courts for civilians, with hard-nosed Nazis as judges and prosecutors for the German population at the 'home front', to keep these folk under tight control. These convinced and fanatical satraps of Martin Bormann constantly grabbed more power and were increasingly given more direct help by the state's secret police, the Gestapo.

These Nazi Party courts were called 'Brown courts' by the German population, and they condemned another 12,000 German civilians to death, ninety per cent by decapitation or hanging. Frequently this was for the smallest infractions of wartime regulations and special Nazi laws and prohibitions, like tuning in to foreign radio stations such as the BBC, the neutral Swiss or Swedish stations or the Voice of America.

In an atmosphere of increasing mistrust, fear and danger the German population was exhorted to report to the Gestapo anybody who might be suspected of almost anything, telling those people hesitant to denounce others that it was the obligation of every German citizen, male of female, to help to strengthen German determination and the will to win the war.

While in other countries the general view was that whatever was not specifically forbidden was allowed, in Germany the reverse was true. What had not been expressly permitted had to be considered as automatically prohibited. Rewards were offered for reporting offenders promptly to the Gestapo.

During the war new Nazi Party courts were put into operation to keep in line all foreigners who had been contracted for work in Germany or had been drafted for heavy labour to maintain industrial and agricultural production. As more and more German workers were inducted into the armed forces they had to be replaced to prevent a complete economic and agricultural collapse in 1942 and thereafter. How many of these foreign workers were punished harshly or condemned to death by these special courts cannot be ascertained any more, although this number was also quite high.

Finally, one must add the people killed after the attempt to eliminate Hitler on 20 July 1944 in his Rastenburg headquarters in East Prussia, the 'Wolf's Lair'. This attempt, led by the Army's Colonel Claus Schenk, Count von Stauffenberg, unfortunately misfired. While the execution of von Stauffenberg and his closest helpers at Army HQ in Berlin took place promptly, another 4,790 men and women were subsequently put to death by drumhead sentencing by the so-called 'people's courts', after the mass arrest of anybody even remotely suspected of being in sympathy with the Army plotters, usually without any evidence or proof whatsoever.

The wives of the principal participants were swiftly imprisoned or placed into concentration camps, just in case they might have known anything about the military conspiracy. Their minor children were taken away, given new names and placed into approved 'foster homes' of Nazi Party members. These almost 5,000 additional persons are not included in the previously mentioned numbers of people exterminated in Germany during the Second World War.

Without knowing anything about these mass killings and the atmosphere of fear they generated in Germany, it is almost impossible to comprehend the Oskar Kusch naval court case.

There lived a poet, Rainer Maria Rilke, who wrote very few texts and poems, as he died young. However, during the First World War the poems he left for the world comforted many soldiers in the filthy trenches of France and Belgium, during the mass butchering around Verdun, in the wretched swamps and the morass of Flanders and the hell of the Somme valley battles of attrition.

Here is what Rilke said about writing: 'If you must write, you have to write as if your entire life depended upon it, so that nothing will stand in your way. But if it does, write anyway, because if you have to think about it first or have to mull it over to look for justification, it would be better to forget writing altogether!'

Therefore this book finally had to be written, after many years of extensive research and communicating with numerous people to double-check details and illuminate the actuality of events.

I have been asked, 'Why now?' 'Why after so many years?' My answer is, 'It would be inexcusable not to bring out the truth even after all these years, because it is never too late for the truth to prevail and become known.'

Let us never forget what Edmund Burke said so rightly: 'The only thing necessary for the triumph of evil is for good men to do nothing!'

Medium Type VII C U-boat

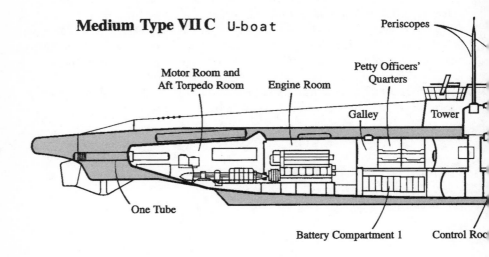

Periscopes

Motor Room and
Aft Torpedo Room

Engine Room

Petty Officers' Quarters

Galley

Tower

One Tube

Battery Compartment 1

Control Roo[m]

(Note: Tower, bridge, and anti-aircraft gun
configurations were often altered during the w[ar])

Large Type IX C U-boat

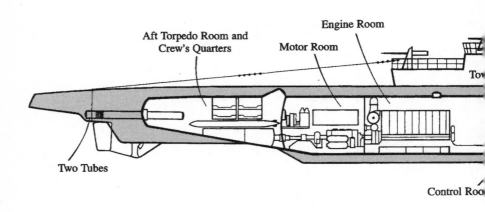

Periscopes

Engine Room

Aft Torpedo Room and
Crew's Quarters

Motor Room

To[wer]

Two Tubes

Control Roo[m]

THE TWO PRINCIPAL

ATT[ACK]

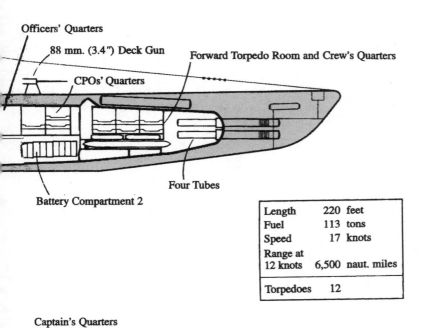

Officers' Quarters

88 mm. (3.4") Deck Gun

CPOs' Quarters

Forward Torpedo Room and Crew's Quarters

Four Tubes

Battery Compartment 2

Length	220	feet
Fuel	113	tons
Speed	17	knots
Range at 12 knots	6,500	naut. miles
Torpedoes	12	

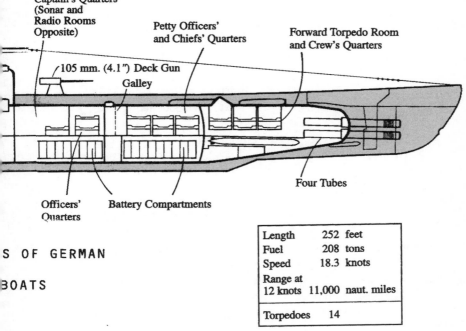

Captain's Quarters
(Sonar and
Radio Rooms
Opposite)

105 mm. (4.1") Deck Gun

Galley

Petty Officers'
and Chiefs' Quarters

Forward Torpedo Room
and Crew's Quarters

Four Tubes

Officers'
Quarters

Battery Compartments

S OF GERMAN

BOATS

Length	252	feet
Fuel	208	tons
Speed	18.3	knots
Range at 12 knots	11,000	naut. miles
Torpedoes	14	

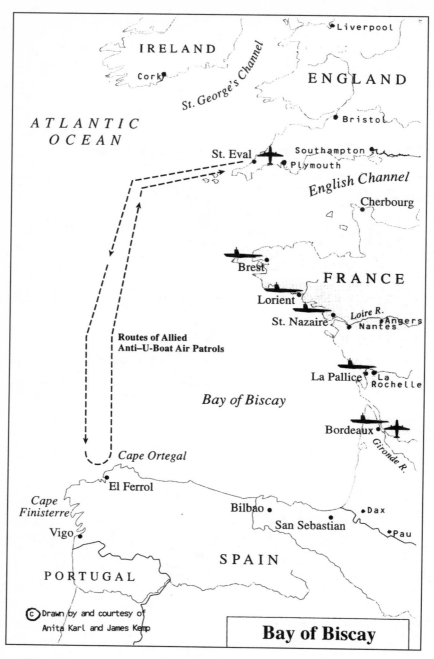

The German U-boat bases in Western France . . . Brest 1st and 9th
U-boat flotillas, Bordeaux 12th U-boat flotilla,
La Pallice-La Rochelle 3rd U-boat flotilla, Lorient 2nd and 10th U-boat
flotillas, St Nazaire 6th and 7th U-boat flotillas.

CHAPTER ONE

From the Shadows
of the Past

It was a sunny day in April 1934, the temperature becoming hotter daily, when a group of thirty-six schoolboys under the supervision of their teachers of ancient history and languages were boarding their motor-coach, which had obviously covered a lot of miles already. They were on the customary art and cultural tour of Greece required in those years for senior high school pupils attending a humanistic high school, where Greek and Latin were obligatory subjects, although English and French were likewise emphasized. The best and most ambitious boys would sign up for a choice of Spanish, Russian or one of the oriental languages in addition. These youngsters were healthy boys, loaded with energy, yet still quite playful. They tended to be rather noisy and liked to play tricks or silly pranks on each other or, if possible, their teachers, provided they might get away uncaught.

Athens and its numerous temples and classical sites had been visited during the previous thirteen days. As usual, many of the boys responded with more tolerance than enthusiasm, not to mention unbounded curiosity, which they often reserved for other matters. They had travelled by several ferries to various Greek islands and enjoyed those trips very much, having a good time aboard the vessels, where the supervision by their teachers was less strict.

They loved some of the beaches and were surreptitiously watching girls with a pair of binoculars that was circulating among them. After all, most of the columns and ruins were almost alike, while the girls were different and more interesting. However, neither the general Greek cuisine nor the sanitary facilities met with their approval, and were the subject of cynical remarks, impolite jokes and at times, unfair comparisons.

But as every day grew hotter, their enthusiasm for climbing hills, walking on dirt roads or steep, cobblestoned streets markedly decreased. They rose earlier every morning to absorb their cultural and visiting programmes while the temperature was still bearable. Green plants, bushes or trees were quite rare and the flowers had already wilted in most places. Any sort of shade or cool breeze was becoming rare. Yet their demanding itinerary, planned by their teachers, had so far been covered as scheduled. Today would be their final day in Greece, and they had advanced getting up by another fifteen minutes.

The boys were a bit sleepy, yet looked forward to their final day with considerable excitement, as they had heard that the ferry steamer from Patras to Italy dispensed free wine to all passengers. Their motorcoach appeared with groaning brakes and blowing black fumes as the driver stopped in front of their small hotel in Sparta. The youngsters boarded quickly, while the two teachers counted heads and settled the bills, making sure no luggage remained behind and that the luncheon baskets were stored in the coolest place possible. After honking repeatedly and loudly the motorcoach slowly started to move, then gradually gained speed.

Soon they left Sparta's outskirts and commenced their climb into the mountains. The motorcoach huffed and puffed, its engine periodically misfiring and coughing, as the altitude increased. The road wound upwards in ever narrower serpentine curves, crossing rocky gorges that alternated with steep cliffs. It seemed that nobody could possibly live here. But there were goats and sheep here and there, guarded by shepherds who appeared to sleep standing up, leaving the work to their huge dogs, who kept the animals in line.

Finally, the saddle of the mountain pass came in sight, the object of the morning's visit. Thankfully, the driver shut off the hot engine and opened the exit doors. The windows were already wide open as there was no air-conditioning anywhere in those days, least of all in Greece. Everybody tumbled out into the sun of the mountainside, some of the pupils cursing silently, others wishing to get it over with quickly. Canteens filled with now warm lemonade were passed around among the group to moisten their already parched throats. Both teachers sweated profusely, and some of the boys used their handkerchiefs quite often. Fortunately, the walk from the parking area was short.

The group stood bunched together before a slab of stone hewn out of the rock of the mountain pass a long time before. The inscription was no longer easy to read and rather dirty. Professor Heller moved as close as possible to the rockside and translated the inscription for his pupils, most of them silently hoping this would not take too long, as the sun was growing fiercer by the minute. The boys just stood and listened as their language instructor read them the story: 'Wanderer, when you reach Sparta, pray tell the people that you have seen us buried here, lying in the ground, dead, as the law demanded of us!'

The name of the leader, Leonidas, who had defended this narrow mountain pass with three hundred Spartan soldiers to the last man, was not even mentioned. Fighting against Xerxes and thousands of Persian conquerors intent upon raiding and raping Sparta in the year 430 BC, Leonidas and his column of men fought to hold the Thermopylae pass, until not a single man of them was left alive. The Persians with their overwhelming numbers prevailed, looting Sparta, capturing her women and treasures.

An eerie silence had suddenly fallen over the group. Professor Lambeck quoted from Roman history: 'It is sweet and glorious to die for your country', adding, 'Even if in vain!' Both teachers now slowly removed their hats. The heat was momentarily forgotten, cold shivers crept along the backs of the boys and cold sweat along those of the two teachers. A few minutes of reverent silence prevailed, before the group walked back to their motor-coach, very slowly. The shadow of death had just touched these youngsters for the very first time.

Surprisingly, the motor caught immediately, to the delight of the driver, and the bus rolled down the other side of the Thermopylae pass in long serpentine loops on the lonely road, with total quiet inside. Only when they approached the port of Patras did the conversation gradually resume. Professor Heller, who had been gassed and severely wounded at the Somme in 1917, when he became a prisoner of war in England, felt that these youngsters needed some further information, and gave them his view of things.

He started thus:

Boys, no such thing can ever happen to you, because our leader Adolf Hitler spent over four years in the trenches of the Western Front, seeing people die and experiencing personally this terrible tragedy of needless and useless war, where the best fellows die while the politicians gain more power and the industrial lobbies more markets. But because Hitler was for so long on the very front line, he will never allow another European war to develop. Therefore, it is an impossibility that Germany and Great Britain would ever again fight each other to the sole advantage of Russia and the Asian powers, as this would be nothing but fratricide.

Professor Lambeck, the history teacher, took a deep breath when he heard this statement, and decided to qualify it gently: 'My friend and colleague is a great believer in many things. Sadly, I am unable to agree with him on that particular point.' The boys' ears perked up to hear every word that was coming. Lambeck continued: 'I shall be very happy if that is what will happen, but I have my doubts, as politicians seldom excel in matching their deeds to their words. The pressure by their followers tends to push them into corners they have problems getting out of again.' Lambeck had served in the last war mainly in Russia, had been twice wounded, still walked with a limp and had one glass eye. He was the most respected supervisor of examinations, as the pupils were never sure where he was looking, and he caught cheats regularly. In 1916, he had been left as dead in the deep winter snow of the Eastern Front, becoming a Russian prisoner of war. He had spent considerable time in rough places, including Siberia, which he nevertheless grew to love.

Lambeck continued deliberately,

Germany has the *Reichswehr* of 100,000 professionals, including officers, and the *Reichsmarine* of another 15,000 men, including officers. These are defensive forces only, imposed by that awful and vengeful Treaty of Versailles and shortsighted, narrow-minded French *petit bourgeois* lawyers and politicians, who occupied pleasant postings way behind the front lines during the war. Such an army and navy are barely sufficient to defend our present borders. But they are also unable to launch large attacks or wage a war of attrition. As long as this remains so, peace will prevail.

However, should Hitler and his party suddenly decide that they want to increase the armed forces substantially and reintroduce obligatory military conscription for all males who have their heads straight on their bodies, peace will quickly disappear, like the snow in the spring, and another European or world war is certain within five years at the most.

Sighing, he added wistfully, 'Just when you fellows are getting to be old enough to fight and die! Though I keep my fingers crossed that this scenario will not materialize, yet I am highly sceptical that it won't happen.'

Heller now chimed in once more:

Let's hope and pray that Dr Lambeck is too pessimistic, due to his past experiences. I would like to emphasize that I do not wish anything like he mentioned to become reality, because it is too dreadful to contemplate. As I said before, Adolf Hitler himself suffered through the horrors of trench warfare, so he will not permit it to be repeated! What you have seen today was warfare of a different time, where the leaders fought at the head of their column of soldiers, unlike nowadays when the top commanders work in pleasant castles behind the front lines and never experience war's frightfulness.

Changing the subject, I should like to tell you that a similar school group of British boys and their teachers will travel with us on the ferry steamer this evening. Many of them, I have been told, are international Boy Scouts. As some of you have been members of that organization in Germany, before they were merged into the various Hitler Youth Groups, perhaps you might encounter former friends from international meetings in the past. As I am acquainted with their teachers, I ask that you do not become involved in things you would be ashamed of later. However, on the ferry steamer there are always huge and long parties with music and a lot of fun. We expect you will participate and join the crowd. But retain control of yourselves, even while you are having a splendid time.

We are now entering the port city of Patras, and tomorrow we shall arrive in Mussolini's Italy, where the trains run punctually. Please act like adults and the civilized, cultured men that you aim to be in a few years. When you are aboard the overnight ferry steamer, don't just hang around with your closest classmates, but mix with the English boys and make some new friends! We shall see you tomorrow morning bright eyed and bushy tailed when we reach Brindisi to board the express train to Rome and beyond. Remember, we have seat reservations in coach number eight. We teachers shall play bridge with the English teachers as a foursome, as we already know the entertainment and music from previous trips.

The boys left the motorcoach in a rush, disappearing below decks to find their sleeping quarters. The teachers checked that nothing had been left behind, handed the driver a bulging envelope of drachmas and embarked on the ferry steamer to find their cabin.

Those advertised free samples of wine aboard were indeed provided, but it was of the weakest type of wine available, as this was cheaper and safer than drinking tapwater, while bottled water was expensive. As Dr Heller had told the youngsters, there was lively music on the ship and two different bands playing with great gusto and enthusiasm, both the latest tunes and many nostalgic oldies. Within an hour of leaving Patras, the two groups of youngsters had mixed easily, and all took considerable advantage of the free wine.

The sailors and musicians laughed about their initial shyness, which disappeared rapidly with the growing consumption of wine. There were no suitable dancing partners, apart from a few older widows of considerable weight. The boys had a great time and calculated they could nap tomorrow on the train, to catch up on lost sleep. Therefore, they talked excitedly and occasionally sang along with the melodies with which they were familiar.

Heller's prediction came true. Several of the boys had met before, during international Boy Scout Jamborees. Two decided to become blood brothers on the voyage, secretly swearing eternal fealty to each other. Several years later they would meet again, unexpectedly and under very different circumstances, but their fealty, their personal faithfulness, would remain firm and unbroken.

Upon arrival, the two school groups stumbled onto the station platform, somewhat hung-over and tired but content. They entered the onward express train to Rome yawning with pale faces. Once the train started to move, most decided to take a snooze until they arrived in Rome to change trains for their respective homelands.

Within a few more months, Hitler ordered the introduction of obligatory military service for all healthy males between 17 and 39 years of age, which was later increased to 55 years of age. As Dr Lambeck had unhappily predicted, the start of the Second World War was nothing but a question of time.

Naturally, the entire development was accompanied by an incredible storm of super-patriotic propaganda, camouflaged as self-defence and protection of the fatherland from evil enemies and political criminals. As the German minister for propaganda and public enlightenment, Joseph Goebbels, said many times, 'The bigger the lies, the more believable they are for most people.'

Having the advantage of hindsight, I can take a look ahead in history, not to speculate, but to let you readers know what would happen to those bright and spirited boys and their dedicated teachers in the war to come.

It is sad to have to report that not one of the four teachers survived. Naturally, they were considerably older to start with. But from the thirty-three English public school pupils nine were still around in 1945, two of them with severe injuries for the rest of their lives; while from thirty-six German pupils only seven survived the war, three of them having war-induced injuries for the rest of their days.

However, those two boys, Telford D. G. Bassington and Frank W. Petersen, who had secretly become blood brothers swearing eternal fealty to each other were among the lucky survivors, as prisoners of war.

CHAPTER TWO

A Somewhat Involuntary Naval Career

Oskar Heinz Kusch was born on 6 April 1918 in Berlin. His parents, Heinz and Erna Auguste Kusch, neé Kohls, had married during the First World War and Oskar was their only child. Heinz Kusch was an executive and director of a large insurance company.

In autumn 1924 Oskar started elementary school, and in 1928 he transferred to the combined junior and senior high school, the Hohenzollern Humanistic Gymnasium, after passing the entry examinations with high marks. Shortly after being admitted to the Hohenzollern High School, Oskar joined the Boy Scout organization called *Wandervogel*, or 'The Migratory Birds'. He made many lifelong friends both in his high school and in his Boy Scout groups.

In 1932, this Boy Scout group merged with several other independent pathfinder groups to strengthen their organization, which was renamed *Bündische Jugend*, usually called *Bündische* for short. This was an alliance of various Boy Scout groups patterned after the International Boy Scouts and Pathfinder organization founded by the former British general, Robert Baden-Powell.

Oskar participated in international meetings, called Jamborees, with campfire nostalgia, secret ceremonies, lots of singing or play-acting and different games in tented assembly camps, where youngsters from several countries met and mingled.

On 30 January 1933, Adolf Hitler became Chancellor of Germany. In his acceptance speech he stated, 'Give me four years of time, German people, also give my party four years of time, and I promise you that you will not recognize your country any more!'

Within two years the Nazi government ordered all existing independent youth groups to be disbanded, and forced them to merge and transfer into the various Hitler Youth organizations. Youngsters between 9 and 13 years of age were placed into the *Jungvolk*, while those from 14 to 19 were put into the different Hitler Youth groups. The *Bündische* Boy Scouts organization agreed to this consolidation reluctantly, but decided to transfer with their entire leadership intact, to remain half-way in control, hoping somehow to preserve their organization.

All groups, organizations and individuals who refused this government order were posted automatically on the black list of the Gestapo, as prohibited groups, outlawed organizations and dangerous individuals hostile to the Nazi state. Such 'unreliable' people would come under permanent police observation and they would be increasingly harassed by the Gestapo.

Many boys started to wear long hair, rather than the Prussian hedgehog haircut favoured by the government. The youngsters grew to dislike the officially promoted type of music and songs, such as marching tunes, military band music and inspirational Party songs, which the young fellows considered dreary. Privately, millions of young Germans turned into enthusiastic fans of the so-called new music, American jazz, Southern Dixieland and related tunes. The Tiger Rag, the Highland Swing and even the Lambeth Walk grew constantly more popular and fashionable among young people. Ella Fitzgerald became one of the most celebrated singers, while the Glenn Miller orchestra and Tommy Dorsey's band rose to status symbols.

Millions of young people looking for niches to escape the Nazi pressure to conform embraced all things American and English as much more desirable than the Nazi standards pushed by the various government agencies. Increasingly, young men reported sick to skip Hitler Youth meetings and the organized Nazi-ordered activities. But the Nazi functionaries caught on quickly. Teachers and youngsters were advised that participation in Hitler Youth meetings, which grew steadily more strident and militaristic, was more important than any type of schoolwork and surpassed the private interests of their homes, regardless of what their parents preferred.

In autumn 1936, Oskar Kusch passed his final senior high school examinations with very good marks and received the *Abitur*, a kind of Bachelor's degree, obligatory for admission to any university or higher technical training school in Germany, all of which were state operated at that time. Since the autumn of 1935, the Nazi regime had made it mandatory that every student accepted or admitted to any university or higher vocational trade school had to furnish a local police certificate of good political standing and desirable personal conduct from the Gestapo in their place of residence. This was to keep troublemakers and other objectionable elements out of the universities and other establishments of higher education in Germany.

As a former *Bündische* Boy Scout who insisted on remaining in close and frequent personal contact with his old friends, Kusch had been placed on the permanent watch list of the Gestapo some time previously. Eventually, he was shifted to the black list of politically unreliable people, as he refused to play by the rules of the Gestapo. Consequently, he was unable to obtain the obligatory police certificate of political reliability and good conduct, and found he could not obtain any academic or other higher education in Germany. While trying to digest this situation, Kusch was called by the local draft board for military registration and medical examination for the now obligatory minimum conscription of two years of military service. The draft board officials informed him that he could become a naval officer candidate, being a registered sport sailor who had participated in many regattas. Kusch applied and was asked to go to Kiel for a ten-day period of personal and medical exams and evaluations, including extensive psychiatric tests.

Until a few years previous, the annual intake of such candidates oscillated between 150 and 250 for all possible careers. But recently the Navy had changed its name and realized that they it had to increase the number of officer candidates to somewhere between 500 and 700 annually. Otherwise it would be impossible to handle the scheduled anticipated growth in manpower and ships.

Yet the selection was still quite careful, and many were rejected for a variety of reasons. While several requirements were desired and top-class physical shape was obligatory, membership of the Hitler Youth, or for older applicants the Nazi Party, was not. Nor was the police certificate of political reliability from the Gestapo required.

Oskar Kusch was among those young men selected and accepted, and he was informed that he would be called in the spring of 1937 for basic training.

He left Berlin by train in the morning of 3 April 1937 for Stralsund, arriving six hours later in this town in Pomerania for training camp service, together with 460 other officer candidates. This number included fifty applicants for the engineering branch, thirty-five applicants for the administrative and paymaster branch and thirty applicants for various specialized technical careers in ship construction, equipment development and ship-yard management. All others were aiming for the career of an executive line officer.

This particular class of naval officer candidates was designated as VI/1937, and called Crew 37-A for short. The young arrivals were met at the Stralsund railway station by the petty officers assigned to drill and train them, and marched directly to the Dänholm, a small island situated in the Strela Sound, half-way between the port city of Stralsund and the big island of Rügen. Here the petty officers were expected to make soldiers out of these civilians.

A high wall had been constructed around the militarily used part of the Dänholm, and a ring of barracks and other necessary buildings had been erected around a big square that was used for the daily assembly of the recruits and for different training activities.

Naturally, the rough drill and basic spit-and-polish activities did not provoke great enthusiasm among the recruits, yet most adapted quite well, because they knew this was a time-limited situation. The main emphasis was on rifle-handling and machine-gun exercises, constant parading on the big assembly square or marching for longer distances and extended time periods with full packs and often gas masks too. Recruits wore greyish-green uniforms during this time rather than navy-blue ones.

As the space was limited on the Dänholm, longer exercises and marches took place on the island of Rügen, primarily on the Drygge peninsula, consisting mainly of dry brush, sandy dunes and thickets of thistles and stinging nettles. These were the preferred spots for the drill sergeants to explore with their groups, if possible creeping along on the ground or crawling around like snakes on their bellies.

Six weeks later, the recruits were sworn in as sailors. It was assumed they could now shine shoes properly, dress correctly and were able to recognize all superior service ranks, to salute as prescribed. The customary jobs prevailed – making beds numerous times, washing and cleaning the rooms and floors of their barracks and other buildings, and endlessly sweeping the parade grounds. Those who displeased the petty officers cleaned the toilets and washrooms with toothbrushes.

Once the basic training period was finished, all rookies considered fit were posted to one of the sailing ships for three months of seamanship training and conditioning.

Oskar Kusch was assigned to the *Gorch Fock*, which was initially visiting various ports in the Baltic Sea, thence proceeding into the North Sea and finally making a trip to the Faeroe Islands in the Atlantic. At the end of the voyage, all candidates who had passed their second examination and had acquired a satisfactory or better rating were named sea cadets, or cadets of their respective special naval career branch.

At the end of October 1937 the cadets were once again shuffled around and transferred to surface ships. The majority were posted on those worn-out obsolete battle-wagons, the *Schlesien* and the *Schleswig Holstein*, which were already out of date in 1916 when they participated in the Battle of Jutland. Over the years these floating museums, often called 'ironing boards', had become the permanent homes of thousands of big tropical rats and millions of obnoxious cockroaches, commonly called *Kakerlaks* in German, which eventually had also become the the enlisted men's nickname for all naval cadets.

However, Oskar Kusch was assigned instead to the light cruiser *Emden*. This was the first post-war construction ship of the German Navy. Kusch participated in a seven-month cruise aboard the *Emden* in the Pacific and the Far East, returning to Germany at the end of April 1938. All cadets evaluated as fit, mature and competent by their petty officers and cadet officers were put on rail transport to Flensburg to report at the Marine Schule, the naval academy at Mürwik, a suburb of Flensburg.

On 1 May 1938 all cadets in good standing became midshipmen, which involved a complete change in their naval uniforms and placed them on equal rank with petty officers.

The summer and early autumn passed swiftly with a full and heavy programme of lectures, classes, lessons and demonstrations combined with a variety of exercises, directed by naval officers and professional civilian instructors, many of them well-known experts in their educational or technical fields. There was a large marina with many types of boat in constant use for training and leisure trips.

At the end of October 1938, all midshipmen who had acquired sufficient points for a satisfactory rating in their different evaluations and tests and an acceptable standard of conduct had to take the extended main examination for future officers. It was imperative for the midshipmen's future standing on the naval ranking list to achieve a good result as it depended largely on this examination and the points obtained.

Kusch passed with good marks and received an excellent evaluation and fitness report regarding his ability, competency, personality and general character. Thereafter he participated in a string of training courses and supplementary weapons exercises for gunnery, torpedoes, anti-aircraft gunnery, communication systems, mine warfare and as a platoon leader.

At the end of these courses, Kusch waited for another shipboard assignment. He hoped to get posted to a torpedo boat or destroyer, but the Navy thought otherwise. On 2 April 1939, to his surprise, he was reassigned to the light cruiser *Emden*, together with three of his classmates. This was owing to his above-average performance and ability to handle groups of men well.

On 1 July 1939 Kusch was promoted to senior midshipman and thereafter evaluated by the entire body of officers aboard the *Emden*, to clear him and his classmates as future line officers. Even one 'no' vote among the secret ballots would have squashed his getting his commission.

One month later, on 1 August 1939, Kusch was promoted to ensign and became a commissioned officer. This was because of a decision by the Naval High Command in Berlin to speed up officers' training considerably. On the secret ranking list, Oskar Kusch was posted in Position 54 of 306 newly appointed ensigns of his naval class.

The main reason for this speed-up in promotions was the growing evidence of a large shortage of subaltern officers. The Navy's leadership had finally comprehended that war was likely to start soon, in spite of promises to the contrary by Hitler. There was an excess of older admirals and fossilized captains in Berlin, many of whom had not been to sea for a very long time. Yet every one of them shuffled files and generated paperwork to demonstrate their importance, if not indispensability. Finally, it had penetrated their over-staffed circles that the Navy would soon be calling-up reservists in huge numbers for the coming war. Such officers were essential, if it was expected that those hordes of reservists could be incorporated into the various naval commands and shore installations smoothly and efficiently.

In the early morning hours of 1 September 1939 Hitler started the attack on Poland. The German Navy opened it at 04.45 hours with an artillery barrage by the old *Schleswig Holstein* moored in Danzig, firing on the Polish fortifications of the Westerplatte, with little effect.

Generaladmiral Erich Raeder, the commander-in-chief of the German

Navy, was rather nervous and feared this attack might turn into a disaster, wiping out the naval cadet class of Crew 1938, now largely manning the *Schleswig Holstein*. He requested that she should be replaced by a more modern vessel, but Hitler turned down such a change as needless. Hitler was in a jolly mood and told Raeder that he should stop worrying about his cadets, because Poland would fold up like a house of cards hit by lightning.

However, the German Navy and most of the officers had another view of things to come. The French papers had fat headlines, asking, 'Who wants to die for Danzig?' Evidently hardly anybody in France. Hitler had recently made his diplomatic deal with Joseph Stalin and the Communists in Soviet Russia, settling the division of Poland, the Baltic countries and the Balkans, and arranging a trade deal by out-promising the British, who had negotiated with Soviet Russia for many weeks without getting results.

Erich Raeder had accepted Hitler's predictions that France and Great Britain would never fight for Poland, much less in Poland, and would merely make a lot of political publicity noise to calm down their socialists and other left-wingers at home. But in the German Navy most officers expected that the British would enter the war, irrespective of geography or local politics in their country, even if the French did hesitate and stall.

The cruiser *Emden* had just been fully overhauled and was scheduled to move into the Baltic Sea as a training ship. However, this order was cancelled for war service preparations and restoration of her full combat readiness.

In the morning of 3 September 1939, the British Admiralty flashed a clear text signal to all commands, units and ships at sea: 'Total Germany!' This uncoded message was instantly intercepted by the German Navy's *B-Dienst* listening service that monitored all airwaves. No time-consuming decoding was required. The Rubicon had been crossed! The die had been cast. The Second World War had started.

The German Navy, while on war readiness and positioned rather widely, was not ready for war, neither in number of ships nor in size of manpower, and would not be able to reach that point for another seven or eight years. Raeder, who had accepted Hitler's prognostications, was deeply shaken and stated correctly, 'The German Navy is in such an inferior position that the men and ships can only die gallantly, but not influence the war, much less hope to win it.'

That very evening the *Emden* sailed with a full load of mines into the North Sea, to participate in laying a big defensive mine barrier named Westwall. Shortly thereafter the *Emden* was transferred to the Baltic, as a training ship for officer candidates and petty officers. This involved a lot of repetitive and tiresome exercises, combined with fighting the heavy ice conditions in the Baltic during the severe winter. Kusch grew bored with this going around in circles, and requested a transfer to some active fighting ship, preferable a U-boat. His request was approved, and on 31 March 1940 he was detached from *Emden* and transferred to Kiel to join the U-boat Command organization there.

Kusch had never before set foot on any U-boat, because U-boats were not allowed to be visited. The only people permitted aboard were the actual crew members, and a heavy screen of secrecy kept all others, without exception, from coming aboard.

A few months earlier, Captain Karl Dönitz, the director of U-boats, had been advised that he was due, after four years in his position, for a command rotation and transfer, either to the Naval High Command in an influential position or to become the commander of one of the battleships.

His replacement, Commander Hans Georg von Friedeburg, had arrived in July 1939 to be broken into the job by Dönitz and assigned as temporary chief of staff. It was expected that von Friedeburg would be able to take over fully sometime between October and December 1939, to free Dönitz for reassignment, rotation and promotion.

However, owing to the start of the war, Raeder decided that such a change in command could not take place without considerable repercussions for the U-boat crews. Therefore, von Friedeburg was appointed as deputy to Dönitz, with the task of managing the entire U-boat organization except actual combat operations, which would be directed by Dönitz while the war lasted.

Immediately Dönitz installed his new headquarters office in a wooden barrack in Sengwarden, a suburb of Wilhelmshaven, situated on a short road named *Am Toten Weg*, meaning On the Path of Dead Men! Might this perhaps become a forecast of the U-boat Command's future? As the Romans said, *Nomen est omen*, the name should become the wish for the future. Quickly a sophisticated communications centre was also set up nearby to stay in radio signal contact with U-boats at sea.

The U-boat Command had only fifty-seven U-boats at hand, and thirty of these were the Type II small coastal U-boats with limited range, called *Einbäume*, or canoes, by their crews. Most of them were needed for school and training assignments. Of the twenty-seven larger U-boats of various types, some had not even undergone their trials, tests and exercises to become combat ready, while others were in shipyards for periodic overhauls. The newest ones had only fairly green and untrained crews aboard and were not yet available for war patrol assignments. This was not exactly an enormous force of U-boats for combat operations.

When Kusch reported in Kiel, he anticipated U-boat training and expedited handling to become assigned to a front-service U-boat. But he was once again put through lengthy tests and had to undergo a long examination for dexterity, medical fitness and his ability to react fast and reliably under heavy pressure and in stress situations, before he was accepted by the U-boat Command. Then he was posted to the First U-boat Training Division in Pillau (Baltisk), East Prussia, to start his actual U-boat training. The various courses and training classes required five months. Kusch finished all schools and classes with a top grade.

But instead of being given a front U-boat assignment as watch officer, Kusch was transferred to Gotenhafen (Gdingen) in East Prussia as an instructor with the Second U-boat Training Division. He remained in that position for nine months, but became restless and managed to pull strings in the U-boat Command personnel department to be appointed as second watch officer of U-103 on 24 June 1941. His fitness reports and evaluations were once more highly complimentary and very good. He had been well liked by his superiors and his groups of students.

He departed the next morning by express trains via Paris to Lorient, France, where U-103 was based, belonging to the 2nd U-boat Flotilla in that port. U-103 was one of the large Type IX-B 'sea cow' U-boats, commanded by Captain Viktor Schütze (Crew 1925), who had commissioned U-103 in Bremen on 5 July 1940.

When returning from his fourth war patrol to Lorient on 12 July 1941, Schütze was informed by Dönitz, when he inspected the crew of U-103, that he was being replaced as her commander and promoted to take over the 2nd U-boat Flotilla in Lorient instead.

Kusch had arrived in Lorient several days earlier and joined the welcoming crowd at the arrival pier when U-103 reached port, observing the brass band reception with showers of bright summer flowers, while baskets of fresh fruit were delivered aboard. A group of singing and dancing girls, secretaries or auxiliaries at different offices and nurses at military hospitals, hugged and kissed the smelly U-boat men.

When the official reception was over, U-103 was shifted to another pier, awaiting the visit of the shipyard engineering specialists. Kusch presented his orders to the security watch and was immediately directed to Schütze. Surrounded by heaps of papers, Schütze had many things on his mind that he had to finish urgently. Nevertheless he welcomed Kusch and told him that he would soon be the only officer in Lorient, and therefore responsible for the security of U-103 for the next couple of weeks. Many crew members would be on leave and others were being transferred elsewhere. Kusch was to look over all replacements arriving to take their places and figure out what the most suitable place would be for them and what battle stations they should be given. Furthermore, he should handle all incoming paperwork once Schütze left U-103, and bring all records, files and instructions up to date and undertake everything necessary to obtain the latest revisions of all secret orders, instructions and manuals and destroy the outdated material safely.

On 13 August 1941 Lieutenant-Commander Werner Winter took over U-103 as her new commander. He had been the admiralty staff officer designated as A-5 in the U-boat Command Centre, now located in nearby Kernevel, and had been responsible for general U-boat security and the protection of the front U-boat crews in France.

Winter was a gentleman officer of the old school who had an independent mind and considerable reservations about the Nazis and the type of people who had risen to power with them. Winter had been very close to Dönitz personally for quite some time. Dönitz had been reluctant to let Winter go, but finally relented after several long discussions of Winter's request to become a U-boat commander once more.

Because U-103 needed extensive repairs and a substantial overhaul, the Keroman shipyard only declared her ready for operations on 7 September 1941. After loading the maximum possible fuel, food, ammunition and other supplies, U-103 departed on 10 September 1941 on her fifth war patrol from Lorient. she proceeded towards the Canary Islands area, and from there into the mid-Atlantic for operations off West Africa.

Oskar Kusch took over the second bridge watch team, as second watch officer. In his team was Peter Marl, an Austrian who had joined the German Navy just before the war started in 1939 and was now a senior enlisted man. Marl is one of the few people still alive who knew Oskar Kusch quite well. Eventually Marl became the U-boat man with the most operational war patrol sea days who survived the war, namely 825 of them, serving also on U-196 and U-195 in addition to U-103. Marl became a prisoner of war in Surabaya, in Indonesia, when U-195 was taken over by the Japanese in May 1945, after Germany had capitulated.

Marl encountered many officers in six war years, and did not like too many of them, to put it mildly. However, here is what Peter Marl said about Oskar Kusch: 'Kusch was one of the finest officers and men I met in the German Navy. A great leader of his bridge watch. It was a pity there were not more of Kusch's type as officers in the German Navy. Kusch inspired his men and never pulled rank or acted the conceited big shot. Kusch convinced his men, had a sunny disposition and cared deeply about the people serving under him. In tight situations Kusch kept his calm and sense of humour.' Marl closed the conversation this way: 'I am still extremely proud that I was privileged to serve on Kusch's bridge watch aboard U-103.'

When U-103 returned to Lorient on 9 November 1941, Kusch was granted home leave on rotation basis, and attended weapons upgrading courses. During the time he spent in Germany, a great many dramatic things happened that drastically changed the military situation.

On 7 December 1941, the Japanese aircraft carrier group and their naval air force attacked Pearl Harbor, in Hawaii, without declaration of war, and caused considerable losses in ships, men and aircraft on the ground. This was despite the fact that the American Navy and Army had cracked the Japanese signal codes by means of their Purple decoding machines and were fully aware of all Japanese intentions and plans. However, the military commanders in Hawaii were not informed about these successful activities and were kept in the dark by the powers in Washington DC for political reasons and considerations of excessive super-secrecy.

Meanwhile, in Russia, the German Army was stopped early in December 1941 in the very suburbs of Moscow by Stalin's Siberian divisions, and suffered a tremendous defeat in the brutal below-freezing weather. The German Army Group B (Mitte) had not been equipped and provisioned for winter warfare in Russia, as Hitler had wasted time with reorganizations and changes in plans, and then gambled much too late on being able to occupy Moscow before the real Russian winter started. Over 250,000 soldiers of the top-quality troops that could never be replaced paid the price and were either killed or froze to death. Berlin was rife with rumours about the terrible defeat in Russia, but the Nazis firmly suppressed the facts.

Furthermore, during 1941 several operational U-boat disasters had occurred. On 9 April 1941, U-110, a Type IX-B U-boat, commanded by Lieutenant Fritz Julius Lemp (Crew 1931), attacked the convoy OB-318 and torpedoed two ships. U-110 was depth-charged in return by the corvette *Aubretia* and damaged, developing technical problems. Lemp ordered U-110 to the surface, creating considerable confusion among her crew, if not a panic. When U-110 was floating on the surface, she was surrounded by British warships. Lemp now ordered, 'Abandon Ship!' His crew jumped into the ocean as quickly as they could, including the second watch officer, Ensign Ulrich Wehrhöfer, responsible for the destruction of all secret equipment and papers. Senior radioman Heinz Wilde pointed out this gross negligence of duty to commander Lemp on the bridge. When he asked Lemp if he (Wilde) should now carry out this job in Wehrhöfer's place, Lemp told him, 'Just forget it! The ocean is very deep here and everything will automatically go down to the bottom anyhow!' So Wilde jumped into the sea, too, followed by Lemp. In the event, thirty-two men were rescued and fifteen, including Lemp, died in the water.

A British boarding team entered the abandoned U-110, led by the voluntary reserve Sub-Lieutenant David Balme, and captured her, taking as booty many secret documents, papers and files, and the Enigma M-3 coding machine, with all instructions and decoding tables, schedules of setting changes, the secret weather report short signal codes, the Navy's general map grid with secret positioning locations, and many other super-secret documents, papers and manuals – a big laundry-basket full of material, apart from the Enigma machine. Just what the British needed! This equipment and material permitted the English code breakers in Bletchley Park to quickly crack and read the radio signals to and from all U-boats.

Whatever one may think about this catastrophe, Britain's King George VI said it best, when he awarded Balme the Distinguished Service Cross during a special private reception at Buckingham Palace: 'The deed for which you receive this reward was the most important single action of the entire war at sea.'

The British tried to tow U-110 to Scotland, but she sank *en route*. However, they now had in their hands what they desired most, and the consequences were tremendous, though kept super-secret.

Because of heavy losses and slow new construction rates, Dönitz, until the beginning of August 1941, had fewer U-boats available than the number at his disposal when the war started. Finally, new U-boats left the Baltic training grounds in larger numbers, and he did a lot of planning how to best utilize the growing numbers. But before he was able to gain any advantage with these higher numbers of new U-boats with mostly green crews, another calamity occurred. On 29 August 1941,the brand-new Type VII-C U-boat U-570 surrendered, first to aircraft and then to speedily appearing British ships. U-570, commanded by Lieutenant Hans Joachim Rahmlow (Crew 1928), was towed via Iceland to Scotland and gone over with a fine toothcomb. The Enigma M-3 had been tossed into the sea, but everything else was still aboard, including the newly improved, wakeless electric torpedoes, another valuable booty for the Royal Navy.

But the most serious consequences were caused by the minute investigation of the pressurized hull of U-570. The British technicians were amazed at the quality, as well as the strength, of that pressurized body, and declared that nothing equal to it could be constructed in Great Britain. While the specialists who interrogated captured German U-boat men who had become prisoners of war had heard about the much deeper diving ability of the German U-boats, they had discarded this information as mere boasting by the U-boat prisoners. Now, examining the real product, they hurriedly reached the conclusion that this was not mere talk, but reality. The British depth-charges had been programmed with the lesser diving ability of British submarines in mind, and so German U-boats often literally underdived the British depth-charges dropped on them and easily got away undamaged.

But this was to change swiftly. As a redesign of depth-charges and exploders would take time, the British ordered the following improvisations: Put heavy-duty grease or lubricants, or soft soap, available on all ships anyway for cleaning purposes, on the sensors of the exploders. This would considerably delay the timed explosions generated by the sensors. Consequently, the depth-charges would sink much deeper than set, and explode quite a bit later too.

This resulted in growing losses of German U-boats, usually with the entire crew, because as the depth increased the water pressure increased and the U-boats just blew to pieces and there was no chance of reaching the surface again. As no U-boat survived these attacks in deeper water with this change in operational conditions, no warning or explanatory information was received of this drastic change, because the U-boats were unable to signal and no survivors were rescued.

And so Hans Joachim Rahmlow became the second-worst U-boat commander, after Fritz Julius Lemp of U-110, in terms of actual U-boat losses resulting from his incompetency. But the British publicized the capture of Rahmlow's U-570 widely, and it became quickly known to the U-boat Command and Vice-Admiral Dönitz, unlike the earlier capture of U-110, which was kept so super-secret that the British naval files of that capture will remain closed until 2041.

Nevertheless, this was not the end of problems for the U-boat Command. Egged on by ambitious generals at his headquarters, Hitler decided to interfere personally for the first time with U-boat operations, and in autumn 1941 ordered Type VII U-boats into the Mediterranean through the Strait of

Gibraltar, removing them from the Battle of the Atlantic and the principal convoy routes. Once the brief initial element of surprise had passed, this diversion turned into a real drain, because none of these U-boats returned to the Atlantic. Both the first batch, and many others that replaced them later, were gradually destroyed in the Mediterranean.

However, even that was not the last blow for the U-boat Command. Hitler became convinced, through mysterious sources, that the British intended to reconquer Norway. Actually, these rumours were spread by SOE, one of the British secret service organizations. Consequently, Hitler now ordered Type VII U-boats into the Barents Sea to defend northern Norway, almost denuding the North Atlantic of combat U-boats late in 1941.

Many admirals at the Naval High Command in Berlin were opposed to the expansion of the U-boat war. They, like Raeder in many ways, belonged to the 'Gun Club', dreaming of artillery fights and battleship lines, like the 1916 Battle of Jutland. These admirals disliked any additional authority granted to Dönitz, and blocked his funding when they could do so. The majority opposed the 'War of the Lieutenant-Commanders', since there was no place in it for older admirals and captains. The enormous physical demands of U-boat service made this an operation primarily for healthy young men.

Lastly, the British code breakers in Bletchley Park made it possible for Captain of the Reserves Rodger Wynn and the submarine-tracking room in the Admiralty to steer most convoys around the U-boat patrol formations and search lines in the North Atlantic, resulting in a substantial reduction of sinkings during the second half of 1941.

In spite of many jazzed-up, super-heroic war reports that the naval propaganda companies generated regarding the so-called *Glückliche Zeit*, or Happy Times, reporters assigned to the U-boat Command were often put under pressure to greatly exaggerate their stories by their supervisor, Wolfgang Frank, who frequently pepped up their reports considerably, to conform to the expectations in Berlin, before they were released to the press, radio stations and the public.

The fact was that since the beginning of the war, Dönitz had lost sixty-seven U-boats on war operations by the end of 1941. Comparing this with the fifty-seven U-boats available to him when the war started, many U-boat commanders protested strongly against this propaganda swindle. But Dönitz decided to disregard these complaints, as he needed the advertising badly, to strengthen his position in the constant fights for turf and influence during his frequent confrontations with the Naval High Command in Berlin.

It was, of course, impossible to keep these various problems and defeats a secret, no matter how hard the Navy tried to sweep them under the carpet. While the men in training in Germany could be isolated and stuffed with propaganda, at the front, at sea, the men were able to recognize the truth and know of the actual facts. In France, in the U-boat bases in Brest, Lorient,

Saint Nazaire, La Rochelle-La Pallice and Bordeaux, things looked quite different from in Germany, where the Gestapo kept tight control of everything and the Nazi-managed censorship clamped down heavily on any type of information considered undesirable by the regime.

In the officers' messes photographs of all U-boat commanders and officers who had remained at sea and did not return from their war patrols or had been posted as missing, presumed dead, increasingly covered the walls. The operational facts were discussed with naval classmates and trusted fellow officers, whom one could depend upon, regardless of the speeches made by the 'Brass', including Admiral Dönitz.

Many level-headed officers had already concluded in the summer of 1941, once Hitler attacked Soviet Russia, that the war was not winnable any more, especially when the Nazis promoted this attack with the propaganda slogan: 'We are beating England in the steppes of Russia', which was something that nobody who knew anything about geography would swallow.

Now the Nazi government had, in addition, declared war upon the United States of America, thereby attempting to induce the Japanese in return to attack the Soviet Union in the Far East and Siberia. This was a total political fallacy, because Japan had contracted for strict neutrality with Soviet Russia and observed that neutrality rigidly until August 1945, despite strong German efforts and heavy pressure to make her change her policy.

On 1 September 1941, Oskar Kusch was promoted to lieutenant, junior grade. On 10 November he was awarded the Iron Cross, Second Class, and the U-boat front service combat badge. As soon as he had returned to Lorient, Winter asked him to become fully involved in the preparation of U-103 for her next war patrol, sailing with the second wave of U-boats to the American east coast, departing on 3 January 1942 and returning successfully to Lorient on 1 March.

After that war patrol Peter Marl left U-103 for petty officer school, and there were a considerable number of other personnel changes when old-timers were usually replaced by greenhorns fresh from the U-boat training commands in the Baltic. Kusch participated in weapons upgrading courses and attended the electronic and radar warfare school in Le Touquet, in France.

On 15 April 1942, U-103 left Lorient on her seventh war patrol sailing to Cape Hatteras, the Florida Straits and the Eastern Caribbean Sea, including the Yucatan channel, returning to Lorient on 22 June.

After this war patrol Werner Winter was awarded the Knight's Cross of the Iron Cross for having sunk fifteen confirmed ships, totalling 79,302 tons, on three war patrols. Kusch received the Iron Cross, First Class, obtained home leave on rotation basis and again participated in upgraded weapons courses.

On 14 July 1942, Werner Winter was replaced as commander of U-103 and promoted to commander of the 1st U-boat Flotilla in Brest. Lieutenant Gustav Adolf Janssen was appointed as the new commander of U-103. There were also quite a few other changes in the composition of the crew. Kusch moved up to executive officer in charge of the torpedo department.

Because U-103 required both a substantial overhaul and the installation of new equipment, including additional anti-aircraft guns, while the 10.5 cm (4 in) gun was removed for weight balance, necessitating an extended yard service time in the Keroman complex, it was decided that Kusch should participate during this time in the prospective U-boat commanders' qualification courses in the Baltic. But once he passed these training courses, he was to make one more war patrol as executive officer of U-103.

On 21 October 1942 U-103 left Lorient for operations in the mid-Atlantic and to the west of North Africa and Morocco. During her time at sea, the Torch landings in Morocco and North Africa took place, a complete surprise for the U-boat Command. Naturally, this landing operation substantially changed the entire shipping pattern. Still, U-103 was able to sink two steamers of, 11,430 tons together, and damaged a third ship of 13,945 tons, which was towed into port for repairs. On 29 December 1942 U-103 returned to Lorient heavily damaged by combat operations, and entered the Keroman U-boat pen complex for another lengthy repair and overhaul stay at the shipyard.

Early in January of 1943, Kusch was detached as executive officer of U-103 and ordered to participate in another updated electronic and radar course and the latest new torpedo and firing system training. Thereafter, he was expected to become commander of a Type IX U-boat, either a new one in Germany or a U-boat at the front in France.

Unrelated to U-boat operations and the changes in sea war strategy in the Battle of the Atlantic, naval operations and events of far reaching consequences occurred in the Barents Sea to the north of Norway. These operations generated changes in the German Navy that shook the officers and men deeply. War is unpredictable and naval operations frequently tend to be imponderable, no matter how well planned on paper.

On 22 December 1942, an Allied convoy left Loch Ewe in Scotland with fourteen fully loaded steamers carrying Lend-Lease war materials and military supplies for Soviet Russia. This was the first such convoy in several months proceeding to Murmansk in northern Russia. The convoy was escorted by seven British destroyers commanded by Captain R. St V. Sherbrooke, assisted by two corvettes, one minesweeper and two armed trawlers. Rear Admiral Robert Burnett with the light cruisers *Jamaica* and *Sheffield* and three destroyers provided close support. Admiral Bruce Fraser was at sea with a heavy support group, the battleship *Anson*, the heavy cruiser *Cumberland* and two destroyers. Finally, there was a submarine watch line of four submarines just off the coast of northern Norway, including HMS *Graph*, the former German U-570, recently renamed by the British.

On 24 December this convoy was spotted by the German long-distance air reconnaissance between Iceland and Jan Mayen Island. This was Convoy

JW-51-B, a half-section convoy. Several days later it was found by U-354, commanded by Karl Heinz Herschleb, a Type VII U-boat of the Barents Sea Force Command, headed on a course towards Bear Island. The alarm bells were ringing in all German commands in Norway and Germany.

The weather was awful, as is usually the case in the polar winter, when the polar night prevails for twenty-four hours around the clock to the north of the polar circle. The sun never rises at all. Snowstorms, ice-cold rain, hail and fogbanks are the norm. The biting winds whip up the ocean and everything freezes rapidly, whenever moisture touches anything fixed. In cooperation with Naval Group North in Kiel and the Naval High Command in Berlin, Vice-Admiral Oskar Kummetz had prepared an operational plan for such an eventuality called Case *Regenbogen*, or Rainbow. If such a convoy proceeded to Murmansk, it could be located by the *Luftwaffe* or U-boats in time for an attack by the German cruiser force anchored at Altenfjord, Norway.

Kummetz, who nearly messed up the German occupation of Oslo in April 1940, expected a quiet Christmas season and thought it unlikely that the British would reopen the Murmansk convoy route in the middle of the polar winter. Therefore, he was rather surprised when the battle standby operational signal was unexpectedly received from Kiel early on 30 December 1942.

Kummetz and his staff were embarked on the heavy cruiser *Admiral Hipper*, commanded by Captain Hans Hartmann. The other ships of this cruiser force were the heavy cruiser *Lützow*, formerly the pocket battleship *Deutschland*, whose name had to be changed on Hitler's orders, commanded by Captain Rudolf Stange and a division of six destroyers. All eight ships proceeded due north, in the direction of the last U-boat convoy sighting received.

Communications with Germany were often interrupted, the landlines by sabotage, bombing damage or winter weather, the radio communications by atmospheric and weather conditions, causing frequent interference and at times lengthy blackouts. Kummetz ordered a pincer attack, where the convoy was to be attacked from both sides, to split the defence. But the atrocious weather conditions made all plans uncertain in their execution. The *Hipper* with three destroyers took a direct course, while the *Lützow* with the other three destroyers proceeded on a circular route, to reach the other side of the expected convoy.

Suddenly the fog blew clear for minutes, and the *Hipper* saw the British destroyer screen. *Hipper*'s De-Te radar equipment became iced up and was useless. The British destroyers attacked boldly and without hesitation, firing torpedo fans and making smoke to shield the steamers. Guns were aimed and fired by direct visual observations. Two British destroyers were damaged by *Hipper*'s gunfire and the destroyer *Achates* was sunk within minutes. Yet *Hipper* managed to outmanoeuvre the torpedo spreads in the heavy seas.

Suddenly, star shells illuminated the polar night. The British light cruisers were firing on *Hipper* without actually getting her in visual sight; having located her on their radar screens, they instantly covered the ship with a hail of shells. Kummetz ordered an immediate change of course. But while turning, the *Hipper* was hit by three shells, which caused substantial damage.

Kummetz ordered maximum possible speed with the prevailing sea conditions. But after receiving the damage report, he decided to break off the fight without attempting another attack on the convoy, and ordered an immediate direct return to the anchorage in Altenfjord.

In the meantime, *Lützow* approached the convoy from the other side and encountered the destroyer screen, firing her heavy guns within seconds and seriously damaging the destroyer *Obdurate*. But receiving the retreat signal at the same time, *Lützow* likewise turned around and headed back to northern Norway at full speed, to get away from this confusing night fighting in the polar darkness.

Owing to their rather higher speed, the German ships gradually gained ground, and the British cruisers lost them on their radar screens. During this turnaround, the German destroyers ran across the British minesweeper *Bramble* and swiftly sank her, while the German destroyer *Friedrich Eckholdt* got lost in the confusion, mistook the British cruiser *Sheffield* for the *Hipper* and was promptly sunk. Pretty soon the icy polar night prevailed again and things started to go quiet, except for the howling wind and the blizzards of snow that come and go.

The British destroyer captain, Sherbrooke, was seriously wounded and lost one of his eyes from shrapnel. The British Admiralty awarded him the Victoria Cross for his intrepid and splendid defence of the convoy against superior ships. A few days later all steamers reached Murmansk safely. The British Broadcasting Service flashed out news bulletins about this night battle, claiming a tremendous victory by the British Navy against the German cruisers, driving the larger and heavier-gunned cruisers back to northern Norway.

Meanwhile, in Hitler's headquarters, all hell broke loose. Virtually the sole information at hand was a radio message from U-354, which did not even reach the actual battlefield and was not close enough for a torpedo attack on the convoy, reading, 'The entire sky is crimson, despite the polar night. A great victory must be the cause of this! Herschleb.' This signal was not based upon visual facts, but merely over-enthusiastic speculation and wishful thinking by Herschleb, but it generated far-reaching consequences in Berlin.

Hitler needed some good news badly, with Stalingrad turning worse daily and Rommel's *Afrika Korps* beaten and in retreat, fighting rearguard defensive actions. Yet many hours passed without an action report, without any signal from Kummetz's Northern Cruiser Force. Only silence reigned.

Hitler became furious and ordered Vice-Admiral Theodor Krancke, the liaison admiral at his headquarters, to get hold of Raeder right away, demanding his presence at headquarters without delay, with a full report of the battle and the events in the Barents Sea.

At the Naval High Command, Raeder really had no other information at hand, except the BBC reports of this fight off northern Norway. When he reached Hitler's headquarters at Rastenburg, East Prussia, he was unable to provide any details or further facts. Hitler demanded that Raeder signal the Northern Cruiser Command instantly to get a full report. But Raeder refused to accept such an order, because it would be suicidal for Kummetz, who was keeping radio silence for security reasons. Raeder stated that the British battleship covering force had just been located.

Hitler yelled and screamed that Raeder was disobedient and must get this information forthwith. In addition, he now told Raeder that he must submit a detailed written report of this battle and at the same time present a plan to dismantle the German capital ships soon, because they were useless and too expensive to keep. This was to be not later than 6 January 1943.

However, nothing was received at all from Kummetz because he decided to sleep off the strain of this operation first, once he had returned to northern Norway. Owing to the communication problems that prevailed, he was unaware how urgently Berlin needed his report. In the meantime, Hitler's impatience grew by leaps and bounds. His naval adjutant, Captain Karl Jesko 'Puma' von Puttkamer, tried hard to pour oil on the waves of excitement and to reduce Hitler's furious outbursts, but it was in vain.

When Raeder reappeared on 6 January, he had still not obtained reliable information from Kummetz regarding this Barents Sea battle. Immediately, Hitler resumed his ranting and raving, periodically egged on by Hermann Göring, who was complaining about the *Luftwaffe* aircraft he had to station in Norway to protect the fleet. Göring shouted, 'I could use these aeroplanes much better elsewhere!'

Hitler carried on and on for over three hours, stating his dissatisfaction with these expensive surface ships, which were practically useless anyway and never did really fight, but ran away instead. When he took his first break for breath, after once more repeating that these capital ships were valueless because they actually never fought for a decision but turned tail instead, Raeder respectfully requested an audience with Hitler privately, without the various headquarter hangers-on being present.

Taken off guard, Hitler agreed and moved with Raeder alone into another room. Here Raeder told Hitler that he had commanded the German Navy since 1928, pointing out that he was turning 67 shortly and was already beyond retirement age. Only because of the war had he stayed on. Hitler had assured him repeatedly that the German fleet would not be needed before 1948 or 1949. Raeder categorically rejected Hitler's accusations regarding the German Navy. All operational orders were issued strictly according to instructions from Hitler's headquarters with respect to policy and all operational fleet orders and fighting procedures.

In order to somewhat camouflage his retirement at this difficult time in the war, Raeder suggested his retirement should take place on 30 January 1943, the tenth anniversary of Hitler becoming Reichs Chancellor in Germany. Furthermore, to smother rumours and gossip, Raeder recommended that he should be named Inspector-General of the German Navy, but only as a purely honorary title and position, without any future duties.

Hitler was stunned and remained speechless for a while. Then he apologized to Raeder and attempted to persuade him to change his mind and keep his position. However, Raeder remained firm and pointed out that his health could no longer bear further abuse, with these constant underhanded political intrigues that originated from Göring regarding the German Navy in general and Raeder himself in particular.

Finally, Hitler agreed reluctantly with Raeder and asked him to propose two admirals qualified to replace him and young enough to bear the strain on their health. Moreover, Raeder should reply specifically to the detailed plan to dismantle the German surface fleet ships larger than destroyers, place their guns into coastal fortifications and distribute their crews on smaller ships. Raeder replied carefully that he had as yet not had the time to study this new plan, but would do so before he retired. Yet on the face of things, it looked to Raeder like handing a bloodless victory to England, dismantling the fleet in the middle of the war!

As demanded by Hitler, Raeder submitted his view of the fleet dismantling plan on 15 January 1943. He succeeded in stretching out some decisions and delaying others over a longer time period. He also handed Hitler a sheet of paper with the names of two suitable naval officers as successors for himself. They were, firstly, *Generaladmiral* Rolf Carls, the commander of Naval Group North in Kiel since August of 1940, and secondly, Admiral Karl Dönitz, the head of the U-boat Command since 1935, stationed in Paris. Raeder told Hitler that he had personally spoken with these men and felt that both were highly qualified to take his place, but Hitler would have to make his own decision and personal selection.

However, he had not mentioned a point of delicacy regarding seniority and the previous personal relations between these two admirals. Both men had served together as younger officers aboard the light cruiser *Breslau* from 1913 to 1916, Carls as the senior gunnery officer and Dönitz as the junior communications coordinator and adjutant of the *Breslau*'s commander in the Mediterranean, Turkey and the Black Sea. Carls was seven years senior and also seven years older than Dönitz. Both officers had become close personal friends in the past, and Carls had sponsored Dönitz several times already, considerably assisting Dönitz in his career climb. Naturally, Carls would find it difficult to serve under the younger Dönitz, should Hitler pick him as the new chief commanding officer of the Navy. Raeder then returned to Berlin and started to clean out his desk immediately to clear the way for his successor.

In Hitler's 'Wolf's Lair' headquarters, his private secretary, Martin

Bormann, who had previously served Rudolf Hess as assistant, had gradually achieved almost total control of all matters within Germany outside purely military undertakings. Yet even on such matters Hitler consulted Bormann regarding the political side of any military action. Consequently, Hitler showed him Raeder's list, to get his view. After staring at the two names for a while, Bormann declared: 'Carls we hardly know at all, except by name. Considering his age, no doubt he will be another one of those stiff-necked, rigid Imperial Navy leftovers. Dönitz we know, at least, as being enthusiastic about our aims and having a positive attitude towards the Nazi Party plans, policies and ideas.' Hitler agreed and just nodded his assent. Therefore, somewhat to his own surprise, Dönitz was selected as Raeder's successor.

Two weeks later, Dönitz was officially appointed as Commander-in-Chief of the Navy and at the same time promoted to admiral of the fleet. Admiral Carls requested retirement to give Dönitz the opportunity to bring his own team into all important positions. Dönitz and his staff had to move from Paris to Berlin Charlottenburg and the Hotel am Steinplatz. He decided to keep his former title as U-boat Commander-in-Chief in addition to his new one, which also included the Navy's coastal artillery. But he realized that he would no longer have the time to look after the daily routine operational grind of the U-boat Command, and his deputy in France, Captain Eberhard Godt, was appointed Chief of Staff and Acting Commander of the U-boat Command. Godt was promoted to rear admiral on 1 March 1943, taking charge of the day-to-day operational business.

It required about six weeks to get all teletype, special telephone and the secret coded typewriter lines installed in Berlin and the additional radio signal circuits put into working order so that the complete move from Paris could take place. In the meantime, Dönitz cleaned out the Naval High Command, the OKM in Berlin. Within a few weeks whole bunches of admirals who had more seniority on the naval ranking list than Dönitz were retired. By the end of March 1943, only four admirals who had more seniority than Dönitz (Crew 1910) remained on active duty because they had technical backgrounds and particular expertise, so that they could not be replaced at short notice. Dönitz also kept a few of the older rear admirals for the same reason or because they had sensitive political connections. This wholesale turnover became known in the German Navy as *Der Robbenschlag*, the Great Cull of Seals, which took place every spring off the Canadian coastline.

Dönitz had never forgotten how so many of these older admirals had put obstacles in his way for years, how they had objected to almost every proposal made by the U-boat Command, how they had diverted funds and manpower from U-boat Command construction planning, how they had deviously attempted to keep Dönitz under tight control and fought every issue that would allow him to gain more authority or prestige, how they had tried to quickly put the brakes on any expansion proposal of the U-boat

Command submitted for approval to Berlin. Now Dönitz was finally able to implement that old naval rule: 'Don't get mad, get even instead.'

A more thorough turnover and change had probably never taken place in any major military organization within such a short time, not to mention in the middle of an extended war, much less in the rather staid German naval administration and its bureaucratic ways.

CHAPTER THREE

Caught in the Revolving Door

rank W. Petersen had just returned from a three-week sailing trip in the Mediterranean. He was still delighted and full of pep when he saw the pile of mail that had accumulated during his absence collected in a shoebox for him. Quickly, he shuffled through the batch of letters and tossed everything marked printed matter immediately in the wastepaper basket, without opening it.

But an official-looking letter in a brown envelope from the regional draft board and Army Command got his prompt attention. Petersen ripped it open and after quickly reading a few sentences, his joy from the sailing vacation started to fade rather fast.

While he had known that such an invitation to present himself for registration and medical examination was unavoidable, since the Hitler government had reintroduced obligatory military conscription for all males, somehow he had hoped it would not come so soon. There was only one small advantage – this registration and check-up took place during the first week of school, meaning a free school day at least. One had to be grateful for small favours in life. He would have to present himself for this examination just prior to his 16th birthday, unless he was mentally or physically handicapped, in which case an exception needed to be applied for right away.

Four weeks later, Petersen joined about eighty other young men. He was put through some medical tests and questioned by tight-lipped fellows about his school situation, being a senior high school pupil, while most others were asked about their vocational or professional status or job-related matters. It appeared that those who were mentally retarded had already been excused and eliminated. His sailing ability and seamanship experience aroused the special interest of these men, who questioned him extensively. When he had passed through the medical circus, Petersen was told to wait somewhere, until called by name for a final assessment and determination by the draft board.

In this way he swiftly learned what soldiers do most of the time: wait. The waiting area got emptier and emptier during the afternoon, until he was finally called. A moustachioed official asked him briskly for his name and took him along a long hall and around several bends and corners to a wide door, knocked and told Petersen to enter.

Inside, there was a long table, a kind of counter with chairs and several desks, three of them occupied by elderly reserve officers in Army, Air Force and Navy uniforms, looking like three oriental Buddhas. They welcomed Petersen with a few rather peculiar remarks. The army officer, being evidently the most senior, informed him that he had been classified as predestined for the Navy, because of his sailing experience and his participation in several regattas.

Then the naval officer took over and interrogated Petersen on his personal habits and his linguistic ability, mentioned in his file. The next question pertained to his contemplated plans for a career once he finished senior high school and had managed to pass his final examination. Considering that this was still about a year away, he was a bit surprised and caught off guard. He told these men that his first choice of a job would be to become a marine biologist and zoologist, and if this did not work out, as it was a brand-new profession, he would consider becoming either a landscape architect or a professional forester. The air force officer bent forward to hear better and asked loudly, 'What in heaven's name does a marine biologist-zoologist do?' Petersen replied, 'They work with animal and plant life in the oceans, especially birds and fish.'

All three officers just guffawed and laughed for minutes about this revelation, which they apparently viewed as the biggest joke ever. When things calmed down again, the naval officer declared that Petersen would be custom-made for the new Navy, as an experienced sailor, and once he joined he would be able to watch birds and catch fish to his heart's content; but, of course, only during his free time or when not otherwise occupied with naval service requirements. Petersen was then asked to explain what a scuba diver did and how this might apply itself to naval needs, as his file contained a copy of his scuba diving course certificate.

It seemed Petersen had made the day for these three old fellows. Then, after telling him that he would be called as soon as he had passed his final school examination, they all laughed again and wished him luck with his combined naval and marine biologist career. Until induction Petersen was admonished to work tenaciously on his swimming and diving abilities whenever he had a chance, and to stay away from girls as much as possible in the meantime, as they usually weakened men far too much! Once more, all three officers laughed uproariously in unison, while Petersen exited rapidly.

Almost a year after attending this draft board, Petersen finished senior high school and passed his final examination with flying colours. A few days later, he reported on the Dänholm near Stralsund for basic training, just a couple of days prior to his 17th birthday. The training schedule for officer candidate recruits had not changed much, except that with the start of the Second World War most shipboard assignments were made on ships in front-line service, rather than school- and training ships. Most cadets served in one of the minesweeping flotillas, some on destroyers or torpedo boats, a few on large warships and a handful on S-boats, the German PT or MTB type of fast-moving boats of small size. Petersen was lucky to get assigned to one of the S-boat flotillas in the North Sea.

After getting ship experience, the cadets were posted to the naval academy in Flensburg-Mürwik, where things had barely changed since Oskar Kusch had attended this institution. Some slight adjustments in emphasis on a few sectors of the training programme had taken place, but nothing really substantial.

Once Petersen and his fellow midshipmen had managed to get through the final examination at the naval academy, they were told to assemble in specific meeting places. Here they were handed a 'Christmas' wish list by their group officers or company commanders – one of the few novelties. They were asked to list in order of preference three different shipboard assignments they would like to get once they left the naval academy.

Petersen, being somewhat of a maverick, completed his sheet as follows: 1, S-boat (PT or MTB boat); 2, Torpedo boat; 3, Destroyer. But his company commander rejected his list and advised him that there was little likelihood that positions were open on those types of surface ships. Why had he not included U-boats, which were at the top of the list for most of his comrades? Petersen answered he would really prefer a ship where one was able to breathe fresh air, but as small as possible. Even minesweepers would be okay with him. The company commander took his questionnaire and dismissed him with some shaking of his head. How could anybody be so headstrong and stubborn, he wondered loudly.

A week later Petersen was handed his ship assignment and given a heavy envelope with rail tickets and instructions where to proceed. He was to report in Lorient to the 2nd U-boat Flotilla for assignment after arrival. His orders and tickets had been issued two weeks earlier. Thus, the whole choice process was really nothing but a sham. He had not volunteered for U-boat service, but was simply assigned to U-boats because he was in good physical shape and fulfilled all the required medical conditions.

The growth of the U-boat Command was faster, in terms of manning needs, than the various U-boat training schools in the Baltic could provide during that period, because nasty winter weather and the icing up of many ports considerably restricted U-boat training classes in the Baltic. At times all available places were taken and no further prospects could be accepted until the training facilities were expanded once more.

Therefore, the decision was made that all midshipmen assigned to the U-boat Command who were not accepted by the U-boat schools would be posted immediately to front-service U-boats, in order to learn by doing. Naturally, this resulted in many mistakes and caused quite a few problems.

But midshipmen were expected to be 'eager beavers', able to learn quickly and overcome such problems. However, as in any group of men, some did learn rapidly, while others did not learn fast enough, even when survival depended upon the pace of such learning. Consequently, midshipmen fresh from the naval academy were not welcomed with open arms on the U-boats they were assigned to, and were often watched closely for quite some time, until they fitted in and were able to act as expected by the U-boat crew, the officers and, especially, the U-boat's commander.

Owing to Petersen's language ability, he was informed that he would get posted to special assignments and confidential investigations, while his U-boat was overhauled in port. During the war, midshipmen could not be allowed to take it easy, enjoying harbour life and having a good time with the crew between war patrols. They were expected to be learning constantly, and they needed to be working at other tasks during slack times.

Consequently, between war patrols, Petersen would get assigned periodic-ally to experienced naval intelligence officers, to give them a hand and assist them to the best of his ability. If and when places became available in the most essential U-boat school courses, these midshipmen would be fed in, skipping the theoretical classes and participating only in the concentrated weapons and technical courses. But exactly when this would be the case was uncertain just then.

Yet this actual front service aboard U-boats would be more advantageous than mere school attendance. It would allow the earliest possible assignment as fully fledged watch officers on front-line U-boats, rather than getting assigned initially either to newly commissioned U-boats undergoing oper-ational training in the Baltic or to school U-boats. After all, in wartime the Navy had to put their men where they were most needed at a particular time, regardless of what their personal preferences might be. There was really nothing else to do, but to salute and yell as loudly as possible, 'Yes Sir, Captain!' and then make the best of it.

As things eventually turned out, Petersen was lucky to be posted aboard a U-boat whose commander liked him and gave him a helping hand when needed, although this was not automatically the case on all U-boats. The watch officers and the directing engineer were also satisfied with Petersen's performance on different type of jobs, and he was admitted to the officers' mess, instead of having to eat and sleep with the petty officers, who were a rather rough bunch and tended to be very noisy.

The temporary assignments between war patrols turned out to be quite interesting because Petersen became involved in things that had little bearing on U-boat service. Usually he had to work for two different senior reserve *Abwehr* officers who had served as junior officers in the First World War in the Imperial Navy. Both took a fatherly attitude and liking to Petersen, allowing him considerable leeway in every respect. Actually, his most time-consuming and demanding duties consisted of going hunting for deer or hare with the one captain, an avid hunter, and going fishing for trout or dorade with the other captain, who happened to be a keen fisherman. Such types of activity were probably healthier and more relaxing than drinking oneself into a stupor in some French bar, raising hell afterwards and getting chased by the shore patrol of the field police, those hated 'chain dogs', as the enlisted men called them.

Petersen made three war patrols, gradually moving up in responsibility and job assignment, becoming an accepted member of the crew step by step. He was also used as a courier for secret documents, travelling with a diplomatic pouch to Madrid, Lisbon, Berne or Stockholm. Here he could buy many things no longer available in Germany, and a few growing scarce even in France. Time passed very quickly that way. Then he was promoted to senior midshipman just before he was ordered to attend the principal concentrated U-boat weapons training courses in the Baltic, required for a full-time watch officer on front-line U-boats.

CHAPTER FOUR

Seeing is Believing

The evening poker game in the U-boat officers' mess located in the Hôtel Beau Sejour in Lorient had just ended when the phone started to ring incessantly. It was picked up reluctantly by Rick Keller, who handed it over to Frank Petersen: 'Paris calling for you.'

Petersen confirmed that he was on the line, and was connected to Commander Günter Hessler of the U-boat Operational Command, the senior staff officer and coordinator. 'Good evening, Petersen, you are needed urgently in Paris for the discussion of a special investigation. I would like you to take the morning express train, as it is already too late for the night express. We shall have a car and driver meet you upon arrival, as taxis are now impossible to find in Paris. Be prepared to be away for somewhere between ten days and two weeks, and make sure that you can be spared from Lorient for that time, one way or another. I anticipate you will need only one day here, but you must plan to stop in La Rochelle for a meeting there. One overnight stop ought to suffice for that. Then on to Spain. The rest verbally. See you tomorrow evening for dinner here!'

Hessler hung up and Petersen finished his drink quickly and proceeded to the office of the 2nd U-boat Flotilla, to have his transportation and travel orders prepared and maintenance expenses arranged. It was already late and dark, and emergency staff were on duty around the clock. In a few more days, it would be 1 September 1942, and the war had already lasted three full years, with no end in sight. Petersen managed to locate his orderly and told him what to pack and put together, as there would not be enough time in the morning to do so. He requested a car to take him to the station in time for the early-morning train from Brest to Paris.

While there were always two or three reserved cars for the exclusive use of the German military forces, crowds of French people invariably jammed the railway stations and platforms for the Paris-bound trains, many with bulky pieces of baggage or unwieldy containers with food items, fish or produce for their relatives in Paris or for sale somewhere.

The 20-year-old Petersen had a huge breakfast in order to fortify himself for the long journey to Paris, because French trains no longer had dining cars. While the railway carriages for the French people were always extremely crowded, those reserved for the German military were fairly empty, as most sailors and soldiers preferred to use the evening express train instead.

The train arrived at Montparnasse station in Paris only fifteen minutes late, less than normal. Petersen was driven to the U-boat Command Centre in Avenue Maréchal Maunoury, where he reported straightaway to Günter Hessler. But Hessler was otherwise engaged, and one of his assistants handed Petersen a pile of prepared reports, papers, documents and messages, with instructions to find an empty desk and work his way through the stuff in order to become familiar with the background and related information then available in Paris.

Petersen ordered a pot of black tea and some biscuits to tide himself over until dinner time. He had nearly reached the bottom of the stack of papers when Hessler entered and welcomed him, telling him to finish quickly and ask whatever questions came to mind after perusing the papers.

Petersen had only a few points where further details were helpful, most concerning technical specifications or clarifications of uncertain facts. Hessler told him that the next morning they would have a meeting with communication technicians, electronic engineers and some others, to get to the bottom of things as far as possible. The rest would then really be up to Petersen.

Hessler also informed him that Lieutenant Peter E. 'Ali' Cremer, commanding U-333, had just returned to La Pallice-La Rochelle after sustaining considerable damage off the Iberian Peninsula. He had made some periscope observations and experienced some new defensive effects by the British escorts that were so unusual that Petersen was to discuss them fully with Cremer in La Rochelle. Hessler had spoken briefly with Cremer and had told him that Petersen would come to see him the next evening and that he was to tell Petersen everything, even the smallest details. Cremer was staying at the Hôtel de France et d'Angleterre, where the offices of the 3rd U-boat Flotilla were then located.

Petersen's head was buzzing with details that did not match up or were even contradictory. Therefore he was happy to accept the offer by one of his naval classmates to visit the Sheherazade Night-Club to get other ideas into his head and circumvent the danger of not seeing the forest for the trees. As always happened to be the case, the Russian nostalgic and sentimental atmosphere relaxed Petersen more quickly and cleared his head better than the four aspirins he had taken earlier.

The naval officers and submariners sat together at specific tables, the Frenchmen at others, while the Russians moved around everywhere. It was the kind of programme young people liked and enjoyed more than those overpriced and overrated shows at the Lido or Moulin Rouge.

After the morning meeting, which did not really accomplish anything of substance and went around in circles, Petersen was seen off by Hessler, after another short conversation summarizing the situation. He was then driven back to Montparnasse station and caught the express to Bordeaux, with cars to La Rochelle. As soon as Petersen reached the office of the 3rd U-boat Flotilla he was welcomed by 'Ali' Cremer.

Cremer had suggested that they should go for a walk after Petersen's long train journey and to make sure nobody overheard their conversation. La Rochelle was a well-preserved, medieval town that had once bordered on the Bay of Biscay, but got silted up over the years, and a new harbour terminal had had to be built in La Pallice, about four miles away, where the concrete and bomb-proof U-boat pens had been constructed. The old harbour of La Rochelle was only used by shallow-draft coastal fishing boats and sport sailors.

At this time, La Rochelle was still out of range of the British bombers, unlike Brest, Lorient and Saint Nazaire. Later, once larger and longer-range aircraft became available, they bombed the La Pallice harbour area, while the old town of La Rochelle was fortunately preserved undamaged for later generations. Today it is a delightful place for visitors who prefer places away from the crowded tourist routes.

Walking in the shade of huge trees grouped into several small parks, Cremer related his recent experiences and observations, to bring Petersen fully up to date. U-333 had approached a convoy from Gibraltar to England off the coast of Portugal, and her sighting short radio signal had clearly been registered by the escorts of this convoy, because within minutes British destroyers appeared coming over the horizon, taking a direct course towards U-333. 'Ali' Cremer and his best lookouts had seen the tops of the destroyer masts grow before it was possible to see the actual ships. Peculiar six-sided birdcage-like antennae could be recognized, looking like some kind of fish-trap from the distance. Because of the immediate response and reaction to Cremer's signal, he felt these were special recording antennae with fast-response equipment, automatically recording U-boat signals. He had had rough drawings prepared and handed them to Petersen.

The only thing absolutely certain was that the German Navy had neither such equipment nor anything even similar for rapid recording or automatic response to radio signals observed on these destroyers, and presumably other surface ships too. Cremer had been able to dive, once the destroyer masts grew larger, but had been located and extensively depth-charged. U-333 had survived these attacks and was able to creep away, running very deep, but the damage forced Cremer to return to base for repairs.

'Ali' Cremer had even photographed these mast tops through his periscope. The pictures were not too sharp, but gave Petersen some further ideas of how one might go about solving the matter and ferreting out what this type of equipment was able to accomplish and what one could try to do to defeat these advantages. Cremer pointed out that the sea had been un-usually smooth and there was no noticeable wind. That, no doubt, was why Cremer had been able to observe these destroyer masts so clearly. In normal

North Atlantic weather, this would have been impossible, particularly when looking at anything over such a distance. Cremer knew that this convoy had been supplied with new escort ships in Gibraltar, but most of the steamers had arrived from other places and were assembled in Gibraltar. Therefore, Cremer stated, to him it would seem logical and most promising to get as close as possible to Gibraltar, perhaps with extra-powerful binoculars to double-check the matter. Petersen grinned and told Cremer that was exactly what he was going to do, continuing onward via Madrid to Algeciras, where the *Abwehr* had an observation post in some villa he was scheduled to get to within a few days. Petersen told Cremer that if Algeciras did not work, he would attempt to get a clear look from La Linea, though the view was more restricted from there. Maybe, as a civilian with fluent Spanish, he could find some way to take concise and sharp pictures or somehow get some more evidential material.

Petersen told Cremer that the technicians in Berlin had already several times rejected the report that the British had radar on their aeroplanes and smaller ships like destroyers. They stubbornly claimed that what the Germans were unable to do would be simply impossible for the English. Furthermore, centimetric short waves could not get beamed sharply enough to get usable results. Cremer cursed the 'chair-farting' bureaucrats in Berlin, who mainly engaged in wishful thinking. Petersen added, 'Amen, provided they are able to think to begin with, and don't merely repeat like parrots what they are taught to say or report.'

Cremer's U-333 had been repaired swiftly, and he had just received his new sailing orders for 1 September to proceed to West Africa. Petersen asked, 'With a Type VII U-boat? To my knowledge we have used Type IX U-boats that far south several times in the past, but the Type VIIs are outside their fuel and operational range, with regard to the distances to be travelled.' Cremer replied, 'I also questioned this right away and called Paris, but was assured that the U-boat Command now has enough U-tankers to supply U-boats in operation and in position to make it possible to refuel Type IX U-boats once, and the Type VII U-boats twice *en route*.'

Petersen commented on this information by stating, 'While this sounds great and I hope it works out as planned, I fear these slow-diving, hard-to-handle "milk cows" won't manage to survive long at sea. When attacked by fast aircraft, they have only a small chance of getting away and diving safely once their position becomes known. But with the constant stream of radio signals required for refuelling meetings, I would not be surprised if such signals get decoded by the British and the U-tankers get targeted for special attention and sunk in short order.' Cremer nodded. 'I think you have a good point there. Consequently, it's even more important that you intelligence experts are finally able to persuade U-boat Command that our signals are being cracked, read and acted upon by the British, which they still seem to doubt.'

On the walk back to their quarters, Petersen brought Cremer up to date on what was new in the Sheherazade in Paris and whom he had met and seen there during his recent visit. 'Ali' Cremer just sighed. 'How I should like to be there tonight, instead of hanging around in the Schepke House, or having to waste my time with boring paperwork.'

'In that case,' Petersen suggested, 'I shall invite you for a lobster dinner at Le Yachtman Hotel. Let's walk there and have a decent meal. Who knows when there will be another chance to do so.' Cremer agreed immediately. 'The paperwork won't run away. Let's enjoy the rest of the evening and not talk about anything connected with U-boats any more.' So they circled the yacht harbour basin and went into the hotel.

When he finally returned to his quarters, a message awaited Petersen that *Abwehr* Dax would send a car for him. He was to be ready for it at 06.45 hours. Another early breakfast would be necessary. He snoozed in the back seat until they arrived. Dax and also Pau *Abwehr* relay stations, at the foot of the Pyrenees, were used to receive and relay radio signal traffic mainly from North Africa and Spain, but depending upon weather conditions, sometimes from South America or South Africa.

Petersen handed over his uniform and received civilian clothing. He turned in his military identity papers and documents and got a passport instead, together with some other papers fitting his projected identity and an envelope of pesetas. The *Abwehr* station manager informed him that he would be driven to San Sebastian, and furnished him with an address and contact there who would handle his onward transportation and operational needs.

It was noon before they reached the place where Petersen was to be dropped. When he rang the bell it seemed as if nobody was at home, but as soon as the car had disappeared the door was opened and Petersen was asked to go inside for a surprise luncheon with Spanish specialities. The contact never mentioned his name, nor did he ask what name Petersen was using. In the afternoon Petersen was handed a case with papers and instructions, and another vehicle picked him up for the long drive to Madrid.

Petersen studied this material and compared the various papers with the information he had been given in Paris and the verbal amplifications furnished during the special meeting there. Some discrepancies were obvious, and these two sets of reports drew differing conclusions in several respects. Petersen realized that there were still a lot of mere assumptions and few definitive or reliable facts. It was clearly up to him to straighten this out and separate the chaff from the wheat and the gossip or rumours from the facts. He would have to depend upon some luck to obtain evidential proof and to document the details in an irrefutable way. This was not going to be a piece of cake.

Hessler had inquired how much help and back-up he would need. Petersen told him that he preferred to work alone as much as possible to remain inconspicuous, but that *Abwehr* Algeciras or the naval staff at the German embassy in Madrid ought to provide him with a high-quality camera and an experienced photographer who would be able to give professional advice and support. Petersen himself was an amateurish picture taker and unable to judge correctly what a camera could do and to what degree. There was no sense in making more fuzzy pictures without clear details, like those taken by Cremer from U-333. Petersen had requested that these should be made available in Algeciras, so that he would not attract attention and undesirable interest while travelling to southern Spain.

In Madrid it was confirmed this would be done and that army Lieutenant Karl Redl in Algeciras would arrange whatever he needed without delays or problems. Petersen did not wish to be spotted by Allied agents or observers, as that would make his job almost impossible and would also put him at considerable risk.

He was asked if he would like to attend a cocktail reception at the Argentinian embassy, which would be a good place for his contact to meet him in the crowd and afterwards simply leave with him unobtrusively. This seemed an interesting way to lose any possible tail in the dark, as the party only started at 22.00 hours.

Petersen did not associate with the German embassy staff at the reception, but became involved in a lengthy conversation with a stupendous-looking girl who apparently worked at the Argentinian embassy as a secretary or something. Her greenish eyes sparkled, her reddish-blonde hair shone and she complimented Petersen on his Spanish fluency and his pertinent, though somewhat spicy, comments about a few of the attending reception guests. The girl had a striking figure and was without a doubt highly intelligent and educated. Her smile would melt almost any heart. Her insouciance was refreshing. Obviously, she was not one of those cloistered Latin girls, sheltered by waspish chaperones.

Suddenly, she asked Petersen directly if he was married or engaged? The girl had not given him her name, nor did she ask his name. Therefore he was amused by her question and considered it a kind of joke. They both had great fun gossiping about the various people at the party, and they evidently had similar tastes and matching views. Petersen told her he was single, but during wartime was not a suitable prospect for any woman. She could not be much more than 21 years old, and she told Petersen that when he was in a position to travel again after this war ended, he must visit Argentina to see her wonderful country. Petersen smiled and replied, 'If all Argentinian girls are even half as beautiful as you are, this will be a very enticing prospect for the future.'

She then whispered to him, 'You can find me through the Dodero Steamship Line, if you ever come to Buenos Aires.' Petersen only nodded because she was suddenly called away and introduced to a group of elderly late arrivals.

He was uncertain what to do next, except to ask for another glass of Mendoza wine, when Captain Leissner, the *Abwehr* head and senior naval officer in Madrid, moved close and told him, 'Your contact has arrived and is waiting for you at the side-door exit. Leave the party without delay.'

Leissner briefly hesitated and then asked Petersen point-blank, 'What got into you? Soft-soaping a woman here in this catholic society. Don't you know who she is?' Petersen replied briskly, 'Captain, Sir, I have not the slightest idea who she might be, because she did not give me her name.' Leissner just shook his head wistfully. 'You young bucks. Fearless at the front and without qualms on land. She is the only daughter of one of the richest families in Argentina. You could never afford her on your salary.' But Petersen replied, 'Captain, Sir, I honestly had no idea whatsoever. After all, it was your office that arranged my presence here and exposed me to this incredible temptation. But I am totally innocent and mightily surprised too.' Leissner just mumbled, 'Off you go now, quietly, before somebody associates you with me and tails you afterwards. For you, the party is over. Good luck in Algeciras!'

The waiting contact had spotted Petersen after this intermezzo, and led him quickly out of the building to a dark car parked some distance away, in the deep shadow of tall trees. The man advised Petersen that he would drive him to Algeciras, where accommodation had been reserved for him at the Hotel Maria Cristina, old but well run. It had been difficult, as the hotel was currently booked to capacity all the time. Petersen stepped into the back seat, snuggled into one corner, grabbed a blanket and was asleep within minutes.

Spanish highways were still in terrible condition, and the ride was quite bumpy in some sectors. They stopped at a country inn for a break, which Petersen used to walk around a bit as he felt rather stiff after the long drive. They arrived at the hotel in the afternoon because the room would not be available any earlier.

When Petersen was shown to his room, there was a complete new set of civilian clothing hanging in the wardrobe, made in Spain. Inside the jacket, a note was pinned, 'Change your clothing. I shall call for you after dark. Get some rest in the meantime. See you later. K.'

Karl 'Charlie' Redl was the *Abwehr* station manager in Algeciras. He got teased by every *Abwehr* man passing through, because he had the same surname as that infamous Austrian traitor, Colonel Alfred Redl of the old Imperial Army, who had sold the plans of all Austrian border fortifications in Poland to Russia to get money for keeping his various homosexual lovers in style. Then, adding insult to injury, Redl was promoted and transferred from Vienna to Prague, as the Austrian director of counter-espionage against Russia. Then he really cashed in to meet his increasing expenses, until the case finally blew up when some of his male lovers got into a jealous fight after getting drunk.

Though Redl had become used to these jocular comparisons, he did not really like them very much. Petersen had never participated in such 'fun', and Redl appreciated this and thanked him by being especially helpful to him and the U-boat requirements. Because Algeciras watched and reported all convoy assemblies and sailings from Gibraltar, they had grown into an important factor for the U-boat Command. However, lately the British had added so many new escort groups to these convoys that it had become almost impossible to attack them successfully.

Petersen took a shower first and then decided to visit the bar, which had just opened. Most chairs and seats were rapidly occupied, many of them by British in uniform, obviously officers on short-term leave, including some junior naval officers trying to get away from shipboard restrictions. Interestingly enough, there were also a few Americans among them, boisterous and free wheeling, while the British were drinking quietly and remained rather reticent. Petersen had little trouble understanding the conversations as long as the people talked loudly enough. Two Spaniards shared his table who sounded like commercial salesmen there to solicit business. He got to talking with them and blended easily into the background.

It was about 23.00 hours when Redl knocked on his door and him picked up. Redl grinned at the Spanish sombrero Petersen now featured. They walked in a roundabout way and a few semicircles before reaching the garden gate of the *Abwehr* Villa San Luis, entering fast.

Redl and two of his men briefed Petersen on the latest observations and rumours. On the balcony, an extra-powerful pair of binoculars had been installed for a constant watch of all ship and air movements in the port and at the airport of Gibraltar. Redl suggested Petersen should use this equipment as soon as it was daylight in order to re-familiarize himself with the layout and geographical details. Redl mentioned that a batch of brand-new destroyers of the new P and Q classes had recently arrived, and had anchored in the bay and were clearly visible. Petersen should study them minutely first, and afterwards decide how to proceed and what he would require.

There is a bed for you upstairs, so you can work on the binoculars as soon as you wake up. Here is the latest batch of messages and reports for you to read and take into consideration. You have all day tomorrow to work on this. However, in the early evening, we have scheduled a barbecue dinner for some visitors from the 'Olymp' in Berlin.

Remember, you are to speak only Spanish from now on, with English as an alternative, if necessary. Good night, old boy. Rest up, so that your head is clear and working on all cylinders. The faster you work and the less time and exposure you need here, the better. The requested photographer will be here at 07.00 hours and stay at your elbow as long as you need him. *Buenas Noches, Amigo*!

Gibraltar and the entire Rock were brightly illuminated, because Spain was fairly well lighted and any type of blackout would therefore be ineffective and useless. Petersen looked at the stars and the sky, trying to get some idea what the weather would be like the next morning. Cremer came to his mind;

he would have sailed from La Pallice by now and already be entering the Bay of Biscay. Then he began reading the various messages and documents that had been handed to him by Redl.

Bright skies and blinding sunshine prevailed when Petersen woke up quite early. Right away he worked on the huge binoculars with enlarging lenses to bring objects closer and to see details more clearly. There could be no doubt, these new destroyers had those six-sided, basket-like, birdcage-type antennae at the very top of their after radar masts, indicating clearly that these Adcock antennae were short-wave limited-range search wave equipment. They had been installed on these ships as high as possible in order to achieve the maximum operational reach, because the curvature of the earth limited their effectiveness to the horizon. In other words, the higher up such Adcock antennae could be installed, the greater the distance they could cover, as their usefulness increased when the horizon could be extended and a larger circle covered.

The photographer suggested certain angles for better pictures because the destroyers swayed and moved somewhat, being fastened to buoys in the harbour. Several shots were made to allow as complete a view as possible. The photographer used three rolls of special film to cover all views. Finally Charlie Redl handed Petersen his personal Leica to take some snaps in addition as a triple safety measure, just in case. All were swiftly developed by the photographic laboratory in the basement of Villa San Luis.

Those taken officially were kept by Redl for onward shipping through *Abwehr* channels. From the privately made pictures, Redl had three sets of copies made, one for the record and two for Petersen to take back. As Redl assumed, U-boat Command in Paris would insist upon one set. He added, 'If that gets lost, destroyed or disappears somehow, you have the third set as reserve, so guard it closely.' Petersen raised his eyebrows when Redl continued, 'Yes, unfortunately we have experienced several cases of mysterious losses of photographic material. Therefore, I want to make sure this time, and am anxious that these pictures actually get to the right people undamaged and not messed up. Verbal reports are one thing, convincing evidential back-ups something else.'

Petersen was flabbergasted: 'Charlie, you mean to tell me some of the shipments have gone astray and have been lost in the past?' Redl replied, 'Unfortunately that is so – not often but frequently enough to be upsetting.' Petersen asked, 'Could the British sneak them away along the transmission line somewhere?' Redl thought not. 'It is the bureaucratic jungle in Berlin where such shipments get lost somewhere in the shuffling. So take another set of pictures, not only of these destroyers but also of those cruisers, further back; they all have radar aboard that is clearly visible. Yet Berlin still refuses to accept the technical facts.'

Redl asked, 'Do you know Air Force Colonel Martini, the head of the Electronic Test Regiment?' Petersen replied, 'No, though I have heard of his outfit on the channel coast.' Redl went on, 'Martini and his technical staff are at present the best-informed people on radar and short-wave applications. Could you not work in a visit to him?' Petersen hesitated a moment, 'Charlie, I doubt that the Naval High Command would give me the authorization for that. As you know, Raeder and Göring are like dog and cat, bitter enemies for a long time.'

Redl thought this over for a moment, though it was not news to him. Finally he suggested, 'Why don't you contact Major Hans Reisinger, who is the top scientific brain of the Kammhuber Radar Defence Command. Reisinger is also an active night-fighter pilot and a practical, nice, cooperative fellow. Furthermore, he is constantly in and out of Martini's office and would be able and willing to get you in for an informal and unofficial discussion. Try Reisinger when you are back in Paris, as he is around there often. Tell him that I suggested this approach to you, and he will set it up so that no paperwork or record keeping will be required.'

Petersen shook his head. 'Where will all this non-cooperation and fighting for personal turf lead us? Surely this is no way to win the war.' Redl replied, 'Since the Americans are in the war, one must consider it lost, no matter what speeches are made in Berlin.' Petersen told Redl that there had been several Americans in the hotel bar, not just British officers as before. Redl replied, 'The Americans will be coming in huge numbers. But we have no idea when, where or how. It looks as if your job is practically done, except to convince the senior staff.'

Petersen agreed that this persuasion would probably be harder to achieve than the taking of the pictures. Redl suggested, 'You should take a swim and a siesta now. Because tonight you must be wide awake for our visitor from Berlin. Maybe you could rope in some help from him.' Petersen was doubtful. 'It would only amount to some promises of aspirin, but fall short of real help.' Redl said, 'Not this time. *Tio* Guillermo, the Admiral himself, is here for the night and he would support you if anybody would. By the way, he will cook the meat and prepare some of his special South American sauces too. Have you met Canaris before?' Petersen replied, 'Yes indeed, and we spoke Spanish together to his delight, because one of my uncles served with him during the First World War and introduced me while I was a high school pupil. However, I have also met Uncle Guillermo several times since. One can talk with him easily if one simply forgets his admiral's uniform and position.' Redl declared, 'Tonight he will be a civilian like you and have on the hat and uniform of a kitchen chef to boot. Until 21.00 hours then. *Adios!*'

The evening was mild and pleasant, the barbecue unusual and very tasty. Petersen had a chance to talk privately to Admiral Canaris, who told him about his ride in 1915 from Chile across the Andes to Argentina on horseback, adding, 'In view of the fact that you have been chasing Argentinian heiresses lately, I thought this would interest you.' Petersen said somewhat lamely, 'I assumed the lady was a consular employee or embassy secretary.' Canaris laughed:

Well my boy, she is, but only to keep her occupied and to gain experience in business. Perhaps, if the war ends one day, once nothing is left standing here in Europe and you do survive through some miracle, you could then become a shipping executive in Buenos Aires. Señor Dodero and his clan are always looking for good men who are workhorses in addition to being responsible managers and conscientious directors for their various companies. So I can only say Congratulations! She is a stunning woman in every way. I hope, you realize, she only will turn 18 next week.

This was news for Petersen, who preferred rather older women to teenagers. Yet she hardly seemed to be a teenager. Canaris finished. 'Naturally, this will remain between Captain Leissner and me and not be passed around. After all, we don't want you to get burnt and become useless for us, let alone shot somewhere. Things will get a lot tougher before an end is in sight, which will be quite terrible for Germany! For me, it will all end somehow some day. But you are much too young yet and should start a new life afterwards.'

Petersen was jolted by the Admiral's pessimism. But in many ways it really differed little from what most U-boat men at the front thought if they were honest and half-way intelligent. Moreover, Admiral Canaris had more information.

Redl called Petersen aside, telling him he would be picked up at 02.00 hours. And so it was time to get back to the Hotel Maria Cristina to pack. Redl informed Petersen that for security reasons he would be driven on another route, which bypassed Madrid.

The journey back was long, slow and tiresome. Petersen was quite exhausted when he left Dax, again in uniform, to catch the Bordeaux–Paris express. He would sleep a full night first, at the Claridge Hotel, before reporting back to Hessler and the U-boat Command, because he had to be alert and ready to fight for what was clearly necessary, so that the U-boat Command accepted the truth.

The other negatives and films had already been flown from Madrid to Berlin and to the Naval High Command for evaluation, after getting approval by the military censorship department.

When Petersen reported to Commander Hessler, he had to wait quite some time. Hessler inquired, 'Back sooner than I expected. Does that mean good news or bad?' Petersen carefully stated, 'This depends upon one's point of view, but only to a degree, because the facts observed and photographed are irrefutable. The British ships have short-wave signal-detection equipment aboard, and short-wave radar as well; evidently not on all ships as yet, but this is unquestionably a mere matter of time.'

Hessler asked, 'What evidence and technical certainty did you obtain?' Petersen confirmed, 'The clearest possible pictures that could be taken, confirming 100 per cent what Ali Cremer has already observed recently from U-333. The Allies have clearly managed to utilize shorter and shorter wave-length equipment, probably in the lower than 30 cm range, if not less.'

Keeping Redl's warning in mind, he reported, 'The negatives of all pictures taken and all films made were dispatched urgently and directly to the Naval High Command in Berlin, with an extra set already developed for the U-boat Command in Paris that will, no doubt, be shipped to them after getting clearance from the naval censorship department. But I have no idea how long that will take.' Hessler replied, 'Generally not too long. Yet sometimes these people ruin the negatives and the pictures by blackening out specific details.' Petersen asked, as if surprised, 'Don't these people dispatch the originals uncensored to you? I understood censorship only applies for any releases to the public and newspapers or radio stations.'

Hessler hesitated, then told him, 'Unfortunately, we often only receive the censored and manipulated material from Berlin, not the originals. This has been the subject of extended disputes for some time. But actually all this takes place with the highest level of secrecy. In fact, officially, I am not even authorized to become involved in this situation, which the Admiral (Dönitz) handles personally, or otherwise Captain Godt occasionally. However, with the Admiral being away so much these days, it became necessary for me to step in, as Captain Godt is already overloaded with work. But I am telling you this under the seal of total confidentiality only. Don't mention it anywhere.'

Petersen responded carefully, 'I have heard rumours about this, but considered them exaggerations and gossip.' Hessler said, 'Leave the information where we can get hold of you with the staff, so that I can call you the minute this material arrives from Berlin.' Petersen replied, 'That won't be a problem, because it seems important that this matter is cleared up as fast as possible, even if it means facing undesirable facts fully and without any reluctance. Otherwise, this will become a deadly danger for our U-boats.'

Hessler nodded. 'I know what you mean, but I can only go so far in this situation. You have seen these things. Seeing is believing, I realize. But the problem will be to overcome the opposition of the technical experts, and you will have to be extremely convincing, and your facts so clear that they can't talk around them any more.' Petersen answered, 'I shall prepare myself as far as possible. I also plan to double-check some technical points with the Air Force scientists who owe me a favour. Maybe they can contribute further evidence to put things across.' Hessler was then called away, and just said, 'Keep this unofficial if possible, as the Admiral would get very upset if we brought the Air Force into the picture to overcome Berlin. See you soon.'

Petersen was dismissed and one of the assistants asked him where he could reach him promptly. He informed him that he was staying at the Claridge. The assistant was surprised. How was this possible? Only higher-rank officers and Knight's Cross bearers were lodged there customarily. Petersen countered that he would just as soon move to the Ambassador or one of the smaller hotels on the Left Bank of the Seine, but the U-boat Command office would have to arrange this for him right away.

The security officer, Lieutenant-Commander of the Reserves, Dr

Gottfried Teufer, nicknamed 'John the Baptist', overheard the conversation and interceded, telling the staff assistant sharply, 'If Frank Petersen is already lodged at the Claridge Hotel, he shall stay there as long as we need him here.' Whereupon Petersen left without wasting more time, before some other bureaucrat could generate more problems.

It so happened that Major Reisinger was in Paris, and he agreed immediately to a meeting, offering Petersen all possible help. They talked for several hours, and Reisinger promised to set up a meeting with Colonel Martini shortly. Petersen learned that most of these electronic factors had been known to the Air Force for quite some time. Reisinger declared, 'If we had had any idea that the U-boat men were interested and concerned about short-wave or centimeter-wave technology, we would certainly have passed our information along to you. But until now nobody has asked or even expressed any interest, much less curiosity, in this.'

Petersen liked Reisinger on the spot, and quickly decided that total frankness would be possible and worthwhile. He told him, therefore, about Redl's extra set of private pictures they had taken in Algeciras. Reisinger had been there several times and knew the *Abwehr* set-up well. Reisinger asked Petersen, 'Do you know if Charlie used official Navy film, which he would have to account for, or a film he had bought personally from some photoshop?' Petersen was unsure, so he repeated that Redl had emphasized to him twice that camera and film were his private property. 'In that case,' Reisinger said, 'don't worry about it, as there are no Navy marks on the pictures and film. Why don't you tell your people here that the Air Force took these pictures when you were in Algeciras a few days ago and gave them to you as a personal favour.

Petersen was delighted with this solution and thanked Reisinger profusely. Reisinger countered, 'Once I get you in and out with Martini, provided you obtain worthwhile information, you can buy me a good bottle of champagne.' Petersen agreed: 'I shall go further and take you to a nice dinner as well. Thanks a lot, Major, Sir!'

The next afternoon Hessler called. 'The pictures have arrived, but they are almost useless because these censorship idiots have mutilated them and blackened out some sections. So the rest was really worthless.' Hessler added, 'I called the censorship division in Berlin, boiling with frustration, and was shifted to five different people before I reached somebody who admitted sheepishly that they had to disguise the origin of any such pictures for secrecy protection reasons. Therefore it was decided to blacken out that prominent Rock of Gibraltar, visible in the background, by cutting it off. But while doing so, these imbeciles also cut off the tops of the destroyers' after masts and with them those six-sided, birdcage-like Adcock antennae too. Then these nitwits disposed of the negatives!'

Petersen felt as if he was being hit with a mallet. 'This is unbelievable.' He cursed grimly: 'How do we overcome these blockheads?' Hessler hesitated a moment and then asked, 'Frank, these Air Force contacts of yours, could they bale us out?' Petersen replied, 'Commander, Sir, I think this might just work, and if your meeting is scheduled for tomorrow afternoon, I hope to be able to manage it somehow. But please don't ask any searching questions during the meeting.' Hessler grinned. 'The less I know, the better it will probably be. We shall keep it confidential. To be on the safe side report here not later than 11.30 hours tomorrow, so that we can plan our strategy. You will then participate in the official luncheon in the officers' mess. Captain Godt will chair the meeting, as it looks as if the Admiral will not be back from Germany, but we don't wish to delay this until he is back here. However, everything has been discussed with him. See you then.'

Petersen arrived a bit early and talked briefly with Hessler once more. When he asked if he should mention 'Ali' Cremer and the observations from U-333 at all, and in what way, Hessler okayed it: 'But keep it brief, as a supporting point. Don't say anything about anything else, except Algeciras. However, don't talk about the routes, the transport or the connections. Because some of the technicians are not cleared for the higher-grade secrecy matters.'

Petersen wore full regulation blue dress uniform to appear very official when making his presentation. Therefore he was sweating in the warm September weather. The luncheon was unremarkable, while some would call it meagre. Petersen had only asked for mineral water to drink, nothing else, to keep a clear head.

A large screen had been set up and a projector with supplementary equipment was available when the meeting opened at 14.00 hours sharp. Hessler introduced Petersen to those he had not met. Godt asked for the lights to be dimmed and the pictures put on the screen. Then he let them run twice, backwards and forwards. The stunned silence was overpowering. A few shy comments were made about the lack of quality of these pictures. One participant, who thought he was being funny, asked if the photographer had had too much vino or sangria. Hessler called him to order instantly. Now the silence became deafening.

Hessler requested the lights to be put on and asked Petersen to tell the meeting about 'Ali' Cremer and what he himself had seen and done in Algeciras, to describe in detail what his eyes had observed, but nothing else for the moment. Once this was done, Hessler requested that he recount exactly how, by whom and under what weather conditions the original pictures were taken. When Petersen had related this in detail, Hessler asked if he would care to add anything else or wished to amplify this unsatisfactory result further with details so far not mentioned. Petersen confirmed that he would indeed do so.

He explained that during his visit to Algeciras, the Air Force had one of their scientific advisers staying there, doing a check-out for the Kammhuber Line Defence Command and the Electronic Test and Teaching Regiment, an extremely knowledgeable man who was an active night-fighter pilot and one of the engineers who worked on the Lichtenstein aircraft search radar equipment. For security reasons, Petersen was not permitted to mention his name. The professional photographer whom Petersen had requested as helper, because he himself was only a amateur in that field, had also worked with this officer, who had flown in from North Africa, but had to inspect other installations in Italy, Greece and the Balkans on his trip. When he heard that Petersen was returning overland and not by air, he entrusted him with one duplicate set of the pictures taken with his personal Leica camera, in case he got shot down returning, or crashed somewhere. Petersen had delivered this batch of negatives to the Air Force liaison coordinator, who had asked what favour the Air Force could do for the Navy in return.

He had just been informed about the disaster the censorship division had generated in Berlin, making the naval pictures for practical purposes worthless pieces of paper. Therefore, he had enquired if the Air Force could make a copy of their set of pictures for him, as a replacement. The Air Force was delighted, but made ten sets, so that the same could be properly distributed to the required key people involved with the short-wave equipment problems. Pulling a thick envelope out of his pocket, Petersen handed out these sets, so that at least every two people in the meeting received one set of photographs to study. They were copies of his pictures of the P and Q class destroyers and some cruisers behind them.

He asked that one set be run through the projector, to give an enlarged view. The effect of this distribution was remarkable, and everybody looked and looked, nobody spoke, until Hessler broke in: 'I assume you all agree that these pictures are clear, unmistakable and irrefutable evidence. Obviously, the Tommies have succeeded where we have failed. Therefore it is essential that we work on countermeasures without delay. Captain Godt and I have briefly informed Admiral Dönitz of this situation, and he demands the fullest cooperation with alacrity. I believe a thank you and well done is due to Frank Petersen in this matter. Now, let us go to work with grim determination to get the job done soon.'

Petersen, sweating profusely in his heavy blue dress uniform, was approached by Godt: 'You have done a magic job on this. I don't care to know how it came about. What counts is the result, even if arranged without close attention to naval rules and regulations. What did you say this short-wave equipment is called?' Petersen replied, 'I did not mention any name. The Air Force calls it High-Frequency Direction-Finding Equipment. I was advised it is very effective and records automatically even the 3–5-second short signals that U-boats send out. The only drawback is the range, which is limited by the curvature of the earth. For that reason, these antennae have been fitted to the very top of the ships' masts to permit maximum range.' Godt mumbled something under his breath, which Petersen did not understand.

Hessler called Petersen away. 'Frank, I hope this will work out with acceptable results. What do you have in mind now? You deserve some leave to recover.' Petersen replied, 'I want to thank the Air Force boys, and have been invited to visit Colonel Martini's command for more information. As you know, Commander, the relations between the Navy and the *Luftwaffe* at the top are not the best. But at lower working levels we usually get very helpful cooperation, such as from Colonel Harlinghausen and his Focke Wulf Condor aircraft in Bordeaux Merignac, and quite a few other Air Force people at the front.'

Because the technical name of this equipment was simply too long and for some folk too hard to pronounce, including the British sailors and petty officers using it aboard their ships, soon it was called 'Huff-Duff' for short. Several improvised countermeasures were tried, but none of them really worked satisfactorily. As long as Dönitz insisted upon the constant use of radio signals to the U-boats and the frequent reports he demanded from the U-boats at sea, there was no possibility of reducing the effectiveness of 'Huff-Duff'.

Petersen took Major Reisinger that very evening to the Sheherazade for a full seafood dinner with all the trimmings. Petersen told Vladimir, the director-manager: 'Vladi, for my guest I should like Bollinger champagne. I mean the real thing, not bubble-water filled into empty Bollinger bottles, you old rascal! And it had better be properly chilled, too. After all, Major Reisinger is the first Air Force guest to grace your establishment with his presence. Therefore, no monkey business with anything!' Vladimir grinned from ear to ear, hearing this. 'Frank, have you been promoted? Acting as the big spender now. I welcome the Major as a customer and hope he and his comrades will return in the future. That first bottle of Bollinger will be on the house.' Then he shouted, 'Musicians! Singers! Dancers! Go to work for our new guest!'

The evening was a success and a memorable event for everybody in the Sheherazade. Major Reisinger was enchanted with the place, its service and the Russian atmosphere of the shows, the music and the staff.

Vladi even managed to get them a taxi, driven by wood-gas. On the way to their respective hotels, Reisinger told Petersen, 'I had always heard that the Navy knows how to party and have a wonderful time. Now I know this is indeed the case. Thanks for introducing me to the Sheherazade.' Petersen replied, 'Hans, you have deserved the visit and the Navy likes to show gratitude and appreciation for all good deeds. If you visit in the future, be a bit selective whom you take along. Don't bring fossilized generals or older reserve officers who fall asleep at 23.00 hours. This is a roaring place for fellows under 30'. Reisinger laughed: 'You bet, Frank, it will only be fighter pilots and front-line pigs. We shall take those old clowns instead to the nearest funeral home, where they really belong. You and I don't have to be concerned about meeting them there as it is highly unlikely we shall reach the proper age for such a visit from the looks of things. So let's enjoy the few good days and nights that we are able to grab somehow. I read the obituaries every chance I get. If my name is not there with a black frame around it, I know I am still around and with some luck alive.'

Petersen, chuckled. 'Hans, that's a new way to find out if one is still alive. But I think I shall imitate it in the future. The very best possible luck to you, nevertheless!' 'The same to you, Frank; we are all gamblers and one of these days we shall hit the jackpot! When you do, say hello to St Peter for me and reserve a spot for me. If I arrive first, I shall do the same for you.'

When they reached the Hotel Lotti, dawn had just started to light up Paris. Reisinger stumbled out of their taxi and yelled loudly: 'Good morning and goodbye to you, Frank. Farewell until we meet again.' He quickly walked into the lobby, while Petersen asked the driver to continue to the Hotel Claridge, hoping somehow to catch up on lost sleep.

CHAPTER FIVE

The U-boat Commander

On 2 August 1941, U-154, a Type IX-C U-boat, was commissioned in the Deschimag shipyard in Bremen by Lieutenant-Commander Walther Kölle. On 7 February 1942, U-154 departed from Kiel on her first war patrol, to reach Lorient on 1 March, as she had been assigned to the 2nd U-boat Flotilla in that base. With Kölle as her commander, U-154 made two further war patrols of longer duration, operating in the Caribbean Sea and the Gulf of Mexico. When U-154 returned to Lorient on 23 August 1942, Kölle reported sick and was relieved as the commander of U-154.

When U-154 was declared ready for the next war patrol, U-boat Command transferred Commander Heinrich Schuch from U-105 to be her second commander, since his own U-boat was delayed in being repaired.

On 12 October 1942 Schuch left Lorient with U-154 for another war patrol to the Caribbean Sea and the Trinidad area. Schuch also developed health problems while at sea and had to be hospitalized as soon as U-154 returned to Lorient on 7 January 1943. A big shuffle of personnel took place aboard U-154, as many crew members were due for promotional training and technical upgrading. The remaining crew members left on home leave in Germany on rotation basis.

Lieutenant j.g. of the Reserves Otto Hinrichs, the executive officer, had left for prospective commander's training in the Baltic as soon as U-154 reached Lorient. The second watch officer, Ensign Heinrich Meyer (Crew 39-B), aboard since commissioning, stayed on for another war patrol. Meyer needed one more patrol to qualify for prospective commander's training.

In the middle of January 1943, a new executive officer arrived in Lorient, assigned to U-154, straight from the U-boat training schools in the Baltic, without any U-boat operational experience. He was Lieutenant j.g. of the Reserves Ulrich Abel, 31 years old. A lawyer by training, but a judge by trade, Abel had been a Merchant Marine officer until he lost his job in the Depression. He had participated in periodic Naval Reserve training exercises before the war, but he was also an old-time Nazi Party member and had been a full-time Nazi functionary in Hamburg before he became a lower court judge.

When the war started, Abel was recalled into service by the German Navy and assigned to one of the new minesweeping flotillas created in 1939 from requisitioned fishing vessels. These were sturdy sea boats, and they usually retained their entire civilian crews, all of them reservists, who were merely put into uniform. Abel became watch officer aboard one of these ships operating in the North Sea and in Norway, mainly escorting merchant ships, clearing mines and getting used in anti-submarine warfare operations. In autumn 1940, he was appointed as the commander of one of these fishing vessels. As far as the Navy was concerned, these were strictly auxiliary vessels and were considered the 'Third Fleet'.

In July 1942, Abel transferred to U-boat training classes in the Baltic and finished these courses at the end of 1942. A few days later, he was appointed executive officer of U-154 in Lorient. When he reached Lorient, he reported to the new commander of the 2nd U-boat Flotilla, Captain Ernst Kals. Kals informed him that U-154 had no commander at that time, and that the directing engineer was on leave but was expected to be replaced shortly.

Abel told Kals that he had been informed in Germany that he would only have to make one war patrol as understudy commander and then he would then be assigned to prospective commander's training immediately. Kals looked at Abel's personal record and informed him that there was no information to that effect in his papers, but that he had been assigned as executive officer to gain operational U-boat experience. Kals added that this was no doubt only because of Abel's Merchant Marine background and age. Otherwise, without U-boat experience, Abel would have had to start as second watch officer.

One week later a brand-new directing engineer arrived, Ensign (Engineering) Curt Druschel, straight from the naval technical schools in Germany, a man who had never filled any position on a ship at sea and was without U-boat front-service experience. Regardless of how inexperienced Druschel was, he told everybody who cared to listen what a big shot Hitler Youth leader he had been before he joined the Navy. Therefore, Druschel hit it off well with Abel, who talked constantly about that wonderful military genius, our *Führer* Adolf Hitler, who was undoubtedly the greatest warrior and leader the world had ever seen!

After two weeks of listening to such tales and looking over these two recruits, the senior petty officers and petty officers got together and requested a meeting with flotilla commander Kals. They pointed out that Druschel was simply too inexperienced to be directing engineer, as well as being a mere loud-mouth. With an inexperienced executive officer, who at least had seafaring experience, but still without a new commander, this would not be acceptable for safety reasons and would be asking for trouble.

Kals listened closely and agreed with the complaining delegation, and called the officer detailer in Kiel to discuss the problem. It was agreed to retain the directing engineer, Lieutenant (Engineering) Fritz Reinicke, on board for some time until he had broken in Druschel sufficiently, instead of transferring Reinicke to another position, as scheduled. Kiel would arrange to have Reinicke picked up at sea by another U-boat on her return voyage to France, once Druschel was able to take over as directing engineer of U-154.

Beginning in January 1943, British bomber groups attacked both Saint Nazaire and Lorient heavily and repeatedly. As a consequence these two U-boat bases became huge fields of rubble within weeks. Practically nothing was left standing in them except the concrete covered U-boat pens that completely sheltered the U-boats during repair and overhaul services. While there was a temporary inconvenience developing for some U-boat crews, more so in Lorient than Saint Nazaire, the folk who really suffered were the French civilians.

The total destruction of Saint Nazaire had little influence upon U-boat operations, because the 6th and 7th U-boat Flotillas based in that port had always quartered their administrations and related offices in nearby La Baule sur Mer, including accommodating officers and crews in commercial hotels. The seaside resort of La Baule, on the shore of the Bay of Biscay, had a big casino for a variety of gambling activities. Around it were the biggest and best four hotels, encircling the casino like a fortress, which had been requisitioned as quarters for the German Navy: the Castel Marie-Louise, the Majestic, L'Hermitage and the Royal.

Here took place the actual scene of that famous opening chapter in Lothar Günther Buchheim's bestseller, *The Boat*, describing a wild orgy by a bunch of rather tight U-boat officers on the Bar Royal premises at La Baule sur Mer. No matter that this description has been attacked as merely a dirty fantasy of the author, it actually pictured reality quite accurately at precisely this time of the war.

In Lorient, the situation was different, because the 2nd and 10th U-boat Flotillas operating out of that base had been lodged in a variety of former French naval barracks and some commercial hotels that had been bombed into smithereens and totally burnt out. It required several weeks to construct alternative quarters and office facilities. At nearby Pont Scorff, open land was converted by the Organisation Todt, the building undertaking that constructed the U-boat pens, into a rest camp surrounded by fences and barbed wire. It was named 'Lager Lemp' after the dead commander of U-110, who had permitted the British boarding team to capture his U-boat, grab the Enigma M-3 machine and many other secret papers. Lemp, who was ultimately responsible for this disaster through his failure to prevent the capture of U-110, was still celebrated as a 'dead hero', and the new compound had been named in his honour.

Gradually, the various U-boat crews and administrative offices moved into Camp Lemp, as additional buildings were erected by the Organisation Todt at a fast pace. Offices and accommodation barracks, eating halls with kitchens, assembly and entertainment facilities, a cinema with stage-equipped theatre and a library, were all built in short order.

The officers' relaxation area was decorated in a scheme that imitated an old watermill in the Bavarian mountains, with a comfortable separate bar section called 'The Old Mill Bar'. Here a big waterwheel kept turning and dropped water noisily into an artificial pond surrounded by scenic views of the Alps. The service was good and provided by friendly French girls with considerable hotel experience, whose places of employment had recently been destroyed by the Royal Air Force.

After a few weeks, sports facilities and exercise areas were added. A month after the destruction of Lorient, this had become just another historic fact, which hardly affected U-boat operations any longer and became, at most, a mere occasional inconvenience.

On 8 February 1943, Oskar Kusch returned to Lorient and reported immediately to Kals, whom he knew from the past. Kals informed him that a teletype had just arrived from Kiel, appointing Kusch the third commander of U-154, then being overhauled. This was the official confirmation for Kusch, who had already been advised over the telephone while still in Berlin about his new assignment.

Kusch decided to take over command immediately after this discussion. Kals suggested he should make a short introductory speech to the assembled men, though the crew was as yet not complete and a few more replacements were still awaited to reach full numerical strength. The older and experienced crew members were pleased to note that their new commander had front service experience with U-boats. Some of them had known Kusch in the past, when he had served on U-103 as watch officer.

Just after the assembled crew was dismissed, Kusch arranged to meet the officers of U-154 individually, to become at least slightly acquainted with them. The temporary directing engineer, Reinicke, made an excellent impression, but he would be gone fairly soon. The second watch officer, Meyer, seemed to be competent and evidently knew his job. Abel, the executive officer, almost seven years older than Kusch, appeared to be a seaman with experience, but promptly assured Kusch that final victory would soon be certain, owing to the *Führer*'s military genius. Kusch almost lost his composure on being so informed. Druschel, initially watch engineer, also felt obliged to tell his new commander what a wonderful job he had done as a Hitler Youth group leader, while Kusch expected a competent engineer instead.

Kusch was rather dismayed and decided to talk to Kals the next day about several matters regarding U-154, enquiring at the same time carefully about these new and inexperienced officers, with regard to their U-boat service. Kals informed him that Abel had mentioned to him just one patrol, then going directly to the prospective commander's training. Kals suggested watching Abel closely and discussing the man with him once the patrol had been finished. Kals told Kusch about the complaining delegation of the petty officers and the arrangement agreed upon, to keep Reinicke temporarily on U-154, until Druschel's experience had been upgraded enough for him to qualify as directing engineer aboard U-154.

The navigator, quartermaster and warrant officer (*Obersteuermann*) Heinrich Lüdmann, who was also the third watch officer on board, spoke at length with Kusch, and brought up the problems that had developed with these two new officers. But Kusch was really a man of good will who believed all officers were gentlemen and cavaliers, even if they had unrealistic ideas, peculiar tastes or unusual habits.

During the next three weeks, all crew members who had been on home leave in Germany returned to Lorient, and replacement crew members arrived in dribbles to bring numbers up to full strength for combat operations. Early in March two additional men arrived and embarked as watch officer trainees on U-154, two midshipmen transferred directly from the naval academy in Flensburg-Mürwik. These were Horst Fröhlich and Hellmuth Kirchammer, both without any U-boat training or U-boat experience, assigned on the 'Learn by Doing' training scheme.

Fröhlich had just turned 18 and Kirchammer would reach his 18th birthday in two months, when U-154 was expected to be at sea. Both of these enthusiastic young men were eager to please and liked Kusch from the moment they met him in Lorient.

While some of the newcomers from Germany still had unrealistic expectations and illusions about the U-boat side of the Battle of the Atlantic, this could not be said of those men who had already served on war patrols. They had personally experienced the steadily growing anti-submarine defences and the ever faster aircraft with constantly increasing range. Moreover, the newer aeroplanes were less and less influenced by bad weather conditions or strong winds, and operated now even during the dark and in the middle of the night. These aircraft had more effective radar and better anti-submarine search equipment. New depth-charges filled with Torpex became deadlier all the time. Greater numbers of new and more efficient destroyers, frigates and corvettes were at sea, vastly better equipped than the older types had been.

It is essential to update the reader on the trends and true results of the U-boat war during the just finished year of 1942, and tell how matters had changed in that year. It had been the most successful year for German U-boat operations, a confirmed total of 1,155 Allied ships having been sunk by U-boats – 6,474,515 tons altogether. The highest total of sinkings –126 ships, representing 802,160 tons – had occurred in November. This was blown up and exaggerated by the German propaganda machine to deflect from the terrible defeats in Russia and North Africa. However, people with inside information were aware that the tonnage battle had already been lost. As in the final quarter of 1942, the new American ship-building programmes had exceeded sinkings for the first time, and kept steadily growing each and every month thereafter, constantly breaking new records, while at the same time the sinkings were dropping more and more.

Crossing the Bay of Biscay increasingly turned into a more dangerous and complicated operation. Nevertheless, to the uninformed it seemed that the U-boats grew in numbers every month and became more threatening weekly.

Owing to the ability of the British to read all U-boat signals, often faster than the U-boats did themselves, secrecy prevailed less and less. Dönitz liked to direct the U-boats very closely, keeping the commanders on short leashes and becoming involved in the smallest details of operations, supplies and both tactical and strategic decisions. The main advantage of U-boats, clandestine operations, was ignored more and more with those group or pack operations favoured by Dönitz. This made putting the cards on the table a necessity, and the British reacted very promptly.

On 17 November 1942, Admiral Max Kennedy Horton had been transferred from his previous position as Flag Officer, British Submarines, to become the new commander of Western Approaches in Liverpool. Horton had been a submarine commander in the First World War, just like Admiral Dönitz, who said wistfully: 'I suppose the British are finally hitting their stride, recognizing that it takes a thief to catch a thief. Things will turn out tougher than ever with Admiral Horton in the driver's seat.'

Swiftly, Horton reorganized procedures at Derby House, the control centre of the anti-submarine operations, streamlining controls and ruthlessly eliminating the last bits of the traditional naval bureaucracy.

He received information from many sources and all commands, not just from the Royal Navy, but also from the Coastal Command of the Royal Air Force and the various secret services too. Consequently, by the middle of March 1943 he had reached the conclusion that Great Britain had finally managed to get over the edge and would now be able to turn towards winning the Battle of the Atlantic, and thus the war. But Churchill and the political admirals in London did not permit him to state his opinion publicly. This was because it would have been possible to reach that point several months earlier and effectively close the so-called black gap of the North Atlantic much sooner, if Winston Churchill and his group of bomber barons had not adamantly refused the delivery of the necessary 120 long-range Liberator aeroplanes to Coastal Command to fight the U-boats and achieve the required wider coverage of the sea. Instead they insisted stubbornly on placing these aircraft in Bomber Command units, intending to bomb Germany into ruins. The official line was to destroy German industry, the admitted purpose to dehouse German workers, so that their morale would be broken. However, nobody talked about the real victims of the bombing campaign: women and children. The fanatical bombers opposed the more logical use of these long-range Liberators elsewhere, especially with Coastal Command to attack the U-boats in the North Atlantic.

This 'revenge and hate crowd' was inspired and directed by Frederick Lindemann, known as the 'Prof', the scientific adviser to Winston Churchill for many years, who later became Lord Cherwell. Lindemann, born in Alsace, and Jewish, thwarted anything that could possibly weaken the British bombing attacks on Germany, without actual consideration of the facts involved and the real effects of the bombing campaign.

The move of the U-boat Command from Paris to Berlin Charlottenburg and the Hotel Am Steinplatz had caused communication problems galore, as well as many delays. The U-boat Command staff was now further removed from the daily grind and operational problems of the U-boat men and commanders.

Dönitz had ordered a far-reaching investigation of the signal and Enigma machine code security, and had been assured by the communication specialists that Enigma could not possibly be read and decoded by the enemy, even temporarily; furthermore, that the British and Americans would be unable to do what the Germans had found impossible to accomplish – build radar sets small enough to install both in aircraft and on small surface ships, such as destroyers. Moreover, the centimetre bandwave was completely impractical and useless for radar equipment because it would be impossible to concentrate the beams sufficiently to make them useful.

They dismissed the claims by U-boat commanders and crews that the British had very efficient direction-finding equipment on their escorting warships that accurately and swiftly spotted U-boats as soon as they dispatched any radio signal, even the five-second automatic short signals. 'We are convinced', these conceited fools said, 'that the commanders are just imagining things and have let their fantasy run wild under the pressure and the confusion of night-time operations, looking for excuses to explain their failures to achieve sinkings as in the past.'

To surpass the blockheadedness and hubris of these admirals would be almost impossible, but Dönitz accepted their expertise, even if he was not exactly pleased with their conclusions.

Shortly before U-154 was fully repaired, Dönitz came to Lorient for an inspection and made one of his typical encouraging speeches to the lined-up U-boat crews. A group of junior officers and petty officers had formed a choir, and presented a show dressed in Roman costumes, made up as slaves and gladiators, singing jointly at the finish, 'Dead men on leave greet you once more, Emperador!' Dönitz liked the presentation, but some of his staff members travelling with him were upset about such 'frivolity'.

About six weeks after Oskar Kusch had taken command of U-154, she left Lorient on 20 March 1943 with minesweeper protection proceeding beyond the 200 m depth line, to make her deep-diving test. When it was satisfactorily concluded, the minesweepers turned around and U-154 started her crossing of the Bay of Biscay, which had now become more difficult and dangerous.

Initially, U-154 was to travel into the mid-Atlantic and then to the Brazilian coast in a westerly direction, subject to reconfirmation by radio signal from the U-boat Command in Berlin. In spite of expectations to the contrary and the experience of most other U-boats, she managed to get across the Bay of Biscay without problems that could not be mastered, and her crew was put in shape with a heavy schedule of diving exercises and action tests. Six times U-154 was forced into emergency dives by British Coastal Command aeroplanes on search patrols. On 23 March, one of these aircraft dropped four depth-charges quite close to her, but with a crash-dive she was already deep enough to avoid serious damage.

Reaching the sea area around the Canary Islands on 1 April, U-154 met U-172, commanded by Lieutenant Carl Emmermann, returning from a war patrol of the mid-Atlantic. Directing engineer Fritz Reinicke was ferried over to U-172 by means of an inflatable rubber boat to return to France, while Druschel now took over as directing engineer on U-154. Druschel was promoted on 1 April 1943 to lieutenant j.g. (engineering).

On 8 April U-154 was directed to proceed to the Gulf of Guinea and West Africa, to patrol from Freetown in a southerly direction beyond the equator. That line was crossed on 13 April, and forty men of the crew underwent the traditional equator-crossing baptism with all sorts of practical jokes. On 17 April U-154 proceeded in the direction of Ascension Island, was twice located by aircraft and later bombed by a third aircraft they had apparently called to the area. However, Kusch had been able to crash-dive, and U-154 was neither directly hit nor damaged.

On 19 April U-154 was ordered to proceed westwards once more towards the middle of the South Atlantic. On 21 April she was attacked by another aircraft but managed to crash-dive safely. Because no shipping whatsoever was encountered, Kusch decided to continue further west towards the Brazilian coast, the area originally contemplated for U-154's operations. On 5 May he approached the coast near the port of Maceio, travelling about twelve miles off the coastline. Kusch decided to enter the harbour to look for ships there. When U-154 was only about 5,000 m away, it could be seen that no ships of any kind were in the port.

Consequently, Kusch turned northwards and proceeded in the direction of Recife (Pernambuco) to find out if ships could be found there. On 7 May U-154 was forced to make another emergency crash-dive when a Catalina flying-boat approached. On 8 May, early in the morning, about fifty miles east of Recife, Kusch located the Panamanian tanker *Motocarline* of 8,900 tons. He started an immediate underwater attack, firing a two-torpedo spread out of Tubes I and IV, but the target turned suddenly and sharply, and the torpedoes missed. Kusch immediately started another attack, and fired a second double fan out of Tubes II and III. One of them misfired or malfunctioned, while the second one hit the tanker with a loud click, yet did not explode. But apparently on hitting the tanker this dud had made a hull penetration. The *Motocarline* radioed promptly for help and reported this attack widely over the airwaves. She also used her deck gun to shell U-154.

Kusch quickly dived to gain some distance, resurfacing when far enough away. U-154 did another plot and started to position herself so that she could run with full speed ahead to reach a forward attack position for a third attack on the tanker. The navigator and Kusch calculated it would take four hours of high-speed running to get to the point where the tanker could be attacked once more. When U-154 had just turned towards the tanker for a new approach, an American Catalina flying-boat arrived, responding to the tanker's attack signal, and dropped eight depth-charges on U-l54, coming steeply down out of the heavy clouds. Only a timely crash-dive saved U-154, and no damage was caused aboard. Under the circumstances, Kusch was forced to break off his pursuit, and the tanker managed to get away.

On 14 May, Kusch was ordered to turn easterly and move to an area about seventy-eight miles off Cabo Sao Roque to be refuelled on 17 May and take on other supplies from the Type XIV U-tanker U-460, a 'milk cow', which was commanded by Lieutenant of the Reserve Ebe Schnoor, who had served in the First World War in the Imperial Navy.

The constant aircraft patrols made a further pullback from the Brazilian coast necessary before it was possible to refuel, and U-154 encountered U-460 only on the evening of 20 May, 500 miles north-east of the Fernando de Noronha Island group. She received 70 cu m of diesel fuel, 2 cu m of heavy-duty lubricating oil and supplementary food and other supplies for an additional twenty days of patrolling. Furthermore, a sick crewman was transferred to U-460, as the U-tanker carried a doctor and had medical treatment facilities aboard. During the refuelling period, special heavy-duty welding equipment, together with a specialist to operate it properly, were brought over to U-154 by means of an inflatable dinghy, to repair and reweld several cracks in Diving Cell 8 that had been caused by one of the depth-charges.

After this meeting, U-154 proceeded again towards the west to get closer once more to the Brazilian coastline. It was reached on 24 May, but constant aircraft patrols dictated staying underwater during the daytime. On 28 May, Kusch spotted a small convoy, BT-17, travelling a northerly course from Bahia, Brazil, to Port of Spain, Trinidad. There were twelve steamers with five destroyers to protect them as convoy escorts. Kusch changed course slightly to approach as closely as possible, underdiving the destroyers. During a turn, she fired all six of her torpedoes, four from the bow tubes and two from the stern tubes, within three minutes, then slowly went deeper, to be able to reload her torpedo tubes as soon as possible. Five detonations were heard by the crew. However, as the destroyers promptly started to search for U-154 and their sonar equipment picked up the U-boat, it was impossible to make visual observations through the periscope, and no detailed report of results achieved was feasible under the circumstances.

According to American records, Kusch actually hit three vessels, some with two torpedoes. They were the *John Worthington*, 8,166 tons, which would be towed into Galveston, Texas, but had to be scrapped there as not repairable; the *Cardinal Gibbons*, 7,191 tons, which was damaged severely but could be towed into Port of Spain, Trinidad, for repairs; and the *Florida*, 8,580 tons, which the escorts managed to tow to Fortaleza, Brazil, to be repaired.

Kusch returned to the area of this attack as soon as U-154 was able to reload her torpedo tubes. But when he did so, another Catalina flying-boat attacked and immediately fired on her periscope, preventing any follow-up approach to attack.

Kusch ordered deep running and silent turnaways, creeping along at 180 m (about 594 ft) and slowly moving away from the destroyers criss-crossing on the surface, searching for him. After six hours he rose to periscope depth and tried once again to locate the floating tanker, but the still circling Catalina flying-boats prevented any close approach.

When Kusch radioed the details of this attack and reported his fuel and torpedo supply situation to U-boat Command in Berlin Charlottenburg,Rear Admiral Eberhard Godt signalled U-154 personally a 'Well done!' on 30 May 1943.

Kusch now proceeded northwards and observed frequent aircraft patrol flights. But U-154 was able to dive quickly every time to remain undetected. About 580 miles north of the Brazilian Coastal Bend, Kusch was finally able to transfer the reserve torpedoes from the pressurized deck containers into the interior of U-154. This was a time-consuming job, with long periods of inspection and adjustment required afterwards, before the torpedoes could be loaded into the tubes, as they had not been serviced since departure from Lorient.

On 7 June the Metox-Schwarzkopf radar observation and detection device became unserviceable and was not repairable. On 8 June smoke was spotted, and Kusch immediately approached for an attack, but when U-154 got close enough to check details, the ship turned out to be a neutral Spanish steamer.

On 18 June 1943 Kusch received orders to return to Lorient and proceed to the Azores Island group to meet U-126, another Type IX U-boat, commanded by Lieutenant j.g. Siegfried Kietz, a naval classmate. U-126 was to hand over a replacement Metox radar detection device to Kusch, essential for the crossing of the Bay of Biscay, and travel jointly with U-154 at close distance for the rest of the war patrol. U-126 had received this Metox replacement set when being refuelled by the Type XIV U-tanker U-487, in the mid-Atlantic.

After some searching, Kusch met U-126 in the afternoon of 28 June about 115 miles north-east of the Azores Islands group. U-l26 was returning from West Africa. One can imagine the considerable amount of radio signals involved in these various meetings, giving the Allies detailed information for locating these U-boats.

Both U-boat commanders were instructed by U-boat Command to travel jointly in close formation, and to support each other with their anti-aircraft guns, a highly questionable order, as U-boats were rather poor gun platforms. Moreover, as a result of extended underwater travel, the flak guns could not be serviced properly, which resulted in frequent stoppages and breakdowns.

Kusch visited U-126 using a small rubber dinghy, to discuss with Kietz how they should proceed and in what manner they ought to act during the different combat and attack possibilities. The commanders agreed to remain on the surface and fight it out if a single aircraft attacked, as ordered by the U-boat Command, using their machine-guns and anti-aircraft guns. Diving was only considered as a last resort or if several aircraft attacked jointly.

Once the U-boats got under way again, U-154 leading and U-126 following close behind, Kusch spotted an American steamer with two funnels, which was moving at a fast rate. U-154 fired a double fan of torpedoes, but they missed because the steamer spotted her, increased speed even more and took immediate evasive action.

On 3 July, the U-boats reached a position about 200 miles north-west of Cape Finisterre, Spain. They had already proceeded for five hours on the surface, since it had become dark enough for that, when suddenly at 02.43 hours a bright and strong searchlight reached after them from a distance of 1,000 m and a height of 15 m above the sea. Kusch was on the bridge. The anti-aircraft guns and machine-guns of U-154 were manned and ready to fire instantly. Kusch ordered them to shoot out the searchlight, but the machine-guns jammed after a few shots were fired. Midshipman Kirchammer was on the bridge, as one of the lookouts.

As the attacking aircraft, Wellington 'R' of Coastal Command's 172 Squadron, with special anti-submarine equipment and the Leigh light with radar combination, rushed closer, the pilot, Flight Sergeant Alex Coumbis, a Southern Rhodesian, saw U-126 too, and immediately changed course, as U-126 appeared in a more favourable location for him. The Wellington had dropped to barely 10 m above the sea. The flak guns of U-154 fired away rapidly, while Kusch ordered hard starboard rudder, to shift U-154 sideways and further away from the flight path of the Wellington. By this manoeuvre the distance between the U-boats quickly increased. U-154 was not hit by the depth-charges the Wellington dropped in a stick throw attack. Two of them fell into the sea between the U-boats, the other two dropped into the ocean on the other side of U-126, seemingly without hitting her or causing her any damage.

Kirchammer observed that the bridge of U-126 was cleared in a hurry and that a crash-dive must have been ordered, against the agreement of the two commanders to fight it out on the surface. The guns of U-126 did not fire a single bullet. As U-126 dipped forward into the deep, Kusch and Kirchammer noticed that the Metox equipment cable appeared to be hung up somewhere and could not be pulled into the U-boat and cleared. Nevertheless, U-126 swiftly disappeared. Kusch ordered rapid fire at the aircraft, while it was flying directly over U-126, to hit the Wellington's underbelly if possible.

However, when the Wellington started to make a short circle and was evidently preparing for a second attack, Kusch ordered a crash-dive, as the Wellington had dropped a smoke-producing marker to get back quickly to the diving spot, which would be visible for some time. Kusch hoped that U-154 would be deep enough by the time the Wellington managed to return to his diving area. When U-154 was settled 40 m below the surface, a depth considered safe, Kusch tried to contact U-126 on her underwater telephone. But there was no reply. Suddenly, several sharp cracks were heard, similar to the firing of a 3.7 cm anti-aircraft gun, yet nothing else whatsoever.

Analysing the various observations, Kusch concluded that U-126 had been unable to close her conning tower hatch completely, owing to the snagged Metox cable. Consequently, water increasingly forced itself into U-126 as she dived deeper. Apparently, she could not reverse or stop the steep dive, nor pull the Metox cable into her interior and close the leaking conning tower hatch-cover to stop the water cascades. She dropped like a constantly heavier rock into the depths, with the growing weight of the water entering her. The implosions and cracks heard were undoubtedly cracks in the pressurized body of U-126, smashed to pieces by the growing water pressure, and dropping to the ocean's bottom with all hands.

Abel, the executive officer, had not been on the bridge during this attack, but demanded that Kusch order U-154 back to the surface after only a few minutes, to search for survivors from U-126. Because the observations of those on bridge watch had not seen any direct hits, and Kusch's instructions called for staying dived one hour as the minimum, he refused Abel's demand.

While there existed no obligation for Kusch to show such instructions for U-boat commanders to his officers, nevertheless this clash rapidly turned into an extended shouting match. The sea was roughing up considerably, as had already been observed through the periscope, and it had grown to about Strength 6 when U-154 returned to the surface. But when no trace whatsoever of U-126 could be discovered, Kusch stopped the circling about and ordered a return to the course for the Lorient entry point.

When daylight started to break, Kusch dived at 08.33 hours to continue the trip under water for the rest of the day, as instructed, when crossing the Bay of Biscay. At 20.22 hours U-154 came back to the surface to start recharging her batteries and to travel at higher speed during the night. A few minutes later a radar contact was reported and she dived again, coming back to the surface at 21.13 hours. Half an hour later there was another radar observation contact, followed by a prompt alarm dive. At 22.26 hours there was a further rise to the surface to continue the high-speed run, but at 23.15 hours the next radar contact occurred and U-154 disappeared once more.

Kusch decided to stay underwater and travel dived for several hours. U-154 surfaced again on 4 July at 05.53 hours in order to crash-dive only twenty-five minutes later. It was problematical to accumulate a full recharge of the batteries, going up and down like a lift in a high-rise building. At 07.11 hours Kusch again tried to surface, yet four minutes later U-154 was once more located and had to dive immediately. She continued underwater until 17.25 hours, before trying once more to surface in the darkness.

Finally, U-154 was able to run for six hours on the surface and recharge her batteries. Shortly before midnight she dived again for a long underwater voyage until 06.10 hours on 5 July 1943. When she reached the surface she signalled, 'U-154 about thirty hours away from meeting point Lucie Two.' At 08.12 hours the message was confirmed with instructions, 'U-l54 should reach pick-up point Lantern Three at 13.00 hours to meet the minesweepers. Under no circumstances to approach the coastline any closer than the 50 m line. U-boat Command is assuming U-126 is arriving with U-154.' As soon as this signal had been decoded and read, Kusch dived promptly at 08.20 hours.

At 21.10 hours U-154 surfaced to acknowledge the signal and directions received, advising that U-126 was no longer with U-154 and probably lost. On 6 July Kusch reached the contact point and U-154 switched to radio circuit 'Küste' for coastal approaches to the mineswept channels, and proceeded from 05.40 hours once more on the surface at high speed. At 14.30 hours she encountered the mine barrier detonator ship and the minesweeper escort group that guided her into Lorient safely in their wake.

At 17.00 hours U-154 reached the arrival pier in Lorient and waved off the minesweeper escorts. Kusch had been at sea with U-154 on his first war patrol as commander for 109 days. He reported immediately to flotilla commander Kals and discussed the war patrol of U-154 at length with him. Kals then studied the KTB, the war patrol journal, closely, approved it and forwarded it to Angers, France, where the Leader of U-boats in western France, Captain Hans Rudolf Rösing, called for short 'FdU West', resided. Rösing had been the liaison officer in Bordeaux with the Italian submarines, which had either been sunk or returned to Italy. In Angers a new headquarters had been under construction for Dönitz and the U-boat Command since the summer of 1942, which was only finished in spring 1943.

After the British Commando raid on Saint Nazaire on 28 March 1942, Hitler had ordered that Dönitz and the U-boat Command must move further inland and away from Kerneval near Lorient at the coast, to make sure the British could not capture and kidnap Dönitz with a landing operation. Therefore, U-boat Command was moved back to Paris again in April 1942. But when Dönitz was selected as the commander-in-chief of the German Navy, he and the U-boat Command moved to Berlin instead of Angers, and the new, but empty, building was no longer needed.

Because communication problems developed with the greater geographical distance, Rösing was appointed to this newly created position in Angers, though it was supposed to be a purely administrative post without operational authority. However, Rösing managed to build up a new intermediate level between the U-boat flotillas in western France and the U-boat Command in Berlin. Within a few months, Rösing had turned his merely paper-shuffling job as coordinator into an intermediate operational position, as personal representative of Dönitz and the U-boat Command in France, and involved himself in operational and personnel matters more and more. Therefore, all war journals were now first forwarded to Rösing in Angers, instead of directly to Berlin and Godt. Thus Rösing received and perused the war patrol journal of Kusch's operation with U-154, fully approving the same, before forwarding the KTB onward to Berlin.

Because Rösing (Crew 1924) will become decisive in the Oskar Kusch case, it is necessary to spotlight him fully. He was the elder son of a former German admiral in the Imperial Navy, born in 1905 and 38 years old in 1943.

It is important to know that sons of admirals received a substantial extra bonus for the preliminary naval examinations, and sons of Army generals likewise, but fewer plus points. Sons of middle-level naval officers, the different captain service grades called *Stabsoffiziere*, were awarded a somewhat lesser bonus point total again. In other words, such individuals received an automatic advance handicap due to the position of their fathers. Therefore, they started the naval examination with a substantial advantage. A number of these men would have failed these examinations without the extra bonus points. The result was that men of average or medium intelligence were accepted on a preferential basis.

When the war started, Rösing was a U-boat flotilla commander. One of the U-boats assigned to this flotilla was U-48, a Type VII-B U-boat with the then top crew aboard, commanded by Lieutenant-Commander Herbert E. 'Vaddi' Schultze. While preparing U-48 for her sixth war patrol in Kiel, Schultze suddenly fell ill and had to be operated on immediately. There was no qualified replacement commander available at short notice. And so Rösing stepped into that position to obviate a delay in the departure of U-48. But this was only possible because of her very experienced crew and her team of outstanding officers, led by Lieutenant j.g. Reinhard 'Teddy' Suhren, one of the best torpedo officers, as executive officer.

U-48 departed on 26 May 1940 for the North Atlantic. During that time of the war, over ninety per cent of all sinkings were achieved by surface attacks at night, when the executive officer aimed and fired the torpedoes, while the commander navigated the U-boat but received full credit for all sinkings achieved.

U-48 made two war patrols with Rösing. The first one lasted thirty-four days, and the second one, which started on 7 August 1940 from Kiel, turned into a transfer voyage to Lorient, arriving there on 28 August after operations in the North Atlantic and to the west of Ireland. On these two war patrols U-48 managed to sink twelve confirmed ships, of 60,702 tons. When she reached France, Dönitz replaced Rösing as commander of U-48 and awarded him the Knight's Cross of the Iron Cross.

Over the years, Rösing had acquired two nicknames that speak for themselves: he was known as 'His Master's Voice', copied from the old RCA gramophone advertisement of the brown and white dog listening attentively to what comes out of the huge horn of that machine; but more and more he was now called 'The Echo of Berlin', which reflected quite clearly what one could expect from him.

For most U-boat commanders and officers who were obliged to come to Angers or who had to deal with his office, there was a kind of saving grace in the persons of his principal staff officers, exemplary men with considerable patience, a strong sense of humour, very witty and dependable. Commander Karl Daublesky von Eichhain was a warm-hearted, charming gentleman of the old Austrian school with a broad horizon, and Lieutenant-Commander Hannes Leinemann, who had a meticulous memory for details and facts, was a good-natured, patient officer, helpful and very sympathetic towards men serving on front U-boats.

Rösing was a fanatical tennis player who had arranged for the construction of a rather fancy tennis court for himself in Angers. This was fortunate, because one could bypass him whenever he played tennis, and deal with his staff officers directly. When Rösing was in Angers, he had his ugly, slobbering pet dog eating in the officers' mess, a mixed-breed boxer that he spoiled dreadfully. During meals, he tossed pieces of meat to his dog sitting on 'his special chair' at the table across from him, and he thought this was very funny. He took this nasty animal along whenever visiting other commands or inspecting U-boat crews, and the brute often misbehaved awfully, to his owner's delight.

Petty officers and enlisted men hated the FdU West intensely, because they quickly found out that his friendliness was superficial and only lasted as long as it suited his purpose. For self-protection one was better off not to rely upon Rösing's smiling face, as the knife would soon be ready to strike the unwary man not on full alert.

Years later in Vietnam, such unpopular officers as Rösing were reportedly often 'fragged out' with hand-grenades or tommy-guns. In the German Navy, it was widely known that some detested officers had accidentally gone overboard in heavy seas. One has to wonder why Rösing had not been dispatched in a similar way.

After American tanks broke out from the encirclement of the Normandy beaches at Avranches early in August 1944, the German defensive front cracked quickly, and Angers was approached by these tanks. Rösing grabbed some trucks and loaded them with the special Kurier communications equipment, the Enigma coding machines, and numerous suitcases and many boxes filled with personal belongings that he had acquired in France, living like a demi-god or king there. His batch of tennis rackets and his nasty dog were loaded on the trucks, too, before they drove rapidly to La Rochelle, to get away from the American troops and tanks.

The U-boat base in Bordeaux had been closed down after Operation Dragon, the Allied landings on the French southern coast, took place. All U-boats that could be repaired and made operable had departed in a hurry. There were some German destroyers, torpedo boats, minesweepers and other smaller surface ships which could not be repaired, and the crews of these various ships and U-boats had been evacuated to La Rochelle. In the other U-boat bases all U-boats that could be made ready for sea were departing for Norway as soon as they were able to leave. While Brest was occupied on 18 September 1944 after considerable ground-fighting, Lorient, Saint Nazaire and La Rochelle were held by German forces until the capitulation on 8 May 1945. Brest was bombed constantly and almost entirely destroyed, except the U-boat pens, which stood firmly in the ruins of that port.

When the surplus naval crews reached La Rochelle, there was no longer any fuel available for vehicles, and trains had been discontinued for lack of coal. These experienced U-boat men were mixed and blended with other naval units no longer required in France, like coastal artillery, watch and security companies or personnel pools, and formed into a special naval regiment commanded by Captain Friedrich Badermann, the naval yard director in Bordeaux. The surplus U-boat men were formed into one battalion of this naval regiment before being placed under the command of the German Army's Major-General Elster. The force was then called Group Elster.

In Germany experienced U-boat men were in great demand for the new Type XXI and XXIII electroboats under construction. But Rösing had neglected to provide transportation to Germany for these men. He made a farewell speech that they were needed by the U-boat Command in Germany and that he expected them to march with determination, utmost speed and without delay. The U-boat men were utterly disgusted by this idiotic rhetoric from Rösing, who was the main culprit for this stupid foot-slogging that was now required. When he talked about final victory for Germany and the U-boat Command soon, no matter what, the marching columns turned totally sour.

In his snow-white summer uniform, crisply ironed with a crease to his trousers that one could shave with, Rösing quickly turned around as soon as the marching columns had passed him, and took a car to La Rochelle airport to board his waiting aircraft, for which fuel had been found and made available for his getaway. All of his many personal possessions had already been transferred to this aeroplane, including his tennis rackets and his ugly dog. As soon as he had slipped aboard the aeroplane took off for Berlin, from where he drove on to Camp Koralle at Bernau, to report to Dönitz.

Meanwhile, the sailors and soldiers marched northwards in the August heat and muddled along as best they could. Once Group Elster was about thirty miles away from Orleans, they found all the bridges over the Loire river had been destroyed by bombing, and American tanks and troops were already on the other bank. As it appeared impossible under these circumstances to reach Germany, General Elster decided to surrender his entire force to the Americans, to become prisoners of war.

This seemed preferable to getting their throats cut by the largely communistic French Maquis resistance bands, who shot soldiers in the back from behind hedges, took no prisoners and expropriated everything they could use, following instructions from Soviet Russia instead of from France and Charles de Gaulle.

When those U-boats that had left the French bases reached Norway, usually Bergen, Stavanger or Kristiansand, they found that the repair and service facilities there were totally insufficient to care for them. Most of them had to continue onwards to German shipyards for repairs and overhaul.

But to the chagrin of the U-boat commanders and the disgust of their crews, who should soon show up in Bergen and elsewhere in Norway? None other than Rösing, again making his sanctimonious speeches and trumpeting loudly that final victory nonsense about new weapons and new U-boats to make it possible.

Rösing arranged with Dönitz that Norway would be split into two commands for U-boats. Reinhard 'Teddy' Suhren continued to direct the U-boats based in northern Norway and operating in the Barents Sea from Narvik, Harstadt, Hammerfest and Trondheim from his communications and command ship *Aviso Grille* in Narvik. Rösing retained his former title and was to direct U-boats operating in the Atlantic from Bergen and the southern Norwegian ports.

When the OKM, the Naval High Command, and the U-boat Command were bombed out in Berlin, the Naval High Command moved initially to Eberswalde, while the U-boat Command moved to Camp Koralle near Bernau, where suburban train connections were available. Shuttle buses and periodic transport was set up. But a lot of time was wasted on the roads and in transit. Once enough new wooden barracks were set up in Koralle, more and more OKM sections gradually moved there, too.

Dönitz had many other tasks to look after with his wider responsibility and the many prestige requirements of the job as head of a German Navy which was still growing. Yet Dönitz constantly felt obliged to involve himself increasingly in politics and political matters, and growing mountains of paperwork made him less and less accessible.

Dönitz had moved with his wife from his house in Berlin Dahlem into one of the only two stone buildings in Camp Koralle, where special visitors or Dönitz's specialized assistants were also lodged. Increasing area bombardments resulted in disruptions of telephone and teletype landlines more and more frequently, requiring constantly more patience and longer periods of time, if they could be repaired at all. Consequently, radio signals handled almost everything, and the British code breakers at Bletchley Park were therefore rapidly and fully informed about everything concerning U-boats.

Thus, Ultra became even more successful and influential in counter-operations, resulting in a rising number of U-boats destroyed. The tendency of U-boat Command to become involved in the smallest details reduced the chances of survival of operational U-boats even more than had been the case before almost everything was radioed back and forth.

The staff officers were overworked and there were never enough of them. They were overwhelmed by the daily grind of routine paper shuffling, lacking

time to think or plan, as they were so enmeshed in administrative requirements and bureaucratic detail that they rarely had time to investigate new
possibilities or to consider new subjects or different options in the constantly
changing and worsening operational picture. And Germany was falling
faster and faster behind in almost all new technical developments.

Because of this additional step in the bureaucratic naval ladder, Rösing's
interference in many details delayed the forwarding of the war patrol journals and other papers to Koralle in Berlin Bernau. If Godt or somebody at
the U-boat Command had questions or needed further input and wanted to
double-check specifics, the originators of the written reports could often no
longer be reached owing to the geographical distance, or only with considerable delays. Frequently, the officers needed for any clarification had
already departed on another war patrol or were even missing, presumed
dead, by then.

Disregarding these complications for the moment, Godt received the KTB
war patrol journal of U-154 prepared by Kusch and studied by both Kals
and Rösing's office, and endorsed it as follows:

> This was the first patrol of this new commander, but with a comparatively
> proved and experienced crew. The U-boat was ordered to operate as a
> single U-boat in the South Atlantic. The attack made on 8 May was unfor-
> tunately not successful, owing to missing and malfunctioning torpedoes or
> torpedo exploders. Extensive aircraft patrols prevented further attacks
> afterwards. The attack on 28 May was very well planned on the spot, with
> time pressure problems, and extremely clever in the execution. Regarding
> the 3 July action, decisions and procedures of the commander were correct
> and the right ones under the prevailing circumstances during the various
> aircraft attacks. But a more extensive and longer search for possible
> survivors of U-126 would have been better and preferable. The first patrol
> resulted in gaining valuable experience, but also brought about a nice
> success for this new commander.

Shortly after U-154 had managed to return to Lorient and was in the process
of being overhauled in the Keroman pens, considerable changes took place
again among her crew. The second watch officer, Heinrich Meyer, was transferred to prospective commander's training in the Baltic. The navigator and
quartermaster, *Obersteuermann* Lüdmann, who had served as third watch
officer, was posted elsewhere. Quite a few of the longer-serving petty
officers, the backbone of any ship, were either transferred to other
commands or to promotional training schools. Both midshipmen were
assigned to upgraded watch officer and weapons training commands in the
Baltic.

As these various men received their travel orders, Kusch spoke individually with each of them, wishing them good luck and shaking their hands.
Those men who were to remain on U-154, took turns with home leave in

Germany, often combined with equipment and weapon upgrading courses. During the overhaul outmoded equipment was removed from U-154 and replaced with newer and improved equipment or newer models that were expected to work better.

While U-154 had been at sea, the Allied forces had managed to turn around the entire U-boat operational situation in the Atlantic. What had been increasingly clear to all observers since autumn 1942 was no longer hidden from anybody now. During March 1943 the largest and toughest convoy battles were fought in the North Atlantic, and it was the last time that the U-boats gained considerable advantages.

After the Torch landings in North Africa, a substantial reorganization took place in the assignment of Allied escorting groups, and several new ones were formed and entered operations. But in March 1943 during these convoy battles in awful weather conditions, fifteen U-boats had been destroyed. In April seventeen U-boats were sunk, and sinkings of steamers dropped considerably. Then in the month of May 1943, soon called 'Black May' by the U-boat men, a total of forty-one U-boats were lost at sea. With reluctance and hesitation, Dönitz had to order an end to U-boats attacking convoys in the North Atlantic, and gradually discontinued his group, or pack, operations at the same time.

Dönitz, eternally optimistic, often disregarding reality for as long as possible, had ordered the factual evacuation of the North Atlantic and a retreat of those U-boats still having sufficient fuel to proceed south into the mid-Atlantic or South Atlantic, where the defences were still less formidable. Though, in fact, admitting defeat, he couched the explanation of his withdrawal order in terms of a temporary retreat until improved and better weapons would make it possible to return to the old battlegrounds in the North Atlantic. But after the heights of March, blown up grossly by the propaganda people, the collapse in May was even more noticeable. Within a few more weeks, U-boat men would more and more refer to 'Black May' simply as 'Stalingrad at Sea'.

While Dönitz and the Naval High Command had put a heavy secrecy cover on both combat losses and the ever smaller operational possibilities, it was simply impossible, no matter how tight that clamp was kept on, to hide the empty spaces in the various U-boat pens, which had been overcrowded before and where U-boats frequently had to wait for dry-docking space for quite some time. During the entire year of 1942, a total of eighty-five U-boats were lost. Now, during May 1943, almost half that many had been lost within a single month.

A considerable number of U-boats were already at sea when this withdrawal order went into effect, many of them the larger Type IX U-boats that usually remained on operations for several months. During June another seventeen U-boats were destroyed, and in July a further thirty-seven U-boats took that final dive. Finally, in August 1943, once more twenty-five U-boats did not return, despite the fact that Dönitz had been forced to put a temporary sailing stop into effect. Departures were halted of new U-boats or those of the older ones that as yet did not have any of the upgraded electronic equipment and the more powerful anti-aircraft guns installed.

All sorts of temporary improvisations were tried by Dönitz and the U-boat Command. However, none of them worked well, if at all. The orders for U-boats to shoot it out with aircraft attacking them had resulted in grievous losses. Now Dönitz and Godt put into effect the so-called group departures and arrivals initially tried with U-154 and U-126. The British quickly caught on, and simply operated their aircraft in groups, too, to overcome the combined anti-aircraft defence of several U-boats travelling as a group. In the summer of 1943 a really peculiar arrangement was introduced. As U-boats did not have the equipment to communicate instantly with other U-boats, apart from the customary semaphore signal flags and Morse code lamps, useless for passing on fast orders, a set of special flags was introduced in a variety of bright colours. The senior U-boat commander in the group was to make the operational decision, like fighting aeroplanes on the surface, dispersing the group or crash-diving, etc., by waving particular coloured flags. Naturally, when actually used it became a complete flop. Not since the ancient Phoenicians had roamed the oceans had such a system been employed.

So-called flak trap U-boats were put into service that were supposed to act as bait for aircraft and knock them down with extra-heavy anti-aircraft gun armament. But after one successful shooting down, one Sunderland flying-boat, the next test backfired, and U-441, which had been converted as the first flak trap, was attacked by three Beaufighter aircraft and shot to pieces. The commander, all officers, all senior petty officers and all gunners were either killed or severely wounded.

Fortunately, U-441 had a naval surgeon on board, *Marinestabsarzt* Paul Pfaffinger MD, who first arranged to look after the wounded and then took over command, diving U-441 and managing to return her to Brest. His sole experience in running a ship was that he had been an avid sport sailor for years. Pfaffinger could only get some operational guidance from the engine-room petty officers who had not been on deck during the fight.

Among several trial-and-error approaches that Dönitz and Berlin attempted, the posting of medical officers aboard U-boats was way overdue, as the number of wounded or killed crewmen increased swiftly once the Dönitz order to fight aircraft on the surface was actually put into effect. The high losses in the spring and summer of 1943 brought about the drowning of many of these naval doctors, who had been assigned in a hurry and without any U-boat training. The naval surgeon-general, *Admiralsarzt* Emil Greul MD, became extremely concerned over these high losses of medical officers, and put pressure on Dönitz to reduce this new practice quickly. The German Navy was very short of experienced medical officers because most of them were reserve officers, so saving the Navy a lot of money.

After some extended arguments, it was decided to give several hundred medical corpsmen supplementary paramedical training, in addition to the usual first-aid kind of training they had previously received. Yet this would require five to six months, if not longer. Therefore, the first truly humane order that Dönitz had ever given – Surgeons aboard the front U-boats! – was soon, to a great extent, cancelled. Only the U-tanker and U-cruiser U-boats usually retained their doctors because they remained at sea for three months or longer.

Consequently, that promise by Karl Dönitz, 'U-boat men are entitled to the same medical care and service that is provided for Army soldiers in Russia on the Eastern Front', quickly turned out to be mainly rhetoric and little else: just another paper promise by the Naval High Command for propaganda purposes. And the paramedics only became gradually available by the middle of 1944.

Like virtually all U-boat officers at the front, Kusch had found out about these changes in U-boat operations directly as well as indirectly. In the officers' and petty officers' messes few other subjects were talked about. The number of photographs on the walls mushroomed, and everybody had friends among those who did not manage to return from the sea.

In actuality, during the first couple of months in 1943, the entire so-called third generation of U-boat commanders and watch officers, groomed as future commanders, together with their experienced crews, were practically wiped out. In most cases, these U-boats were lost with all hands, and only in a few instances were a couple of U-boat men rescued and taken prisoners of war. It was not possible the German Navy and the U-boat Command to recover from these losses, or replace these experienced men.

While the U-boat men at the front became gradually more and more resigned and many often turned completely fatalistic, the really upset men were those who had returned from home leave in Germany, particularly after the fire-bombing attacks on Hamburg, where the families of many U-boat men had lived and been burnt.

All U-boat men returning from Germany talked about the quickly growing problems of their families, if they had somehow survived the bombing attacks. Others found that their families had been evacuated in a rather arbitrary way and had been moved elsewhere, by orders of the local Nazi functionaries and 'bigwigs'. As housing became less available in the cities, many had to move into the countryside as the only alternative. Yet this invariably meant considerable problems for their families in the services. Quite a few U-boat men returned from their leave and had been unable to even trace their families and relatives. In fact, many naval people were drafted for rubble clearing and fire-extinction labour and forced to work with emergency crews.

Oskar Kusch participated in another electronic updating course and the latest technical torpedo tests in the Baltic because new electronic and counter-electronic equipment was being installed during the repair and over-haul stay in the Keroman U-boat concrete pens. Moreover, he had been informed that a new and improved type of torpedo would be provided for the next operation of U-154, which required additional training and participation in test firings.

No matter how technically obsolete U-boats had become in 1943 and thereafter, and regardless of the true situation at sea and the smaller and fewer chances for operational successes, U-boats periodically departed on war patrols once they were repaired, fuelled, ammunitioned and had been manned.

CHAPTER SIX

Tilting at Windmills

From the newly constructed compound of the 2nd U-boat Flotilla, and now the Tenth U-boat Flotilla as well, about six miles away from the ruins of Lorient near Pont Scorff, called *Lager* Lemp, U-boat crews were shuttled daily in buses to and from the huge Keroman U-boat pens in the harbour of Lorient.

While there was a full line of eating facilities, recreation halls and entertainment places, they were often frequented by senior base officers. Most were older reserve officers no longer in physical shape for shipboard assignments. Quite a few of them were not connected with the U-boat Command, using courtesy privileges to visit the bars and dining halls. Many of the subaltern officers preferred to eat outside the naval compound area, in one of the many French seafood restaurants in various close-by fishing villages. These older officers cramped the style of the U-boat officers, who were fed up with having to listen to the same tiresome, boring stories mouthed endlessly by them. The younger officers had different interests and other expectations. They liked parties with jazz music and dance tunes, instead of boring drinking sessions. They preferred the smaller French restaurants, or taking a drink here and there in the local bars instead.

On 23 September 1943, after some delays, U-154 was declared ready again, fully repaired by the shipyard engineers, called shipyard grandees by the U-boat men. She had been loaded, provisioned and ammunitioned to the gills, but because of the constant dropping of air mines by the British, it was now impossible to make the customary deep-diving test near Lorient. At 18.00, U-154 left with a batch of shipyard technicians still aboard and a minesweeper escort to enter the Bay of Biscay, and proceeded to the 200 m line, going even somewhat further for the deep-diving test. Kusch had been instructed to continue onwards to Brest if there were any technical problems, instead of returning to Lorient, because of the air mining situation. Problems did develop and U-154 proceeded to Brest on 24 September to iron out the various shortcomings that had shown up during the deep-diving test.

Once all technical and mechanical problems were straightened out to

Kusch's satisfaction, U-154 departed from the U-boat pens in Brest, with minesweeper escorts, at 15.30 on 2 October 1943 on her sixth war patrol. The initial destination was again the mid-Atlantic and the Azores Islands area.

During Kusch's absence in Germany, another big turnover had taken place in the crew of U-154, most of the new people being inexperienced recruits from the U-boat training schools in the Baltic. A new second watch officer arrived late in July, another former Merchant Marine officer, Lieutenant j.g. of the Reserves Arno Funke, older than Abel and thirteen years older than Kusch. Funke was another noisy Nazi type, too, and a former SA (Storm Trooper) leader. He had no U-boat operational experience and was assigned directly from the U-boat training courses, which had recently been shortened and accelerated. As a convinced Nazi Funke was welcomed with open arms by Abel and Druschel, and all three became close friends.

As soon as Kusch had returned to Lorient, several U-boat officers warned him about this bunch of officers and told him about the impertinent way they had shot their mouths off about him. Funke had not even met Kusch, which did not hold him back in the least from joining Abel and Druschel in slandering their commander. Naval classmates recommended that Kusch have these officers exchanged and replaced with experienced U-boat officers. Some officer friends suggested that Kusch ought to contact the officer retailer in Kiel, Lieutenant-Commander Harald Jeppener-Haltenhoff, who would promptly arrange for suitable replacements. But Kusch was convinced that he could somehow manage to get along with this bunch assigned to U-154. He wanted to avoid the possible court-martial case that might have come about had this been handled through official channels.

The newest addition, Funke, had done nothing at all with the paperwork that had accumulated and was part of the responsibilities of the second watch officer. Kusch had to take care of everything himself once he reached Lorient, as Funke told him he was not competent to handle office work.

Erich Raeder had tried to keep the German Navy free from political impulses and political influences and ideas. His firm conviction had always been that the Navy first and foremost served Germany and her interests, rather than the political aims and plans of the many and often clashing Nazi factions and suborganizations.

Undoubtedly this view had become gradually something of a delusion in many ways. Nevertheless, it was accepted at the naval headquarters in Berlin, largely dominated by older officers who had served in the Imperial Navy, that younger officers had a right to their own opinions. It was known they often held beliefs not in line with the official Nazi ideas and views. Therefore, there existed among officers a definite atmosphere of free expression that extended into politics, foreign relations and the general conditions in Germany as seen and experienced by these officers, both while on assignments in foreign or occupied countries and also when serving within Germany.

It was fairly common knowledge that many of the younger officers listened to foreign broadcasts, both because of the musical programmes and also for the news coverage. Yet in addition to radio stations like the BBC, the Voice of America, Radio Beromünster or Radio Stockholm, more and more officers tuned in the so-called 'Black' radio programmes operated by the British under the direction of Sefton Delmer Jr, a convinced socialist. These were stations like Siegfried Eins, Radio for Soldiers Calais, or the newest of them, Radio Atlantic, specifically run for U-boat men and their preferences and interest. Here news was included about prisoners of war as soon as they were taken, while official notifications usually required several months to reach the U-boat Command. *Abwehr* officers listened to these stations as part of their work.

Yet there was a small number of officers, petty officers and enlisted men, particularly those who had only recently arrived from Germany, who still believed the official Nazi propaganda completely, and defended Adolf Hitler or the Nazi Party in every possible way. Abel, Druschel and the newcomer Funke belonged to that minority. When Druschel was posted to U-154 in Lorient he had never been outside Germany, spoke no French and found the French disagreeable, dirty and dishonest.

A well-educated and widely read officer like Kusch was unable to swallow such Party propaganda, and refused to waste his limited free time on anything connected with such matters, like Nazi publications or the various naval propaganda sheets constantly distributed without cost.

Once Karl Dönitz had become the Navy's supreme commander, replacing Erich Raeder, matters had quickly taken a turn towards a much closer relationship of the German Navy with the Nazi Party organizations and the entire Nazi regime. One of the first orders promulgated by Dönitz and addressed to all naval officers, petty officers and enlisted men read: 'Our lives belong entirely to the state. Our honour lies in our fulfilment of our duty and constant readiness for action. None of us may claim the right to a private life any more. All that must concern us is the winning of the war. We must pursue this goal with fanatical devotion and the harshest will to win!' Such kinds of pronouncement one would expect from the Nazi minister of propaganda, Josef Goebbels, but hardly from the Navy's commander-in-chief. They would have been an impossibility under Erich Raeder's direction.

Meanwhile, U-154, under Kusch's command, moved underwater, and once darkness fell, on the surface, in accordance with the latest operational instructions. These had a tendency to change frequently and drastically during that summer and autumn of 1943. Cape Finisterre was reached and rounded on 6 October 1943, and Kusch proceeded along the Portuguese coast in the direction of the Azores Islands once more. He intended to search for ships off Ponta Delgada, just outside the Portuguese three-mile territorial limit. However, apart from two small Portuguese harbour patrol boats, nothing was encountered.

On 17 October U-154 continued her voyage travelling further south into the mid-Atlantic area. When she had proceeded another 500 miles, she met U-123, a Type IX-B U-boat commanded by Lieutenant j.g. Horst von Schröter, which was returning from Trinidad and the Caribbean Sea area to France. The commanders exchanged the latest operational information and shared their recent experiences at sea, which changed rapidly and constantly, swiftly making knowledge and information stale and equipment obsolete after several weeks of use.

On 22 October Kusch received radioed orders to proceed towards the Brazilian coast and to operate as far as 10° latitude south of the equator. According to the message from U-boat Command in Berlin, lightly escorted convoys could be expected in that area, offering good chances for attacks by single U-boats. The signal advised U-154 that immediately after any attack many aeroplanes would appear promptly, searching for the attacking U-boat. Lastly, the message furnished this cautionary advice: 'Be alert constantly for surprises. Best possible men on bridge watch are imperative, even if the tropical heat grows tiresome and the weather conditions almost intolerable. Usually aircraft only show up in numbers once the U-boat has been discovered, but then additional support is quickly activated to enforce the defences.'

When reading and considering this specific operational and tactical advice, one can only reach one conclusion. Success in sinking any target could only be expected if one was able to fire torpedoes without the slightest delay, and preferably before the enemy could activate sonar contacts to ascertain the U-boat's position. Once the escorting warships had been alerted and the air patrols were operating at full strength, it would appear preferable to break off an attack to preserve the U-boat for a better opportunity, rather than taking questionable chances.

On 2 November U-154 reached her new operational area, about 100 miles north of Cabo Sao Roque on latitude 3° south and about thirty miles east off the Brazilian coast. On 3 November Kusch stayed dived during daylight, but rose to periscope depth at 08.57 to get the sound-detection devices activated. At 10.00 they picked up propeller noises of a small convoy. Kusch checked the surface situation by periscope. A convoy travelling in a southeasterly direction could be seen very faintly, somewhere between twelve and fifteen merchant ships, including tankers and ore freighters, plus one combined passenger-freighter. An airship, a small blimp, was leading the convoy and there were three escorting frigates or corvettes. In addition, a Catalina flying-boat was circling around the convoy. After careful observation of the various movements from a distance of somewhere between nine and ten kilometres, Kusch decided to let the convoy continue until it was below the horizon, then to surface and commence a bypass overtaking operation with maximum speed, trying to get into a forward attack position ahead of the convoy for an underwater surprise attack.

Kusch and the new navigator, Karl Hoffmann, calculated it would require between twelve and fourteen hours, depending on how often the convoy changed course. Kusch aimed to reach that attack position about 02.30, when the moon would have just disappeared. Subject to the prevailing sea conditions, he decided that he would then make a final determination as to the type of attack and the most favourable direction for it to succeed. Furthermore, that way U-154 would have enough time to reload her batteries to maximum capacity. Kusch expected the assault would generate lengthy and tenacious underwater searches and depth-charge attacks, making it essential to have the batteries fully charged.

After high-speed surface running for about six hours, one of the Catalina flying-boats made a much wider circle and approached on a course that would undoubtedly detect U-154, particularly as she was running at high speed with a long and visible wake. Consequently, Kusch ordered an emergency dive to remain undiscovered. Once underwater U-154 continued at slow speed for a while in accordance with operational instructions. But now the speed of the convoy was considerably faster than the speed of U-154 underwater, and so the convoy moved further away again. After one hour U-154 rose to the surface and resumed high-speed surface travel, attempting once more to catch up with the convoy. Yet less than one hour later, another Catalina flying-boat approached in a direct line, attacking out of the sun and coming through cloud formations, quickly dropping deeper. When the aircraft was still 2,500 m away, but only 100 m above the sea, Kusch ordered the flak guns and machine-guns of U-154 to open fire as soon as practical. When the tracer bullets came close to the Catalina, the aircraft immediately turned away and changed course to fly parallel to U-154, trying not to overfly her directly. After this course correction, the Catalina dropped a stick of four depth-charges. Kusch had ordered full speed and hard starboard rudder to twist U-154 around to a new course. The depth-charges dropped into the ocean, the closest one 20 m from U-154, while the aircraft fired her machine-guns at her and multiple rounds splashed into the sea around the U-boat.

The very moment when the Catalina had passed, and before the aircraft had any chance to turn around and circle back for a second attack, Kusch ordered a crash-dive so that U-154 would be able to reach a safe depth and avoid a second attack. He went deep for thirty minutes, then rose slowly and remained under water for another thirty minutes, as instructed in the U-boat commander's manual.

Abel and Druschel argued with Kusch to rise to the surface more quickly, or even immediately, in order not to lose this convoy. As Kusch did not agree with their arguments he showed them the signal received and the U-boat commander's operational manual. But these officers continued to grumble and curse, with Funke joining them. Kusch had asked the navigator to re-calculate and refigure the possibilities remaining, with the delays encountered. It appeared that U-154 was unlikely to catch up with the convoy while it was still dark.

When one hour had passed, U-154 rose to periscope depth and Kusch immediately observed the still circling Catalina over the original diving spot, waiting for U-154 to rise to the surface. As it was by now after 20.00, it was clear that U-154 would be unable to catch up with the convoy, even if able to move at full speed and burning up a lot of diesel fuel doing so. Kusch had been advised that it was unlikely that U-154 could be refuelled on this war patrol, because most of the U-tankers and suppliers had been sunk. Therefore, he decided to discontinue the pursuit and turned around, resuming a northerly course once more.

Proceeding on the surface at night to reload her batteries, and underwater in the daytime, U-154 reached an area about 130 miles north of the French territory of Cayenne on 19 November. Kusch kept criss-crossing the shipping routes between Brazil and Trinidad, but ten days of cruising in this area did not bring a single target in sight. The sea was empty.

Consequently, on 29 November 1943 Kusch decided to change course towards the east for the return trip to Lorient, after having triple-checked the diesel fuel supply on hand, which Druschel measured at 76 cu m in the fuel tanks. This was just sufficient for a slow return voyage to France. No ships or aeroplanes were met on the return trip through the mid-Atlantic and along the coast of Portugal. On 17 December U-154 rounded Cape Finisterre, Spain, northbound.

They entered the dangerous Bay of Biscay in very heavy weather, which restricted the British aircraft patrols. Nor did U-154 encounter any enemy surface ships on anti-submarine sweeps or U-boat search patrols. After signalling her approach to the mine-free channel entrance, she reached the meeting point during darkness on 20 December 1943. Here she was picked up by a mine detonator ship and two minesweepers for a closely escorted trip back into Lorient, where she arrived at 11.50, after a war patrol of eighty-nine days at sea without refuelling, but also without sinkings.

During the time U-154 spent off Brazil and Cayenne, several loud and lengthy arguments had developed between Abel, Druschel and Funke on one side, the convinced Nazis, and Kusch on the other side. Whenever political questions were raised and the name of Hitler was mentioned, instantly noisy verbal fighting started anew. Abel told his commander that it was forbidden in Germany to tune in and listen to foreign broadcasts, which Kusch did more and more, the further away U-154 operated from Germany. Kusch showed Abel the commander's handbook and operational manual which specifically authorized U-boat commanders to tune in to foreign radio stations and news sources whenever German stations could no longer be received on account of the distance involved. But Abel complained that Kusch listened to music programmes and others not essential for operational information. Abel told Kusch that in Germany people would be beheaded if caught listening to foreign broadcasts.

Considering the nearness of the Christmas and New Year period, Captain Kals requested all officers to stay in Lorient for about a week to take care of all pending odds and ends with the shipyard technicians and engineers, only starting to take their home leave on or after Christmas Day. By then it would be clearer and easier to determine how long U-154 would require for her overhaul and the modification of equipment or installation of new equipment. Kusch had several long discussions with Kals regarding the various technical problems and the documented repair requirements and needs of U-154.

The KTB, the war patrol journal, had at once been closely studied by Kals, and was speedily forwarded, via Rösing's office in Angers, to the U-boat Command in Berlin Bernau at Camp Koralle. Godt had ordered that all KTBs must be forwarded to him quickly and in the most expeditious way because U-boat Command needed more and more input while U-boats, increasingly operating singly, dispatched fewer and fewer radio signals. Some commanders, doubting the security of the Enigma circuits, only made a signal after having received a direct order from Koralle to report without delay. The Dönitz-type wolf-pack group operations had been discontinued in stages, though the final such operation took place in February 1944, turning, however, into a complete failure.

Therefore, Kusch's second war patrol report with U-154 had been received in Koralle a few days after U-154 had returned to Lorient. Again it was studied carefully and evaluated personally by Godt. Godt was a matter-of-fact officer, unemotional and businesslike, who was considered a 'cold fish' by most U-boat commanders.

Here are Godt's comments and observations of Kusch's second war patrol, as reflected in the war patrol journal of U-154:

The U-boat had been ordered into the mid-Atlantic for a single U-boat operation. The only opportunity that the commander had was totally unexpected, namely to surprise a suddenly appearing convoy on 3 November 1943. But it was thwarted by an aircraft attack. At 10.05, after catching sight of the enemy, the only possibility might have been to retreat promptly underwater and to pull back far enough to be able to surface safely outside the range of both the escorting warships and the patrolling aeroplanes, and thereafter attempt a speedy but wide-area roundabout approach to get ahead of the convoy outside its protective aircraft screen, getting perhaps a chance for a possible surprise attack after dark.

The attempt to catch up with the convoy after the aircraft attack should have been tried and undertaken by any and all means possible, regardless of how slight the chances were. The unpredictable fortunes of war took revenge for this omission, and it did not offer another chance to this commander thereafter.

On 23 December 1943 all officers present in Lorient were asked to attend a pre-Christmas officers' meeting, where Kals would speak to them and pass along some holiday greetings from Dönitz, who had been scheduled to spend Christmas at the U-boat base of Brest. However, when Dönitz had reached

Paris, he decided to cancel that visit and turn around post-haste to return to Berlin instead, because of the Barents Sea operation of the battlecruiser *Scharnhorst*, which ended in another huge naval calamity.

To start his Christmas messages and speech, Kals first read an older message to the assembled officers, issued by Dönitz on 9 September 1943, but held back by Kals until now. The other holiday messages and greetings were the customary stuff, but this admonition stated:

1. Decree against criticism, complainers and belly-achers. Complainers, who are voicing their own personal wretched and miserable opinions and force them openly on their comrades and other German people and reduce thereby their willingness to fight with all their might and their determination for self-assertion, are to be made fully responsible for their irresponsible actions and must be held accountable unmercifully and relentlessly by the military courts for criminally undermining our fighting abilities!

2. Ideological conviction is obligatory for military officers. It is therefore necessary that a soldier fulfils his duty with his soul and all his spiritual strength and willpower. And this includes his conviction, his view of the world, too. Because it is utter nonsense to say the soldier or officer must be non-political. The soldier embodies the state in which he lives, he is the representative, the outspoken advocate of the state. Therefore, he has to stand behind this state with all his might. Your Supreme Commander, Dönitz.

One can leave it to the imagination how this message was received by the majority of officers assembled in Lorient. What was worse, these threats with the naval military courts were an outright insult to every serving officer of the U-boat Command. The joker was that the attending officers were asked to communicate this information and repeat the contents of the special message from Dönitz to their petty officers and enlisted men, as it was considered impractical to read these inspiring greetings to them directly.

After this speech, everybody returned to their units, ships or commands. A couple of hours later the U-boat crews were driven to *Lager* Lemp for a Christmas party. All U-boat men going on leave were handed a gift parcel with food items and some bottles for their Christmas holidays to upgrade the food rations of their families. Some men tried to get on the BdU special express train that very evening, but most went the next day.

The officers of U-154 had organized a farewell party for Abel, who was being transferred to prospective U-boat commander's training in Germany. Abel, Druschel and Funke were in high spirits after listening to the speech by Kals, and enthusiastic over the Dönitz greetings. Druschel and Funke were visibly the worse from too many drinks, and declared loudly that they would support Abel 100 per cent in anything he would do with respect to Kusch.

Abel shouted that Kusch ought to be removed as commander of U-154, as he was a negative defeatist who did not believe in German victory any more.

Officers at some of the nearby tables tried to calm down the noisy trio, who decided to leave for the railway station in Hennebont, where Abel was to get on the express train to Paris, with connections to Germany. Abel muttered and grumbled that the speech by Kals that afternoon had strengthened his conviction even more that Kusch should be put up against the wall and shot.

Kusch had been seeing off the petty officers and enlisted men who were leaving U-154, either for other assignments or on home leave. Then he looked after some shipyard requirements and completed the necessary paperwork. Lastly, he spoke once more with Kals in his office regarding pending matters and needs. Finally, Kusch proceeded to the Old Mill bar section of *Lager* Lemp to talk to some of his naval classmates celebrating there. Shortly after he had joined this group, Druschel and Funke returned from the station where they had seen Abel off. Immediately they ordered more drinks, though it was rather obvious that they were already fully loaded.

Kusch was in a jolly mood, because he had received great news in the accumulated mail. Admiral von Friedeburg in Kiel had approved Kusch's request to get married. Kusch had applied for approval before leaving on the last war patrol in September, wishing to marry Miss Inge von Foris. While the approval had been granted, a few paperwork snags remained to be ironed out before the wedding date could be set. This concerned two of her grandparents, for whom documentary proof had to be furnished that they were of pure Aryan stock and bloodlines.

This was a real surprise for the officers present, and everybody congratulated Kusch. Even Druschel and Funke wished Kusch well, though they were hardly able to stand up straight any more. The senior administrative officer of the 2nd U-boat Flotilla, who also handled welfare matters, offered Kusch and his officers and their families, as a surprise present, a skiing holiday at the Navy's expense, at a naval R & R hotel in Zürs, Austria, in the Tyrolean mountains.

Kusch was as surprised as the others over this unexpected offer. He stated that he would be happy to accept, provided he was able to first spend about a week in Berlin with his parents, his bride and his future in-laws. He added that no doubt both his bride and her parents would like to come along, too, so he would need two single rooms, as they were as yet not married, and a double room for the in-laws. Druschel also agreed to come, and would bring along his girl-friend, while Funke accepted if his wife and children could come too. Owing to these different plans, it was decided to start the holiday on New Year's Eve, 31 December 1943. The flotilla administrative officer made the required room reservations and arranged for the rail tickets for all participants. As things turned out, Funke had to cancel on account of family problems.

On 24 December, as his last job before going on leave, Kusch prepared and finished the evaluation and fitness report for Abel, turning it over to Kals without delay for further handling. Here is the fitness report and Abel's evaluation, as written up by Kusch:

1. General exterior appearance: Short, stubby, tight when moving, but stocky when not moving. Bodily strong, tenacious, but reluctant to accept advice or recommendations. Polite when it suits his purpose and he is still unsure of people. Good general behaviour and manners, tending sometimes towards complacency.

2. Mental attitude and abilities: Abel has completed an academic education. He holds a degree as doctor of jurisprudence and has been admitted to the bar as a lawyer. His civilian occupation has been judge in a lower court but he is expected to be transferred to a higher court eventually. His thinking and acting are somewhat rigid, inflexible and often rather one-sided in his approaches and views.

3. Abel was aboard as executive officer, as torpedo officer and as division officer for the non-technical crew members, including the torpedo mechanics and the radio shack and signal men.

4. On account of his long service in the Merchant Marine, Abel has outstanding knowledge of seamanship and used his experience in all situations in a remarkable way. Approaches all tasks with calmness and determination but a bit slow at times. Abel has outgrown the position and the requirements of an executive officer, appearing sometimes as not energetic enough and less than swift in his reactions.

5. Simple, uncomplicated and quiet character but sometimes a bit slow in his reactions, having outstanding ways to do his duty and to comply with his service obligations and responsibilities.

6. Suitable as U-boat commander of an operational U-boat.

7. A straight, clear-thinking, quiet officer with a developed type of personality. During attacks and in combat situations he is determined, unwavering and acts without hesitation.

   Combined summation of officer's fitness and ability: Average officer with good abilities to get his way, practically minded.

This evaluation and fitness report had been endorsed by Ernst Kals and afterwards by Hans Rudolf Rösing, U-boat leader for western France, without any changes. Then the file was forwarded to Neustadt, Germany, where Abel was to start the simulator U-boat school course on 2 January 1944.

Kusch departed via Paris to Berlin, requiring several train changes, arriving with some delay because of Allied bombing of railway stations and tracks. Kusch visited his parents and his bride, Inge von Foris, and her parents. Inge von Foris was 23 years old, an art student and even more anti-Nazi than Kusch. She opposed the whole Nazi Party programme and considered Adolf Hitler a monster and mass murderer.

Kusch met some of his old friends in Berlin on Christmas leave from their respective units, including Lieutenant of the Air Force (*Oberleutnant LW*) Hans Dietrich 'Dieter' Berger, who had lost one arm fighting in Russia and was doing light administrative work in Berlin since his release from the Air Force hospital.

Berger brought Kusch up to date with respect to many of their mutual friends and former Boy Scout comrades. The majority, it turned out, were dead already, most of them buried in Russia. Others had been put into concentration camps, either as malcontents or because they were anti-Nazi. Some had been released from jails once they 'volunteered' for military service in one of the penal companies on a probationary basis.

It was precisely this keeping in touch among old friends and former youth group members that the Gestapo feared. They had frequently encountered the determination and loyalty of these young men towards their friends and old comrades, who had been associated with these now prohibited, and thus for the police illegal, underground organizations. The steadily deteriorating military situation was the subject of many conversations Kusch had in Berlin with his old friends.

During this time he tried to work on the documentary paper problems to expedite his wedding, but with the confusion caused by the bombing attacks and the general disinclination of low-grade government civil service clerks to work during a holiday period, his follow-up attempts were not successful. Nevertheless, Kusch, his bride and her parents arrived at the naval R & R ski hotel in Zürs, Vorarlberg, on New Year's Eve. Druschel and his girl-friend arrived a bit later because they used different train connections.

As Inge von Foris and Kusch were not yet married, they occupied two separate single rooms. But Druschel moved into a double room with his girl-friend. Kusch dressed him down, stating, 'An officer and gentleman would not share a room with a lady, unless they were married.' This made Druschel angry, becoming almost incoherent in his fury, yelling, 'We are here on leave and not under naval rules. Kusch should mind his own business. Because Kusch is not in command here.' Walking away, Druschel mumbled that he would now report Kusch without fail, and get in touch with Abel as soon as possible to arrange it.

While the snow conditions were perfect, the weather fine, the hotel facilities very good, with friendly service and first-class food, this was hardly a great way to start the New Year 1944.

CHAPTER SEVEN

An Interlude of Fate

The calendar swaying on the wall with the ship's movements announced 25 March 1943. Ensign Frank W. Petersen moved restlessly in his rolling bunk, as the heavy sea did not allow him to sleep very deeply. His subconscious mind had almost automatically registered the whistling in the voice tube from the conning tower, followed by the call, 'Captain to the bridge!' This was the voice of Ensign Johnny Bascha, who headed the first watch. Petersen knew instinctively that it would be only a matter of a few minutes before his presence on the bridge would be requested by Lieutenant j.g. Hans Hartwig Trojer, the commander of U-221, a Type VII-C U-boat. Trojer's nickname was 'Count Dracula', as he had been born in Transylvania, deep in the Carpathian mountains of the Balkans, now part of Romania.

Trojer wore a thick black beard from being at sea for a month without shaving, nursing his beard and his reputation as a gruff and tough guy with outsiders. In reality, he was a fun-loving practical joker, who looked after his men very well, patiently listened to their individual problems and helped them in a natural, friendly way. Trojer had been a watch officer on U-34, a Type VII-A U-boat commanded by Wilhelm Rollmann, and U-67, a Type IX-C U-boat commissioned by Heinrich 'Ajax' Bleichrodt. Petty officers and enlisted men simply adored Trojer, who was frequently just called 'The Count', dropping even the Dracula. 'Hansi' Trojer was seen among U-boat commanders as a coming ace. He was invariably referred to as 'The Old Man' by his crewmen, though he was only 26 years old, younger than some of the members of his crew.

Petersen mentally prepared himself for getting up, though he was rather tired, after some of the toughest and most confusing convoy night-battle operations in the North Atlantic. He searched with half-closed eyes for his seaboots and his grey leather trousers and jacket, the latter four sizes too large for him, though the extra length kept his kidneys protected. Petersen wound a thick terrycloth towel around his neck, tucking it in tightly, fished around for his hat, then slapped it firmly on his wavy hair, much too long by Navy regulations on shore, when the whistle sounded again and the call came through the voice pipe, 'Petersen to the bridge on the double!'

Petersen sighed, rose off his bunk, grabbed his binoculars, slung them around his neck and pushed through the circular, pressurized compartment door, bending down and looking into the control room to get the drift of things. Directing engineer Lieutenant j.g. (Engineering) Charlie Kolbig looked half asleep leaning against the control desk, but fooled nobody, always being wide awake and alert, never missing a thing. The third watch officer and navigator, Warrant Officer Georg Buschmann, working with his calculating tools, just pointed upstairs with his left hand. Petersen climbed the shining steel ladder like a well-trained fireman, entered up and stepped onto the back side of the bridge, the only space not already occupied by others. Here was the so-called winter garden with one rotten and usually malfunctioning 20 mm anti-aircraft gun. Petersen straightened up and Trojer told him in a few words:

> We've spotted a life raft or rubber float and have changed course directly towards the sighting, but the seas are preventing constant observation. We don't know if there are any people on this float, but should be able to tell shortly. Blume and Kamp with one helper each are coming up. Have them tie a knotted safety line, then get down on the deck and catch the rubber dinghy with a shooting line. Pull that rubber boat over and don't waste any time. Get moving, shake your legs!
>
> Here are your four men coming up. We're within Coastal Command range, about 100 miles off Cape Ortegal. Don't fiddle-faddle around, but check if there are any people on the float, dead or alive, grab them and bring them back quickly, so that we shall be able to crash dive if necessary. Everything clear?

Petersen nodded. 'Yes Sir, everything clear.'

The five men now descended to the deck and moved in single file, holding the safety line and stringing it along as they moved forward. Blume, who was the 'Walking Newspaper' of U-221, bubbled over with excitement: 'The radio shack has just decoded a message, that we should look for some shot down Ju 88 aircrew. Perhaps they are on this rubber float.'

Trojer yelled: 'If there are only dead bodies take off their identification, but put them back into the sea. However, if you're not certain, haul them aboard.' Petersen waved with one arm, signifying his comprehension of the instructions.

The shooting line was ready for firing as soon as they approached the rubber dinghy close enough. There were some figures in it, holding on tightly to ropes. But when the shooting line was clutched by hands, Petersen knew there were live people on that float. They hauled the shooting line in as rapidly as possible to bring the rubber float closer and pull it on deck with the movement of the waves.

Three haggard men were dragged aboard, obviously almost at the end of their tether. But they were not part of the Ju 88 *Luftwaffe* crew. These were Englishmen, wearing British uniforms, or what was left of them, anyway. The howling of the wind made conversation difficult, so sign language seemed more practical under the circumstances. Petersen waved his arm towards the bridge, indicating: Get ready to pull in the safety line. He held one of his gloved hands in front of his face, to shield himself somewhat against the wind-driven, biting sea spray. The men were shakily swaying and their knees seemed to be buckling, so the seamen of U-221 just grabbed the exhausted men with one arm, holding the safety line with the other, signalling: 'Pull us back.'

Petersen had jerked the last man towards himself to prevent his lurching back into the sea, as U-221 rolled heavily. Instinctively he switched to English without thinking about it. Instantly he felt like an idiot, yelling: 'Good Morning!', adding: 'Welcome aboard!' The soaked and filthy figure hung on to him tightly. The sailors had already dragged the other two men towards the conning tower when Petersen thought he had been hit by lightning. A familiar voice croaked in his face: 'For heavens sake, Frank, is that really you? What the devil are you doing out here?' Petersen's mouth fell open but not a sound came out, yet he kept pulling and dragging this man gradually towards the base of the conning tower.

He could not organize his thoughts, wondering how this poor creature knew his first name. But the croaking voice continued: 'Thanks, by the way, for picking us up in this awful weather. We'd almost given up all hope and thought we were for the chop!' Petersen trembled and thought, 'I must have a fever or some hallucinations. This just can't be true!' But it really was true. His old Boy Scout friend and blood brother, Telford Bassington, was being dragged by him onto the winter garden of U-221. The other men had already been lowered into the control room, and Trojer yelled at him: 'Get moving man, step on it. Get this man below deck quickly.' Petersen went through the motions like an automaton.

He was momentarily disoriented, but happy that Bascha still had bridge watch duty for another hour before he had to relieve him and the first watch. When they hit the floor of the control room, Bassington asked Kolbig: 'Permission to come on board, whatever ship this happens to be.' The directing engineer almost flipped out, and shouted for the Sani and some medicinal revival water. Paramedic Petty Officer Erwin Arndt, already working on the other two British, answered: 'As soon as possible. The Old Man has authorized a double shot for everybody who got drenched, but the flyers first.'

Now Trojer came down into the control room. The sailors and stokers had swiftly undressed the men, cleaned and dried them and wrapped them into somewhat smelly, mildewy blankets, as there were no others. Arndt fed them the cognac and they were carried into warm bunks that had been hurriedly vacated by their customary occupants.

Trojer asked Petersen: 'Are you all right? Did you swallow too much seawater? Or did you see a ghost? Because you look as pale as the walls of the Sheherazade's urinal stand.' Petersen just nodded, then declared he would be fine shortly, and told Trojer in a few words about Telford Bassington, his old Scout friend and pilot officer with the Royal Air Force. Trojer shook his head, mumbling surprised: 'What will happen next on this operation?'

Trojer, who always had his antennae out for anything unusual in the works and was sensitive to the feelings of his crew, had known immediately that something extraordinary had occurred, and just added: 'Take care of him; who knows, the next time the position may well be reversed. We would also prefer to be rescued rather than drowning.' Petersen was startled by Trojer's remarks, but nodded gratefully. What a great guy my captain is, he thought, realizing how he admired him more every day.

The runner approached: 'Time for the second watch to get dressed and ready in fifteen minutes.' Petersen was practically dressed for bridge duty, so he moved to the tiny kitchen and asked the cook to heat up a bowl of chicken noodle soup for him right away. He felt the need to fortify himself for these four hours on watch. Kolbig told him in a low voice: 'All three are now sleeping, but I shall arrange for some unobtrusive watchers, when they are awake again; after all, we don't want accidents or sabotage. Some of my control room stokers can keep a close eye on them and still do their other duties, except if we get attacked, of course.'

Petersen's three watchkeepers trooped into the control room. He checked their safety-belts and then moved up to the bridge. Bascha informed him about course, speed and weather, then all four took their positions and relieved the first watch smoothly. Johnny Bascha winked and told Petersen: 'I hear you picked up a friend from the sea. What a pity, no mermaid. I hope these men make it', and then dropped below.

When the third watch, with navigator Buschmann in turn, took over four hours later, Petersen was weary and his back ached. In addition, the old bullet wound in his leg hurt and he was grateful for the warmth of the control room. Bascha had already taken his usual place in the narrow officers' mess section that also served as sleeping quarters. Petersen, after cleaning up and removing the salt spray from his face and hands, just worked his way sideways beside Bascha.

Then Trojer joined them and talked about some radio signals that had just come in, which Petersen was to read first – and before eating. He added: 'See to it that our English guests are fed, once they wake up. Delegate this to Scheuer and Schink for the time they are with us'.

With one thing and another, paperwork, record keeping, inventory lists and updating handbooks, the time passed fast. While everybody else on U-221 drank coffee, Petersen always had black tea from captured supplies the Navy had found left behind by the British Army when they left France in June 1940. After the cook delivered his huge pot, the aroma woke up the prisoners, and he filled some mugs for them that they swallowed eagerly.

Bassington asked Petersen: 'Do many of your men speak English?' Petersen was surprised, but answered: 'How many, and if so how much, I really don't know for sure, but probably more speak some French.' Bassington nodded: 'That's understandable, but as we both speak Spanish, we can always do that to be on the safe side, because my Greek has become rather rusty since Patras.' Petersen replied: 'If that is your preference, okay with me, but what about your two men?' Bassington said: 'They can only speak and understand English, though one has a Midlands and the other a cockney accent.'

When the teapot was fetched for a refill by the cook, who had probably never seen any enemy soldiers before, Bassington quietly inquired: 'Your captain, what kind of a man is he? One of these U-boat pirates and free-booters, or . . . ?" Petersen smiled: 'No, Telford, he is one of the finest naval officers I know and a swell guy. But he hides behind a screen of gruff talk and his beard to justify his nickname, Count Dracula'.

Bassington grinned: 'In that case we're among friends. I wonder, was he also a Boy Scout, like both of us?' Petersen did not know. It was not customary to check out superior officers. Then he said: 'If he wasn't, he ought to have been, but he is a gentleman in any case.'

He now remembered that Bassington had some kind of title, or at least his father did. Maybe he was a real count. He thought, 'I have forgotten.' Reading his thoughts, Bassington said: 'What a joke, Count meets Viscount!' Both of them burst out laughing. The ice was broken for good.

Petersen cautioned the three Englishmen:

Fellows, please don't do anything stupid. Submarines are just as tricky as aeroplanes. Keep your hands to yourselves and step out of the way if the alarm bells ring and an emergency dive commences. Otherwise, you might get knocked down or pushed over unintentionally. Curiosity kills the cat, don't play at being heroes! Your mothers and girlfriends will appreciate it very much. As prisoners of war, the fight is over for you, for now. You will be treated fairly as you deserve, almost like one of the crew. However, once we reach base in France we have to turn you over to the *Luftwaffe*, the German Air Force, because you are Royal Air Force people, and then you had better watch out for yourselves. Most of these airmen are all right; the younger ones are maybe a bit too much of the 'I only follow orders type'; the older reservists are usually more easygoing and reasonable, if one is patient with them. The in-betweens one can't ever tell for sure in advance.

Bassington just said: 'Seems to be about the same as in the RAF. Some nice, some nasty, some helpful, some lazy, a few big-mouth types, but most others just trying to do their job and follow orders.' Petersen nodded: 'That's what I would assume.'

Time seemed to fly along between one thing or another. Signals to request port clearance, confirmation of minesweeper escorts to enter Saint Nazaire, navigating to reach specific marker points at fixed hours for the mine-free entry channels, and bringing all records up to date kept Petersen busy. Bascha, who spoke only a limited amount of English, worked on the personnel records since several men and a few petty officers were due for promotions and transfers to qualification courses. The schedule of leave rotation had to be worked out, the travel orders prepared and the need lists for the shipyard repairs coordinated. Before long 28 March had arrived. Kolbig warned his technical men: 'Full attention and no goofing off as yet, we are not in the barn at this point; those last fifty miles are always the most dangerous.'

Soon the minesweepers appeared, led by a large mine-detonator ship looking like a floating mountain of anti-aircraft guns. Quickly U-221 moved behind these ships and continued in their wake towards the delta of the Loire river, with its many tricky shallows and wrecks. Petersen had arranged for a collection of warm clothing and other useful items for the three prisoners of war. All crew members had contributed generously. The feeling was that these poor fellows should be able to dress and look like soldiers, but most of all they should not get cold. Who knows where they would put them in the East, where most prisoner-of-war camps were located, as there was lots of room and open spaces compared to the industrial western regions. Kolbig had found three empty seabags (one never asked him where such things came from), so the prisoners of war could pack them with their newly acquired possessions and carry them properly.

Petersen talked in a low voice with Bassington:

Telford, we shall reach Saint Nazaire soon. Officially, I'm not supposed to tell you this, yet that's a load of rubbish. The base staff of our flotilla takes over immediately in port. These are not all men of the front, a lot of base wallahs are among them, and the flotilla boss is a particularly strange bird. I suggest that you tell nobody, either in Saint Nazaire or elsewhere later, that you understand and speak German quite well. It would only cause you a lot of problems. The Air Force interviewers in Oberursel, near Frankfurt, where you will be interrogated and classified would certainly consider this dangerous. Pilots are already in the highest security category in terms of prisoners of war. Therefore you would be placed in an extra-high-security camp, where things are handled quite strictly.

As you probably know already, enlisted men and petty officers are placed in separate camps or compounds from officers. So say farewell to your men early enough and prepare them, if required. Since I am due to travel to Madrid very soon, I could drop a letter into the commercial mail there to your mothers or families. Just a short text, use as signature a nick-name or pet name that they will recognize, but not other people like censors. It will be a while before you will be able to notify them that you are no longer missing, and where as well as how they can write to you all.

Petersen pushed over three sheets of writing paper and envelopes, plus pencils: 'But don't include anything that would sound suspicious to censors and such people. Instruct your men accordingly.' In no time all three scribbled away and waited for the things to come.

The low outline of the coast of Brittany rose gradually over the horizon as they steadily approached. Petersen wanted to mention that they should thank the captain when saying goodbye, but Bassington asked in the same moment: 'Could we thank your captain and wish you all well?' Their inner thoughts had again coincided.

The minesweepers turned away sharply, and U-221 reduced speed and switched to electric motors, stopping the diesels. She glided slowly into the flooded lock basin, the sluice gates closed behind her, and she moved into the actual port area and reached the arrival pier. Here a big crowd of people waited, quite a few girls among them, nurses, secretaries and female auxiliaries from the various commands and hospitals in the area. A brass band opened up, flowers were tossed at the men of U-221, and some naval people carried baskets and boxes of fresh fruit aboard. Bascha ordered the lines to be properly fastened and the crew to line up on the upper deck, sailors in one group, stokers in another. A harbour watch was immediately activated.

Trojer climbed down from the bridge and Bascha yelled: 'Attention!' Trojer looked at his crew, shook his head slightly, grinned and commanded: 'Eyes left!' The petty officer of the watch piped the side on his whistle. The officers and senior petty officers raised their right hands to their hats to salute a bunch of officers coming aboard, led by the unpopular commander of the 7th U-boat Flotilla, Commander Herbert Sohler, wearing a rather weird-looking uniform, with odd-looking riding boots. The enlisted men blinked catching sight of him. Several of the staff officers followed him closely, like assistant doctors trailing after the head surgeon during a hospital visiting inspection.

Petersen recognized the senior paymaster, the chief engineering officer and the adjutant of the 7th U-boat Flotilla. There were several others, plus film and press people at the rear of the group. On the pier a sergeant of the field police with three men showed up, waiting for the prisoners of war.

Sohler had earned the Iron Cross Second Class as commander of U-46, when he managed to sink two ships, together 7,952 tons, at the beginning of the war, which placed him in 341st place on the commanders' confirmed sinking list. In order to fill up his breast a bit more, Sohler wore the golden Reichs Sports badge, one that almost any able-bodied man would be able to earn.

The 7th U-boat Flotilla had been looking after some of the highest decorated U-boat aces, like Günther Prien, Herbert Schultze and Otto Kretschmer, to mention a few. Sohler seemed to have some sort of inferiority complex, which he compensated for by being a super-stickler for naval and military order and discipline. Petty officers and enlisted men hated him without exception. Many officers had considerable reservations about him. Sohler was the type of officer who always arranged for schemes to keep the men busy, ordering night alarm exercises, upgraded infantry training or marches and saluting brush-ups. Trojer cursed through the side of his mouth, while still saluting: 'Shit! Sohler is still here. I was hoping they'd transferred him to Kirkenes [northern Norway], or even better, to the island of Spitzbergen [Svalbard].'

The band played the England Song, the unofficial U-boat hymn. Sohler stopped across from Trojer, returned his salute, stuck his other hand into his pocket and pulled out a ribboned medal: '*Oberleutnant* Trojer, the *Führer* has just awarded you the Knight's Cross of the Iron Cross for sinking on this patrol five ships of 30,476 tons and damaging others.' He wrapped the ribbon around Trojer's neck, then pulling the Knight's Cross straight: 'Congratulations, Trojer, from all of us here. I have also received a message that you will be promoted to *Kapitänleutnant* [Lieutenant] on 1 April 1943.' The adjutant added: 'This is no April fool's joke, either! Please accept the warmest wishes from us all here, in Saint Nazaire.'

Kolbig whispered to Bascha: 'Johnny, what a party this will call for tomorrow.' Sohler marched along the lined-up crew, and turning around declared: 'There will be a huge celebration tomorrow in La Baule. See you again then.' Bascha ordered: 'At ease, dismissed!' Petersen looked around for the Englishmen to guide them to the pier. Time for good byes.

Petersen said in a low voice: 'Take care, Telford, stay healthy, don't try anything foolish. These field policemen are not Gestapo, but they will shoot you without compunction if they believe you are trying to escape. Once you are in your Air Force camp, things will get better and you will be with your people mostly, including Australians, Canadians and South Africans. Lately Americans, too, from what I hear.' Petersen slipped each man a small paper bag: 'There are vitamins in there, make sure they are not taken away when you get processed and searched. You might need them until you get your Red Cross packages regularly. Good luck, you three! Telford, whenever this war is over, don't forget your old Boy Scout friends like me!'

Now after the crowd had dispersed, the waiting field policemen approached, whom the sailors called 'chain dogs' and detested fiercely. Petersen admonished them to treat these prisoners of war correctly and in accordance with the Geneva Convention rules, and to deliver them to the *Luftwaffe* in Oberursel as fast and as directly as possible. The second administrative officer came towards them and handed every man, German and British, a food parcel for the long rail journey, telling the policemen: 'We shall drive you all to the station in Savenay for the express train to Germany. This is easier than taking the old local trains from here.' Bassington saluted, as did his men. A big car stopped in front of them. All the men got in, the driver honked, everybody waved and the vehicle disappeared.

The administrative officer observed to Petersen: 'It looked to me as if you were already old friends.' Petersen replied: 'In more ways than one', adding:

'But who knows if we shall ever see each other again?' The administrative officer gave Petersen a lift, as the bus with the crew members of U-221 had departed, dropping him off at the Hôtel L'Hermitage in La Baule-sur-Mer, about twenty minutes' drive away. Here Petersen just rolled into a huge double bed after tossing his hat on a chair, and fell asleep instantly, fully dressed.

The party at the Hôtel Royal was a blast to end all parties. After having soaked for two hours in a huge bath, Petersen still had a headache and had been unable to get rid of his diesel oil U-boat smell, though he was now shaved, massaged and with a new haircut. The evening in the Hôtel Royal was memorable, but sooner or later everybody went to sleep sitting or standing up. Trojer arranged for the flotilla doctor and his paramedics to transport his men to their respective hotels and rooms in one of their ambulances, bribing them with some bottles of Scotch.

Petersen tried hard to get his senses together and clear his head after a hearty breakfast on the balcony overlooking the Bay of Biscay, when the phone rang so long and so loudly that he picked it up resignedly. The hotel's head porter was on the line, and pleaded with Petersen: 'Please come down just as fast as possible. Your driver has already been waiting for some time and is getting quite concerned why you are so late and don't come down. Don't bother about checking out and such things, all this will be taken care of automatically. Your clothing and personal possessions will be packed and stored neatly for you by the hotel.'

Grumbling, Petersen quickly tossed a few things into a travel bag and walked downstairs. The car took him to Dax, a small French town near the Spanish border. Here he was fitted with civilian clothing, handed a passport and some other pieces of paper and an envelope with Spanish pesetas. Then he was given the courier pouch for Madrid and Lisbon. The vehicle continued to Hendaye, crossed the Spanish border and dropped him off at the Irun railway station to board the express train to Madrid. There were always some delays, as the gauge of the railway tracks changed. He entered his reserved compartment, locked the door with his pass key and wrapped himself in a blanket. Snuggled into one corner, he had a few moments to think about Telford Bassington and his two men. Had they already reached Oberursel? Were they perhaps in the pressure cooker of the Air Force interrogations? In what prisoner-of-war camps would they finally be placed? While such questions still buzzed through his head, Petersen quickly fell asleep, as his backlog of missed sleep was still considerable. He did not wake up until the guard knocked on his compartment door when the train pulled into the Chamartin station in Madrid.

Petersen grabbed his things and walked directly to the post office at the station, which he remembered from previous visits, pulled out his three letters, bought airmail postage and continued to a mailbox to deposit his letters unobtrusively. Then he stepped out of the rail terminal building, walked to the parking area, where his car and driver were waiting, greeted the driver, entered the vehicle, rolled into the corner and immediately resumed his sleep.

When they entered the grounds of the German embassy, the assistant naval attaché met him in the garage. Petersen turned the courier bag over to him against a receipt, and was told: 'Report to Captain Leissner immediately.' Being a 'civilian' now, Petersen did not salute, but just nodded, smiled and walked with long strides into the lift. The driver told the naval officer: 'Lieutenant-Commander, he slept solidly all the way from the railway station and snored like some mad bull entering the bullring arena!' The officer shook his head and replied: 'Oh well, that's a submariner for you. They are a special breed of cat and unpredictable in their reactions!'

Three days later Petersen returned to Dax, turned in the courier pouch, reclaimed his uniform and personal papers and handed back those received for the trip to Madrid. The *Abwehr* officer on duty informed him he was to pick up his personal belongings in La Baule and continue as fast as possible to Rennes in Brittany to work again with Lieutenant Hermann Rasch, assisting him with an urgent special investigation of captured British equipment.

When Petersen reported to Rasch, 28 years old, he was pleased to get Petersen's help once more as they worked very smoothly together, supported by a changing small team of specialists and technical assistants, depending upon the requirements of the matter under investigation.

This time it involved the brand-new British Magnetron-type radar. It was essential to ascertain the exact centimetre wavelength used in that equipment and to determine its possibilities and effectiveness. On 3 February 1943, a Short Stirling four-engined bomber had been shot down near Rotterdam in Holland. From the wreck such a new Magnetron radar had been recovered, marked 'Experimental Number Six'. A working set had been reconstructed from recovered parts and shipped to the Telefunken Electronic Research Laboratories in Berlin by the *Luftwaffe* technical recovery team. But severe damage caused by air attacks had first delayed the investigation, then damaged parts could not be reconstructed and the radar could not be made to work.

The real joke was that a fierce and extended political and military battle had taken place in Great Britain prior to the use of the Magnetron radar equipment, between the Admiralty and Coastal Command on one side and the 'bomber barons' and political yes-men on the other side. The inventing scientists strongly recommended that the new Magnetron radar should initially be employed only over the ocean and at sea, because it would just be a matter of time before one or more sets were lost. That would be aggravating when such new sets sank to the bottom of the sea, but a real problem, limiting their widespread future use, if they were lost over the European continent and recovered by the Germans. But again, the 'Bomb Germany to Hell' crowd prevailed, and Bomber Command first received the new radar sets for trial use towards the end of January 1943.

At the end of March 1943, a Handley Page Halifax four-engined bomber was shot down and crashed in the countryside of Brittany. Three men of the crew survived and managed to get away from the burning wreck. These British airmen had been deeply shocked when they were captured by French Gestapo auxiliaries, who immediately turned them over to the SS/SD. Consequently, these men were extremely nervous once the Navy had succeeded in taking them over. Rasch informed Petersen that they had been 'bought' from the SD with a car-load of wine, champagne, and cognac, but that this had only been possible because the SD had not yet set up a written file for the men. Otherwise it would have been out of the question.

Rasch and Petersen had worked almost two weeks with these prisoners of war, before they had gradually managed to calm them down sufficiently and gain their trust somewhat, in small steps. During this time a completely new set of the Magnetron centimetre wave radar had been rebuilt from several partially destroyed sets, and the wavelength had been determined as 9.75 cm with minor oscillations. The German Navy called this equipment the Ten Centimetre Radar.

During their last discussion and interrogation Rasch carried the reconstructed Magnetron radar set casually into the room and put it on the table. The British airmen were instantly convinced that the Germans knew the exact wavelength and other technical details when they observed the rebuilt set, and they confirmed that the wavelength was 9.80 cm, as it was obvious to them that this was no longer a secret. At the same time they insisted that Rasch and Petersen must make absolutely sure they were not turned over to the Gestapo again but remained regular prisoners of war.

That kind of approach was often used by British intelligence officers when they interrogated captured U-boat men in England, as in the Kensington District prisoner-of-war 'cage'. It was easier to confirm something already in evidence rather than getting squeezed for information and being put through the wringer.

Rasch had been executive officer of the Type IX U-boat U-106. In autumn 1941 he became her commander. He had sunk eleven confirmed ships, totalling 73,423 tons, and had been awarded the Knight's Cross of the Iron Cross. He was a big fellow with great bodily strength, who liked to smoke cigars, much to the disgust of Petersen. He overwhelmed many people with his blustering ways, and was an eager and practical joker, which did not delight everybody. In reality his bark was a lot worse than his bite. Moreover, he was a great party organizer who loved to have a ball.

Nevertheless, he had greatly intimidated the three prisoners, though he had never even touched them, while Petersen had eventually gained their confidence with his quiet, understanding way. They had been a very successful team. But Berlin, with the unrealistic wishes and expectations they still nursed, did not like their findings.

Therefore, the armchair warriors around Dönitz arranged to dissolve their team once more, and transferred everybody to other duties or ordered their return to former commands, where this was possible. Rasch was moved to Berlin and Petersen returned to La Baule and Saint Nazaire to rejoin U-221 as second watch officer.

Before Petersen returned to his old command, he arranged for the immediate transfer of the three British airmen to the *Luftwaffe* and fixed up the required paperwork, backdating their capture by a month. Hopefully, this would circumvent questions by the *Luftwaffe* about the month not accounted for, because they would be unlikely to accept such a delay without explanations from the Navy.

Furthermore, Petersen suggested to them that they should play dumb and act as ignorant as possible to sneak through the Oberursel compound near Frankfurt as fast as possible, to get transferred to a regular *Stalag* prisoner-of-war camp without hold-ups or complications. This special sorting-out camp had been set up as an initial interrogation camp for all Allied airmen, and had been copied from and patterned on the Royal Air Force and British Army interrogation compound called Cockfosters Teacher Training College, at Trent Park, Middlesex, near London. Here listening devices, recording bugs and equipment of many types were everywhere, mostly hidden in trees or bushes, in toilets or washrooms, in all walking areas and both the sleeping and resting areas. The Royal Navy had access to the Cockfosters facilities whenever German naval prisoners of war were held there for classification.

But in 1942, an even newer and larger Listening Centre was built at Chesham, Buckinghamshire – the Combined Services Detailed Interrogation Centre UK, at Latimer House, to deal with a far larger number of prisoners of war. They were anticipating numerous German Army prisoners of war from North Africa and later from Europe, once the Allied landings in France and Italy took place. Here the latest electronic devices and the most up-to-date equipment was employed in every possible way.

On 3 May 1943, U-221 sailed from Saint Nazaire on her fourth war patrol in the North Atlantic, later operating to the west of Portugal, and returning to Saint Nazaire on 21 July 1943.

The spring and summer of 1943 had passed slowly and with hammer blows for the U-boats at sea. The height of the fierce convoy battles had been replaced by that terrible 'Black May', which was soon widely known as 'Stalingrad at Sea'. The operational situation in the Battle of the Atlantic had been decided, and Germany had lost completely.

On 1 August Frank Petersen was handed new orders, and he was reassigned for special duties. His replacement aboard U-221 as second watch officer was Ensign Horst Steinhauer, who had arrived on 29 July to take Petersen's place. Consequently, it was possible to turn over all records, files and other important and pertinent pending matters to him in an orderly way before Petersen packed his personal belongings and travelled to Paris for further instructions.

On 20 September 1943, U-221 left the U-boat pens in Saint Nazaire on her fifth war patrol for operations in the North Atlantic. On 27 September she was bombed about 150 miles south-west of Ireland's southern coast by a Halifax B of the RAF's 58 Squadron, commanded by Flying Officer Eric Hartley. But the increased anti-aircraft armament shot down the Halifax before U-221 sank with all hands.

Two men of the Halifax flight crew died in the crash, but six other crewmen, including the pilot, managed to get out of the burning aircraft alive and inflate a rubber float. They drifted for eleven days in the Atlantic before they were spotted and rescued by the destroyer *Mahratta* on 8 October 1943.

However, 'Hansi' Trojer, that fun-loving Count Dracula, just 27 years old, ended on the ocean's bottom with his men. He had sunk eleven verified ships, totalling 69,589 tons.

CHAPTER EIGHT

The Building of the Avalanche

Abel had arrived in Neustadt Holstein on time and was busy with simulator exercises and attack training games. There was a small group of officers who participated in this first course for prospective U-boat commanders. It was the initial test for them, cheaper and less time consuming than firing exercise torpedoes. Discussions of tactics and operational approaches filled the long days.

In the German Navy it was normal practice that periodic fitness reports and personal evaluations of officers, petty officers and enlisted men were never shown to the man evaluated unless he performed very unsatisfactorily, in which case the reports were discussed with the person involved. Such evaluations and reports were forwarded by sealed, heavy-duty military mail envelopes, containing the individual's complete personal file, and marked in big red letters, 'Confidential'. These shipments were dispatched for the attention of the commanding officer of the next or new command or school to which the man had been transferred or assigned. Only in rare cases were there problems or delays in this system. But in such cases, the error was usually corrected quickly.

Abel's personal file had been expedited precisely in this way. Yet owing to holiday mail congestion or delivery problems caused by bombed railway tracks or mail facilities, his sealed package arrived late in Neustadt, on 15 January 1944.

Abel happened to be in the administrative office of the U-boat School to pick up his onward travel vouchers and transportation orders when the delayed parcel arrived from Lorient. He somehow managed to snatch his personal file and studied it thoroughly. He had never before read his file, and grew furious the more he read. His rage increased as he perused the various evaluations and fitness reports, particularly the last one prepared by Kusch, but fully endorsed by Kals and Rösing.

He decided to report in sick and requested the rest of the day off, skipping the final simulator summation and the tactical evaluation of the training course participants. Then he called Druschel at his R & R hotel in Zürs. When he reached Druschel, he yelled into the telephone: 'I've now decided to report Kusch to-day, without any further delay. It's high time for Kusch to get what he deserves and has had coming for a long time. I expect that you will support me fully!' Druschel only managed to say: 'Yes, of course', when Abel hung up and rushed into his quarters to write up his report.

As a trained lawyer and judge, Abel had the necessary professional experience and the required bureaucratic vocabulary to prepare the report quickly. Three hours later he asked to see the commander of the U-boat School, Captain (Engineering) Heinrich Schmidt. Schmidt read Abel's report slowly, as soon as Abel had handed it to him, without any preliminaries.

After reading the report and considering the serious implications of the contents, Schmidt suggested to Abel that he should sleep on his report and reconsider it. It would undoubtedly have nasty repercussions for Abel himself. Many officers would cut him dead, as a political denouncer. However, Abel refused to listen and rudely rejected Schmidt's advice out of hand.

Schmidt's irritation and consternation was considerable. He pointed out to Abel that all of his allegations and claims had taken place in his previous command, either in Lorient or at sea. He finally told him that he would have to forward the report to Captain Kals in Lorient for further handling. But Abel stubbornly refused to pay any attention, and demanded loudly that his report should be registered officially that very afternoon and a copy should be dispatched expeditiously to Lorient. Schmidt had no alternative but to go through with the matter, in accordance with prevailing naval rules and regulations.

As soon as Abel left Schmidt's office, Schmidt decided to call nearby Kiel to talk to the legal adviser of the admiral commanding U-boats, von Friedeburg, to get the view of that lawyer and automatically inform the senior level of command, just to be on the safe side. The adviser turned out to be *Marine-Oberkriegsgerichtsrat* (naval judge advocate) Karl Heinrich Hagemann. Employed by the Navy since 1936 and currently assigned on the U-boat tender *Erwin Wassner*, a former banana steamer originally called *Gran Canaria*, Hagemann got very excited about the information that Captain Schmidt passed along, and requested a full copy of Abel's report by teletype.

For the reader it is essential to know some legal and technical details regarding the naval judge advocate and naval military court system in Germany during the war. In 1939, there were thirty full-time naval judge advocates. But by the fifth year of the war, this number had increased to over 300. Many had been drafted and held reserve status only for the duration of the war.

These judge advocates were full-time naval employees with civil service status, wearing uniforms with everything in silver that was in gold on officers' uniforms. Therefore such people were generally called '*Silberlinge*'. They were disliked by all soldiers and officers, as they were arrogant. The increase in their numbers had been gradual, and most of the newcomers were former associates or acquaintances of the naval judge advocates already working in the Navy's legal department. So they generally knew one another well. Periodically, circular letters of instruction were issued in Berlin for all judge advocates and distributed as Secret.

In addition, there were regular guidance meetings, where the judge advocates were brought up to date and firmly instructed in Berlin, since it was considered imperative that all judge advocates be informed about the requirements, views and the thinking prevalent at the Naval High Command. They were all supervised by Admiral Walter Warzecha, head of the general naval administration since 1938, of which the growing legal department was a division.

All purely legal aspects of this department were coordinated and directed by *Admiralstabsrichter* Dr jur. Joachim Rudolphi from 1937 right up to the German capitulation. Whenever any naval court sentenced anybody to death, Rudolphi would automatically receive the entire file and discuss the case with Admiral Warzecha.

Warzecha, the main speaker during these periodic meetings, encouraged the judges always to keep the viewpoint of the Navy and the interests of the Navy foremost in their minds, as these were more important than mere legalistic, pettifogging technicalities. Warzecha never neglected to warn the judges that the fleet revolution of 1918 must never again happen in Germany. This was the Navy's most important ground rule: To suffocate without hesitation any development in that direction immediately and with all means at its disposal. Warzecha stated that the Navy would firmly support the judges and stand fully behind them, regardless of legal technicalities, if they stuck to these firm instructions.

Rudolphi, 45 years old at the time, preferred to work behind the scenes whenever possible, and stay out of the limelight. Nevertheless, his influence was profound. With such a tightly directed and largely uniform group of judge advocates it was easy to influence their decisions, whenever required, to support the Navy's policies and ideas.

The average case, drunken misbehaviour and the resulting problems, was processed within one hour, often in less time, when many cases were lined up. Naturally, a case that could involve substantial matters would get more time on the docket.

Rather bewildering to naval outsiders, including lawyers acting as defence counsel who had not dealt with naval cases before, was this: owing to the closeness of this group, the judge advocates constantly changed their position, being prosecutor in one case, judge or pre-trial judge in the next, case investigator and directing judge in the third. While this saved the Navy time and money, it also opened the door wide for ambitious men who could turn up as pre-trial investigator and then prosecutor, leading judge and pre-trial judge, in sequence in the same case. This was like the American Old West, where hanging judges did everything but personally string up the accused whom they had sentenced to death.

The various naval stations had a list of approved defence counsel that the accused would be given, should he wish to pick one from that list, though many accused soldiers rejected such official legal help as almost useless.

In trials not involving matters of substantial importance, defence counsel were dispensed with entirely. Most enlisted men and petty officers preferred to have one of their own superior officers as their defender, especially when crew members from U-boats or smaller ships were involved. Such officers would fight tenaciously for their men, as they needed them aboard, even if they had got stinking drunk in port and involved in fights with the hated field police. In the case of accused officers, most preferred to have either a naval classmate or one of their direct superiors defend them, instead of using the naval list.

There was the possibility that such officers, acting as defenders of their men, could manage to convince the two naval *Beisitzer* judges, or 'Assessors', and make them see their point of view. In that case, the *Beisitzer* would vote in opposition to the judge and the judge advocate prosecuting the case.

Officially, all naval courts had a nominal court president, who happened to be the naval officer in command of the naval organization to which the court was assigned or had been temporarily attached. Such officers had plenty of other tasks and could rarely sit in court and supervise trials, although their signature was solicited after the case was over to confirm the judgement.

But this was a routine formality, unless the case was appealed and went to a higher command for review. But when the official president of the court decided to interfere or to demand a specific case decision and sentence, it would generally be granted by the judges without a lot of argument. Under this system, he would not even have to appear in court to get his way, or to get the decision desired by the naval command he headed.

Civilian lawyers permitted to act in naval courts were, of course, well aware of this situation, and considered in advance whether to accept or refuse a case in terms of protecting their legal reputation instead of fighting the naval system without any real chance of winning.

The reasoning of the court presidents did not need to be made known in court. Naval ideas of what constituted justice or fairness could be difficult to understand for outsiders, as neither logic nor common sense was taken into consideration, but only what the Navy viewed as best and necessary. Usually such input was by telephone or through a brief personal conversation, so that the judges could be guided correctly but without any reference to the input from above being reflected in the court file.

Schmidt arranged to have complete copies of the Abel report teletyped to Kals in Lorient and Hagemann in Kiel. In Lorient, the copy was received on

16 January 1944 and promptly delivered to Kals. After studying the report and discussing it with two of his staff officers, Kals called Rösing in Angers and talked to him about the information at length. Rösing was the official court president of the naval court in western France, serving on a rotation basis all five U-boat bases.

Rösing was quite aroused that such a case had happened in his command region, though he stated that he had met Kusch only on social occasions. But as the FdU West court's president, he felt this case had to be prosecuted, to make an example of Kusch, as a warning to other U-boat commanders and officers who might think in a similar way. The matter must be processed as a clear warning to others, and Kusch would just be the vehicle for that purpose, so that nothing like it would happen again.

Rösing called in his resident naval judge advocate and legal adviser, *Marinekriegsgerichtsrat* Dr jur. Hans Egon Breinig. He gave him the copy of Abel's report and instructed him to investigate the matter in Lorient forthwith; he was to talk to any witnesses still reachable in Lorient and afterwards prepare an indictment and quickly set the case for expedited hearings.

Breinig pointed out that most of the witnesses were no longer in France, but in Germany. Would it not be better to try the case in Kiel? The HKU court, the court of the Higher Command of U-boat training, was in Kiel and would have more personnel to expedite the case, once he had done the pre-trial collection of evidence in Lorient and put witnesses still in France under oath, taking their depositions on the spot. Rösing gave Breinig full authority to get the case under way, telling him to report periodically by telephone as things developed, so that he, Rösing, was fully informed and could contribute input, if necessary. He called Captain Viktor Schütze in Kiel, the president of the HKU court, informed him about the report and enquired about the possibility of trying the case in Kiel, because of the number of witnesses now in Germany.

Schütze agreed, but told Rösing that he would not wish to head the court case himself, since he knew Kusch quite well. Schütze pointed out that this would become a point of objection for any clever defence counsel. He recommended that the Kusch case be tried on the HKU court premises as a case of the Western Regional U-boat Command, on a courtesy basis. Rösing accepted this proposal and informed Breinig accordingly.

Once Breinig had reached Lorient, Kals had done some preliminary checking on which of the people named in the report were available in Lorient, so that they could be interrogated promptly. It turned out that Funke had returned that afternoon from his leave, so he would be available the next morning. Druschel had called to advise the 2nd U-boat Flotilla that he would arrive the next day, if his train connections permitted this. He reported that Kusch was still in Zürs, but he did not know for how long. They had had another fight, and Druschel decided to leave earlier than at first contemplated. He was instructed to report immediately to Kals's office in Lorient when he arrived.

Breinig asked Kals to arrange for a call-back order for Kusch, so that he would appear as fast as possible in Lorient, but he was not to tell Kusch the reason. Should Kusch ask why he was recalled, he was to be told that U-154 would be ready earlier than scheduled for her seventh war patrol, requiring his presence sooner. Rösing had instructed Breinig not to inform Kusch about anything in advance, so that he could not prepare himself in any way.

Breinig talked to a number of people while waiting for his witnesses to become available. Quite a few U-boat commanders and other officers, including several naval classmates of Kusch's, told him they were outraged and utterly disgusted at how this matter was being handled, and how it had started. They knew the officers involved and called them pure Nazi trash and dirty denouncers. Others stated that Abel had made this nasty report only for personal reasons and to revenge himself on Kusch, because he had not cleared Abel for the prospective commander's courses after the first war patrol.

Funke was only able to present himself at the office of the 2nd U-boat Flotilla during the morning of 20 January 1944. Druschel returned to Lorient later that day and came to the flotilla office straight away. Consequently, Breinig was able to take the depositions from both of them consecutively, with assistance by clerical staff from the 2nd U-boat Flotilla staff.

Once these depositions had been registered and copied, Breinig called on Kals and requested an immediate order to arrest Kusch as soon as he returned to Lorient, preferably right at the railway station, to obviate any help for Kusch by other officers. He then phoned Rösing and brought him up to date on developments. He also informed Rösing about the objections by many officers and U-boat commanders in Lorient with respect to the handling of the Kusch case.

Rösing immediately ordered that the entire Kusch file and case, including all papers and connected documents, were to be stamped 'GeKados', a 'Supersecret Command Matter', in order to stop any further objections.

Breinig was astonished about the secrecy upgrading, but had to comply with this direct order. Kals was informed and was stunned about such a procedure, yet had to obey too.

Once Kusch received his telephone recall from the 2nd U-boat Flotilla, there were problems in rearranging the train reservations for his bride and in-laws, as well as his own. They separated in Munich for different destinations.

Kusch reached Lorient in the late afternoon of 20 January 1944 and was met at the Hennebont railway station by two officers in full dress uniforms who, to his surprise, placed him under arrest. He had assumed they were meeting him to welcome him back. Both were embarrassed, and informed Kusch they were only acting under direct orders from Kals, and they showed Kusch the arrest order. Breinig was immediately informed that Kusch had been picked up at the station and was being held at the 2nd U-boat Flotilla's office.

Breinig had been told by Rösing on the phone to arrange for Kusch's transport without delay to the armed forces' jail in Angers, where a section was held for the Western Regional U-boat Command. Kusch should be placed under tight security and guarded. A car was ordered and Kusch departed with two security guards for Angers, where the vehicle arrived at 20.25, and Kusch was turned over to the jail administration of the general army prison at 20.35. Here he spent the night in a cell by himself.

Breinig returned to Angers the next morning, 21 January 1944, and interrogated Kusch in the dreary, depressing interrogation room of the army prison. He arranged a recording protocol of the entire conversation with Kusch, but permitted him only one phone call. Kusch managed to reach Dieter Berger in Berlin, bringing him up to date and asking Berger to find a good defence counsel without delay. Breinig had informed him that he would request a trial as soon as possible, to take place in Kiel. Berger was shocked, but confirmed that he would do everything in his power to help Kusch. He told him he would get the wheels turning and also arrange for the necessary financing.

After Rösing had spoken with Breinig, he contacted Kals, to inquire about the overhaul status of U-154. He instructed Kals to relieve Kusch immediately as commander of U-154 and replace him with Lieutenant j.g. Gerth Gemeiner, who had recently arrived in Lorient to join the personnel standby pool as an emergency or sickness replacement commander.

Kals called Druschel to assemble the crew of U-154 in the evening, to introduce their new commander. Several crew members, particularly the petty officers, asked pointed questions about why Kusch was being replaced. Druschel told them Kusch had suddenly fallen ill and had to be hospitalized. However, some of the petty officers had got wind of Kusch's arrest and were furious that Druschel lied to them so crudely.

Rösing then contacted the U-boat personnel department to cancel Kusch's promotion to *Kapitänleutnant*, full lieutenant, which was due and already in the pipeline.

After Breinig's interrogation of Kusch in Angers, Kusch insisted that a supplementary personal declaration of his must be made part of the record and incorporated into the court file. It read as follows:

I strongly protest about this collection of twisted and false remarks by Abel, Druschel and Funke. Particularly, the reproaches in their reports of an unsoldierly, unpatriotic attitude on my part towards Germany's naval leadership and war direction. There are numerous witnesses available who know better and also know me far better than these conspiring denouncers. As three such witnesses I name herewith:

(a) Commander Werner Winter, 1st U-boat Flotilla in Brest.
(b) Lieutenant-Commander Gustav Adolf Janssen, commander of U-103.
(c) Lieutenant j.g. (Engineering) Otto Strelow, formerly directing engineer of U-103 and at present instructor with the Second U-boat Training Division in Gotenhafen [Gdingen].

Breinig left Angers by train for Kiel on 22 January, but had another long conversation with Rösing before doing so, to obtain final instructions and bring Rösing fully up to date on developments as president of the FdU West naval court.

In the evening of 23 January, after dark, Kusch was taken by two armed guards of the field police to the railway station in Angers and transported with a change of trains to Kiel, arriving on 25 January at 12.20. He was immediately turned over to the chief warder of the naval investigative prison, in the Wik section of Kiel. He was again placed in solitary confinement.

In order to be able to prepare his indictment, Breinig asked the Gestapo office in Kiel to contact its Berlin branch to obtain a complete copy of Kusch's police dossier and also that of his father, particularly regarding his past record and political views. He asked for a swift reply as the trial was already scheduled for the morning of 26 January. This had been arranged by putting other cases off the docket, in order to hinder the defence in locating helpful witnesses or obtaining mitigating evidence and documents.

The HKU court in Kiel shared staff, equipment and offices with the higher appeals court, presided over by Admiral von Friedeburg, the admiral commanding U-boats. This was arranged to maximize utilization and hold down operational costs. Therefore, copies of all files, documents, court papers and decisions were automatically forwarded to von Friedeburg too, being the next highest command and court. Any HKU court decision that was appealed or reviewed would later be handled by the higher court, with von Friedeburg as official president to that court.

Von Friedeburg was horrified when the copy of Abel's report reached his desk. He immediately requested from Koralle Bernau complete copies of the war patrol journals of both war patrols by U-154 under Kusch. These were teletyped to Kiel within thirty minutes. He then asked one of his staff officers, Lieutenant-Commander Wilhelm Franken, to study thoroughly both journals, plus all claims and reports, in order to prepare an expert evaluation of the entire matter.

Then von Friedeburg requested a true copy of Kusch's personal file and all past fitness reports on him. He just could not believe that a U-boat commander could be in charge of a front U-boat for eleven months without anyone reporting anything negative about him in that time. Nor apparently had any other officer, crew member or Kusch's superiors noticed or even suspected any possibility of misconduct. His chief of staff, Rear Admiral Ernst Kratzenberg, with whom he had discussed the Kusch case, also considered this impossible.

Both admirals were quite upset, because Abel had included the two midshipmen in his report without their knowledge or agreement, and had involved them in this court case. Both admirals insisted that these two young men must not be forced to testify unwillingly, nor should they be placed under oath, as they were too young and inexperienced to understand the implications of such testimony concerning their former commander. This would become a terrible black mark on their respective service records and would have to be included in their fitness reports, prejudicing their future careers as naval officers because no commanding officer would wish to have them serve under him.

Once the Kusch case had been fitted into the adjusted court session schedule for 26 January 1944, Judge Advocate Hagemann was assigned as presiding judge, while Breinig, the pre-trial investigator, became the prosecutor. Hagemann agreed reluctantly with Kratzenberg that the midshipmen ought to testify only voluntarily, and definitely not under oath. He thought the reports and depositions of the three officers would suffice to get Kusch convicted, regardless of what defence he put up.

Hagemann was anxious that no additional witnesses should be brought into the case, especially petty officers or enlisted men who had served on U-154 while Kusch had been her commander, as with additional witnesses the case would become broader and less predictable for the prosecutor and the judges. He pointed out that Breinig barely had enough time to prepare his indictment of the Kusch case, and that he was still working on it.

Franken started right away with the job given to him. As a former U-boat commander with combat experience, he was naturally much closer to operational matters and details than the two older admirals. Franken had been executive officer on Type VII U-331, under Lieutenant Hans Dietrich von Tiesenhausen. Afterwards he commanded a Type VII U-boat, U-565, in the Mediterranean, and was awarded the Knight's Cross of the Iron Cross on 30 April 1943.

Franken's investigative report was delivered to Admiral von Friedeburg and Judge Advocate Hagemann for court guidance, reading as follows:

Kiel, 25 January 1944
The U-boat specialist Lieutenant-Commander Franken as expert declares:

After triple-checking the war patrol journals of the last two war patrols and this entire file, I have reached the following view and opinion regarding these two war patrols by U-154 with respect to those accusations made by Lieutenant j.g. Ulrich Abel:

1. It would have been possible on 28 May 1943 after the first attack at 04.45 to manage a second attack on the convoy, before it got light, if the reloading of all tubes had been possible quickly enough and the weather had not turned heavier.

But such absolutely perfect attack operations can't realistically be expected from a new commander on his first war patrol. The actions and reactions as well as his behaviour during the period when a coup de grâce was attempted on the already torpedoed tanker, I see as indecisive or irresolute. That the commander operated on and attacked the already torpedoed and damaged tanker, instead of tenaciously following the convoy, could be seen as a false tactical decision by the commander . . . maybe. On the basis of the facts and files I have in front of me, I am not in a position to believe that it would be possible to conclude that the accused did not pursue the convoy because he was afraid to do so.

2. When double-checking and reviewing carefully the facts and submitted files with respect to the action(s) on 3 November 1943, I have reached the conclusion that the accused did not act with a lot of decisiveness. The claim(s) and statements by Lieutenant j.g. Abel are not suitable or helpful to contradict the conclusions of the commander regarding this operation. While it is correct that with an angle of around 253° and a course by the enemy of 120° the attack angle would eventually reduce itself to less than 70°, such small differences can be explained and must be excused as erroneous observations and estimates through the periscope.

The fact that Commander Kusch did not attempt to approach the enemy closer to make an attack because the distance(s) were too great, and did not do so promptly, I likewise consider as indecisiveness or hesitation, before judging the situation clearly. To me there is no obvious appearance of cowardice to be found nor any facts to reach that conclusion. To the contrary: the surfacing in the afternoon at 15.30 in that area and the prevailing conditions actually calls for different conclusions altogether.

But from the determination and the reasoning, why no immediate following of the convoy was attempted, and why the U-boat then reached a position ahead of the convoy only at 10.15, is not clear, nor explained fully. However, perhaps there is an error in calculations involved or a mistake in dead-reckoning, in view of the fact that the navigator arrived at the same calculation results. But again, there is no evidence whatsoever that the commander wanted to shirk an attack that was possible.

3. In the war patrol journal of U-154, there is no inclusion of the radio signal that is cited by Lieutenant j.g. Abel. When double-checking for comparison the war patrol journal of U-662, commanded by Lieutenant Heinz Eberhard Müller (Crew 1936), I found on 26 March 1943 at 15.00 the receipt of signal number 1320/26/43, reading:

Our own air reconnaissance reported a convoy consisting of 35 ships and 4 escorters in grid square CF-6669 with course 0° [due north] speed 8 miles.

No explanation or reason for this missing radio signal is made. Why U-154 did not operate on that particular convoy is not reflected and covered in the war patrol journal. Owing to lack of any further evidence or more supporting facts, I am not able to reach the conclusion that the commander did not operate against this convoy through cowardice. However, I can't find any reason why this radio signal is not recorded in the war patrol journal or why no mention is made of this signal, nor what decision was made after receipt of same anywhere in the war patrol journal.

On the other hand there is the fact that the accused attacked a convoy on the same war patrol on 28 May and fought it success-fully, suggesting he acted in the first case not out of cowardice but some lack of decisiveness. Furthermore, with a convoy of that size and with such a limited small escort, it seems unreasonable and unbelievable that he should have been afraid, in that particular case, to attack it. That would certainly make no sense whatsoever.

Franken determined there was need for further clarification of Point 7 in Abel's report, a point also mentioned by Funke, though Funke had not even been aboard U-154 at that time and had resorted to hearsay or gossip. The codeword 'Rose', which appeared in the report, was unknown to Franken, and he could not remember if he had ever heard it in the past. Therefore, he ordered a back file check and requested a true copy of the specifics that had been signalled under that special code.

It turned out that it involved a long signal, by Karl Dönitz personally, that had been sent out on 21 May 1943, just three days before Dönitz had to withdraw the U-boats from the North Atlantic, during Black May. It had been coded in the special 'For officers only' key, which required decoding by the watch officer in charge of signals, usually the second watch officer or the commander himself. But Bletchley Park in England had also decoded, cracked and read this signal quickly, and was fully informed. The signal was directed to the U-boat commanders of Group Moselle. But it had been sent to other U-boats at sea, too.

The signal read:

Anybody who now believes it is no longer possible to fight and attack convoys is nothing but a weakling and not a real U-boat commander! The Battle of the Atlantic is growing tougher, but it is the decisive battle of this war! You will have to be fully cognizant of your enormous responsibility and must be very clear about the fact that you will have to assume full responsibility for your actions and decisions! Do the best you can with this convoy. We simply must hack it to pieces and destroy it. If conditions are favourable, do not dive for aeroplanes, but fight them hard and shoot them down! When destroyers are involved, whenever possible don't dive, turn away on the surface to get away. But stay rock-hard, push tenaciously ahead to reach a forward attack position and attack harder than ever! Then attack again and attack once more after that! I believe in you!

Your naval commander-in-chief, Dönitz.

Because of the 'For officers only' classification of this signal, Franken ordered a true copy attached to his evaluation report, as an appendix. This was in case questions came up with respect to Point 7, in connection with the special codeword 'Rose' included in the Abel report.

When the admirals received a copy of Franken's expert evaluation regarding the military and operational view of the Kusch case, they had also obtained copies of his fitness reports since he joined the Navy in 1937. The admirals suggested that they should become part of the court file and ought to be presented during the hearings, but Hagemann objected that this was not customary and contrary to court rules.

Since Hageman succeeded in suppressing Kusch's fitness reports for information of the court, they are shown here for the reader. On 26 June 1942, Werner Winter wrote the following evaluation of Oskar Kusch:

> Lieutenant j.g. Kusch was assigned as second watch officer aboard U-103 of the 2nd U-boat Flotilla from 25 June 1941 to 26 June 1942 and participated in three long war patrols in that position. Kusch turned out to be an excellent young officer. He matured greatly in the war and during combat operations, has conducted himself perfectly and has an outstanding clean character. His considerable ability and rapid reaction in any situation made him an increasingly valuable assistant to the commander. As superior he exhibited a lot of heart and cheerfulness towards his subordinates, but at the same time a firm hand and determination. He is creative, with artistic ability, and has an unusually broad and fine educational background. In front of the enemy, he always demonstrated considerable tenacity, daring and, after smart deliberation, unusual boldness, great responsibility and total dependability.
>
> His knowledge of seamanship is very good. He handled all tasks with resolution and stayed on top of his job in all situations. As weapons director, he always acted with precision, calmness and consideration of all possibilities, as well as being extremely dependable. Kusch has been awarded the Iron Cross First Class for his outstanding performance. After another war patrol as executive officer, he should be suitable and competent as U-boat commander.

On 5 January 1943, Gustav Adolf Janssen, who had followed Winter as commander of U-103, prepared this evaluation of Kusch, who now served as executive officer in charge of the torpedo department:

> Kusch is a well-behaved young naval officer with way above-average ability. He has a very high educational level combined with good knowledge of seamanship and the handling of people. His courage, quiet determination and vigour were outstanding during combat operations of U-103, when serving as executive officer on the U-boat commanded by me. His cheerful brightness in confusing situations was remarkable. When

dealing with superiors and his comrades, Kusch showed a certain reserve and cautiousness, rather than acting excessively or demonstratively close. Though he is not a loner by any means, but appreciates some privacy, as far as that is possible on any ship. He is unusually curious about many things and feels a very deep responsibility for his men, events and all operational problems.

As officer and superior Kusch was liked by his men and subordinates, owing to his cheerful and pleasant, but always very correct, ways in dealing with them. They appreciated his competency and the way he treated them, firmly but comradely too.

I had always outstanding support from Kusch, whenever this was required and expected. I found him absolutely dependable and very responsible in all of his actions. Kusch has already successfully passed the prospective commander's training classes with very good results and is now suitable as U-boat commander in the near future – both of a front U-boat, but also of a training or school U-boat too, because he is an excellent and patient instructor.

After discussing the various documents and papers in front of them, the two admirals decided that the cowardice and fear issues had to be stricken entirely from the case. Abel seemed to be personally prejudiced against his former, but younger, commander, having clearly brought personal motives into his report not supported by evidence. Therefore, the trial would have to go forward. But the judges as well as the pre-trial investigator, now prosecutor, had to be firmly instructed that all the military and fear aspects were to be deleted from the indictment and only the entirely political complaints were to be retained and presented at the court martial.

While these matters came to the fore in Kiel, events elsewhere were finally bearing fruit. Kusch's friend Dieter Berger in Berlin managed to ferret out a civilian defence lawyer, in spite of the extraordinary shortage of time available, which almost precluded any effective defence, as purposely arranged by Hagemann.

Not only had Berger been able to reach both Winter and Janssen to inform them of the trial and the incredibly close date set for it, but both officers agreed to appear as character witnesses for Kusch. Breinig and Hagemann had intentionally done nothing to locate these officers or request their presence in Kiel.

Berger had talked to a large firm of old-established lawyers in Berlin, where several former imperial naval officers were partners. They had waved off the persistent Berger, declaring that they would not accept cases where they would have to work against the Navy, regardless of reasons. Finally, they would simply be unable to take on a case that was already set to be processed within a day or two. One of the partners guided Berger to the front door, apologizing to him. Suddenly, he pulled an envelope out of his pocket and put it with a sheet of paper in Berger's hand, as he shook it to say goodbye.

The front door closed swiftly. Berger looked at the sheet of paper. It featured the names of two lawyers in Kiel, indicating that both were experienced in naval court cases. Berger walked around the corner and opened the envelope absent-mindedly. It contained 20,000 Reichsmarks with a slip of paper saying, 'Our contribution for legal defence expenses. Good Luck.'

Within the hour Berger was at the railway station, fighting his way to Kiel among the masses of people wanting to get on the trains. He reached Kiel during the morning of 25 January and went to see the first of the law firms listed. The firm explained that there was not enough time to become familiar with the case, much less to prepare any kind of defence, which would be considerably restricted by the Navy regulations anyway.

Without wasting time, Berger immediately called on the second lawyer on his sheet, who was Gerhard Meyer-Grieben, working as a civilian lawyer, and not accepting criminal cases. Meyer-Grieben had to step rather softly, because he had been involved in politics as a Social Democrat before the Nazis took over power in Germany. He rarely accepted cases where political considerations were foremost. But since the war had started, he had gradually accepted more and more military and naval court cases, though preferably smaller ones, mostly involving misbehaviour while being drunk, and situations that had originated owing to soldiers being under the influence.

Meyer-Grieben slowly obtained more clients and became familiar with the judges and the lower-ranked court personnel in Kiel, particularly at the naval courts. He had thereby gained quite a thorough inside view of the naval court system. For Berger the fact that Meyer-Grieben had been opposed to Nazi politics in the past had considerable value, because Berger did not at this point trust anybody tainted by Nazi political doctrines. He did not explain this to Meyer-Grieben specifically, but rapidly realized that he had found a competent and trustworthy lawyer to defend Kusch sympathetically.

After Berger had talked to Meyer-Grieben for half an hour, the lawyer agreed to accept Kusch's representation. The lawyer asked him for a copy of the indictment, but Berger did not have it as yet, since Breinig was still working at it. Meyer-Grieben went immediately to the naval investigative jail to see Kusch, after getting a visitor's permit from Hagemann. As both lawyers knew each other, the permit was given swiftly. Meyer-Grieben had a twenty-minute conversation with Kusch in the jail's meeting area, and asked him to sign a quickly prepared Power of Attorney. There simply was no time to discuss defence procedures or court tactics.

Kusch was informed that *Marinekriegsgerichtsrat* (Judge Advocate) Ernst Meinert had been assigned to keep Kusch under observation, control access to him and censor all of his communications until further notice. Meinert would sit in court, too, as a legal expert to become familiar with the Kusch case and to observe the entire court proceedings, in case the Kusch case should go to appeal later. Meyer-Grieben was informed that Breinig would be the prosecutor and had also been the pre-trial investigator of the case.

Meyer-Grieben and Kusch were told the trial would take place the next morning, 26 January 1944. As Breinig was still working on the indictment, he allowed Kusch's defence counsel a first, cursory look at the reports and the file, as far as this could be done under the pressure of time. It would be difficult to imagine a case where the defence was given less time and advance information. In any normal court, unquestionably, the defence lawyer would immediately ask for a postponement of the trial, to have enough time available for preparations and independent research to ferret out helpful facts and locate more witnesses for the defence.

Meyer-Grieben had asked Breinig why there were no petty officers or enlisted men from U-154 listed as witnesses, and why none had been questioned in Lorient or elsewhere. He was told there were enough witnesses involved already, as this would be treated as a trial of an officer, without subordinates being brought into the case. Meyer-Grieben was surprised, but could not understand why that would be so. Then one of the naval clerks whispered to him that the Navy did not want crew members in the court to create possible difficulties or make problems with uncontrolled testimony or evidence.

Meyer-Grieben immediately realized that this would be a closed case, regardless of what would be said or presented in court, with the conclusions already pretty well determined, and few alternative possibilities were left for any defence. Nevertheless, Meyer-Grieben asked Meinert about this peculiarity, too, when he had to get a second visiting permit in the evening. Meinert said that U-154 was in the middle of preparations to depart on another war patrol, so nobody could be spared as witness, as that had higher priority than any trial anywhere of anybody.

Finally, Meyer-Grieben was told that the trial would take place in the Villa Forsteck on Niemandsweg in the Wik section of Kiel – a house that had so far remained undamaged by bombing and had been requisitioned by the Navy as a courthouse.

Meyer-Grieben had recently reached his 60th birthday, and he did not find it easy to prepare any defence under such pressure, while rushing about in a town that was destroyed to a considerable degree, with the consequent traffic complications and delays. Berger was with Meyer-Grieben until late in the night to give him some more background on Kusch, who was for practical purposes unknown to the lawyer.

Like anybody who had ever dealt with the naval court machinery, Meyer-Grieben was astonished at the record speed and determination that prevailed to rush this case into court. Meinert mentioned to him that the pressure for this rush originated from the court's official president, Rösing, in agreement with others of the senior staff in Kiel. Now that the case had been stamped and declared a super-secret command file, the judge advocates could employ extraordinary means to hurry the Kusch case along.

CHAPTER NINE

The Court Martial

At 08.15 Meyer-Grieben showed up at the designated trial location. At last he was given access to the finalized indictment prepared by Breinig, and he had twenty-five minutes to peruse most of the papers and depositions.

Funke had been scratched from the witness list because he was indispensable in Lorient. But Breinig had his interrogation and deposition at hand, anticipating that possibility. A small group of spectators was admitted, after a close identity check, including several officers from the various departments working under von Friedeburg. Wilhelm Franken was among those spectators.

Breinig had tracked down Lieutenant j.g. Heinrich Meyer, second watch officer on the first war patrol under Kusch, in Memel (Klaipeda), and had requested his presence in court as witness. But Meyer, recently promoted, had not been informed in advance what the trial was about. He had successfully passed the various courses for prospective U-boat commanders in the Baltic, and now commanded the Type VII U-boat U-287, which he had commissioned on 22 September 1943.

Breinig had also located the two former midshipmen who had been promoted to senior midshipmen in the months since serving aboard U-154, Horst Fröhlich in Swinemünde, and Hellmuth Kirchammer in Flensburg.

While Abel had named them in his report, neither of these three men had been asked about their concurrence. No pre-trial depositions had been arranged, nor had any preliminary interrogations of them taken place. The two midshipmen would be included in the procedures only if they agreed voluntarily to be questioned. But by the order of the admirals, they would not be placed under oath.

However, regardless of how soon U-154 would be getting ready for her next war patrol with a new commander, or how busy everybody would be with preparatory matters, Druschel, the directing engineer, had insisted on travelling to Kiel. After the fights in Zürs, Druschel hated Kusch even more.

He declared prior to his departure from Lorient that he would make sure Kusch finally got what he had coming.

At 09.00 sharp the doors were opened by armed guards, and the various small groups waiting around were admitted, after another identity check. To Kusch's surprise, both his former U-boat commanders, Winter and Janssen, were present, having been tracked down by Berger in time to come to Kiel, no mean feat during those times, in the middle of a cold and nasty winter in Germany.

Hagemann as presiding judge declared the court in session and stated that in his estimation the testimony would probably take up the entire day. Meinert was sitting in as standby judge and legal expert on military technicalities that might pop up unexpectedly. Meinert would also interpret the naval and military laws, rules and regulations to the folk who were not lawyers, should this be necessary.

Hagemann swore in those witnesses who were to testify under oath, telling them to wait in the witness chambers, but not to discuss their testimony or anything they overheard in court among themselves. The witnesses were advised that they would be called back into the court individually, and were admonished that the Kusch case was now a super-secret command file. Consequently, it was forbidden to talk afterwards to anybody about it, on account of the existing secrecy regulations, which called for harsh penalties of any infringement of that secrecy.

Hagemann had discussed the Kusch case with Otto Kranzbühler, the senior judge advocate at Naval Group West, known among the naval judge advocates as 'Prince Otto', who was very influential and exercised his strong inside connections carefully. In addition, Hagemann had talked about the case in detail with Naval Judge Advocate Helmut Sieber, who had worked in Kiel for a long time as judge for the U-boat Command, to get Sieber's view of the case. Sieber had the reputation among the naval judge advocates of always having a right nose for the wishes of the Navy's Top Brass.

At 09.12 the witnesses moved to the witness room. Breinig then read aloud the prosecution's indictment:

The naval court of the Leader of U-boats, Western Region, on 25 January 1944 meeting in Kiel, has issued the following indictment:

Against Lieutenant j.g. Oskar Heinz Kusch of the 2nd U-boat Flotilla Command, born on 6 April 1918 in Berlin, Protestant, single and not previously convicted, who entered the *Kriegsmarine* on 3 April 1937, the following charges are made and he is herewith accused of:

He is sufficiently suspected during the year 1943 to have acted continuously in this manner:

1.   Attempted publicly to undermine and to paralyze the determined will of the German people for successful self-assertion and tried repeatedly to sabotage the discipline of the German armed forces in a malicious way and with evil purpose, to wit:

He ordered during two war patrols that the picture of our *Führer* Adolf Hitler be removed, and as commander of U-154 to have it taken away, making the following remark: 'Take this away right now, as we are not pursuing any idolatry here!'

He furthermore stated publicly during several conversations in the officers' area: 'Only the fall from power of Hitler and his party can possibly allow the German people any kind of peace and another cultural ascent in the future. If the German people themselves are able to find the strength for such a political overthrow, the other countries will be most willing to work out a peace treaty with us. In so many ways the population suffers heavily and bears a tremendous load caused by the present political regime, and only after its elimination will the true abilities and the strength of the people rise again to full growth and a much better life.'

In the same vein and aiming in the identical direction, he ordered the following joke put into the onboard radio news sheet. 'Question: What have the German people in common with a tapeworm? Answer: Both are surrounded by brown shit and in danger of suffocating in this mess.'

During another discussion he told the two midshipmen that our political and military leadership's orders and announcements should not always be automatically accepted at face value, and ought to be viewed with caution. 'Concerning our present regime,' he said, 'you as higher educated human beings and prospective officers must be above their ways and views.'

During other extensive conversations with his officers he referred to the *Führer* as being an insane utopist, who was in fact a megalomaniac with extreme delusions of grandeur, and sickeningly ambitious too. He said he had heard from a reliable source that the *Führer* suffered frequent attacks, when he tore down curtains and drapes and rolled around on the floor throwing fits.

When talking to his officers on several occasions he stated that the defeat of the German Reich would surely take place before the end of 1943, because the German

Reich just did not have enough raw materials and resources or skilled labour to win. He said that the chances of our opponents are much more favourable, and the German propaganda undertakings deliberately enlarge everything in the grossest way.

World Jewry he refused to recognize as some sort of world-wide conspiracy or any sort of political force interested in the destruction of Germany. He declared that this was pure invention by our own propaganda ministry. The very same would be applicable for the terror-bombing attacks; he emphasized several times that any bombs hitting residential areas were merely accidental mishaps, rather than intentional hits.

Concerning the present U-boat Command's direction of the tonnage war, he pointed to radio signals under the codename 'Rose', that were made purely as orders for even more relentless attacks, used as a slave whip was employed by slave drivers in the past, but now by our U-boat leadership instead.

2.   Intentionally having tuned in and listened to foreign broadcast stations illegally, in that he listened to them during war patrols when this was really not required or essential. Nevertheless, he listened constantly to the enemy's news services.

This is a crime in line with Paragraph 5, Subsection 1 and 2 of the War Direction Orders and also Paragraph 1 of the general prohibition regarding extraordinary radio broadcast measures against tuning in to hostile radio stations of 1 September 1939.

Evidence: 1. The admission of the accused.
2. Declaration under oath by Lieutenant j.g. of the Reserve Ulrich Abel and Lieutenant j.g. (Engineering) Curt Druschel.
3. Written statement under oath by Lieutenant j.g. of the Reserve Arno Funke.
4. Verbal testimony by Senior Midshipmen Horst Fröhlich and Hellmuth Kirchammer (not under oath).

An agreement was reached to delete accusations according to Paragraphs 84, 85 and 86 of the Military Justice Code:

Cowardice in action in front of the enemy and shirking duty owing to fear to attack.

Herewith follows the official transcription of events in court:

Reported as personally present in the court for the purpose of:

In the criminal matter against the *Oberleutnant zur See*, Oskar Kusch, from the command of the 2nd U-boat Flotilla:

For undermining of the Military Fighting and Defence Ability of the German Armed Forces and sedition of other officers p.p.

As Presiding Judge: *Marine Oberkriegsgerichtsrat* Hagemann

Senior Officer (*Beisitzer*) for courtroom procedures: *Korvetten Kapitän* [Lieutenant-Commander] Dittmers

and for military expertise: *Oberleutnant zur See* [Lieutenant j.g.] Westphalen

The main hearing began with the calling up of the accused, the defence counsel and of the witnesses.

In person appearing were:

The accused: Brought into court on order.

For the reader's guidance, I will discuss the military *Beisitzer* officer judges and their military background, because they appear here for the first time. On paper, they were to balance their experience and knowledge of naval and military activities and regulations against the purely legal expertise of the judge advocates. In reality, such men were ordered into court on the shortest of notices and usually without any information about the case and the person involved. Ignorance of the case details was supposed to allow a decision without prejudice on the part of the two military *Beisitzer* judges. However, this also favoured the naval judge advocates in many ways.

The senior *Beisitzer* judge was Lieutenant-Commander Wolfgang Dittmers, 34 years old, who had not held any shipboard position since early 1941, for reasons of impaired health. Dittmers had undergone partial U-boat training in the Baltic, but did not finish it and was transferred with medical problems to a shore command, first as company commander, then ground service unit commander of the permanent watch, security and administrative groups at two different U-boat training commands. Officers assigned to such units were generally not fit for shipboard or U-boat service. Dittmers was marking time in a dead-end assignment, and continued to do so to the end of the war.

Such officers frequently developed an exaggerated 'orders are orders' complex and become narrow-minded martinets, to demonstrate they were just as competent as officers serving on shipboard commands at the front. Eager compliance with instructions from superiors and the growing requirement to follow Nazi policies with enthusiasm and excessive strictness were invariably part of the picture.

The junior *Beisitzer* judge was Lieutenant j.g. Otto Emil Westphalen, 23 years old. He had attended a boarding school, which had been converted into a school for Nazi Party functionaries in 1933 (Napola), to educate children of the Party faithfuls. But other pupils previously enrolled were initially kept, until it was possible to set up full classes of uncritical admirers of the Hitler regime. Westphalen claimed that his type of education did not transform him into an uncritical enthusiast of the Nazi regime or a fanatical supporter of Party policies and ideas.

From April 1941 to March 1942, Westphalen served as second watch officer on the Type VII U-boat U-566, commanded by Lieutenant Dietrich Borchert in the Barents Sea and the North Atlantic. Thereafter Westphalen commanded the Type II school boat U-121 in the Baltic for ten months, before he commissioned the Type VII U-968 on 18 March 1943. He had led that U-boat through the Baltic trials, exercises and mechanical tests required to prepare it for front-service operations. Those trials were nearing their end, and Westphalen had come to Kiel to arrange for the final shipyard overhaul of his U-boat, prior to departure on her first war patrol. He was a rather short man, who barely cleared the minimum height requirement of 165 cm (just over 5 ft), when he was accepted by the Navy in 1938 as an officer candidate. When he called at the U-boat Command in Kiel, he was roped in off the street and at random for duty as a *Beisitzer* judge for the Kusch case.

Generally, such assignments were unpopular with most officers, and few volunteered for them. The two *Beisitzer* judges had not read or been shown anything whatsoever about the Kusch case, and had to wait for developments in court.

Meyer-Grieben, Kusch's defence counsel, had already gained the impression that innocence on the part of Kusch was considered impossible by the judge advocates and so could not be assumed as even a remote possibility. For these judge advocates Kusch was practically convicted, and only the final penalty might not yet have been fixed.

Consequently, it would be a very difficult case for any defence counsel, especially if he wanted to remain in business and handle further naval court cases in the future. Based upon his considerable experience with naval courts, Meyer-Grieben knew that the best he could hope for were mitigating circumstances coming up during the questioning of the witnesses, or some unexpected new facts being discovered during interrogations in court.

There was no time to look for new witnesses. It would be a tough case, with only a slim chance of overcoming the rigid naval court system.

The transcription of the court proceedings continues:

As witnesses were present:

Lieutenant j.g. Ulrich Abel
Lieutenant j.g. (Engineering) Curt Druschel
Lieutenant j.g. Heinrich Meyer (Crew 39-B)
Senior Midshipman Hellmuth Kirchammer
Senior Midshipman Horst Fröhlich

Commander Werner Winter
Lieutenant Gustav Adolf Janssen

The accused was questioned about his person and his personal situation, and confirmed the correctness of the information read from his personal naval file by the prosecutor. In addition he stated the following: Since 1 April 1940, I have served with the U-boat Command and became commander of U-154 on 8 February 1943. Until some time in 1935, I was a member of the Hitler Youth and have been a platoon leader of a musical instrument group called a 'Spielschar'.

The accused was asked if he wished to make any comments or remarks with reference to these accusations. He declared this:

I intended to have the Führer's picture moved to the control room, where it had been placed on my former U-boat U-103. In its place I wanted to put a picture that I had painted, which was in better condition. In the event, the Führer's picture remained in the officers' section, but was shifted to another spot. I can't remember now having made remarks then or remember precisely what I might have said at the time. But I doubt that it was, 'Take that picture away, as we do not wish any idolatry here.'

The assertion that I talked about the overthrow of the Führer and the entire regime has been spliced together by the witnesses and taken out of context from a considerable number of discussions.

To the contrary, I actually wished that nothing of the kind should take place. From our many conversations the witnesses have simply picked out specific phrases and words and combined the negative points from them. I deny that I used those specific expressions and comments that I am accused of. Evidently my words were grossly misinterpreted and misunderstood by the witnesses and are cited out of context by them now.

With respect to the joke that had been put into the radio informational sheet, I have to say that it had become customary to include some jokes in these news information sheets. I had told that particular joke in the radio shack. The next day it had been incorporated into the daily news bulletin, but I did not give an order to have it done. I see clearly that I should have prevented this from happening.

My remarks and observations to the midshipmen were made to point out to them that propaganda appears necessary in some respects, but as prospective officers they should take the trouble to differentiate between rumours and facts and form their own personal opinions based on the truth. However, I don't believe I made these statements exactly as reflected in the indictment.

My observations regarding the *Führer* have been grossly misunderstood and misinterpreted by the witnesses and are wrongly quoted. We talked in a general way about the border between craziness and genial behaviour. I certainly did not state verbally that the *Führer* is a megalomaniac or has delusions of grandeur and is an utopist. I said that I had heard rumours and stories that the *Führer* suffered such types of attack. However, I can't remember now where I picked up that kind of rumour and so can't say anything more about it.

The prosecutor then demanded further specifics on these points.

Unfortunately, I simply can't recall who told me these stories. At the time I was told about this, it was reported to originate from someone close to the *Führer*, who had personally observed these attacks. With reference to the defeat of the Reich in this war, I have not put it in those words specifically. Neither did I state that the war was already lost with certainty, and the words are taken out of context.

Upon further questions by the prosecutor:

I have never emphasized a particular tendency, nor have I put special stress on my position as U-boat commander to strengthen my remarks regarding world Jewry. I did not put things as alleged and as I am reproached here. I have said that international world Jewry are not our only opponents, that there are other important powers, like the Catholic Church. I did say that propaganda exaggerates everything strongly.

Naturally, I was aware that my officers had different opinions. Our conversation regarding the terror air attacks occurred during the huge air attacks on Hamburg that shocked everybody. But I stated that the enemy intended to bomb only industrial targets.

In connection with the codeword 'Rose', I should like to comment thus: We received a flood of radio signals, some of them attempting to lift our spirits and to encourage us. I can't imagine that I talked as it is claimed here. I may have said something about getting whipped into shape or something similar.

I only tuned in to foreign radio stations when our German ones could not be heard well or reception was totally impossible. I wanted to hear what was taking place in Berlin. Mostly, I listened to music programmes, though some included news bulletins. The prohibition and regulations with respect to listening to foreign broadcasts are known to me.

Upon further questions by the prosecutor:

> My father is not a Nazi Party member. I do not have any brothers or sisters, but am a single child.

With reference to the operational situation and events, the accused declared the signal and contact report was received.

> According to my calculation, shared by the navigator, we were 240 miles further west than the reported convoy. Perhaps I could have turned around, but doubt that this would have been successful. However, such comments really do not belong in the war patrol journal as they were nothing more than operational deliberations, not actual facts.

Now the court coordinator called the witnesses to be heard one by one, with none of the other witnesses being present.

> First Witness Abel: As to myself, my name is Ulrich Abel, I am 31 years and 10 months old and was born in Leipzig. I belong to the New German Church, *Gottgläubig*, and am currently assigned as *Oberleutnant zur See der Reserve* to the 23rd U-boat Flotilla, participating in the upgraded torpedo-firing course for prospective U-boat commanders in Eckernförde. I am not related in any way to the accused.
>
> To the facts: I was at the time in question executive officer on U-154, commanded by the accused. The accused entered the officers' section and gave the order to remove the *Führer*'s picture hanging there that had been furnished by the Deschimag shipyard. In its place was hung some other picture the accused had painted of a sailing ship. I remember very clearly that he stated at the time: 'Take this picture away, we do not carry on idolatry here!' While the *Führer*'s picture remained in the officers' section, it was shifted to another place less visible. There was no talk whatsoever that it ought to be moved to the control room section.

Accused: I did not give the order to move it to the control section.

Witness Abel: I can take this on my oath that the accused said: 'We don't carry on any idolatry here.'

Accused: I am unable to recall whether I made that remark. My first thought was that it would be preferable to have the *Führer*'s picture in the control room, as that was the spot it had been placed on my previous U-boat. I considered that spot more suitable and dignified.

Witness Abel: The accused spoke disparagingly of the *Führer*. He said, as I heard clearly, the *Führer* was an insane utopist. The debates took place on several occasions about that. We other officers all contradicted him. I had the firm impression that the accused was convinced that we would lose the war.

Accused: I doubt that I have made precisely that statement.

Witness Abel: The accused asserted again and again that we simply had not enough raw materials to win. I am of the opinion that some of the enlisted men could overhear these talks. Sometimes the arguments were so loud they could easily be heard in the senior petty officers' section. I believe it happened in the officers' section when the accused stated solemnly and dead seriously that only the overthrow of Hitler and his party could bring about peace for the German people and a cultural ascent. He thought that such an overthrow could be imminent. The accused asserted that we live under the sign of bondage while living under the present regime. He told us that he had been involved in some political legal proceedings just prior to joining the *Kriegsmarine*.

Accused: I probably made the last one of these statements.

Witness Abel: The accused told the midshipmen that the regime was transitory and that they, as well-educated humans and prospective officers, had to be above the present low-quality, nasty and ugly events. I ordered the midshipmen afterwards to come and report to me and informed them otherwise, putting them straight promptly.

With reference to the various radio signals under the codeword 'Rose', the accused stated that such messages to encourage the timid and to warn the cautious were the equivalent of slave driving, and each one of these signals was nothing but the lash of a whip to drive on slaves.

He also said once that nothing much could really happen to the German people, as the English and Americans would see to it that communism would not be able to take over Europe. Furthermore, he asserted that there does not exist a world Jewish conspiracy or similar organizations in various countries, like the Freemasons, as these were pure inventions of propaganda. We talked indeed about the terror-bombing attacks. The accused declared that they were just not taking place as reported by our propaganda. But if here and there some bombs fell on residential areas, this was a case of unintentionally missing their targets.

I know for certain that the accused tuned in and listened to foreign broadcasts. I personally have noticed that sometimes when my watch term was to start shortly and I entered the radio shack to check through the last received radio signals, that this was so. He discussed the information and news afterwards with the other officers. The accused was warned, and it was pointed out to him that he could be punished in accordance with Paragraph 2 of the extra-ordinary radio-listening regulations and prohibitions.

At this point a lunch break was announced, and the court reconvened for the afternoon session at 14.00.

Immediately the afternoon session opened, the second witness, Druschel, was called to the stand.

He declared: My name is Curt Druschel, I am 23 years old, of Protestant belief, lieutenant j.g. (engineering) and the directing engineer of U-154. I am not related to the accused in any way.

With respect to the matter before the court: We wanted to hang the *Führer*'s picture in the middle of the officers' section. The accused said, 'What nonsense, we don't carry on idolatry here!'

Accused: I can't in any way remember that particular expression.

Witness Druschel: Except for the U-boat commander, we officers were all of the identical political conviction and opinion. I had the impression of the accused that he rejected the regime and was in general an opponent of Nazism. He said when the war was lost, he would be among the very first men who would march on Berlin to clean it up completely. He said we can only bring this war to a good end if we overthrow this regime and erect a military dictatorship in its place.

Accused: I simply can't remember whether I did say this. In no case did I say exactly that and in those words, or I had intended it quite differently and in another connection.

Witness Druschel: To the midshipmen the accused stated that they as prospective officers would have to form their own opinions, not influenced by propaganda in any way. He also said once that he had in the past belonged to the '*Bündische*' Youth organization. He criti-cized the Hitler Youth strongly.

He said he had heard from a trusted source that the *Führer* suffered attacks and threw fits. That he was actually a crazy utopist, who would tear down drapes and curtains during his attacks and roll around on the floor.

Accused: These comments were not made just like that and as the witness states them.

Witness Druschel: With reference to the codeword 'Rose', I am unable to say anything specific any more. The accused said something like: 'The U-boat Command (BdU) is chasing us out into the sea without giving us enough defensive weapons.'

The accused was of the opinion that we would lose this war for sure, but the English and the Americans would prevent Bolshevism from conquering Europe. He disdained propaganda and claimed the people would no longer believe in propaganda, nor would they continue to be influenced by it. They were only interested in facts now.

I know for sure that the accused did tune in and listened to foreign radio stations. I have the definite impression that the accused rejects the Third Reich and all of the connected or associated organizations!

Third Witness Meyer: My name is Heinrich Meyer, I am 21 years old, Roman Catholic, lieutenant j.g. serving as commander of U-287 in the 24th U-boat Flotilla. At the time in question, I was second watch officer aboard U-154 during the first war patrol under the accused. I am not related in any way with the accused.

To the facts: We did discuss the general political situation several times. The accused always had a completely different opinion. I have been a member of the Hitler Youth. As far as I know, the accused belonged instead to the '*Bündische*' Youth organization. He once stated that the *Führer* had a morbid ambition and also had attacks too. He knew this from an absolutely reliable source.

I recall that the picture of the *Führer* had been hanging in the officers' mess section. But suddenly it had disappeared and was replaced by another picture showing a sailing ship.

Fourth Witness Kirchammer: My name is Hellmuth Kirchammer, I am 19 years old, Roman Catholic, I am a senior midshipman currently assigned to the command of the U-boat Torpedo Training School in Flensburg. I am not related with the accused in any way.

Regarding the facts: I had the impression that the accused is anti-Nazi in his views. During various conversations one noticed this. Once he told us midshipmen we ought to form our own opinions, and these should not be influenced by propaganda. The executive officer did tell us differently afterwards.

Fifth Witness Fröhlich: My name is Horst Fröhlich, I am 19 years old, Protestant, a senior midshipman, currently assigned to the command of the Anti-aircraft Training School Number 7 in

Swinemünde. I am not related in any way with the accused.

Regarding the facts: I did not hear any discussions of the commander regarding the *Führer*. On one occasion, while serving as helmsman, I overheard the commander having arguments with the directing engineer. However, what was said and argued about, I do not recall any more, as I was too occupied as helmsman with staying on the ordered course during the heavy seas and weather.

The accused once told us midshipmen that we ought to form our own opinions and should not let ourselves become influenced unduly by the usual government propaganda. Afterwards the executive officer called us aside and told us that we should not pay too much attention to anything the commander told us.

Sixth Witness Winter: My name is Werner Winter, I am 31 years old, Protestant and lieutenant-commander. At present I am the commander of the 1st U-boat Flotilla in Brest. I am not related to the accused.

Regarding the matter at hand: To the facts under consideration and in dispute I am unable to say anything as I was never on U-154. Otherwise, I can only say that I am able to give the accused the highest grade of recommendations. When we on U-103 talked in the officers' section about politics at times, he was always just as positive in his views and opinions as the rest of the officers aboard U-103.

Seventh Witness Janssen: My name is Gustav Adolf Janssen, I am 28 years old, Protestant, I am a naval lieutenant and commander of U-103. I am not related to the accused in any way.

Regarding the facts: To the case under consideration and review I am unable to say anything at all because I was never on U-154. While he served on U-103 the accused always made the very best impression on me. In fact I can tell you that he was a top officer in every respect and can only say good things about him.

Then the written statement under oath of Lieutenant j.g. of the Reserves Arno Funke was read by the prosecutor, as he was unable to appear in person. His affidavit had been taken while he was under oath on 20 January in Lorient and his deposition is reflected on Pages 7 to 9 of the indictment.

The accused declared in this regard: I shall not give any explanation or make any comments on this statement by Funke.

Then Breinig, the prosecutor: Read off a teletyped message he had just received through the local office of the Gestapo from their office in Berlin Charlottenburg, that Kusch had already been under observation by them for several years, as a suspect still having connections with the former '*Bündische*' Youth groups, a long since prohibited and therefore illegal organization.

Once all the evidence listed had been produced, presented and discussed fully, the prosecutor was heard once more, and spoke about particular legal points and details.

Neither of the military *Beisitzer* judges asked any questions, nor did they talk at all during the entire hearings.

The prosecutor requested the following:

> Because of sedition and undermining of the fighting ability: 10 years' imprisonment, plus the loss of the ability to be allowed to serve in the armed forces, and the complete loss of all civil rights and individual privileges. On account of listening without authorization to foreign radio broadcasts: 1 year's imprisonment. Combined penalty being requested: 10 years and 6 months in prison.

The defence attorney made his presentation, but did not make specific requests nor an application for reconsideration. The accused was then asked if he had anything to add in his defence or wished to offer further information.
He stated: Nothing to add or say.

Now that the accused had had the final word, the court withdrew for deliberation and consultation.

After the court's return from these deliberations, which required forty-three minutes, the court's presiding judge Hagemann announced the following judgement:

Sentence: By unanimous FdU court decision and determination:

> In the name of the German People:
> By reading the formula of the sentencing and disclosure of the essential points of the judgement and the reason for same in the presence of the accused:
> The accused is being sentenced on account of sedition and continuous and repeated undermining of Germany's fighting ability and the prohibited listening to foreign radio stations repeatedly, to:
> DEATH
> and additionally to one year of imprisonment.
> Furthermore, he will be denied the privilege of serving further in the armed forces and all civilian rights for the rest of his life.

The presiding judge advised the accused that this sentence and judgement would only become final once reviewed by the *Führer* personally and confirmed by him. The clock on the courtroom wall indicated 17.54.

ADDENDUM: [handwritten addition]
File to be destroyed in 1975.

When the unexpected death sentence was passed on Oskar Kusch, he had not shown any noticeable emotion. Even his defence counsel, Meyer-Grieben, was surprised, indeed highly astonished. Oskar Kusch just rose, saluted and requested permission from the court to say farewell to his friends and the witnesses in court testifying for him.

But since the disliked field police had already entered the courtroom to take Kusch away, he was only able to shake hands with and thank the senior midshipmen Fröhlich and Kirchammer for their honesty and support, wishing them the best of luck in the future.

Witness Heinrich Meyer approached Abel, who had not bothered to obtain his permission to include him in his report, saying rather angrily, 'You had no right whatever to include me without my advance agreement in your report on Kusch!' Abel went red in the face and shouted back at Meyer that he was compelled by naval regulations and obliged by the general laws in effect to bring Meyer into the case, with or without his consent.

Now Meyer really got angry, and shouted back that Abel should in future mind his own personal and dirty business and never again bring Meyer into it. Least of all to denounce a fellow naval officer with an outstanding and clean record, and kill him. Then he just turned around and walked off the court's premises.

Winter and Janssen were not given the chance to say anything to Kusch, not even farewell.

It was unusual that a deliberating military court would totally reject the sentence requested by the prosecuting judge advocate (Breinig) and alter it substantially. They usually considered mitigating circumstances instead, and if possible reduced or adjusted the sentence requested.

Therefore it was imperative to ferret out what actually transpired during the court's closed deliberations. Why and at whose demand was the jail sentence changed to a death sentence? Because this was not recorded and reflected in any way in the court's protocol or the court file.

However, it was possible to ascertain that during the court's withdrawal, Judge Advocate Hagemann overturned the prosecutor's initial request for a prison term. Records were discovered explaining why Hagemann did this. He had telephoned the Navy's chief judge advocate in Berlin, *Admiralsrichter* Peter Paul Becker, to consult him on the Kusch case judgement.

Becker pointed out to him a recently approved law for civilians that would soon apply for military personnel also:

'In all political cases where the *Führer* Adolf Hitler is personally insulted, degraded or slandered in any low-grade way . . . only the Death Penalty will be appropriate.'

While not yet formally included in the naval legal regulations, this was under way and should already be accepted as a definite order.

Hagemann announced this information from Berlin, somewhat to the surprise of several participants in the deliberations, including Breinig, who was unaware of this new law imposed by the Nazi political administration on the Navy. Dittmers stated that if this was the case, they really had no alternative except to fully comply under the prevailing circumstances and change the sentence. Breinig agreed, saying that they clearly had to go along with the new regulations from Berlin.

But Hagemann did not include or incorporate this reasoning from Berlin in the protocol, nor did he reflect it anywhere in writing, because Judge Advocate Becker had cautioned him to only verbally inform the court members and not put anything in writing before the new naval regulations had been printed.

Naval Judge Advocate Ernst Meinert, who had been present during the hearings and the deliberations, likewise went along without objection.

Meinert, who was responsible for Kusch's custody after the trial, kept him in close confinement and as isolated as possible from visitors and occurrences in the outside world. Meinert allowed Kusch's mother only a single visit, and Inge von Foris, Kusch's bride, another single visit in jail. Apart from Kusch's defence lawyer, all other requests to see him were rejected by Meinert, including several requests by naval classmates of his and other personal friends. Meinert censored and restricted Kusch's mail and correspondence, and confiscated many of his letters to prevent them reaching the people they were addressed to, claiming that security reasons made it essential to hold Kusch practically incommunicado.

As indicated in the trial record, the two military *Beisitzer* judges did not open their mouths even once during the hearings. But they talked in the closed session afterwards. Dittmers declared his agreement with Hagemann's unexpected demand without any objections. Westphalen felt Dittmers, as senior officer, should carry the can and take full responsibility. Westphalen thought Kusch did not defend himself effectively and that his defence counsel should have asked for a review of the judgement and a change to probationary service in a penal unit in the lowest service grade.

However, Hagemann had rejected such a possibility out of hand because Kusch had personally insulted Adolf Hitler, the German *Führer* and supreme commander, in the most degrading way. Therefore no mitigating circumstances could be considered. Berlin had instructed him clearly in that respect.

CHAPTER TEN

The Aftermath

Before Winter returned to Brest, he wrote a long personal letter to Dönitz, pointing out that he had attended Kusch's trial, that a couple of things happened which hardly made sense and were contrary to standing naval regulations, and that the Kusch case should be fully reviewed. Actually, he suggested a new trial ought to be set up, where the various shortcuts and errors would be avoided and both the defence counsel and the witnesses would be allowed more time for preparation. Furthermore, the court had refused to hear any crew members of U-154, and rejected as witnesses senior petty officers and petty officers. Winter therefore respectfully requested that Dönitz authorize a retrial, once he had made himself familiar with the file. U-boat officers were quite furious about the case, even though it had been made a Super-secret Command Matter.

A large part of Abel's report consisted of hearsay and rumours, while evidence, facts and confirmation of specifics were totally amiss. Winter suggested that the Kusch case could generate more problems and future complaints within the U-boat Command.

Many commanders and officers grumbled that the U-boat Command had become far too remote from the front since moving to Berlin. This growing distance could turn more problematical yet. Only somebody who had been very close to Dönitz would be in a position to write such a letter.

Dönitz replied after a long delay that he was unable to do anything in the Kusch case, because he could not change the laws and regulations. All legal reviewers insisted that no exception must be made in the Kusch case. However, Hermann Göring would review the sentence once more in the near future. The matter had been taken out of his hands.

Gustav Adolf Janssen went even further. He had ascertained where Dönitz was expected to be during the next few days. Janssen had recently transferred U-103 to Germany to be used as a school and training U-boat, because of her age and poor mechanical state. He was informed that Dönitz was inspecting the U-boat bases in France, ending in Lorient. Janssen managed to find some reason for a trip to Lorient, which was plausible because U-103 had been based there so long.

Janssen had been posted to the original BdU U-boat Command staff at the beginning of the war, as coordinating signal control officer and, for some time, as Dönitz's adjutant. So Janssen also knew Dönitz personally very well. He had just been told he was to take command of one of the new Type XXI electro U-boats, U-3037, in the near future.

As Hitler had forbidden Dönitz to use his Ju 52 aircraft for any flights outside Germany itself, Dönitz now made his inspection visits with his special armoured Mercedes car, driven by *Obermaat* (Petty Officer) Prior. Dönitz had never driven a car himself. By that time of the war, motor travel within France or Italy took place only at night. During the daytime, Allied fighter planes shot up every moving vehicle they caught sight of. Janssen greeted Dönitz and mentioned he was due to return to Germany, but that the trains were now so unreliable and were constantly attacked by aircraft.

Dönitz immediately told Janssen to be ready at 22.30, and he could ride with him back to Germany, where he could make better connections. Dönitz seemed glad to have a chance to talk to one of his old band of U-boat officers. The car reached the Rhine valley in Germany early the next morning. But if Dönitz had hoped to get some sleep *en route*, Janssen made this impossible. All night long he talked about the Kusch case, about the incredible legal manipulations, about the arbitrary limitation of witnesses, about the considerable amount of hearsay evidence presented, suggesting to Dönitz that he should schedule a review and arrange for a retrial, as the case might well do a lot of harm to his relations with the U-boat commanders at the front.

Janssen talked and talked and talked until his throat became dry. But Dönitz made only vague promises and remained uncertain about the case. Naturally, Janssen had to be quite careful what he said. Dönitz was getting irritated about his insistence, and then became quite furious, but Janssen just did not give up. Dönitz finally told him, when he stepped out of the car, 'This is very decent of you, Janssen, to stand up so firmly for your former officer. Friends are rather rare these days! I shall ask to talk face to face to your boy, whom I do not know myself, to look deep into his heart and test him thoroughly. Then we shall see what will be possible and what the next step will be'.

Janssen was happy that he had managed this concession from Dönitz. Though dead tired, he felt he could not have done less for Kusch, whom he considered not only as his former watch officer, but as a reliable and good friend. While he had reservations about such verbal promises, he hoped that Dönitz would stick to his word. But once Dönitz got back to Camp Koralle in Berlin Bernau and the often unrealistic, hypocritical and servile atmosphere that prevailed there, he evidently forgot his promises to Janssen.

Here Judge Advocate Rudolphi ruled the legal bureaucracy firmly. Rudolphi repeatedly pointed out to Warzecha and Dönitz that the *Führer* himself had been insulted and crudely besmirched by Kusch, and consequently no mitigating circumstances could be considered. Dönitz got cold feet and once more became wavering und undecided. Instead of ordering a new trial to take place in Lorient, he stalled and postponed making any decision. The Kusch file passed several times backwards and forwards between the desks of Warzecha, Rudolphi and Dönitz, with Dönitz asking Warzecha to review it once more, while Warzecha refused to sign the final decision and insisted Dönitz himself had to sign that decision, not Warzecha, regardless of what the final outcome would be – clemency, a retrial, any kind of pardon, or the confirmation of the death penalty.

Other more urgent matters buried the Kusch file on Dönitz's desk, and things were held in abeyance for almost two months. However, during this time Rösing and Godt called on Dönitz several times, demanding that no exception of any kind be made in the Kusch case, insisting that his execution should be confirmed. Eventually, supported by von Friedeburg, too, they wanted to set a warning example for all U-boat commanders.

While it is surprising that Dönitz had never become acquainted with Kusch, this has been verified as correct. Kusch had seen and heard Dönitz during several U-boat crew inspections in Lorient, but only from a distance, and never spoken to him personally in any way about operational matters as a U-boat commander.

Now, when U-boat commanders, especially newly appointed U-boat commanders about to leave on their first war patrol, were asked to report to Camp Koralle, they rarely had a chance to talk to Dönitz any more, but were briefly instructed by Godt and then turned over to one or two of the staff officers. Dönitz, known at one time as either 'Uncle Karl' or 'The Lion', had turned into another 'High Brasshat', constantly tied up with other matters.

One must marvel at the courage of Janssen and Winter and admire their insistence and determination to help Kusch. When there were delays in getting a response, both officers approached Godt at Camp Koralle several times, informing him about the various errors and legal manipulations during the Kusch trial and the obvious shortcuts taken during the pre-trial investigation. Winter told Godt the entire Kusch case had been mishandled from the very start for political considerations, had been unseemly rushed and the facts had been twisted. Under the circumstances, a complete retrial would be the only fair and reasonable way to handle this case for future considerations.

When, following up on their efforts, Winter and Janssen called on Godt once more on 11 May 1944, to present their views firmly, Godt promised them he would recommend a retrial and complete review of the Kusch case.

However, Kusch's execution had been confirmed by Hermann Göring on 10 April, and the file had been returned to the Navy a few days later, descending the bureaucratic naval ladder step by step. The official naval order to shoot Kusch had been issued on 3 May 1944, and had been seen by Godt before it was forwarded to Kiel.

Furthermore, with Godt's pressure on Dönitz to execute Kusch, it is hard to reach any other conclusion except that Godt had paid only hypocritical lip service to Winter and Janssen, even twenty-four hours before Kusch's execution, unless Godt simply lied for his own personal convenience, to get Winter and Janssen out of his hair. Because the Navy executed Oskar Kusch under cover of total secrecy and without any kind of announcement, the next day, 12 May 1944.

In the U-boat Personnel Bureau, Lieutenant-Commander Harald Jeppener-Haltenhoff, the detailer for U-boat officers in Kiel, who had attended the Kusch trial as an observer, was shocked that any U-boat officer would denounce his commander in such a conspiratorial way. He could not understand why Kusch had never contacted him directly, or through Captain Kals in Lorient, to have that sorry lot of U-154's officers promptly replaced, stating: 'Even in the worst of Nazi times, there has been general acceptance of the saying, "The most despicable bastard in the land is and remains the political denouncer!" I would never have anticipated such abominable behaviour on the part of any naval officer, including any Reserve officer.'

When the various highly placed legal specialists in Berlin kept pointing out that the *Führer* was both entitled as well as destined to review each and every case where a German officer had been condemned to death, Dönitz decided to reject any pardon and to pass the file to Hitler for a final decision.

However, Judge Advocate Rudolphi came up with an emergency release by Hitler's headquarters stating that any case where the *Führer* had been personally insulted and grossly slandered should be passed to *Reichsmarschall* Hermann Göring, whom Hitler had appointed as his deputy, for a final review, the reason being that one should shield the *Führer* from such matters, which would only upset and aggravate him strongly and should be avoided.

Therefore, both Dönitz and Rudolphi finally put their initials on the file and asked Warzecha to deliver the Kusch file to *Feldmarschall* Wilhelm Keitel at Hitler's Army HQ, in order to submit it to Hermann Göring for review and final determination.

Göring, largely responsible for the technical and operational decisions of the *Luftwaffe*, including many errors of considerable consequence, lived like a medieval king in his special train not very far from Hitler's headquarters, the 'Wolf's Lair' armed camp, near Rastenburg in East Prussia.

Keitel, always eager to keep Hitler in a passable mood, was immediately convinced that this was the right way to proceed, and called the chief of the *Luftwaffe*'s legal department, Ministerial Director Dr jur. Christian von Hammerstein, who was the legal adviser of Göring as chief of the *Luftwaffe*. Von Hammerstein handled his required paperwork and reportedly studied the file superficially, as naval peculiarities and shipboard conditions were alien to him.

In this way, the Kusch file reached Göring's desk on 10 April 1944, together with a prepared decision for Göring to sign, accompanied by a legal evaluation in a condensed note suggesting there was no reason for Göring to issue a pardon or commutation of the naval court's decision and to confirm the rejection of any such possibility without further explanations. Göring, habitually lazy, signed.

In this way the death penalty had literally been rubber-stamped all the way, without anybody really looking at the facts. Significantly, Dönitz, Godt and Rösing had in this way managed not to be finally responsible for Kusch's execution in any direct way.

The conclusive review order read:

> CERTIFIED COPY:
> The *Reichsmarschall* of the Great German Reich
> 10 April 1944
> To the Chief of the High Command of the Armed Forces:
> Reference: Confirmation and consideration for review and mercy of the judgement by the court of the Leader of the Regional U-boat Command Western Region, dated 26 January 1944, issued for sedition and continued undermining of the ability to sustain our capability to fight, sentenced to death:
> And due to listening and passing on of news broadcasts of foreign and prohibited radio stations condemned to one year of imprisonment and also the loss of the honour to serve in the military forces and permanent loss of all civilian rights and honours:
>
> > Naval Lieutenant j.g. Oskar Kusch
> > commander of U-154 of the 2nd U-boat Flotilla.
>
> I herewith confirm this judgement.
> I reject and decline any possibility of reconsideration or mercy.
> The death sentence is to be carried out.
> Signed: H. Göring
> The chief of the High Command of the Armed Forces
> Signed: W. Keitel
> [seal of the OKW Command]

When this order arrived in Kiel by teletype, Judge Advocate Meinert, Kusch's custodian, took over the handling of all further requirements.

Owing to a sudden shortage of single cells, Kusch for a few days had been given a cellmate, who was the first human being with whom he was able to talk for an extended period of time without restrictions or censorship. This was Senior Midshipman Karl Hans Seemann, whose trial had been invalidated and who was waiting for a second trial. After a while, the second trial was cancelled and Seemann was suddenly released.

As soon as the Kusch file had been returned to Dönitz, a copy of Göring's final decision was teletyped to von Friedeburg, Godt and Rösing, then passed along to Meinert, who would be responsible for setting all requirements for Kusch's execution in motion and issuing the necessary paperwork, including the actual execution order.

Protocol and report of the announcement of his time of execution to Oskar Kusch on 11 May 1944.
Naval Detention Jail, Kiel-Wik at 21.30
Present:
Marineoberstabsrichter Meinert [naval judge advocate]
Attorney Meyer-Grieben
Telephone: 14676
[added by hand by *Marineoberstabsrichter* Meinert afterwards]
In the Navy Detention Jail appeared under guard the *Oberleutnant zur See* Oskar Kusch.
He was informed that the sentence and judgement passed on him on 26 January 1944 has been confirmed in place of the *Führer* by *Reichsmarschall* Hermann Göring. The *Reichsmarschall* has refused any consideration of clemency and has ordered the execution as a consequence. Furthermore, this execution will take place tomorrow, 12 May 1944 at 06.30.
When asked if he had anything to say or declare on the subject, the condemned stated:
    NO, NOTHING.
[signed by the prisoner] Oskar Kusch
confirming that he understood this order:
Meinert [full signature]

Naval Judge Advocate Meinert only permitted Oskar Kusch one single and final letter either to his mother or to his father, but not both.

As soon as Meinert had informed him of his execution, Kusch wrote to his father as follows:

Kiel, MUG (Naval Investigative Jail)
    12 May 1944 at 01.30
    Dear Dad,
    All hopes have come to nothing! The judgement will be carried out today at 06.30. I find it difficult to write to you under the pressure of the last walk ahead of me. Unfortunately, we were unable to talk together for a last time, but in view of the imminence of death there is really very little to say. Life could have been great, but a senseless fate has torn it to pieces. Thus I can only wish you in this moment all the best for the future. In my thoughts I am with you and wish to thank you once more deeply for all the love and support that you have always extended to me. It is rather hard and wretched for me during these last hours when I only think about you now, your huge pain and also the future that I shall no longer experience.

All that is now gone for ever and lost for good. My dear Dad, please forgive me if I ever hurt you unintentionally.

It is so sad that fate has caused us this end against our wishes. Please accept herewith my most sincere greetings and deeply felt thanks for everything you have done for me. I shall always be with you in spirit, until it is possible to be connected again or reunited somewhere sometime. Regardless of circumstances, you, nevertheless, had always the top place in my heart that you wanted to have. It was the restlessness of youth that drove me around in circles. To catch up on things we have missed is now no longer possible for lack of time. Kindly accept it as if it did happen, nevertheless. I embrace you, press your hands and I shall be your faithful son for ever and ever eternally. Yours, Oskar

This letter was forwarded to Heinz Kusch, together with the shipment of Oskar Kusch's few personal belongings that Meinert had permitted Kusch to keep with him in the Kiel naval prison.

The recorded protocol of the actual execution of Kusch follows:

> Naval Shooting Range, Kiel-Holtenau, 12 May 1944.
> Report for the Record:
> With respect to the carrying out of the death penalty on *Oberleutnant z.S.* Oskar Kusch from the 2nd U-boat Flotilla Command
> The following were present:
>
> > Lieutenant, Naval Coastal Artillery, Wilhelm Gerdes, *Kapitänleutnant M.A.* [name added by hand]
> > As the leading officer
> > *Marineoberstabsrichter* Meinert
> > As judge-advocate and acting judge
> > *Marine Oberassistenzarzt der Reserve,*
> > Bloebaum MD [name added by hand]
> > As medical officer
> > *Marinepfarrer* [naval chaplain] Lucht
> > As military chaplain
>
> In addition a platoon of the naval watch and security company was standing by to act.
> The accused was positioned at 06.30 on the place of execution. The standby unit of the firing squad stood still, with rifles at the ready. The Judge read to the condemned the judgement once more and also the confirmation of his sentence, and then asked him if he had anything further to say or declare. The condemned stated:

NO [added by hand]

The chaplain was given a last opportunity to offer encouragement.
The firing squad of ten men had positioned themselves five paces
away from the condemned, facing him.
The order to fire was given at 06.32 [added by hand]
The medical officer present confirmed the death at 06.37 [added by
hand]
The body was immediately put into a wooden naval casket for
removal from the place of execution.
Gerdes, *Kapitänleutnant MA* [full signature]
Lieutenant Naval Coastal Artillery
Bloebaum MD [full signature]
Marine Oberassistenzarzt d.R.
Meinert [full signature]
Marineoberstabsrichter

This preparatory form for execution was entirely preprinted, with only the
names and titles left open and the signatures added as applicable. The three
times: 06.30, 06.32 and 06.37 were left blank on the form and filled in by
hand. In other words, this was a piece of paper frequently used by the Navy,
because otherwise it would not have been worthwhile to have it printed in
tear-out books. This was not a form used only occasionally.

Incomplete records of the shooting gallery in Kiel Holtenau confirm that
more than forty naval men were executed there alone by naval firing squads
during the Second World War.

On 18 May 1944, the following notification was received in the mail by
Kusch's father in Berlin:

The Court of the Higher Commander
of U-boat Training Kiel, 12 May 1944
GEHEIM [SECRET]
To: Director Heinz Kusch   Berlin Schöneberg

Berchtesgadener Strasse 26

The judgement against Lieutenant j.g. Oskar Kusch on account of
the misdeeds that he committed, passed on 26 January 1944 by a
naval court martial, the death penalty, has been carried out after
confirmation by the pertinent higher court's review, on 12 May
1944.
Announcement of the death or obituaries and notifications in any
form in newspapers, magazines or any type of publications is strictly
forbidden!

J. A. Meinert [signature], *Marineoberstabsrichter*
Authenticated/Certified by:
[name and signature illegible], *Marinehilfsjustizinspektor*

There was also a preprinted note attached reading:
> The wearing of black ribbons or black armbands on outer clothing
> in public is prohibited, as this could generate questions from other
> folk. Recipient will be notified in time, where the urn with the
> remains will be placed and information will be received as to the final
> disposal including handling expenses. These will be billed separately
> in the near future, at the actual cost for the Naval Disposal Service.
> Heil Hitler!
> [Illegible signature by means of a worn-out rubber stamp]

After cremation in Kiel, the remains of Oskar Kusch were buried on 24 June
1944 in the general cemetery of the city of Kiel. They were placed in the
public field for urns, Field Section 14 and Gravesite Number 631.

In order to understand the difficulties for the defence, which the naval courts
and judge advocates tried to increase as much as possible, it is imperative to
know more about the inside of naval court policies and the permanent directions given to the naval judge advocates.

In the first year of the war, on 29 December 1939, the legal department
of the Naval High Command in Berlin had already issued the following
directions and guidelines for naval judge advocates: At a time when our best
men are killed in action at the front for our fatherland and victory, it is incomprehensible to the people why we would at the same time preserve
cowards, saboteurs and shirkers in our jails, so that they survive.

Furthermore, when the above instructions were distributed to all judge
advocates and the various courts, there was forwarded to them another over-
riding guideline from the director of the armed forces' central department
for legal affairs, Rudolf Lehmann, reading as follows:

> It is not the task of any court, nor the job of any judge, to search diligently
> for the truth, which frequently does not even exist in a definite and specific
> way. It is instead the purpose of any military court to protect the interests
> of the entire people and with its decisions and determinations to conserve
> and protect this common interest of the people, if necessary with force,
> tenacity and all means at the disposal of the military courts. Especially
> necessary, it appears, is the most severe and merciless sentencing of any
> individual who has already acted contrary to this common spirit of the
> German people.

These guidelines were sharpened by a follow-up directive issued by Admiral
Warzecha in February 1942, for all naval courts and judge advocates:

Our military courts have a directing function, and this in two different ways: they are a tool of the general government policies and aims and intentions, and they protect all political directions of the state with the full rigour of the harshest punishment, in order to shield and safeguard the government's purposes in all areas of life.

But in addition to these requirements and beyond their limits, the military courts are basically different from civilian courts and their procedures, because they are also a tool of the military leadership whenever it is imperative to demonstrate the need for such an instrument of power and execution.

Kusch's rejection of the Nazis, the *Führer* Adolf Hitler and the type of people connected with the Nazi Party and what they had made out of Germany, was based on his upbringing and liberal education and his respect for individual freedom, dignity and a humane view of other people.

Though often warned by his friends, Kusch had absolute confidence in the traditional and long-existing comradeship among naval officers, where an open and candid exchange of ideas and information was considered normal, customary and safe; where, until Abel stepped out of line, nobody had ever been denounced before for purely political points and matters.

Here is what happened to these denouncers, Abel and Druschel. Abel finished the various training courses for prospective U-boat commanders in the Baltic at the end of March 1944. On 1 April 1944, he was appointed the new commander of the Type IX-C U-boat U-193. She had been commissioned by Lieutenant-Commander Hans Pauckstadt on 10 December 1942, and captained by him until he brought her into Lorient on 24 February 1944. Pauckstadt was relieved as commander a few days later, and promoted to commander of the 8th U-boat Flotilla in Danzig instead.

Consequently, he did not meet Abel, nor was he able to transfer anything to him. As soon as Abel reached Lorient at the beginning of April, he insisted on taking over command of U-193 immediately and officially. The repairs required for U-193 were substantial, and the overhaul lengthy, and it was only finished on 21 April 1944.

On 23 April U-193 departed from Lorient with Abel as commander, but was never heard from again. For several years, there had been assumptions that U-193 hit a British air mine in the Bay of Biscay, or that she was bombed to pieces near the delta of the Loire river west of Nantes. But this was due to a mix-up in radio signals. Eventually it was concluded that U-193 was lost with all hands because of a diving accident or some technical mishap, but the actual cause was never determined. U-193 was posted as missing, presumed lost, for a long time.

One of the old hands in the Keroman U-boat pen complex, who had known Abel and had dealt with him, commented on the loss this way: 'Good riddance to that bastard Abel. What a pity that another fifty-eight good men had to share his fate.'

Druschel remained the directing engineer of U-154 under her fourth commander, Gerth Gemeiner. U-154 departed on her seventh war patrol on

31 January 1943 and operated off the Panama Canal and in the Caribbean Sea, but did not see any targets and returned without sinkings to Lorient on 28 April 1943.

On 20 June 1943, Gemeiner left Lorient with U-154 on her final war patrol, with the mid-Atlantic as her initial operational area.

The Tenth Fleet decoding room in Washington DC put the hunter-killer task force group of the auxiliary aircraft-carrier *Croatan* with four destroyers on the track of U-154, based upon intercepted operational instructions from the U-boat Command to U-154, by means of the Ultra system. U-154 was located west of Madeira on 2 July 1944, but managed to escape once more and get away.

Yet on the next day, 3 July, U-154 was found again by the task force destroyers *Frost* and *Inch* of the *Croatan* group, and sunk with depth-charges with all fifty-seven men aboard.

The third denouncer, Funke, made the seventh war patrol of U-154 as executive officer under her new commander. Funke was transferred to the prospective commander's training courses after that patrol. He finished last of all participants but was allowed to repeat the courses, owing to his age and long seafaring experience. Otherwise he would have been washed out. Funke had been unable to handle the required reports and related paperwork on account of his low-quality school education. However, again he barely managed to pass, and he was judged to be incapable of becoming the commander of any U-boat for the time being.

Consequently Funke was posted aboard U-2536, a brand-new Type XXI electro U-boat, as understudy commander in training. U-2536 was commanded by Lieutenant j.g.Ulrich Vöge, who was sixteen years younger than Funke and not thrilled about Funke's addition to his crew. Funke served on U-2536 from March 1945, during the initial trials and tests in the Baltic. But U-2536 could not finish these exercises and was scuttled near Laboe on 3 May 1945. The entire crew was placed in prisoner-of-war camps, except Funke, who as an old Nazi Party member had somehow obtained forged identity papers and disappeared without trace in the prevailing confusion.

CHAPTER ELEVEN

Skating on
Ever Thinner Ice

W hen Oskar Kusch was executed, the final year of the Second World War and the War at Sea came into sight, in fact with a rapidly accelerating pace. Therefore, it is important to bring the reader up to date on the true situation which prevailed in the sixth year of the war with respect to the U-boat war, because the official government propaganda became constantly more ideological and tended towards gross misrepresentation of the truth in the crassest way. This was not limited to the noisy Nazi propaganda machine, but applied almost equally to the Allied powers, too, particularly the Soviet Union.

Until 1941 Dönitz had not permitted any U-boat officer, no matter how experienced and competent, to become the commander of a U-boat unless he was at least 25 years old. Since then circumstances had forced him to make changes in these inflexible restrictions. In 1942, the first Reserve officers had moved up and become U-boat commanders. In addition to Reserve officers, an increasing number of *Kriegs Offiziere*, or KOs, were given commissions for the duration of the war and started to be promoted to command U-boats. Most of them were former senior petty or warrant officers.

Gradually, more and more former watch officers became U-boat commanders, with shorter and less extensive front experience. This resulted automatically in less-qualified commanders, but also frequently younger ones too. By 1944 it was not exceptional to see U-boat commanders who were 21 or 22 years old.

In order to overcome the shortage of qualified executive line officers to some extent, former special branch officers were induced to undergo navigational training courses and supplementary weapons training, especially for torpedoes, to convert them from technical weapons specialist, administrative/paymaster officer or even coastal artillery officer into executive officers. Such officers increasingly became U-boat commanders during 1944 and

1945. Many lacked sufficient seamanship experience, apart from actual U-boat combat experience.

Most petty officers and enlisted men greatly disliked this trend, but they were likewise promoted faster and with less experience and training. Therefore, a reduction in operational and combat ability could not be avoided. The British, and soon the Americans, did not fail to observe these changes, and swiftly drew their own conclusions.

While Germany had eventually managed to build new U-boats in growing numbers, their technology was largely unchanged. Lack of special alloys and rare metals, like copper, more and more required 'ersatz' materials for both original and spare parts. This resulted in soaring maintenance complications with torpedo tubes, anti-aircraft guns and virtually everything else, with more frequent malfunctions or operational disorders, particularly when equipment was most needed, in combat. There were growing shortages of specialized lubricants, wearing out machinery parts sooner and more frequently, no matter how hard the technical men worked at keeping equipment and machinery in working order. Eventually, even fuel became short.

At the end of 1932, the German Navy had fewer than 1,200 active officers in all branches, including engineering and shipbuilding specialists, and medical as well as administrative officers. This was a smaller number of officers than even the restrictive Treaty of Versailles had authorized. And so it is easy to understand how the rapid growth of the naval officer corps was influenced by these different factors.

Since the U-boat Command had been reactivated in 1934/5, with Captain Karl Dönitz appointed as its director, until April 1945, a total of 1,418 naval officers had passed the different training courses for prospective U-boat commanders, and had qualified to take over the command of a U-boat.

A total of 538 of these officers died in wartime operations, and another twenty-seven were killed in accidents while on duty or committed suicide. Two, Oskar Kusch and Heinz Hirsacker (Crew 1934), who had commanded U-572, were executed.

Naturally, quite a few commanders received their training before the war started, and they were used in shore positions during the war, for health reasons or age, though some did still command school and training U-boats in the Baltic. Others commanded only U-tankers or pure supply and transport U-boats, not equipped for combat operations, or U-boats operating in geographical areas where no sinkings could be achieved. Quite a few commanded U-boats only used for weather reporting or reconnaissance war patrols.

At the beginning of the war U-boat construction was slow, and until 1941 did not replace the combat losses in the Atlantic. Thereafter, Admiral von Friedeburg brought additional shipyards into the construction programme, and the numbers were forced up sharply. Eventually, 1,167 U-boats of the different types were built and commissioned, and fifteen foreign submarines were taken over and placed into service, mostly as training U-boats.

But only 859 U-boats made actual war patrols. From these, 603 were lost at sea through hostile actions. A further twenty were lost for unknown reasons. Seven had to be scuttled or decommissioned after collisions at sea or similar accidents. Eighty-one U-boats were destroyed in various German shipyards or ports by Allied bombing attacks. Thirty-five U-boats were decommissioned because of old age or serious combat damage. Lastly, eleven U-boats that could no longer reach their bases became interned in neutral ports after battle damage, but some of these were sold or turned over to foreign navies.

From all U-boats making war patrols, 429, or fifty per cent, were sunk with their entire crews, while 215 U-boats, or twenty-five per cent of those undertaking war operations, were lost on their very first war patrol.

After the summer of 1943, the only U-boats that had a chance to succeed were those on single, clandestine activities, which had been the original purpose of all submarine operations. The stubborn adherence to outdated operations, combined with the short-leash handling by Dönitz with the excessive radio signalling required for this, played directly into the hands of the British, and later the Americans, who had cracked the Enigma codes and often read such signals faster than the U-boats themselves.

Thus, Ultra turned out the biggest killer, followed by the various short-wave (centimetre) radar-sonar systems and the High-Frequency Direction-Finding Equipment ('Huff-Duff', for short).

Moreover, for practical purposes ever faster aircraft made U-boat operations an impossibility in many areas. After that summer of 1943 it was already an accomplishment to return at all from a war patrol, even without sinkings.

Despite the horrible losses, many on their first war patrol, U-boats continued to be built and manned. Once they had been crewed, they were ordered into the Atlantic, the Barents Sea or the Mediterranean BECAUSE THEY WERE AVAILABLE, regardless of whether they had any chances of accomplishing anything.

Instead of dropping the pack operations, outclassed since spring 1943 at the latest, what was pushed without substantial changes was called '*verheizen*' in German, meaning tossing men and ships into the fires under the boilers, frequently sacrificing them.

Whether it made sense or not became totally immaterial. The men and the equipment happened to be available and were therefore utilized, reason, responsibility or logic be damned, not to mention humanitarian grounds, which were ignored by the Nazis, anyway.

The highly skilled U-boat crews were only a drop in the bucket, when one compares the 30,226 dead U-boat men with the more than three million German soldiers killed in Soviet Russia alone. Nevertheless, this represented the highest percentage loss of any armed group in the entire war. Furthermore, 5,038 men became prisoners of war, when they were rescued by Allied ships after their U-boats had been sunk.

In politics in general and in the German Navy in particular, appearances were often more influential and important to many people than the facts. For others, prestige was more essential than getting results. In many respects the Old Russian charade known as 'Potemkin's Villages' had been adopted to keep those in power satisfied and stop them from asking too many undesirable questions. Quite a contrast to the Old Prussian habit, a main point of order in the Imperial German Navy, 'To be more than what one appeared to be', which had been dropped by the Nazi regime as no longer fitting.

Many reports from the front-lines were polished and embellished step by step, as they worked their way up the naval hierarchy, as intermediate people were forced, often in self-defence, to protect their own backs and behinds as much as possible. This is another reason why many German naval documents and files can't be accepted at face value in many cases, and the historian is forced to read between the lines.

By 1944, most people with any brains had concluded that it would be preferable to reach an end of the internal terror, but what kept Hitler and his regime in power much longer than necessary was the 'Unconditional Surrender' slogan that Franklin D. Roosevelt insisted upon and had handed to his favourite reporters at Casablanca in January 1943. This was like water on the dry waterwheel of the Nazis, and it prevented an earlier termination of the war, putting tens of thousands of American soldiers under the ground who should have remained alive.

It was a grievous error to institute such a policy in Europe, no matter how great the headlines that could be generated with this unrealistic demand. Eventually, the sole beneficiary turned out to be Stalin's Soviet Russia.

In this connection, it is interesting to list the various Lend-Lease supply shipments that the British and Americans transported to Soviet Russia, paid for entirely by the English and American taxpayers, including the transport and insurance involved. While the convoys to Murmansk and Arkhangelsk (Archangel) got the press coverage, these were the smaller part of all shipments made.

The Persian Gulf ports in today's Iran and the Siberian port of Vladivostok handled the major percentage of these shipments. The Iranian ports were out of reach of the Axis forces, and Vladivostok was wide open because the Japanese had agreed to observe strict neutrality towards Soviet Russia. The Trans-Siberian railway consequently transported the largest part of the shipments onwards to Moscow and points beyond in Russia.

With food items excluded, the free gift shipments included:

Trucks	376,000
Submachine-Guns	131,633
Jeeps	51,500
Motorcycles	35,000
Aircraft	22,206
Tanks	12,755

Anti-aircraft Guns	8,218
Anti-tank Guns	5,003
Projectiles (shells and ammunition)	473 million
Explosives (various)	350,000 tons

The ships sailing the route to Murmansk and northern Soviet Russia did carry 22.7 per cent of the shipments for Soviet Russia. Many of these supplies were later utilized by the Stalin regime to foster and strengthen the Cold War against America and Great Britain.

Whether one likes it or not, the internationally used measure for the success of submarines is the actual number of ships sunk and the amount of tonnage definitely destroyed by them in wartime operations.

During the entire war at sea, in all ocean areas and by all possible causes, 5,150 ships of all types were lost or damaged to a point that did not make repair practical. The combined tonnage amounted to 21,570,720 tons of shipping, which included accidents and collisions, surface ship and aircraft attacks, losses due to mines or submarines and weather-related losses.

Italian submarines sank in the various areas of their operations a combined total of 714,433 tons, including a few warships.

Japanese submarines managed to sink altogether a confirmed total of 962,961 tons of shipping, including some warships.

German U-boats sank a total of 2,828 ships in all sea areas where they operated, for a combined total tonnage of 14,687,231, including warships.

YEAR	SHIPS	TONS
1939	114	421,156
1940	471	2,186,158
1941	432	2,171,754
1942	1,160	6,266,215
1943	463	2,586,905
1944	132	773,327
1945	56	281,716

The actual German U-boat losses in combat or at sea were as follows:

YEAR	LOSSES
1939	9
1940	23
1941	35
1942	87
1943	242
1944	241
1945	152
Total	789

In addition, 221 U-boats were scuttled by their crews in May 1945, rather than be surrendered at the end of the war. But 166 U-boats were surrendered to the various Allied countries. An additional six U-boats were taken over by Japan in south-east Asia when Germany capitulated, and were incorporated into her navy.

From the 2,828 ships sunk, as listed above, it is remarkable that only thirty U-boat commanders, who managed to sink more than 100,000 tons each, for a combined actual total of 818 ships adding up to 4,495,205 tons, sank more than thirty per cent of the total tonnage. Another twenty-six U-boat commanders each sank more than 75,000 confirmed tons of shipping, amounting to 445 ships and 2,224,508 tons, or more than fifteen per cent of the total combined sinkings. A third group of thirty-two U-boat commanders each sank more than 50,000 confirmed tons for a combined total of 393 ships and 1,983,740 tons, amounting to more than thirteen per cent of the tonnage sunk by all U-boats.

To summarize, eighty-eight U-boat commanders managed to sink altogether 1,656 ships, of 8,703,453 confirmed tons between them, representing just over fifty-nine per cent of the total tonnage sunk.

This confirms clearly and convincingly that the competency, determination and experience of the individual commander was paramount in combat operations, as long as he was supported by a fully trained and experienced crew. One must remember that such abilities were extremely restricted when U-boats had to work within a search group network with rigid directions for almost everything. This became another factor in reducing results whenever wolfpack operations were involved.

A further 449 U-boat commanders did sink some ships, although many of them sank only one or two. However, 881 qualified U-boat commanders did not sink any ships at all.

Quite instructive and significant is the breakdown of sinkings achieved by commanders with different types of U-boat, especially the medium Type VII compared to the large Type IX. This demonstrates clearly that U-boats on single operations were the actual achievers, not the U-boats ordered into U-boat packs, so highly touted by the propaganda people and so strongly supported by Dönitz. Based on numbers of U-boats involved, those operating singly, or at most in very small groups, were mostly those that got the best results.

The different models of the Type VII U-boats, excluding the minelayers and torpedo transport subtypes, built in very small numbers, sank 1,581 ships altogether, a total of 7,394,357 tons. Sinkings by commanders of the various Type VII U-boats were achieved by 343 different officers. Yet, from the Type VII U-boats, a total of 689 were commissioned, though not all of them made war patrols eventually.

However, of the larger Type IX U-boats, excluding the U-cruisers, only 164 were commissioned. Again, not all of them made war patrols. But with these Type IX U-boats, excluding the U-cruisers, 1,098 ships were sunk, with a combined tonnage of 5,768,539. These results were achieved by 128 different commanders.

1. Lorient, February 1943, Oskar Kusch commander *U-154.*

2. The author, Peter C. Hansen, in the spring of 1943 in Lorient-France.

3. Lothar von Arnauld de la Pèriere, summer of 1917. The ace of aces of all submariners in the world to whom this book in dedicated. A true gentleman.

4. Werner Winter, who commanded U-103, while Oskar Kusch was watch officer aboard and attempted to get a retrial for Kusch, but in vain.

5. The author as watch officer trainee in St. Nazaire-France.

5. Training U-boats of a school flotilla in Pillau, East Prussia returning to port after exercises in spite of below freezing conditions.

7. While operating on the surface, the bridge watch acting as look-outs. Watches rotate in four hour shifts around the clock. In rough weather, it was almost impossible to get enough sleep.

. A group of German U-boat officers as prisoners of war in Camp Bowmansville, Canada. The fourth man from the left is Otto Kretschmer, the most successful submariner of the Second World War. Known as 'Silent' Otto, he was captured on the 17 March 1941, when his last U-boat, U-99, was sunk by the British destroyer *Walker*, captained by Commander Donald G. F. W. MacIntyre.

9. Herbert A. Werner, a friend of the author, as commander of *U-953*. He wrote the bestseller '*Iron Coffins*'. Werner also commanded *U-415*, served as executive officer on *U-230* and *U-612* and was aboard *U-557* as midshipman.

10. Günther Hessler, the senior U-boat specialist at the U-boat Command. As commander of *U-107* Hessler sunk 14 steamers, (a total of 86,699 tons), the most successful single war patrol. A man with common sense and the ability to think logically and fairly.

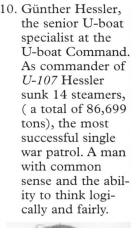

ermann Rasch, mmander of ·106, spring of 42. Later director two-men mini-bmarines of the al (Seehund) type.

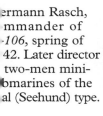

12. Johann 'Jochen' Mohr, commander of *U-124*, spring of 1942. Known as the best looking lieutenant in the German fleet. Killed in action on 3 April 1943.

13. U-572 in heavy seas in the winter of 1941. Her commander at that time, Heinz Hirsacker, was relieved of command and shot by a naval firing squad after being sentenced for cowardice in the face of the enemy for his refusal to enter the Mediterranean through the Straits of Gibraltar.

14. After a ramming by a British destroyer *U-333* reaches La Pallice for repairs. Her commander, Peter-Erich 'Ali' Cremer, discussed his observations at sea with Frank W. Petersen in the Autumn of 1942.

15. Reinhard 'Teddy' Suhren as commander of *U-564* entering Brest. His sign for good luck: three times the black cat. One of the maverick types in the U-boat Command.

The anti-aircraft gun crews of U-309 are awaiting aircraft attacks in August of 1944 while waiting for minesweeper escorts off La Pallice. Commanded by Hans-Gert Mahrholz, she had left Brest a few days ago and Lother G. Buchheim, the author of the bestseller 'The Boat' was also aboard.

. Heinrich Lehmann-Willenbrock, autumn of 1941, commander of *U-96*. The 'Old Man' of Lothar Buchheim's book: '*The Boat*', also made into a film.

aint Nazaire pring of 1943. -226 returning om the fiercest onvoy battles the North tlantic to a wn bombed to mithereens hile they were sea.

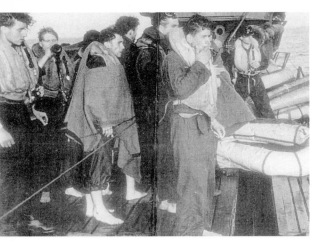

19. On 12 August 1944, *U-891*, commanded by Günther Keller struck a mine of the British air-*Cinnamon* minefield off La Rochelle. Twelve crewmen were killed, but *U-309* rescued 40 cr members and took them aboar where they had to remain on d due to lack of space underdeck *U-891* had left Lorient only five earlier and was scheduled to re in La Pallice. *U-309* was very c. when entering the minefield for rescue, trying hard not to get b up herself while picking up the survivors from the Bay of Bisca

20. Officers' mess of the 11th U-boat flotilla in Bergen, Norway, autumn of 1944. The officially ordered cheerfulness is rather dampened by the constantly increasing number of black framed photos (on the back wall) of those commanders who had died at sea. Everybody had close friends and naval classmates amongst them, who were hard to forget.

21. Recreational activities between war patrols were organized by the onshore st. of the U-boat flotillas in Brittany, using a French countryhouse for barbecuin and 'forget everything' parti

Moreover, the Type IX U-boats were technically more complicated, dived considerably more slowly, were much harder to operate under water, less sturdy and less able to sustain heavy battle damage and survive than the medium Type VIIs. They were also unable to dive as deeply as the medium Type VIIs could.

Consequently, the larger Type IX U-boats were gradually withdrawn from group convoy attack and group search operations in the North Atlantic, and shifted into single U-boat clandestine operations in more remote sea areas, requiring a greater range and longer war patrols.

The most successful U-boat commanders, who sank 100,000 tons or more, were called 'Aces'. Most of them operated U-boats in the earlier war years. After the Black May of 1943, the Aces were either dead, had become prisoners of war, or had been transferred to shore positions.

The sole exception was *Kapitänleutnant* z.V. (Lieutenant) Werner Henke, commanding the Type IX-C U-boat U-515. Henke sank twenty-seven ships, including several warships, of 163,098 confirmed tons, reaching tenth position on the U-boat commanders' sinking list. Henke was awarded the Knight's Cross with oak-leaf cluster. But he had several fights and serious run-ins with various SS bullies, Nazi functionaries and the Gestapo, all demanding harsh punishment of him by the Navy. Therefore, Henke was removed from the active naval officers' ranking list by von Friedeburg and Dönitz and discharged, but immediately recalled as a standby reserve (z.V.) officer for the war's duration. His scheduled promotion to *Korvettenkapitän* (Lieutenant-Commander) was cancelled.

Werner Henke became an American prisoner of war when U-515 was sunk on 9 April 1944. Henke was put under pressure to reveal secret information at the unlisted secret interrogation compound of Fort Hunt, Virginia, and shot on 15 June 1944 by camp guards, allegedly while trying to escape.

In these computations U-boat types were omitted that were only built in small numbers. These were Types VII-E and VII-F, the Types IX-D-1 and IX-D-2 U-cruisers, the large Type X minelayers, often converted to supply or freight U-boats, the Type XIV U-tankers and the small Type II coastal U-boats, mostly used as school or training U-boats. The Types XXI and XXIII electro U-boats were excluded, as too few made war patrols. U-boats of purely experimental type, such as the Walter-engined U-boats, were left out entirely.

CHAPTER TWELVE

Muddling Through Somehow

S everal busy naval doctors, including the head surgeon, surrounded by a flock of nurses in all sorts of uniforms, crowded into the departure lobby of the naval hospital to say goodbye to one of their patients who had just been checked and medically cleared again for U-boat service, after having been in their care for six weeks. Some of the girls had tears in their eyes when Frank W. Petersen handed each a small gift and one single rose. The men received practical things, like different bottles of booze, a box of cigars or several packs of cigarettes.

In summer 1944, it was a mystery how Petersen managed to ferret out such things. But he seemed to have valuable connections, and many of his numerous visitors brought along boxes of food and cases of presents, as they knew that rationing in Germany was tight and men trying to get back on their feet again were unlikely to manage this on the official hospital meals. Nevertheless, Petersen had lost a lot of weight. But at least he could now walk with a supporting cane, and had been able to drop his crutches a few days previously. For practical purposes, he had had to learn to walk again like a baby, but his tenacious determination to get well had helped him, supplemented by these presents of eatable things constantly delivered to him during his recovery period.

He shook hands with the men, kissed all the women, and just as he finished, a black naval car pulled into the entrance way and stopped. The driver jumped out, grabbed the baggage Petersen had stacked next to the exit door and then helped him into the rear seat and put his luggage in the front seat.

Petersen had been wounded during an aircraft attack, and had almost been given up by the doctors, after extensive emergency treatments and procedures. His loss of blood was heavy and quite a few pieces of shrapnel had been removed from his body. He was convinced that only the extraordinarily dedicated nurses had eventually pulled him back from the edge. Considering that this was his third injury, and the previous ones had been caused by clean and simple bullets that had not done too much damage and the wounds had healed comparatively fast, this last one had been an extremely close call.

The medical board had just decided that Petersen was able to do inside administrative and instructional work again, effective from the beginning of September, and would be fully rehabilitated within four to six weeks. But he needed to undergo torpedo-firing retraining with the various new torpedo types, so that he could serve again in the near future on one of the new Type XXI electro U-boats coming off the shipbuilding yards in growing numbers. That is, unless a final medical recheck early in October reached another determination.

Originally, Petersen had been supposed to be discharged from the naval hospital four days later on the Monday morning and proceed directly by train to his new interim command in Danzig. But his naval classmate Wally Neuhaus had decided to get married, and was able to get four days' leave to do so. The wedding was scheduled for a small country estate in East Prussia, where a tiny village church had been selected for the marriage ceremony. Because Wally had to be back in Bremen on the Monday morning, where he was executive officer on a new Type XXI U-boat recently commissioned, the wedding took place on Saturday, so that the groom and bride could entrain for Bremen on Sunday morning and hopefully get there on time. Wally had managed to find a Navy-owned apartment, and both he and his bride Helga arrived late on Friday. Frank Petersen was scheduled to be his friend's best man.

The bride's mother, a fairly young widow, had arrived several days earlier to make the wedding arrangements, accompanied by her younger daughter Vicky, who was barely 16. Naval friends of Petersen's had arranged for the car and fuel, which by now was very hard to find. This way, Petersen was driven in style to the celebration, as a special favour by one of his former superiors.

Accommodation was limited and on the simple side. Petersen was given a small room, where in the past household help had been quartered. Although he was worn out and considerably underweight, Petersen immediately liked Wally's future mother-in-law. But to his disappointment, the smart-looking widow, who could not be more than in her late thirties, had other ideas. Apparently, she considered Petersen a good catch for her younger daughter, based upon information that Wally had given her. She tried to match her up with Petersen, to his consternation, as he disliked teenage girls and preferred a more experienced type of woman: that is, somebody like the bride's mother, rather than her sister.

Consequently, this turned into a weekend of misunderstandings and confusion, mixed with quite a bit of fun and many laughs. Wally was concerned that he would not manage to get back to Bremen on time because of the constant bombing attacks on cities and railway lines, which caused interruptions of service and big delays. Therefore, the bridal pair decided to consummate their wedding night somewhat in advance of the actual ceremony. They would have to depart immediately after the wedding, and trains were so crowded that one had to be happy to get on them at all.

Because the walls were paper-thin, Petersen spent most of the night reading two new books he had received as gifts. Otherwise he would have become far too distracted by the joyful activity of Helga and Wally in the next room. A bottle of genuine French Cointreau helped him to pass the time.

A horse-drawn wagon took Petersen to the closest railway station early on the Monday morning to catch the local train to Danzig, where he had to report to the office of the 8th U-boat Flotilla for temporary duty. The widow came along and would return with the wagon. She asked Petersen if he did not like her daughter Vicky, and why he didn't. Petersen had to resort to some excuses, and told the widow that he was still having a lot of pain from his injuries and was generally very weak. His present interest was only to get well as rapidly as he could manage. A fervent hand-kiss as a final goodbye at the railway station was all Petersen would be able to get out of the wedding.

When he and Wally talked regarding the military situation in general and about the reality of U-boat warfare in particular, both were mighty gloomy about things when they discussed matters on a one-to-one, confidential basis, without any civilians being in earshot.

Petersen presented his orders and was introduced around from one person to the next to become at least superficially acquainted with the staff and the operational set-up, including torpedo-firing practice schedules. Commander Hans Pauckstadt, formerly commanding U-193, was the flotilla commander. He immediately questioned Petersen about things in the U-boat bases in western France still in German hands – Lorient, Saint Nazaire and La Rochelle-La Pallice – but Petersen was not really up with the latest developments since he was wounded and hospitalized. Pauckstadt arranged that he would be assigned to all torpedo test-firing exercises and be present whenever any of the new 'miracle' torpedoes were fired, without having to queue or take his turn. This was quite a concession to his experience, more so as he still limped somewhat and was forced periodically to utilize his walking cane in support.

The 8th U-boat Flotilla was a transit flotilla, composed of a frequently changing number of Type VII U-boats in Baltic training and preparatory exercises for future front-service assignments. This meant there was little permanency, as new U-boats arrived while others transferred elsewhere.

Since June 1944, a section of the 8th U-boat Flotilla had been made a front-service U-boat flotilla, supplying and coordinating up to eleven fully trained Type VII U-boats on operations in the Eastern sea area of the Baltic, usually along the huge anti-submarine mine barrier between Finland and

Estonia. This was a triple net, mine and obstacle barrier to bottle up the Russian submarines and surface ships in Kronstadt, the port of St Petersburg and other ports on the Gulf of Finland.

But recent defeats on the Russian front had pushed the German Army back quite a bit. The Russians had reconquered Estonia and the front lines were no longer firm but changing. Soon Latvia would return to Soviet rule, and Finland dropped out of the Eastern war entirely, concluding an armistice with the Soviet Union, and bringing about the second defeat of Finland since the 1939–40 Winter War.

These developments created considerable problems in keeping those sea barriers effective, and it had become impossible to retain a close watch and observation set-up along them, particularly once Finland dropped out of the war, since the Finnish Navy had been mainly engaged in these watch, observation and barrier defence operations.

Because the German Navy was criminally short of effective escorting ships and suitable patrol vessels in the Baltic, Dönitz had ordered German U-boats to watch and protect these barriers in the best way possible, though U-boats were not very suitable for such operations in fairly shallow waters. However, it was considered important to maintain the effectiveness of the barriers to the greatest extent possible, to keep Russian submarines and other ships from breaking through them and entering the Baltic Sea west of the Gulf of Finland and attacking German shipping there.

New minefields had been laid to repair the spots the Soviets had cleared and to block further breakthroughs. But these U-boat operations were seen as a temporary emergency situation, to last only until the Eastern Baltic froze over, with the beginning of the coming winter.

These combat U-boats were based in Danzig and provisioned, serviced and looked after by the 8th U-boat Flotilla in every respect, except actual operational assignments and their planning. This responsibility had been given to the admiral commanding the Eastern Baltic, Vice-Admiral Theodor Burchardi, already overloaded with many different tasks, including the charting of the mine-free, or rather recently mine-swept, routes and shipping channels.

To stay on top of that type of work and to utilize the far too few escort vessels available and arrange for their operational distribution, the 9th Escorting and Security Division had been created, commanded by Commander Adalbert von Blanc for the Eastern Baltic area. It was the only organization that was as current as possible on the minefield locations and the available shipping routes and channels. Therefore, for any ship movement outside the close-in Bay of Danzig area, this coordinating office had to be consulted and informed, to minimize shipping losses or operational problems. This included the U-boats of the 8th U-boat Flotilla, whether they were assigned as front boats or only engaged in exercises and tests.

When such advance consultations and safe routeing requests had been disregarded, several serious mishaps had occurred and a number of ships had already been lost that way. The 9th Escorting and Security Division became ever harder to reach, owing to insufficient telephone lines, which caused a growing delay in the assignment of the inadequate number of escorting vessels. Many were damaged, but repairs were slow because of a lack of spare parts and shipyards. Moreover, the Navy had removed too many suitable escort vessels from the Baltic and transfered them to Norway, Denmark, France and Holland on orders by Dönitz.

One of the losses involved U-250, a Type VII U-boat commanded by Lieutenant Werner Karl Schmidt (Crew 1935), posted to this Russian section of the 8th U-boat Flotilla in July 1944. U-250 left Kiel on 15 July, but did not call in at Danzig at all, proceeding instead directly to Reval, Estonia, and thence to Kalasika, Finland. Consequently, U-250 did not receive the latest information available, but left Finland on 26 July for a watch type of patrol along the net and mine barrier, which called for an observation operation within a limited area.

On 28 July, Schmidt sank a small Soviet harbour patrol boat, the MO-105, of only 56 tons, with an acoustic torpedo. But this brought sister ships belonging to the same group to the scene, once a German U-boat had been spotted. The MO-103, commanded by Lieutenant A. P. Kovalenko, found U-250 in the narrow Koivisto Strait on 30 July and sank her with depth-charges. The Baltic was only 42 m (138 ft) deep in that area. Forty-six men of the crew drowned, but Schmidt and five other crew members managed to get out of the wreck, using their Draeger-type escape gear, and rose to the surface. Here they were promptly caught by the Russians and made prisoners of war. The MO-103 immediately took the six men to Kronstadt and turned them over to Russian naval intelligence interrogators, who quickly put the screws on them to obtain information.

The Russian Navy swiftly dispatched divers, who entered the wreck of U-250 and recovered the naval Enigma machine M-4, the required coding and decoding tables, operational instructions and all the other secret papers and documents. These included the U-boat commander's instruction books, the maps of all obligatory shipping routes and the mineswept channels in the Baltic, as well as the location of all German-laid minefields.

Very soon the Russian Navy decoded and read the German naval radio signals with increasing speed and effectiveness. Russian submarines laid mines into these mineswept channels, and other submarines were posted directly into the obligatory shipping routes, to attack German ships that could not detour or take evasive action, owing to the narrowness of those rigid routes. The captured material became largely responsible for the huge shipping losses and terrible sea disasters in 1945.

The Russians also recovered the latest model of acoustic torpedoes, improved from the T-4 Falcon and T-5 Wren. They brought lifting cranes and raising equipment from Kronstadt to bring the sunk U-250 up from the bottom, towing her to Kronstadt for a close inspection and minute investigation. A decision was reached to repair and rebuild this U-boat and to put her back into operation as a Russian submarine after complete reconditioning. She was renamed TS-14 on 14 April 1945.

None of this became known to the German Navy, because the Russians imposed total secrecy in such matters and the information only seeped out to Western Europe many years later.

Russian armies entered East Prussia in January 1945, when German forces were already surrounded in Courland and Latvia by the Russians. Dönitz had fiercely opposed the timely evacuation of these armies to Germany. Once the huge mass exodus of civilian refugees started, after criminal delays caused by the East Prussian Nazi Party functionaries, it completely overwhelmed the available shipping capacity. Because of the irresponsible shortage of escorting vessels and the super-secret material recovered by the Russians from U-250, especially the maps of the German minefields and the mine-free shipping channels to Germany, more than 33,000 people drowned during these evacuations. The transports were terribly overloaded and took place in bitter-cold weather, well below freezing point.

On 30 January 1945, the liner *Wilhelm Gustloff* sailed from Gotenhafen (Gdingen) with 10,582 persons aboard, including 918 men of the 2nd U-boat Training Division, 373 female naval auxiliaries and a civilian crew of 173. The Russian Submarine S-13 torpedoed her and 9,343 persons died, most of them women and children, more than six times the number of people who drowned when the Titanic hit an iceberg in the North Atlantic in 1912.

On 10 February 1945, the liner *General von Steuben*, used as a hospital transport ship for military wounded being evacuated from Latvia, was torpedoed, and 3,608 soldiers and medical staff drowned. Then, on 17 April 1945, the freighter-transport *Goya*, already damaged by bombing attacks by Russian aeroplanes, was torpedoed, and a further 6,666 persons drowned, all of them civilian refugees.

In all of these shipping disasters the German Navy was unable to provide the necessary escort vessels for these and many other ships. Therefore, irresponsible chances had to be taken when they finally sailed without sufficient escorting ships, apart from the constant communication delays and the severe winter weather problems. Nevertheless Dönitz was later lauded by the naval propaganda crowd as the 'Saviour' of the East Prussian refugees, although he had actually strenuously opposed the evacuation of any civilians until it was often too late. Frequently, he was simply confronted with irreversible facts orchestrated by other naval officers that he was forced to accept, often with great reluctance on his part.

Petersen spent three weeks in daily training and special torpedo-firing exercises, and felt he was again fully on top of things. Pauckstadt agreed, and was quite satisfied with his performance. These tests had included the firing of the latest T-11 acoustic torpedoes and also the LUT- and FAT-equipped electric torpedoes.

To fire, oversee and check another series of new torpedoes during test firings under simulated combat conditions, Pauckstadt ordered Petersen aboard the Type VII U-boat U-297, commanded by Lieutenant j.g. Wolfgang Aldegarmann. Her executive officer had been involved in an accident, requiring hospitalization, and no qualified replacement was available at short notice.

The commander of U-297 was no U-boat man, but had served a long time on minesweepers before undergoing the U-boat training and prospective commander's schooling. Pauckstadt wanted a front-experienced torpedo officer aboard to undertake these important test firings, scheduled to run for six or seven days.

The group of U-boats assigned to participate in these exercises was moored in a long line along a dirty pier, fenced off with rolls of barbed-wire, but within easy walking distance of the offices of the 8th U-boat Flotilla. Therefore, Petersen just tossed enough personal laundry for a week into his travel bag and set off to find U-297. Because all of these U-boats were painted alike and had no identifying marks whatsoever to distinguish one from another, he had to enquire at each one as he moved along the pier until he found U-297, almost the last U-boat in that row.

He reported aboard and was shown to the commander below deck. U-297 was in the process of making ready for departure, and everybody was busy with different tasks. Aldegarmann said he was quite happy to have an experienced torpedo officer on his U-boat for these important tests. To Petersen, U-297 appeared beaten up rather than new, and some of the crew members a bit sloppy. However, as he considered himself a temporary replacement aboard, he felt he should not make quick judgements based upon those first impressions.

In addition, he swiftly got involved in operational matters, because U-297 left Danzig ten minutes after he had embarked, together with the entire group of U-boats. Aldegarmann, her commander, turned out to be a quiet fellow who appeared somewhat depressed to Petersen. Therefore, Petersen concentrated on his job and largely minded his own business. The operational exercises were tiresome and demanding, and soon sleep was getting a bit short.

When the group of U-boats returned to Danzig and their pier in the early morning, Petersen was occupied with the completion of the torpedo logbook entries, the reports about each firing and the results achieved, or, for that matter, not achieved. Then he packed his travel bag and requested permission to leave U-297. Her commander asked if Petersen would not care to have a leisurely breakfast aboard before leaving, as there was always a lot of confusion and aggravation on the pier when the U-boats returned to port.

But Petersen wanted to report to Pauckstadt as soon as possible, and decided to get off U-297 quickly, especially as he had not managed to develop much personal rapport with the officers and crew, who probably viewed him as an outsider. However, they evidently respected his competency and experience, because there had been no problems with having orders unhesitatingly complied with.

Lieutenant j.g. (Engineering) of the Reserves, Ernst Friedberg, the directing engineer, guided Petersen to the pier, overcrowded with people, all screaming and yelling in different languages incomprehensible to Petersen. Most of these people wore striped two-piece suits, or what was left of them, dirty and torn in many places, but they were dreadful to look at. Emaciated bodies, they were a real shock to Petersen when he approached closer. Though he had seen and experienced many frightful things during the war, this sorry spectacle was really more than he could stomach.

He thought for a moment that he would have to throw up, as he confronted the incredible horror of this milling crowd. Then he decided to turn around and return to U-297, instead of walking onward. Most of these people appeared to be mere human skeletons, rather than human beings, acting like animals. When the white-faced Petersen again reached the control room of U-297, Aldegarmann was waiting for him and simply handed him a mug full of brandy. When Petersen had managed to swallow it, he was still unable to talk. Aldegarmann said:

So, Petersen, now you have experienced the reality of the German home front! These are either Russian prisoners of war or inmates of the nearby Stutthof concentration camp. I have faced this horror show every time we returned to Danzig. Frankly speaking, I can't wait to get U-297 ready for her next assignment and leave Danzig as soon as possible. These people are used to load or unload ships and work in the warehouses along the pier. They are trying to grab the leftovers of our U-boat food and any edible items that we drop into those rusty oil barrels used as garbage cans, standing along the pier, within their reach from behind the barbed-wire fence separator. I can't stand this terrible mess any more. That is the reason why I stay below deck. Want a late breakfast, after all?

Petersen just shook his head quickly. By now he had lost any kind of appetite. However, this information had so stunned him that he decided to hang around for a while to recover from the shock.

When he debarked for the second time, he asked Friedberg, the directing engineer: 'Aren't such methods of disposing of leftover food liable to generate all sorts of epidemics, and thereby represent a serious health hazard for the U-boat crews?' He was told, 'Several other disposal systems have been tried, that were less inhuman and filthy. But the Nazi functionaries have not permitted them to be put into effect.' He added, 'They rule things beyond the barbed-wire fence and the Navy has no influence on the other side of that separator, though the Navy has tried several times to implement some changes.'

The directing engineer was a typical technician, much more interested in machinery or equipment and their ways of operating than in people. Yet even he said to Petersen: 'This certainly is hellish, like some spectacle from Dante's *Inferno*.'

Petersen arrived just before lunch time. Pauckstadt berated him for not having arrived earlier to deliver his report and the paperwork, and enquired if he had gone to the emergency treatment room of the naval hospital, having developed medical problems during the voyage. Petersen hesitated a moment, then he could not keep his mouth shut any longer with respect to those occurrences on the pier and the shameful things he had seen in the port that morning.

Naturally, Pauckstadt was aware of them, and declared: 'The Navy had tried repeatedly to clean up this horrible mess. But the local Nazi functionaries have different ideas and hold opposing views, on direct orders from Martin Bormann in Hitler's headquarters. The Navy in Berlin had been told they must not become involved in purely civilian affairs.'

Petersen listened intently and finally replied: 'Now I understand what Admiral Canaris referred to last summer, when he stated:

It is terrible, the Russians never signed those Hague and Geneva Conventions for prisoners of war, neither the imperial Russians nor the bloody Bolshevists. Their people are suffering unbelievably for that refusal. Germany will be paying for at least one hundred years, and not less than five generations, for the criminal way these Russian prisoners of war are treated, not to mention the concentration camp inmates and the Eastern Jews!

It required more than a hundred years before Napoleon was recognized by other European nations, apart from the French, on a factual and fair basis. In April 1801, the British fleet under Admiral Hyde Parker bombarded Copenhagen, unexpectedly and unprovoked, while another part of the British fleet, under Vice-Admiral Horatio Nelson, attacked and destroyed the Danish fleet anchored off Copenhagen at the same time, as a purely preventive measure, to make it impossible for Napoleon to take over the Danish ships. Denmark and the Danes have not forgotten, much less forgiven, this outrage for over a hundred years; in fact not until 1940, when Denmark was occupied by German troops, which eventually wiped out that memory'.

Pauckstadt finally managed to calm Petersen down a bit and told him he would be liable to lose his head if he continued to talk like that and got reported by people he could not trust absolutely. Then, changing the subject swiftly, he told Petersen: 'Your time in Danzig is finished, you will be assigned to Pillau, East Prussia, for a few days, to speak in front of the officer training classes of the First U-boat Training Division about the new torpedoes and their possibilities. Report to Captain Fritz Poske the day after tomorrow.'

After that Petersen would be posted to the anti-aircraft school in Swinemünde, for a refresher course in anti-aircraft gunnery, as several new models of flak guns were coming into use. This was to be followed by a final medical re-examination in Kiel by the U-boat Command's medical board. Anything else beyond that was uncertain. Lastly, Pauckstadt added: 'I hear you did an outstanding job as torpedo officer on U-297 during these important exercises.'

When Petersen arrived by train in Pillau (Baltisk), he was met at the railway station and welcomed by one of his naval classmates who was both the adjutant and an instructor, and then introduced to the other staff members and informed about the anticipated schedule of his speeches.

As the training classes in Pillau were filled to capacity, no sleeping space could be provided for Petersen aboard any of the accommodation ships of the First U-boat Training Division. Therefore, he was placed in one of the wooden transient barracks of the nearby 3rd U-boat Personnel Pool Command, where crews for new U-boats were assembled and assigned as needed.

The officer in charge there was a rather elderly commander (engineering) by the name of Kurt Hohnwaldt. But Petersen was immediately told in confidence by the adjutant, another naval classmate of his, that he was for practical purposes never in his office. He was also in charge of a company of female naval auxiliaries and tied up chasing them around all day long. Evidently this tired Hohnwaldt out so much that he could hardly handle any other work any more.

Most of the routine paperwork was handled by an even older Reserve officer, Lieutenant-Commander von Stein, who was at the same time the newly appointed Nazi doctrine political officer, called by the enlisted men simply 'Commissar', or 'Politruk', modelled after such political guidance officers in the Soviet forces. This was one of the new developments ordered by Dönitz, after the attempt to kill Hitler on 20 July 1944 had failed.

Captain Poske had divided the officers into groups, so Petersen had to make three different speeches, which meant he could personalize them more, compared to talking to one huge assembly. This permitted some question-and-answer periods afterwards, and all were pleased.

When Petersen returned to his sleeping quarters for the last time, the adjutant took him aside for a walk in a nearby grove of old oak trees, to be able to converse confidentially with him, which rather surprised Petersen. Yet what he was told by the adjutant aroused his interest greatly.

When they had walked around a bend in the sandy road and could no longer be seen from the administration barrack, the adjutant just handed Petersen a teletyped sheet marked: 'Super-secret Command Matter, just received from Kiel, under the signature of Admiral von Friedeburg', and marked in large letters: 'for senior staff officers (captains) only!'

It stated:

In the past two months, civilians in bombed cities have been so mad about the enemy terror fliers that they have grabbed shot-down flight crews by force and either tossed them into the still burning houses or otherwise lynched them without compassion, in revenge for having lost their living quarters. The Nazi propaganda minister, Goebbels, has declared and repeatedly announced that Total War is now in effect in all of Germany, and previously observed niceties in the conduct of the war can and should no longer be observed. To the contrary, these murdering terror airmen ought to be punished and killed on the spot, whenever there is a chance for the German population to do so. But their justified fury over these flying killers and murderers has been interfered with by anti-aircraft and Air Force soldiers in uniform who have caught some shot-down airmen and protected them with their arms, as prisoners of war, whenever they have reached them before the general populace.

This has generated some real fights in the still burning cities, when shots have been fired by soldiers to prevent the mad crowd from killing such prisoners of war. The Nazi Party functionaries in these cities have strongly protested against such actions by the military to Hitler's headquarters, and orders have been passed to the air defence units to immediately cease such protective actions and to discontinue forthwith standing in the way of revenge on the part of the incensed people, who are bitterly opposed to these military acts of protection of these criminal terror airmen. Since such orders have been given, an estimated two hundred such airmen have been lynched by the outraged population in different metropolitan areas.

Therefore, as far as the German Navy was concerned, though they are rarely involved in land operations, the following strict order is now given:

> In any such cases that might occur in the future, when any naval soldiers are involved, they have to turn around and disregard any possibility of protecting or sheltering such terror fliers and let the people take their justified revenge, killing and disposing of such flying gangsters!

This teletyped instruction order had a secret registration code number with limited distribution. The prompt total destruction of the order was to be reported at once by teletype to the commanding admiral of U-boats in Kiel. But the content of the order was to be passed on to subaltern officers, petty officers and enlisted men in an immediate and suitable way, VERBALLY ONLY!

Petersen was extremely disturbed, and the adjutant asked him: 'What shall I do and how should I handle this order? Commander Hohnwaldt is too tired and too uninterested to handle it or take any action. He told me, against express instructions in this teletype, to read it anyway and to arrange announcements. The Nazi doctrine officer, von Stein, is unreachable. He got totally boozed up after some party and is fast asleep.'

Petersen suggested: 'If I were you, I would just burn this entire message immediately. Then confirm and report the destruction to Kiel, before one of these two old codgers gets into the act, and causes very serious problems.

You will, of course, have to take this on your conscience. But would you, as a U-boat man, wish to encounter situations when enraged merchant mariners or other civilians would like to murder you on the spot, instead of making you a prisoner of war?'

The adjutant just nodded and thanked Petersen for his candid and straight answer, adding: 'I can't trust any officer of this command to give me an honest reply, as all are still extremely Nazistic in their beliefs and ways.'

Petersen left early next morning, as he had a long day ahead of him, changing trains several times to reach Swinemünde. The ten-day anti-aircraft gunnery exercises and courses passed rapidly, and a lot of live ammunition was most likely wasted. Another participant in this upgrading course was Lieutenant j.g. Fritz Strecker, an old friend of long standing. They had not seen each other in over two years, and were delighted when it turned out that Strecker was likewise ordered to proceed to Kiel for a new assignment. This way they could travel together, talk about a lot of things and shorten the long and boring journey ahead of them.

Both officers had done well with target practice firings. The commander of the anti-aircraft school called them into his office to talk to them at length and tell them how pleased he was with their performance. But he had caught them literally at the exit-gate, when they were about to leave for the railway station. Consequently, they missed their train, which would have been the last one allowing onward connections to Kiel without having to stop overnight somewhere.

The train they did manage to catch after this delay was a local milk-train that reached Stettin so late they were unable to make any kind of express train connection beyond that town that had been heavily bombed. It was quickly growing dark. They contacted the railway station security office and were informed that no commercial hotel space was available so late. He was sorry about that, but the officers would have to fend for themselves, the best they could. The old Army sergeant running the office could not care less, like so many of the older Reserve type of men in the Army, for whom naval soldiers were some kind of exotic birds with strange ideas.

It looked as if it was going to start to rain shortly. The two officers discussed what they could do and how they might find a place to spend the night. Strecker brought up the possibility of staying in one of the military brothels. But Petersen objected that sanitary conditions were usually terrible, and in places like Stettin the girls were worn out and quite awful. Furthermore, owing to bomb damage, it was difficult to find one's way around with detours and closed sections around the station.

Petersen pulled two packages of cigarettes out of his travel bag and suggested they go back to the station's control office and offer them to that Army sergeant if he could come up with a place to bed down for the night before they got soaked by the approaching rain. They had hardly spoken to the sergeant when he grabbed the cigarettes firmly and grinned: yes, indeed, if the officers had something to barter, he could help them, and wrote down a name and address on a piece of paper. When he realized they did not know their way around, he provided directions.

It turned out that the place was only two minutes away from the damaged railway station. They rang the bell, then knocked loudly and shouted at the same time. Finally, a light was switched on on the second floor, visible despite the blackout. After they had waited some more, the door opened and a woman waved them into the dark hall, led up worn-out stairs and into an older type of apartment, with the toilets still outside, between the floors. Petersen felt like turning around, but Strecker pointed out that they had no alternative.

And so they entered, handed the woman a bottle of booze as payment, and she lit a candle for them. There were two beds along the wall. The woman said they could have them, and she would spend the night in some kind of chair. This seemed unfair, so Strecker said that one of them would sleep in the chair instead. They decided to toss a coin to find out who would get the bed and who would end up with the chair. Petersen lost.

While they got ready to sleep, the woman suggested that for another bottle they could both spend the night with her, alternately, the turns to be taken as their throw of the coins dictated – Strecker first in the front bed and Petersen second in the rear bed. But Petersen was so tired he just dropped into the rear bed and fell asleep immediately, neither hearing the action in the front bed nor waking up once his turn was supposed to start. Strecker tried really hard to wake Petersen up but he could not do so. Then he decided to take over Petersen's turn too, and returned to the front bed.

Once daylight came they swiftly packed their things together, handed over some small presents and departed in a hurry, without breakfast being offered.

When they returned to the railway station, there was a lot of activity going on. The Army sergeant was pleased to see them, as he needed help, and led them to a small office cubicle where an officer in a rather weird uniform was sitting. The sergeant spoke only German, and that with a strong accent. Petersen tried some of his linguistic abilities on the officer, who finally seemed to respond and showed him a letter of introduction, rather artistically prepared, but so obviously faked that Petersen had to laugh.

The letter stated that Lieutenant Jan Buggeroff of the Royal Bulgarian Navy was on a visit to Germany, intending to inspect shipyards in order to ascertain the opportunity of purchasing some small ships. All the help possible should be extended to him, and cooperation would be greatly appreciated.

Petersen looked at Strecker, then asked the Army sergeant where the officer had come from and how he had ended up in his office. The army sergeant explained: 'The officer was walking around the piers in the harbour area looking at ships there, and was brought in because nobody could communicate with him. I have tried to locate an Army officer of influence, but now that you naval officers are here, no doubt you can settle the matter and resolve this communication problem.'

Petersen suddenly started to talk in some gibberish, and Strecker thought that perhaps he had totally flipped, after the previous night's experience. However, Petersen had simply made up some phrases in Greek that he was able to remember, to test the Bulgarian naval officer. Petersen did not speak Bulgarian, and the officer made big eyes, yet obviously did not understand anything. Then Petersen switched to English and said: 'If your name is Jan Buggeroff and you are Bulgarian, my name should be changed to Joe Fuckoff and I shall become a Zulu chieftain instantly.'

The officer in his fancy uniform knew when his poker hand was worthless, and admitted sheepishly that he was not Bulgarian, but an escaped British Royal Air Force officer, who had tried to sneak onto a Swedish ship in port, to get away somehow. He also happened to be hungry and without sleep. Petersen laughed. What a joke! He suggested that the Army sergeant should take the officer to the guardroom, feed him, give him a bunk and watch him closely, then call the nearest local Air Force representative, probably some anti-aircraft gunnery officer, requesting him to pick up this Bulgarian fellow and arrange a fast return to his Stalag prisoner-of-war camp.

Petersen told him: 'Whatever your real name is, this certainly was a nice try, for which you ought to get an A for effort. But what cheek, to select such a phoney name and get-up for it.' The British officer replied with a sad grin: 'Well, that was the best we were able to come up with. It worked for a couple of days anyway. If I had been able to get aboard one of these Swedish steamers, I might have made it back home.' Petersen smiled and replied: 'Well, now you'll have to wait until this war is finished, which can't be too much longer, from the looks of things. Good luck to you until then!'

The Army sergeant was pleased that his problem had been cared for, but he was rather baffled by what had transpired, and mumbled that if there were fewer aliens and other peculiar foreigners in Germany these days, life surely would be easier for everybody, adding somewhat more loudly and with a sly grin on his face: 'Did you find your accommodation satisfactory? The woman is clean and actually the wife of a local pastor serving on the Russian front as chaplain.' Because the delayed departure of their express train was finally announced, the two naval officers skipped any reply and just snatched their luggage, rushing to the appropriate platform.

They had to change trains in Hamburg Altona for their onward train to Kiel. During the wait, Petersen suddenly spotted Lieutenant Hermann Rasch getting off another train arriving to make connections. Both were overjoyed to meet unexpectedly. Petersen introduced Strecker to Rasch, who invariably carried a hip-flask for such emergency situations. Rasch immediately offered a quick drink to celebrate their chance encounter.

Petersen knew that Rasch had been transferred to the super-secret KdK command for testing new equipment and small battle weapons, being in charge of the two-man mini-submarines, called *Seehunde* (seals). When Rasch's train pulled into the station, Petersen asked him point-blank:

'Hermann, tell me, would that new outfit you work for be suitable for me?' Rasch was surprised Petersen knew about his super-hush-hush assignment, and replied: 'Certainly not, Frank, this is no command for you. We only accept volunteers under 21 years of age. They still follow orders without asking too many questions, being too young to be able to think for themselves. You are already too old for the KdK command.' Rasch got on his train to Neustadt Holstein, found a window that could still be opened, yelling cheerfully, 'Take care of yourselves. Keep your noses in the wind and clean.' Strecker and Petersen left ten minutes later for Kiel. Passing their medical re-examinations they were then cleared for new assignments.

U-297 soon left Danzig for Kiel and a final overhaul, then got loaded and ammunitioned for her first war patrol, thence continuing to Horten, in Norway, for snorkel exercises. On 26 November 1944, she departed with seven other U-boats for the Pentland Firth area to search for British aircraft-carrier groups assumed to operate from Scapa Flow, participating in Operation Diana.

On 6 December the aircrew of Sunderland flying-boat NS 'Y' based at Castle Archdale on Loch Erne in Northern Ireland, commanded by Flight Lieutenant Denis Hatton of 201 Squadron of the 15th Coastal Command Air Group, was on a long low-altitude anti-submarine search flight. In the late afternoon the aircrew spotted smoke from U-297's snorkel, and shortly afterwards the wake made by the snorkel head. The Sunderland made two attacks with six depth-charges during the second approach, sinking U-297 with all fifty men aboard.

CHAPTER THIRTEEN

Last-Minute Games and Gambles

W hen Oskar Kusch was shot, one would assume this was the end of his story. But things turned out otherwise, because after the war the Kusch case again rose to the surface, as the truth has a way of doing eventually, growing into an important political and moral issue, in spite of the fact that a conspiracy of former naval judge advocates tried strenuously to prevent this from happening.

Consequently, it is necessary to introduce another person who was not involved in the Kusch court martial in 1944, but became instrumental in it after the war: Naval Judge Advocate Kai Nieschling. In 1944, Nieschling was *Oberkriegsgerichtsrat* in Berlin at the Naval High Command. He worked as legal adviser for the naval leadership, and was assigned to the Naval High Command's appeal court when it was in session. As this did not require Nieschling's full time, he was also in charge of the personnel department of the naval judge advocates, arranging their transfers, new assignments, promotions and other changes. In May 1944, Nieschling was promoted to *Geschwaderrichter*, squadron judge advocate, but remained in Berlin. Outside the naval judge advocate circles, he was unknown, but he had strong political connections and considerable internal influence, being a convinced Nazi.

Dönitz decided that for self-protection the Navy must become involved in the Richard Sorge espionage case in Tokyo. Admiral Warzecha argued strongly against such meddling in Japanese affairs, and pointed out the great obstacles that existed. Yet Dönitz, always stubborn and determined, insisted on having his way. Nieschling was ordered to take over the prosecution and investigation of the Sorge case personally, and to proceed to Japan to do so. To make this decision by Dönitz comprehensible, it is necessary to delve into the historical background of the Sorge case and the means of transport selected for Nieschling to move to Japan.

When Dönitz made the decision to become involved in the Sorge case, Sorge had already been executed by the Japanese, though he had expected, and hoped to the end, that the GRU, the Russian military espionage service, would exchange him for several Japanese spies captured and held by the Soviets in Siberia.

As so often in such matters, the devil was in the minor details, which had made it possible for the Kempetai police to catch Sorge and his informants, helpers and assistants. His least important sub-agent was arrested for another matter and squeezed in police custody. When his house was searched as a consequence, compromising material was discovered.

Sorge's cover was working as a journalist, a foreign reporter for several German and other European papers and magazines. He supplied keen political and economic previews, reports and stories that were paying very well, owing to their extraordinary inside information. As he initially only had contracts for German newspapers, he had built up a very close relationship with the German embassy in Tokyo and all the military representatives working there. He was considered to be outstandingly informed, and so unusually knowledgeable about Japanese politics and military affairs that he was viewed as an expert on Japan and China, a man who knew more of what was actually going on than all Western embassies combined. This was an extraordinary achievement for a Caucasian in Asia.

Prior to his posting to Tokyo, Sorge had worked for the Russian military espionage service, the GRU, in other Asian countries. Once he was recalled from China, he was promoted to colonel in the Red Army by the famous GRU director, Lieutenant-General Jan Karlovich Berzin, whose real name was Peter Kyuzis. Berzin intended to employ Sorge next in Belgium and France in western Europe, for his linguistic abilities. But unexpectedly, the Japanese secret police caught and eliminated the previous GRU resident in Japan and destroyed his net of informers. Therefore, Berzin transferred Sorge instead to Tokyo to replace him. Thus Sorge had to start from scratch during the pre-war years that he worked in Japan. His mentor, Berzin, was shot on Stalin's order during the 1937 military liquidation campaign, after directing the Soviet involvement in Spain, organizing the international Communist brigades and arranging the supply of Soviet weapons to the Spanish Communists.

Germany attacked Soviet Russia on 22 June 1941. Sorge, like other GRU representatives, had warned Moscow well in advance of this attack. However, Stalin overruled the GRU and the general staff of the Red Army, regarding this information as a purely political British provocation. Churchill also warned Stalin directly, based upon intercepted German radio signals read by Bletchley Park. But again Stalin rejected the information. His reasoning was interesting: 'No doubt Hitler and the Germans want more economic support and a better trade deal. But Hitler would NEVER be so crazy as to attack Soviet Russia before Great Britain and her Empire have been defeated or Hitler has made peace arrangements with England, at the least.'

Many different sources informed Moscow about this attack, which could hardly be entirely concealed. But for Moscow, the real bonus turned out to be Sorge's advance information and dependable confirmation that Japan would not attack Soviet Russia in Siberia and the Far East, but remain strictly neutral.

This permitted Stalin to pull out his first-line troops from Siberia and feed them, as the decisive factor, into the battle for Moscow in December 1941, beating the German Army, which had already reached the suburbs of the city but was not equipped for winter warfare. The defeat was so crushing, killing the best divisions, that the German Army never recovered from it.

When the Japanese Kempetai police found out about Sorge's activities and his radio system, they did not believe he worked for Soviet Russia, as Sorge had only once visited the Russian embassy in Tokyo, in an emergency situation, but had otherwise acted generally like an anti-communist for effective cover. The Japanese police, automatically watching all foreigners, including the various foreign embassies and consulates, but especially the Russian ones, had never suspected Richard Sorge in any particular way, least of all as GRU spymaster. Rather, they considered him a boozer, a womanizer and a big party man. His camouflage had been outstanding in every respect, and his effectiveness as a European in an oriental country made him the most effective spy in Japan.

The revelations that the Japanese secret police had made belatedly, and with great reluctance on their part, to the German embassy, involved virtually every military officer, in addition to Eugen Ott, who had been replaced as German ambassador in Tokyo by a reliable Nazi type. But when this whole affair blew up, there was no longer any direct and reliable transport available to take Ott back to Germany for a court martial, and he was allowed to retire in Japan until the war ended.

In 1934, a new German naval attaché arrived in Tokyo, Captain Paul Wenneker, who held this position for four years before returning to Germany. But in March 1940, Wenneker was again transferred to Japan as a rear admiral to become the senior German military representative in the entire Far Eastern area, directing all other German military officers in the region. He was soon promoted to full admiral to work more effectively with the status-conscious Japanese. A bachelor, he quickly made many friends, and turned into a great and popular party organizer and tiger on the cocktail-party circuit.

Ambassador Ott had introduced Sorge to Wenneker soon after his first arrival in Japan, and the two party goers hit it off well in every respect. Because Ott had vouched for Sorge's reliability and competency, Wenneker had no reason not to trust him, and talked openly to him about everything of interest, Sorge in turn furnished him valuable inside information about Japanese conditions, including army and navy politics, something Wenneker had to learn about in a hurry. Much of what Wenneker managed to absorb originated from Sorge.

Wenneker was put in charge of the loading and scheduling activities of the blockade-running merchant ships, known as 'Black Ships'. But the general introduction of radar on the Allies' aircraft and ships finished that programme. Wenneker coordinated the operations of the German auxiliary cruisers in the Pacific and later set up the U-boat base plan for the Far East, with bases in Penang, Singapore and Surabaya, arranging the cargo loads of all U-boats managing to reach the Far East without getting sunk *en route*.

Wenneker worked well with the Japanese, but his close friendship with Sorge had compromised his position greatly as far as the Nazis were concerned. The Gestapo undertook a thorough investigation of events in Tokyo, and turned the findings over to Keitel at Hitler's Army headquarters. However, Keitel concluded there was nothing that could be done at that time, but added that Wenneker was a second target for such a future investigation, in addition to Ott.

Naval Judge Advocate Nieschling, trying to score points with Dönitz, obtained the secret Army file and passed it on to him. Dönitz was horrified about the implications for the German Navy, and an extensive exchange of signals was generated. Captain Werner Vermehren, the naval chief of staff in Tokyo, an old *Abwehr* officer, tried hard to defuse the various implications of the Gestapo report and the misgivings of Dönitz, who was never able to understand how foreign-based intelligence officers worked, and wanted to suspend Wenneker from his position immediately. But as a result of strong pressure by the Japanese military representatives in Berlin and Tokyo, Wenneker was retained until Germany capitulated.

During these hassles and the required paper shuffling, Nieschling had become involved in the exchange of signals regarding the legal aspects of the situation. He sensed that he could use the Sorge case as a springboard to gain recognition from Dönitz and a promotion. Therefore, he heated up the case with new legal problems, asking further questions and generating a lot of 'visibility' activity.

Suddenly he was relieved of his position in Berlin and ordered to proceed to Japan to clean up the mess and institute court-martial proceedings, first against Ott and subsequently all German citizens involved, whether military or civilian. Nieschling considered this a future assignment, largely on paper, for political window dressing.

But Dönitz floored him when he arranged for his passage aboard U-234 to Japan as special judge advocate to process the matter in Tokyo as soon as possible. He was flabbergasted, as he had never been aboard any warship, much less a U-boat. As it turned out, he would travel with a very unusual group of passengers on U-234.

This U-boat was one of the only ten large Type X-B minelayer U-boats built. U-234 had been heavily damaged by bombs in her building yard, requiring lengthy repairs, and then had been converted into a pure supply and freight U-boat. Once this rebuilding was finished, U-234 was commissioned on 2 March 1944 by Lieutenant Johann Heinrich 'Hein'

Fehler. But because of further technical modifications ordered by the U-boat Command and the replacement of some equipment, U-234 only became ready for operations a year later, in March 1945.

'Hein' Fehler had managed to get U-234 out of the shipyard undamaged and fully loaded in Kiel. He was anxious to leave Kiel before U-234 was bombed once more. On 24 March 1945, a final special freight shipment was received from the Japanese embassy, accompanied by two Japanese officers, secret intelligence service Army Colonel Genzo Shosi who was, an aeronautical engineer and Navy Captain Hideo Tomonaga, a submariner and multiple inventor of technical equipment. The shipment in leaden boxes was marked U-235 and contained Uranium Oxide. Tomonaga checked and sealed each and every box personally.

In addition to these two Japanese officers, U-234 embarked the following VIPs in Kiel: Air Force Colonel Fritz von Sandrart, anti-aircraft specialist; Air Force Captain Erich Menzel, aerial torpedo specialist; Lieutenant Heinrich Hellendoorn, naval anti-aircraft gunnery specialist; Gerhard Falk, naval construction specialist and commander of the Reserves; Heinz Anton Schlicke, another naval *Silberling* and electronics engineer travelling as commander of the Reserves; and Lieutenant Richard Bulla, as air-sea coordinator.

On 20 March, 'Hein' Fehler returned early from a meeting scheduled by von Friedeburg's staff, and coming aboard U-234 he discovered his executive officer, Lieutenant j.g. of the Reserves Albert Klingenberg, *in flagrante* with one of the sailors. Fehler had already suspected that Klingenberg might be a homosexual, and was so incensed that he arrested him on the spot and personally transported him to the naval prison. Then Fehler continued to the U-boat Command's Personnel Bureau in Kiel, requesting an immediate replacement. Fehler demanded a front-service experienced executive officer, in view of his imminent departure for Japan.

Both U-boat personnel officers, Commanders Harald Jeppener-Haltenhof and Wilhelm Müller-Arnecke, tried to calm Fehler down, and patiently attempted to make it clear to him that nobody with such qualifications was available at short notice, nor were such officers sitting around waiting for assignments elsewhere.

At that moment one of their assistants directed an officer to them who carried a file that needed signatures. It was Frank Petersen, interrupting this heated conversation. 'Hein' Fehler had become well acquainted with Petersen in Lorient earlier in the war and called out, 'My search is over, my problem is solved, because here comes my new executive officer!' Petersen was quite surprised at this outburst of Fehler's enthusiasm, and immediately told the three officers that the Medical Board of the U-boat Command had just judged him as no longer fit for U-boat service. Owing to the after-effects of his latest war injuries Petersen could no longer tolerate the constant changes in air pressure aboard dived U-boats when they utilized their snorkel equipment for extended periods of time. He emphasized that he had been ordered by the Medical Board to have Commander Jeppener-Haltenhoff sign his release from the U-boat Command and arrange his immediate transfer to the Personnel Department of the Admiral Baltic, for further assignment. Fehler was stunned, but there was nothing he could do. After getting the necessary signatures, Petersen wished Fehler lots of luck and quickly left for the nearby office of the Admiral Baltic.

After some further arguments, Fehler finally agreed with the suggestion made by Jeppener-Haltenhoff that he should accept Lieutenant Richard Bulla as his new executive officer. Bulla was already aboard U-234 and Fehler had known him for many years. Bulla lacked U-boat experience and training but he was a qualified torpedo officer for surface ships and a very experienced pilot for catapulted aircraft. Considering that U-234 no longer carried any torpedoes, the U-boat Command in Koralle-Bernau approved this change.

On the morning of their departure from Kiel three more passengers boarded. These were August Bringewald and Franz Ruf, aircraft engineers of the Messerschmitt aircraft works, with a boxed model of the Me 262 jet fighter plane and additional boxed spare parts and blueprints, and Naval Judge Advocate Kai Nieschling with lots of luggage, proceeding to Japan for his court-martial assignment as ordered by Dönitz.

U-234 made an intermediate stop in Horten, Norway, for snorkel exercises and final load distribution and weapons tests in the Oslo fjord. When she had left Horten, U-1301, a Type VII U-boat, collided with her. The damage caused could not be repaired in Horten or Oslo, and Fehler did not want to return to Kiel because of the constant air bombings of that port. Therefore, he decided to continue to Kristiansand, hoping to find repair facilities in that port, arriving on 6 April. However, their were none, and Fehler arranged for some load shifting and the cranking of U-234 to get the damaged area welded over with steel plates, to at least make U-234 watertight again.

Here a final passenger embarked for Japan, Air Force Lieutenant-General Ulrich Kessler, the *Luftwaffe* commander in Norway, who was being transferred to Tokyo as the new *Luftwaffe* representative in the Far East, replacing Major-General von Gronau, who was also involved in the Sorge case.

U-234 had the following cargo load aboard, according to Ensign Karl Ernst Pfaff, second watch and load officer of U-234: 74 tons of lead, 26 tons of mercury, 12 tons of special steel, 7 tons of optical glass and special lenses, 43 tons of aircraft instruments, parts and arms with blueprints, 5 tons of new flak ammunition and parts of new anti-aircraft guns, 6 tons of special U-boat equipment for the German U-boat bases in Asia, 1 ton of courier mail, films, medical supplies and naval mail, 1 dismantled twin-jet Me 262 fighter plane in boxes and 1,232 lb of uranium oxide, in lead containers each marked 'U-235'.

General Kessler, a user of monocles, imitated and parodied Göring, the detested Air Force commander, to the amazement of the U-234 crew. On 16

April 1945, Rösing showed up unannounced in Kristiansand. He gave one of his final victory-is-just-around-the-corner speeches, leaving most crew members disgusted and the rest furious at having to listen to such claptrap.

Fehler had been given a single U-boat Enigma code and signal circuit for this war patrol of U-234. He had topped off his diesel fuel supply in Kristiansand to the maximum possible, then departed in the late afternoon of 16 April 1945 with minesweeper escort to the 200 m depth line. Her destination was Kobe, Japan, without intermediate stops. As soon as the minesweepers turned around, Fehler dived U-234 and started on a sixteen-day underwater snorkel voyage, but on a totally different course from the one ordered by Rösing.

After the German capitulation, and once the order to cease operations was received, telling U-234 to return to base or surrender in an Allied port, an extensive debate took place aboard U-234. The two Japanese officers suggested that U-234 should continue to Japan. But Fehler decided to surrender and proceed to the USA instead. Consequently, the two Japanese officers committed suicide, as they did not wish to fall into American hands under any circumstances.

When U-234 proceeded on the surface, Fehler reported his position and was contacted by a Canadian signal station, advising him to proceed to Halifax, Nova Scotia. But American signal stations that had picked up and read the position report of U-234 interfered with the Canadian directions and ordered Fehler to take a course towards the American coast instead. Fehler accepted these new instructions, and U-234 was located and approached after some hours by the American destroyer *Sutton*. A boarding party came aboard and took over U-234, directing Fehler to proceed to Portsmouth, New Hampshire, for surrender.

The bodies of the Japanese officers had been buried at sea with their personal belongings and their secret papers and files. Fehler had disposed of the brand-new Tunis radar equipment, the experimental Kurier express signalling machinery and the Enigma coding machine, plus all related papers and devices, before being boarded.

When U-234 with her escort entered Portsmouth on 19 May 1945, the crew of U-234 was surprised to see three other U-boats moored at the pier side-by-side and guarded. They had surrendered individually, and were U-805, a Type IX-C U-boat commanded by Lieutenant-Commander Richard Bernadelli; U-1228, a second Type IX-C U-boat commanded by Lieutenant j.g. Friedrich W. Marienfeld; and the Type IX-D-2 U-cruiser U-873 commanded by Lieutenant Friedrich Steinhoff. Another Type IX-C U-boat, U-858, had surrenderd in Philadelphia, commanded by Lieutenant Thilo Bode, and was transferred to Portmouth, New Hampshire, a few days later.

Because there existed one of those illogical, bureaucratic deals that often grow up between various sections of the armed forces, the American Navy was not permitted to hold any prisoners of war, including those captured by the Navy, but had to turn them over to the American Army.

Therefore, all German naval prisoners who were not selected to remain aboard their U-boats as technical specialists were turned over to US Army representatives, who placed them in Boston's Charles Street Jail, instead of a prisoner-of-war camp, a very unfortunate arrangement that was disliked by the American Navy.

Most of the crews were shipped initially to Fort Mead in Maryland for classification and sorting out in preparation for transporting them to a prisoner-of-war camp – for most U-boat men Papago Park near Phoenix, Arizona. However, senior petty officers, officers and some technical specialists were instead secretly trucked at night to the unlisted Army installation of Fort Hunt near Mount Vernon in Virginia, about seventeen miles south of Washington DC, for extensive interrogations, in spite of the fact that the war had ended.

The quarters for the prisoners of war were bugged with hidden microphones, as were the toilets, the outside areas and the eating hall. The teams of interrogators were directed by Navy Commander John L. Riheldaffer, associated with the naval intelligence group OP-16-Z.

Officially, Fort Hunt never existed. Any enquiries by the International Red Cross, the Swiss embassy or the American Red Cross, looking after German prisoners of war, were bluntly lied to, and the existence of this secret installation was repeatedly denied.

Geschwaderrichter (Squadron Judge Advocate) Nieschling, in his '*Silberling*' uniform, was a novelty for the American Navy. Nobody had ever encountered anybody with such a service grade. Therefore, Nieschling became a sort of mystery man to the interrogating Americans, who initially assumed he might be some sort of chaplain or civilian specialist whom they could not properly classify. This resulted in considerable bafflement for a while. Eventually, when those clandestine recording tapes were checked, Nieschling was found to be an interesting prisoner, who knew a lot about the internal ways of the German Naval High Command in the bureaucratic area, not only in regard to legal matters, but also personnel decisions by Dönitz, about which Nieschling was well informed.

Soon he was transferred to a preferential prisoner-of-war camp. Because of the information he had provided, he was classified as cooperative and cleared for early repatriation to Germany, even though he was a confirmed Nazi, and he was discharged much sooner than any of the others who had been aboard U-234 or any other U-boat that had surrendered in the USA.

When Germany capitulated, one by one the U-boats still at sea on or after 8 May surrendered, unless their commanders had decided to scuttle them prior to that date. Eventually, all U-boats were accounted for, except for two, which seemed to be lost somewhere.

One was U-530, a Type IX-C U-boat commanded by Lieutenant j.g. Otto Wermuth, which had departed from Horten, Norway, on 3 March 1945 and operated alone off the American east coast. She had a pretty good fuel supply aboard, and Wermuth decided to proceed into the South Atlantic, trying to reach southern Chile. But weather problems caused excessive fuel consumption, and he took U-530 into Mar del Plata, in Argentina, instead, on 10 July 1945, and surrendered there to the Argentinian Navy.

The second U-boat was the Type VII-C U-977, commanded by Lieutenant j.g. Heinz Schäffer, which had left Kristiansand, Norway, on 2 May 1945, one of the very last U-boats departing before capitulation, with a supplementary fuel supply obtained by bartering and trading booze and tobacco. U-977 had been ordered into the area west of the English channel by Godt and Rösing. When the order to cease operations was received, Schäffer returned briefly to the Norwegian coast to disembark those crew members who wanted to return to Germany rather than remain aboard.

Then U-977 left for the mid-Atlantic on a 66-day snorkel trip with a reduced crew. The crew members dropped in Norway were captured, but remained silent regarding U-977 and Schäffer's plan. On 17 August 1945, U-977 entered Mar del Plata, Argentina, and surrendered there, as the last U-boat. The crews of U-530 and U-977, after extensive interrogations, were transferred to the USA as prisoners of war, while the U-boats were moved as war booty to the USA.

The yellow press and sensationalist reporters created wild stories about these two U-boats, claiming that valuable treasures and many Nazi bigwigs had been aboard, including even Adolf Hitler – all of it pure invention and crazy speculation.

By now the war in the Far East had ended too, after the dropping of atomic bombs on Hiroshima and Nagasaki had forced Japan to surrender. Shortly afterwards, Japan was occupied by American troops. The question arose as to what had happened to those 1,232 lb of uranium oxide aboard U-234, which had somehow disappeared. If correctly condensed and properly handled, it could have been converted into 7.7 lb of purified U-235 uranium and provided one-third of the load of one of the American atomic bombs.

Why was it shipped to Japan? Intelligence and scientific sources concluded that Japan, unlike the Germans, was quite close to building a workable atomic bomb. But all traces of the Japanese research, their laboratories and records, had been destroyed before the Americans landed, while the scientists inconspicuously melted into the civilian population, leaving no traces whatsoever.

However, one of the top scientists disobeyed orders to destroy all records, and hid a box with his secret papers in the country house of his youngest assistant, with instructions in his will that this box should be opened only when he himself had passed away, thereby preserving the Japanese atomic secrets and facts for more than fifty years.

CHAPTER FOURTEEN

A Very Surprising Survival

It was shortly after 12.00 when Petersen left the U-boat Command Personnel Bureau and headed for the building where the Admiral Baltic, *Generaladmiral* Kummetz, was located, a mere five minutes' walk away. After a close identity check at the front door, Petersen was instructed to proceed to the second floor and report at the very last office at its end. An elderly administrative officer inquired what Petersen needed and told him that the personnel officer, Captain Hans Dominik, was out for lunch. However, he would start the necessary transfer paperwork right away. Petersen's ears perked up when he heard that name, as Dominik happened to be his former cadet officer. He was informed that Dominik had been the commander of a torpedo-boat flotilla in the Eastern Mediterranean, consisting of requisitioned former Italian torpedo boats, all of them gradually sunk. Dominik had been awarded the Knight's Cross for his leadership and had been transferred from the Aegean to Kiel only a few days earlier.

While the paper-pusher busied himself at his own pace, Petersen asked him what positions were available and needed to be filled in the Baltic. He was told that at present only some naval infantry jobs were open on shore, either in Pomerania or possibly in Mecklenburg. Petersen was quite upset at that unwelcome news, as he had no intention of fighting the Russians on the ground in trenches and foxholes, with insufficient supplies, lacking guns, tanks and other heavy supporting weapons.

At that moment Captain Dominik returned. He was quite pleased to see that his former cadet had survived U-boat operations, and wondered why Petersen was on the premises. Once the reason was explained, he became rather glum when Petersen emphatically requested a shipboard assignment instead of being shifted to infantry warfare. Petersen pointed out that he was still periodically undergoing ambulant medical treatment in connection with his past injuries.

Dominik, a tall, reddish-blond man, scratched his head and suddenly blurted out: 'I know you have served on S-boats [German PT or MTB boats], and that you are a qualified torpedo officer. Let me make a phone-call and check something out that I just heard about at lunch from Admiral Kummetz.' Ten minutes later he reappeared smiling. 'Boy, do you have luck! There is an immediate posting available with S-boats in the Eastern Baltic. The Admiral is not certain how many of them are still afloat. They operated in the Finnish Gulf and escorted ships to and from Libau [Liepaja] and Windau [Ventspils]. Kummetz thinks there were five at the last count, but more might have been lost. The S-boats are on their way to Hela, the last naval base we have in East Prussia, to refuel, get their flak ammunition restocked and have emergency repairs made. The group commander was killed and Kummetz believes there is now only one officer alive. They are expected to reach Hela tomorrow, 21 March. How long will it take you to be ready?' Petersen said he was as ready as he could be, as whatever he carried in his hands was his entire property. Dominik replied: 'Let's finish the necessary paperwork quickly, and you can leave as soon as Admiral Kummetz has finished the secret mail for the Eastern Baltic region. At 15.00, a special courier aircraft is scheduled to leave for the island of Bornholm, because no landing strip is available any more in East Prussia. A fast minesweeper will meet you and take you to Hela to report to Captain von Blanc.' Dominik then added: 'I understand these S-boats still carry torpedoes, although they were also used to put down mines occasionally. I can't see any further need for them. The Russians use a huge fleet of heavily armoured aeroplanes to attack our ships, so torpedoes are useless, and ships as targets don't exist in the Eastern Baltic. I suggest that you ask Captain von Blanc to authorize the transfer of your remaining torpedoes to the destroyers or torpedo boats operating out of Hela. Perhaps they will have some opportunity to use them. Try instead to get as much additional flak ammunition as you can grab and find room for it on board, as you'll need it in the worst circumstances. Try to top up your fuel whenever and wherever you have the chance to do so, as fuel is becoming increasingly hard to find and you'll need every drop to get back to northern Germany. After all, you will be operating hundreds of kilometres behind the Russian front lines, and the situation can only get worse in the remaining weeks of this war. Here comes your mailbag now. Take care, my boy. Come back in one piece. May you have fair wind all the way!'

Petersen saluted and followed the petty officer, who carried the mailbag and led him to the back entrance, where a naval car waited to take them directly to Holtenau airport.

Upon reaching Hela, Petersen reported immediately to von Blanc and repeated what Dominik had suggested to him. Full clearance was given, and Petersen was told that the S-boats were expected early the next morning, as daytime operations had become very difficult with the great number of Russian aircraft about, many of them American and British made. Von Blanc brought Petersen up to date on the military situation in the Eastern Baltic and recommended that he should get a good night's sleep, as this might well be the last one for quite some time. But he should be on the pier when the

S-boats arrived, determine their operational state and have the torpedoes removed right away, as the destroyers and torpedo boats were quite short of torpedoes and eager to get them.

Shortly after dawn, three S-boats pulled into Hela and tied up at the pier. Von Blanc welcomed them and introduced Petersen to their crews. The men looked somewhat demoralized, and the S-boats heavily used and quite beaten up. Von Blanc announced the torpedo transfer, and groups of men from the destroyers and torpedo boats stood ready to remove them without delay. The sole surviving ensign ordered the crews to assemble on the pier, as two of the S-boats were commanded by senior petty officers who were qualified navigators. Von Blanc told them to get their personal laundry ready, because they had not been able to get anything washed while operating off Courland and Latvia for weeks, and they had been forced to live in their clothing. Here in Hela laundry was still washed and finished within twenty-four hours. Moreover, while in port, they should get their uniforms cleaned, their hair cut and take hot showers. Then he turned over the men to Petersen for further handling.

Von Blanc had suggested that Petersen ought to give a short speech to the assembled crews, pointing out certain facts that would result from the removal of the torpedoes and inform them candidly about the prevailing military situation, because these men had been rather isolated while at sea, as far as the worsening situation was concerned. Then Petersen should dismiss the men and arrange to talk to each of them individually, after first studying their personal records to become at least slightly acquainted with them. If Petersen felt some men needed to be replaced or exchanged for either more experienced or more dedicated crew, this should be done forthwith, because Hela still had a big personnel pool at hand.

During his speech Petersen told the men that he had served on S-boats in the North Sea and was not a pure U-boat man who was inexperienced as far as S-boats were concerned. He also stressed the fact that both flak ammunition and fuel would have to be taken aboard at every opportunity, keeping supplies as high as practical – all the time, because of growing shortages of both. Petersen shocked the crews by stating that it might well become necessary to barter for the needed supplies or even to trade their alcohol and tobacco rations for them in the future, as had already been required here and there, to remain fully operational. He went on:

> In view of the fact that we are now over 400 km behind the Russian Army front along the Oder river, it is imperative to keep the tanks topped up and the ammunition stacked wherever there is space. The removal of the torpedoes and the weight and space gained thereby will have to be used to the maximum, even if this restricts the already limited room for the crews even further.
>
> Should any of you men feel this is not his kind of thing, he is free to leave immediately and transfer to other naval units in Hela, without prejudice

as to his motives. However, if we are to have any chance to return to northern Germany, all orders must be carried out promptly, with the utmost dedication to the job and undertaken without the slightest hesitation. You men have already experienced the swarms of Soviet aeroplanes. It is expected that this situation will grow worse, as the Soviets are starting to use the former German airfields in East Prussia, giving these aircraft an even longer range over the Baltic. You don't know me as yet, nor do I know you, but we shall get to know each well during the forthcoming days, fighting for our survival! Otherwise, we shall end up either at the bottom of the Baltic or in Siberia. I promise you that I shall do anything in my power to bring you back home and keep you out of the hands of the Soviets, where prisoners of war are not exactly pampered.

I have been informed we must get ready as fast as possible again to escort more hospital and supply ships into those ports of Latvia and Courland still held by the German Army. All repairs will be carried out on an expedited basis. Full readiness for sea duty is expected to be restored within seventy-two hours. At 10.00 tomorrow I should like to see you three commanders to discuss future operational needs and tactics. Try to catch up on your sleep here in Hela.

After dismissing the assembled crews, Petersen talked to Admiral Theodor Burchardi, the head of the Eastern Baltic Defence Command, on the radio-telephone as von Blanc had suggested, to bring him up to date on the operational status of the S-boats. Burchardi questioned him closely with respect to their mechanical state, the service needs of their engines and requested his impression of the three commanders. Petersen told Burchardi that he had not had enough time to evaluate them. All three had served with S-boats for several years and certainly had enough experience. Burchardi then wanted to know if Petersen would like to get some additional officers, in view of the fact that only one S-boat had an officer as commander. Petersen said he would prefer to keep the two senior petty officers, because of their years of experience, instead of having to try out young officers with little operational experience. Burchardi agreed and added: 'There are no suitable officers available anyway, and with the pressure to perform no chances could be taken with untried men in the present situation.' Then the Admiral wished him luck and success in every respect.

After this discussion Petersen walked to the officers' mess, where he met several friends and acquaintances. Soon the conversation became quite lively. When Ensign Dietrich 'Dieter' Garbers appeared, the sole surviving officer aboard the S-boats, and commander of one of them, Petersen called him to his table and asked if he would care to make any suggestions or would like to pass on helpful observations for the future. Garbers was somewhat surprised, and told Petersen: 'Your speech was the frankest I have heard since joining the Navy, but just what the men needed to hear.' Petersen could depend upon his fullest cooperation in every respect. Petersen then asked

Garbers to discuss with the other two commanders their respective crew members and find out if there were any men who ought to be replaced, and to advise him during the meeting the next morning, so that the necessary steps could be taken to obtain competent replacements without delay.

The afternoon passed rapidly with various meetings and visits required to expedite the repairs needed and to get the supplies requested. Russian aeroplanes repeatedly attacked the ships waiting to board refugees and to take on wounded military personnel. The anti-aircraft guns were constantly in full action to hold the aircraft at a distance. Petersen talked with von Blanc about the contemplated escort operations and the available communication arrangements, which grew less dependable as the military situation became more confusing. The Russians were pushing steadily further into Germany, and the lines of supplies and communications became longer and less reliable.

Von Blanc told Petersen that the minefields in the Eastern Baltic were now so many that the few remaining bigger warships had been limited operationally to the East Prussian coastline. They also had serious problems in obtaining ammunition resupplies. He anticipated that shortly even destroyers and torpedo boats would no longer be permitted to operate in the Eastern Baltic off Courland and Latvia – only minesweepers and S-boats, owing to their shallower draft. Petersen requested the installation of additional anti-aircraft guns to utilize the weight and space gained by the torpedo removal, which was approved by von Blanc and immediately authorized, because it would have to be done right away, while the S-boats were still in Hela.

The meeting with the S-boat commanders went well. A complete understanding on priorities and operational procedures was achieved. A small number of men were exchanged, based upon the experience and knowledge of the commanders. Petersen obtained qualified replacements from the personnel pool in Hela. There were many volunteers for the few positions available. There simply was no time to train new men, they had to be able to perform reliably from the outset.

On the evening of 25 March the S-boats departed from Hela crammed with ammunition and supplies. They were ordered once more to escort ships into and out of the Eastern Baltic, and expected to operate for several weeks without major breaks. The military situation turned steadily worse and became hopeless in April 1945. Petersen made absolutely sure that no opportunity to refuel and to obtain additional flak ammunition was allowed to pass, no matter how tired the crews were. This generated some griping at times, which was quite normal for sailors and soldiers.

The attacks by Russian aeroplanes increased daily as the weather improved, and the expenditure of flak ammunition rose correspondingly. Fortunately, the Russians only used small-calibre bombs, and when attacking with their machine-guns their aim was generally poor. The S-boats managed to stay out of harm's way for several weeks, although they were constantly at sea. However, towards the end of April, their luck ran out and one of them was hit by a bomb, which was a dud but holed the bottom of the vessel, causing leaks that could not be stopped. Petersen divided the crew between the other two S-boats, creating standing room only, then scuttling the damaged and sinking casualty. Fortunately, they were only a few hours away from Hela, where most of the rescued men were put ashore.

At the end of April, Hitler committed suicide and the Nazi regime finally collapsed. But almost the last order given by the Hitler-Bormann clique in Berlin was completely unexpected, even to insiders, much less the general population: that was that Karl Dönitz was officially named as Adolf Hitler's successor, and instructed to take over as Germany's last *Führer* and President!

Reportedly, even Dönitz himself was not quite prepared for this last-minute promotion. However, he did not waste any time in taking over the position, although the communications confusion and transport chaos were formidable and it had become almost impossible to reach many still existing military commands.

But Dönitz insisted that those still reachable, as well as all ships at sea, must immediately swear a new oath of allegiance to him, Karl Dönitz, personally, copying the oath of military allegiance that Hitler had imposed on the military forces and all soldiers since 1935. Not one single word was changed, except that the name of Karl Dönitz was substituted for Adolf Hitler.

This did not matter a lot in the general military situation on or after 1 May 1945, nor did it make any difference whatsoever in the last-minute senseless fighting that was still demanded here and there. Yet this incredible hubris by Dönitz is fairly unknown to most people, including historians, up to this day.

A few days later even Dönitz had to concede that there was nothing else to do except capitulate and surrender unconditionally. The war had finally ended, though the demand of unconditional surrender had extended it far too long and needlessly killed a huge number of people, including many thousands of Americans, Englishmen and Jews.

Yet during those last few months and weeks, even in the first few days of May, untold thousands were still shot, hanged or murdered within Germany, or at least in the few parts not already occupied by foreign armies. All this was under the slogan: 'To uphold resistance and discipline in the German forces, no matter how hopeless the situation has actually become.' Thousands were hanged from trees, telephone poles, barn doors and even church towers.

Men who considered further resistance useless and insane, if seen or over-heard, were declared to be deserters, cowards or men who refused to fight tenaciously for the final victory of Germany, the *Führer* and so on and so forth. Most of these atrocious murders were ordered and consummated by so-called *Schnellgerichte*, 'Express', or 'Flying' Courts, which settled cases in less than five minutes, including the hanging – all in the name of Germany, to defend the Fatherland until there was literally nothing left to defend. Several hundred of these express courts were activated and hard at work. The German Navy furnished a substantial percentage of them, on the direct order of Karl Dönitz.

Because the express courts had no time to keep records, and did not have paper and supplies to do so, to this day nobody knows how many thousands were executed in those final weeks, naturally only to uphold discipline, military order and a totally senseless last-minute defence to the final bullet and the last man.

Strong attempts were made to enforce desperate resistance from un-enthusiastic, tired and hungry men, who were completely worn out, had no ammunition, no usable weapons, no supplies or provisions. Most were barely trained as soldiers and were put into uniform under duress. Thousands of them were sacrificed and needlessly butchered to prolong the hopeless fighting by days or even hours. The luckier ones managed to dodge these express courts, and became prisoners of war instead.

The S-boats made two more round trips to Libau, and managed to return, in spite of almost continuous attacks by Russian aircraft, during the morning of 7 May. Petersen used every man who could be spared aboard to grab more anti-aircraft ammunition in Hela, because they had almost fired their entire supply when returning from Latvia. In addition, he ferreted out fuel at several places and had the tanks filled to overflowing, by hook or by crook, greasing palms if necessary.

When the S-boats arrived from Courland, the final group of destroyers and torpedo boats were just leaving Hela, overcrowded with refugees and military wounded, and proceeded to Copenhagen, because the northern German ports were either occupied by Allied troops or were closed to ship arrivals once the Armistice went into effect. Admiral Burchardi asked Petersen on the radio-telephone to embark von Blanc and his staff, although he knew how extremely limited the available space was on the S-boats. However, von Blanc had already boarded the old coal-burning coastal steamer *Rudgard*, overloaded with refugees. He told Petersen he would stay on this vessel and take his chances, wishing the S-boats luck with their break-through to northern Germany.

Consequently, the two S-boats were the last German vessels pulling out of Hela, minutes before the Second World War officially ended in Europe. They were so heavily loaded that there remained hardly any freeboard. Petersen had ordered the engine-room petty officers to remove the safety seals of the motors to squeeze out some extra speed if attacked by Russian aircraft or ships. Fortunately, the Russians only attacked during daylight hours. Petersen had made it crystal clear to the engineers that this was their last voyage, and if the engine valves got burnt, so be it. The slight extra speed obtainable might well make the difference if they were able to get out of this trap, almost 600 km behind the Russian lines, or ended up sunk in the Baltic.

They travelled a good distance during the night, covering half the mileage necessary to return to northern Germany.

It turned out to be a decisive measure, because they were attacked incessantly, the minute it became daylight, and pursued for several hours by rows and rows of Russian aeroplanes, approaching very low and in straight lines one after the other, stolidly disregarding the anti-aircraft fire from the S-boats. Petersen ordered snaking turns at the highest possible speed whenever these armoured aircraft started to drop their bombs, which gave the S-boats just enough time to manoeuvre and avert any hits. However, these frequent speed bursts also used up fuel in the worst way.

Once the S-boats had passed Cape Arkona on the island of Rügen, a signal was received from Admiral Baltic: 'Don't enter Kiel, Flensburg or any other German port. Change course for Copenhagen. Enter the freeport harbour area.' They had reached a point where the attacks by Russian aeroplanes gradually ceased. Petersen immediately ordered the necessary change of course to comply with this signal. In view of their excessive fuel use, it had already become questionable whether they would still have been able to reach a north German port. To reduce fuel use, Petersen ordered slow speed once it got dark, and they reached their new destination the next morning with almost empty tanks. After looking around and informing himself about the local situation, Petersen visited the various German minesweepers and fast mine-clearing boats tied up along the pier to find out what their commanders intended to do.

After the British cruisers *Birmingham* and *Dido* arrived in Copenhagen, accompanied by four destroyers of the Z class, word came down the line that the S-boats would be taken over by the Royal Navy, while the minesweepers were ordered to leave for Flensburg, as they still had enough fuel. When Royal Marines showed up on the pier to take over the S-boats, Petersen distributed his men among the minesweepers and accommodated himself aboard a fast minesweeper (R-boat) commanded by a naval classmate, to make the trip to Flensburg as his guest. Trucks were waiting upon arrival for those men no longer required aboard, to drive them to a temporary prisoner-of-war pen nearby, located in a school building surrounded by rolls of barbed wire and guarded by the British Army.

During the summer of 1945, the weather had been warm and pleasant. Frank Petersen had been repeatedly shifted from smaller prisoner-of-war pens to increasingly larger camps.

The British Army had patiently tried to observe existing regulations and to implement sanitary conditions and food requirements, as stipulated in the various international treaties signed by Great Britain. Naturally, there was considerable confusion and disorganization during that summer. But great efforts were made gradually to upgrade the prisoner-of-war camps to reach prescribed standards. With each move the size of the fenced-in area had increased, but so did the number of prisoners of war concentrated in such larger camps and compounds. From Denmark, Norway and Holland all German prisoners of war had been transported to Belgium, France or northern Germany. Many of the larger camps were established in former German military training areas or otherwise in the open countryside.

After having been in six different camps, Petersen had gained a lot of practical experience about how to get grouped with reliable fellow prisoners, how to pick the more suitable buildings or barracks and how to get through periodic searches, sudden inspections or medical examinations. Because Petersen had been wounded three times, the last time quite seriously, he had no problems with medical re-examinations, where attempts were made primarily to select the more able-bodied prisoners of war for heavy construction labour in France or elsewhere.

While earlier the British camp administrations and soldiers involved in handling the prisoners of war changed frequently, with the consolidation into larger camps the British administration in charge remained and the people of the smaller, closed-down camps returned to England. It was a lot less trouble to become familiar with a camp with an established administration in place.

With these transfers and moves the summer had passed, the autumn had arrived and the autumn leaves were turning colourful. Petersen was quite aware that the winter would be coming sooner or later, resulting in problems with heating, cooking, doing laundry and being dressed warmly enough.

The word had just been passed that they would be trucked the next day to an even bigger camp, although this would not entail a long ride, because the new camp was located fairly close by. The British top sergeant, with whom Petersen had become quite friendly, after having him in charge of work assignments in the last two camps, told Petersen: 'This will probably be your last move.' Prisoner-of-war Camp 'S', for submariners, was well established and located not far from a town called Heide in northern Schleswig Holstein. A lot of former naval men had been concentrated into this multiple compound camp.

Top Sergeant Ferguson, unofficially called Tommy, but officially 'Tops', had suggested to Petersen that he ought to apply in the new camp to become the German confidence officer, the camp interpreter/translator or the work assignment coordinator, informing Petersen that the officers who had filled these positions had been transferred for shipboard service with the German minesweeping administration. But Petersen was uncertain if he should do so, holding off any decision to see first what type of British officer would be the commander of the new camp. Petersen wanted to look over the remaining German officers in the camp administration, too, before committing himself, as he had heard some rather unpleasant stories about them. Petersen did not wish to find himself in the middle of some power struggle between different interest groups with established privileges and inside connections.

He had been unable to establish any contact with his family and wanted to wait and see what was cooking in Camp 'S' before making definite decisions about the future. After all, time was what prisoners of war had in excess. Petersen had learned that volunteering blindly or eagerly for anything in the Navy or military was usually foolish and had a tendency to backfire. He had grown tired of doing favours for fellow prisoners of war, then finding out later that it was a one-way street. It would be no exaggeration to say that he had become quite weary of other prisoners of war and increasingly longed for some privacy, something quite problematical in any prisoner-of-war camp. He had pulled back more and more from the various organized activities by different groups in the camps, using his war injuries and the frequent ambulatory medical services he required as a legitimate and accepted excuse to mind his own personal business.

By and large, Petersen had stayed together with his naval classmates who had been detained for a long time in prisoner-of-war camps in Canada, the USA, Great Britain and even Australia. They respected his medical problems and did not impose on him with special requests or demand personal favours. They had become real foxes, were totally dependable and always able to give valuable tips and reliable practical advice.

The convoy of trucks got under way with jeeps as vanguard and rear-guard, and pulled through the main gate of Camp 'S', stopping in a single row alongside the guard building. Everybody descended with their personal possessions, lined up in platoon-sized groups and did what soldiers do most of the time – waited for something to happen.

Tops Ferguson reported to the administration office and reappeared with another top sergeant, whom he introduced as Tomlinson. Both together checked off name lists and assigned sleeping locations. Once everything had been ticked off and assignments agreed with the number of prisoners of war standing about, they were told to proceed to their new quarters.

But Petersen had been daydreaming, watching a pair of kestrels circling in the sky, wishing he were able to fly away with them, thinking how unbearable this world would be without trees, plants and flowers. Suddenly, there was nobody else standing around with him any more.

Tops Ferguson called him: 'Please follow me and put your stuff into the waiting room temporarily.' Petersen, surprised, only nodded. Ferguson knocked at a door in the fairly dark hall. A loud voice called out: 'Come in, Ferguson.' He opened the door and asked Petersen to pass ahead of him, closed the door, then reported to a major of the British Army: 'Here is Lieutenant Petersen as ordered, Sir.'

Petersen grew instantly attentive, an automatic self-defence, although he had not done anything forbidden, much less been caught doing it. The major rose, stating in a Scottish brogue: 'I am Major McIntosh, the camp commander here. Tops Ferguson has reported you are fluent in English and some other languages and would like to become camp interpreter and confidence representative for the German officers here.' Petersen swallowed hard, searching for words that would not put Tops Ferguson on the spot, as he would be the wrong man to upset and could cause unpleasant problems.

Petersen hesitated, when Major McIntosh added: 'I understand your friends call you Frank. Would you prefer that?' Petersen replied, 'Major, Sir, while this possibility was once mentioned to me by Top Sergeant Ferguson, there was nothing definite about it, much less a firm decision reached, just some conversation really.'

McIntosh stretched out his hand, quite unusual for a senior officer, and more so when a prisoner of war of lower rank was involved. Then he said: 'I am a personal friend of the Bassingtons. Telford is my godson. Yes, he's fine and sends his regards to you. I was not satisfied with the German officer who acted as interpreter and camp liaison representative for me, and we transferred him to Camp Munsterlager. Tops Ferguson looked you over and believes you are honest, fair and competent. Therefore, we would very much appreciate it if you will accept this position of trust and importance.' He continued: 'I know that you have medical and health problems. Both Tommy Ferguson and I shall see to it that you'll get the necessary time for all your medical needs.'

Petersen was flabbergasted and searched for words, when McIntosh grinned and added: 'I take it you have agreed and accepted this unusual offer. I want to thank you for having looked after Telford. His mother told me that without you it would have been unlikely that he and some of his Wellington crew would have survived.'

Ferguson cut in: 'Frank, old chap, you could not find a better camp commander than Major McIntosh, so say yes, instead of wavering. Let's all shake hands on this and have a spot of 'spiked tea' together. This stays between the three of us. We don't want you to have difficulties with the hard-nosed Germans. Some of them are still in this camp, but we'll try to ship them to Camp Munsterlager in the near future.'

Petersen just nodded, and they shook hands solemnly. Tommy Ferguson said: 'Tomlinson has assigned you to Building 226, which is fairly empty at the moment, so you'll have plenty of room for the time being. I'll take you there now.' All saluted. Then McIntosh said: 'I understand you've not found any family members as yet, nor they you, for that matter. We shall help you, and also look for a place to live and a job. However, both Ferguson and I have applied for a transfer to another assignment. Although when that will come through, who knows? We should like you to stay here as long as we do. I shall arrange for your discharge when we get reassigned. Meanwhile, make sure you get all the medical help you need. And please, don't try to escape or go over the fence, as long as we are in this camp.'

Petersen managed a, 'Thank you, Sir, Major', and departed, trailing after Tommy Ferguson, who told him on the short walk to his building: 'I've never heard the Major talk that long and say so much to anybody, and we've known each other for many years. The Major has no children himself, but loves his godson like one of his own. You've made a friend for the rest of

your life, Frank. I thank you for having been a good guy in 1943!' Petersen
muttered: 'All this happened so long ago, almost in another time, or even in
another life. But I am happy Telford and his men made it back home.'

They entered the assigned quarters and Petersen spotted a pile of books
on the table. Tops Ferguson pointed to them: 'Some presents from Telford's
father, who was quite ill but fought to hang on to see his only son once more
before taking off. He had heard you like to read.'

The winter passed slowly. However, after every November there eventually arrives a May. Things had worked out well in every possible way. Major
McIntosh was pleased at how much better Petersen was as his interpreter-
translator. Tops Ferguson had acquired two girl-friends in different villages.
Petersen assisted him with his love letters and dates. He also gave him lessons
in basic German. He kidded Ferguson: 'I've often heard about the sailor with
a bride in every port, but you make me laugh, a top sergeant who can't make
up his mind and reach a decision about one girl or another.' Ferguson
grinned: 'This only applies when women are involved, otherwise I have no
problem making quick decisions.' Petersen knew this well and replied: 'Just
teasing you, Tommy.'

Ferguson turned now quite serious again: 'I've been informed that six
more pieces of shrapnel have been removed from your legs. You should soon
be climbing mountains again.' He closed the curtains, pulled out a hip-flask
and offered it to Petersen first, then said: 'Frank, the major's and my own
reassignment have just come through from London. We shall be flown to
Singapore shortly to be transferred to Malaysia to fight the Red rebels there,
who are working with the Chinese Communists.' Petersen swallowed so hard
on the unaccustomed drink that he almost choked. Ferguson continued:
'Major McIntosh has already signed and sealed your discharge papers, for
medical reasons, to be on the safe side. A sponsor has been found for housing
and a job in Munich. Our highest recommendations will go with you for the
outstanding job you've done here. Rail tickets will be furnished, but let's wait
until our written orders for Malaysia have arrived and we'll see you off
officially. You know, you have many friends here, old Scout.'

Petersen answered: 'Tommy, that's no longer so, most of them have died
and left me fairly alone in the world.' Ferguson winked, 'Another drop, old
chap? Do cheer up. Pretty soon you'll be chasing pretty girls again, while the
major and I shall be chasing Communist rebels instead, in some rotten
jungle!'

But as military matters often do, things dragged on for over two weeks.
However, in the morning of 3 July 1946 Major McIntosh showed Frank
Petersen the signed and sealed discharge papers, and explained briefly some
things about his sponsor, as Petersen was curious about him. He had not the
slightest idea who this happened to be, nor why anyone would select him or
volunteer to sponsor a prisoner of war whom he had never met. When he
raised this question with Major McIntosh, he replied: 'It works somewhat
like an adoption in many ways.'

Petersen pointed out that he was no longer a minor, and was still searching for his family. McIntosh grinned and said: 'You'll like him and he'll no doubt get to like you, too. However, once you get back on your feet and into the swing of things, you are free to make your own decision whether this should remain a temporary situation or whether you wish it to continue for longer. By the way, tomorrow morning the discharge commission is arriving, so you'd better get your things together and get packed to leave for good.'

Petersen replied with a loud laugh, 'Major, as you know, I don't need much time to pack and to get ready, considering that I came out of the war with nothing, except the clothing I was wearing; though I have acquired a few other things since.'

McIntosh then added: 'I never know who all the members of such commissions happen to be. However, you will be discharged, period, regardless of what they decide. If they ask too many questions, just play dumb and say as little as possible, no matter how awkward one or other of these fellows may become.'

On 4 July, the discharge commission arrived and they did handle a considerable number of people. Petersen had been informed by Ferguson that he would be processed towards the end, so that he would not have to wait too long, standing around with his injuries. Three tables had been set up in a row, with some distance between them to allow for conversations or questioning, minimizing noise interference. These tables were in a barn-like building that had two small side-windows and was illuminated by some electric bulbs hanging down from the ceiling. Three Englishmen were seated at each table. Because Petersen was obviously the last person to be put through the procedures, some of the men at two of the tables had already started to pack up their files, equipment and instruments.

The first table, a final medical check-out, was easy. Petersen almost got waved through, and a medical officer just declared: 'We've read your file, all okay.' At the second table Petersen's personal and identifying details were rechecked and found in order. He moved on to the last table. Two officers and a sergeant waited for him. He had never before seen any of them. This smelled like trouble to him. His limp instantly increased a bit more to indicate that he would hardly be a case for reconstruction labour. The two officers mumbled something, and one of them said with a high voice: 'Here are your discharge papers', handing him two envelopes. 'Also your rail ticket and 222 Reichsmarks discharge money. Sign here! Once you walk out of that door, you become a civilian again, Lieutenant Petersen. We have received a present for you, that Sergeant Jenkins will hand you. Good luck to you!'

Petersen marched towards the indicated door, hoping that nothing unexpected would happen before he passed through it. But Sergeant Jenkins grabbed his elbow and told him: 'Please don't forget your suitcase standing over there. You'll probably need the stuff now.' Petersen tried to shake off the man, convinced this was nothing but some last-minute dirty trick to keep him a prisoner of war longer. He immediately thought that they just wanted to pin something on him, such as stealing British Army property, or whatever kind of trap they had prepared, to hold him longer as a prisoner of war. Maybe even to punish him for illegal possession of whatever happened to be in that wretched suitcase. Jenkins held him back, pleading: 'Lieutenant Petersen, this is no trick, this suitcase really belongs to you.'

Petersen snapped: 'I entered this camp without luggage, except what I have in my hands, and I have no intention of stealing anybody else's baggage either, Sergeant Jenkins.' Jenkins was perplexed, and added: 'The suitcase was delivered for you from London. It has a letter taped to it, explaining this. Please take it along, it really is yours.' He forced the suitcase on Petersen firmly.

The two English officers just roared: 'Look at that Jerry. Suspicious straight away, whenever somebody wants to do him some good.' Jenkins pulled the door open and literally shoved Petersen through it, together with that strange piece of luggage.

The door closed with a bang. A jeep was parked only a few feet away, Ferguson at the wheel, smiling and calling: 'Get in Frank, toss your luggage in the front, but sit in the back.' Petersen pulled the side-panel open and there was Major McIntosh in the rear seat, grinning. 'Well, Boy Scout. What kind of fancy baggage have you already acquired? Very fast for a civilian, I should say.' Petersen knew he was just pulling his leg, and laughingly replied: 'They even handed me 222 marks, so that I can buy twenty-two Lucky Strikes in Hamburg while changing trains: this as a farewell present for a confirmed non-smoker.'

Ferguson broke in: 'We're taking you to the railway station, so you don't have to lug that heavy suitcase yourself, as a final gesture among friends. This really is goodbye. Perhaps for ever. Who knows if we shall ever return from that godforsaken Malaysian jungle country!' McIntosh added: 'I suppose you'll remain in touch with Telford, once postal services have returned to normal again. Please keep us posted too. He'll know how to contact us. Goodbye, old chap, we shall often think of you.' Petersen replied in a low voice: 'I shall be thinking of you, too.'

They reached the small railway station. Petersen hopped out, grabbed the suitcase and put it down on the ground to wave goodbye. The jeep accelerated jerkily, the tyres squealing loudly while the vehicle turned the corner, leaving a cloud of dust in the air, settling slowly. Petersen's eyes itched and he had to dry them quickly, much to his embarrassment. They had become moist for the first time since 1939.

The train arrived, Petersen got aboard and found it was fairly empty this far north, but it would fill up as it proceeded towards Hamburg. Once the train rolled along, Petersen remembered the envelope that was supposed to be pasted on the side of the mysterious suitcase. Carefully he pulled it off, opened it clumsily and slowly started to read:

London W1. 22 June 1946

Dear Frank,

Having ourselves experienced the many problems that prisoners of war invariably encounter with many things, including decent clothing, we have organized a collection with contributions by every one of us in some way. Even my mother insisted upon adding some things that women consider important. We hope that most of these items will half-way fit you, especially the shoes, but if that is not the case, we suggest that you exchange, trade or sell them on the black market.

You have lived or more likely survived for many years in a purely male world with little privacy. Now you are returning to the civilian world, which will eventually become civilized again, and in time even orderly. As we have returned from Germany ourselves, we know into what a mess things have turned, what with the mass bombings and the street fighting. Therefore we are aware of what you will have to deal with. But all of that will pass at some time in the future – hopefully sooner rather than later. We realize that you, Frank, are not exactly the type for the present black market economy or the current wheeling and dealing. However, that will also end eventually.

You are re-entering a country primarily full of war widows and hordes of females, many of them, no doubt, keen to grab a man: probably any man at all! Therefore we say: Watch out, Old Scout, don't get roped in too easily. Take care of yourself first. Get in touch if and when this is feasible and communications have returned to normal.

We seventeen ex-prisoners of war wish to say to you from the bottom of our hearts: Thank you, Frank, so very much! We all appreciated the practical advice that you gave us voluntarily, and the personal encouragement which you offered us when we badly needed it. Your personal example considerably reduced our individual fears and apprehension in trying situations.

Finally, we are especially grateful with hindsight for your low-key, honest and practical suggestions that no doubt kept some of us out of serious trouble. You were a fair, candid and understanding fellow, with human sympathy. In other words, Old Scout, a true friend under difficult circumstances.

Be sure to stay in touch. Call us when possible and necessary. Scout's Honour Always!

Most gratefully yours,

Telford Bassington, Harry J. Osborne, Kenneth F. Alford, Marvin S. Black, John D. Stratchey, Henry L. McCurdle, George A. Williamson, Arthur E. Manning, Terence H. Coulter, Joseph T. Follesly, Clive B. Graham, Bernard A. Traynor, Thomas H. Greenley, Nigel R. Holcombe, Clyde S. Symington, Charles F. Sharp, Anthony C. Tucker.

PS My dear mother will write to you separately, once she receives your new address, as she wishes to thank you in the name of my late father.

Petersen was quite overcome emotionally, and almost speechless at this information. What a day this had turned out to be. You lose some friends, but unexpectedly gain others. Although by now he hardly remembered any of these men any more, except for Telford Bassington.

The other passengers in the compartment left Petersen alone, ignoring his soft humming of some of his favourite melodies. He thought, 'After all there are still angels around nowadays. But how did they find me?' However, he was very glad and mightily content that those angels had managed to find him. And he knew he would need all the help he could get in the near future.

In Hamburg, he had to change trains. The Interzone Express departed from an isolated platform, where a close identity and travel-permit check took place before passengers could proceed to that platform. The train was full, but not crowded. The people already in the compartment just moved a bit closer together to make room for Petersen, somewhat shyly and without making a fuss about it.

Once the train left the station, several of them said, 'Welcome back, sailor! All the best to you!' Soon the other passengers asked him in low voices whether he needed something to eat or drink, and offered him a share of whatever they had brought along. But Ferguson had furnished him with a travel luncheon, so he was all right. It was obvious that his 'modified' uniform had given him away. But he didn't really care. It was getting fairly late, and after a few hours, everybody either took a nap or snoozed contentedly. In the early morning hours the Interzone Express entered a long tunnel and suddenly emerged from it into a glaringly illuminated area, braking hard. The passengers were woken up by bright circulating searchlights. Petersen rubbed his tired eyes and noticed a long sign giving the station's name: Eichenberg.

Loudspeakers immediately started to blare: 'Everybody must get out here for a baggage inspection! Have your personal papers ready! Hurry up and get moving now!'

Cursing silently, the passengers complied. Several teams of constabulary and American military police appeared with hand-guns in their holsters, ready for use. They also carried extra-powerful flashlights, two feet long, to examine the entire train, including the locomotive; then they searched under the carriages and finally on the roofs, too.

The waiting people wondered what they were looking for. Whom were they trying to find? Evidently, it was an exercise in futility, because they found neither stowaways nor whatever else they were searching for. Other teams double-checked documents and identity papers again. Apparently neither criminals on the loose nor other wanted folk had been on the train.

At 04.00 the train continued its journey. When it picked up speed, Petersen noticed a banner proclaiming, 'Welcome to the American Zone of Occupation'. All passengers had just entered Hesse, the land where the Hessians had once come from many years before, who had been sold like cattle by their feudal rulers to the British Crown and King George III as mercenaries to defeat the colonial rebels in North America. Fewer than half of them had eventually returned to their homeland, and the rest were buried in America, were prisoners of war or simply deserted to become Americans themselves, joining General George Washington.

But Hesse was now just another place on the way to Bavaria, which had reportedly become the new colony of the former colonials, and the destination of most passengers in that compartment was Munich, her capital.

Petersen sighed and pulled from his inside pocket the 'iron rations' emergency flask that he had closely guarded until now – a bottle of real Benedictine from Fécamp. He offered a swallow to all his fellow passengers in the compartment, exclaiming: 'Cheers!' The other folk smiled, even at such an ungodly hour, and replied with 'Prosit!' All of them now looked forward eagerly to what the future might bring. Spontaneously, they started singing, 'In Munich stands a royal court brewing house.' They laughed uproariously and yelled: 'Munich watch out, here we come!'

When the train pulled into the Munich station, it was just after 11.00. The travellers dispersed, wishing each other well, and went their individual ways. Several people in the compartment had asked Petersen if he had a place to sleep or needed some initial help to get back into things. Major McIntyre had given him a letter of introduction to a name and address in the Bogenhausen section of Munich, and he enquired at the station how to get there, and was told which tram to take.

After a very short walk from the tram stop, he found himself in front of a somewhat old-fashioned villa, which had largely escaped the bomb damage of its neighbourhood. Two bells with various names listed were at the garden gate. He rang the bell indicating Kowalski, his sponsor, there was no response. He reckoned Kowalski worked during the day, and decided to try the second bell, to find out if anybody was about, because he didn't wish to wait all afternoon in the street for the man.

Suddenly the front door opened slightly, and an American-sounding voice enquired, 'Who are you and what do you want here?' Petersen replied, 'I'm Frank Petersen and I'm here to see Mr Kowalski. But he seems to be at work, and I should very much appreciate it if you could let me wait inside for him, as I'm tired from a rather long train journey.' The door opened fully, and a lady waved Petersen inside and told him, 'Please come in, Colonel Kowalski won't return before 6.00 p.m. from his office. However, he has mentioned to us that you would be arriving in the next couple of days. My name is Carol Kelleher, we occupy the first floor, while Colonel Kowalski uses the ground floor whenever he happens to be in town. Put your things down and make yourself comfortable on his sofa. His housekeeper should return shortly from shopping.'

Petersen was momentarily stunned. Looking at the lady he wondered if she might be one of those angels who had guided him, though she did not have wings. Her shining raven-black hair contrasted with sparkling eyes of the most brilliant deep blue, tinged with a shade of violet. Petersen felt thunderstruck, what the French call hit by a '*coup de foudre*', and he hesitated to enter. The lady encouraged him and said, 'Do come in, please; don't worry, I don't bite! How about some coffee to pep you up?' Petersen informed her about his preference for tea. 'That's no problem, we have both. I'm an Army lieutenant from Santa Rosa, California. Today is my day off. I share the first floor with Lieutenant Belinda Hollingsworth from Tampa, Florida, and Lieutenant Harriet Wilson from Greenville, South Carolina. But both are away for several days on Army business.' Petersen had recovered somewhat from his shock, and asked: 'You mean to tell me, you come from the town where Luther Burbank lived and worked, Mrs Kelleher?' 'I'm Miss, not Mrs, Kelleher. I'm mighty surprised that you know anything about Luther Burbank, because you are the first person in Germany who seems to have heard of him. I shall be tickled pink to talk to you about him and California, the Golden State. Although most people have only heard of Hollywood, the movie companies and San Francisco, or the historic gold strikes.' Petersen replied, 'Miss Kelleher, there is a first time in life for everything. I learned about Luther Burbank at high school, and look forward to hearing more about him from you.'

He sat down on the sofa. The housekeeper came in loaded with packages. Miss Kelleher told her, 'Please make tea right away and look after Mr Petersen until Colonel Kowalski arrives.' 'Colonel Kowalski told me you were a submariner. I get the shakes and claustrophobia whenever I just hear the word Submarine.' Petersen smiled and replied, 'Fortunately, that's all over and done with. We can talk about more pleasant things and what the future might have in store.' She asked: 'What do you have in mind? Colonel Kowalski will undoubtedly need you as his personal interpreter and a translator for his mountains of paperwork. By the way, he is from the Chicago area, and a lawyer in civilian life, married with three children. I think he has enough points for overseas service to return home and get discharged from the Army. Although he seems to like it in Bavaria and hasn't mentioned that he is keen to return to civilian life and his old firm. The Colonel is extremely busy and a very demanding boss, who expects top performance from his subordinates.'

The tea was poured by the housekeeper, and the conversation stopped for a while. Petersen sipped his tea and silently thanked those two 'Scottish rascals', Major McIntyre and Tops Ferguson, for this arrangement that they had set up for him. He could not quite understand how, and especially why, they had done it. Nevertheless, he was certainly going to like it very much, no matter what sort of person Colonel Kowalski turned out to be. Petersen had had quite a few difficult superiors and had always managed to get along without becoming aggravated to a point where things became intolerable. Therefore, he was convinced that somehow he would also get along passably with Kowalski, at least temporarily, if the worst came to the worst.

CHAPTER FIFTEEN

Post-war Changes and Cold War Switches

Once the war ended in Europe, it became obvious that something had to be done about the half-million mines laid in the North Sea, the Baltic and connecting sea areas during the war. A meeting of naval experts was organized in London to solve the problem. They decided to create the International Mine-Clearing Board at the end of May 1945.

It was quickly determined that there was a great shortage of minesweepers and experienced men to crew and operate them. Minesweeping was not the preferred type of assignment for ambitious naval officers, because it was considered a largely defensive activity, without distinction and visibility, while naval officers build their reputation with aggressive operations to gain recognition and promotion.

The ever-practical English decided that there was only one solution to the problem: reactivate the German minesweeping flotillas and employ them forthwith. The surviving German units had been assembled in Flensburg and Kiel in the Baltic, and Cuxhaven and Bremerhaven in the North Sea area. They had been well maintained and had skeleton crews aboard. Because of language problems, the British experts rapidly realized that these ships would have to be managed and directed by experienced German officers and administrative officials. Consequently, they quietly reactivated these German minesweeping units in the summer of 1945 under a British director, to get this pressing job done in the shortest time possible, and organized the German Minesweeping Administration. Former commanders and officers were retained if they had a clean record and were willing to stay on voluntarily.

Among the administrative staff hired were the former naval judge advocates Helmut Sieber and Otto Kranzbühler. When they had been confirmed in their new positions, they started to set up a legal assistance organization on the side for former naval judge advocates and a few others.

In autumn 1945, Kranzbühler was selected by Karl Dönitz as his defence lawyer in the Nuremberg War Criminal Trials. Commander Hans Meckel was hired as coordinator of personnel. Meckel was pleasant to work with, clever and reliable. He had been the communication director of the U-boat Command for many years and was a former U-boat commander. Meckel, fluent in English and French, organized the naval and technical support for the defence of Dönitz, ferreting out witnesses, supporting documents and providing travel assistance, while Kranzbühler handled the legal side and persuaded reluctant witnesses to come forward in Dönitz's defence. Any effective defence of Dönitz would have been impossible without the strong support of these men, who worked as a secret vanguard and rearguard for Dönitz and looked out for his personal interests in all possible ways.

The British combed out the various prisoner-of-war camps to pick up enough experienced men to run the ships with full crews and set up a personnel replacement pool in Hamburg, to take care of the constant fluctuation among the crews. As men left or did not renew their working contracts, new men had to be provided to fill their positions. The changes among the officers were less frequent, particularly when they commanded ships, because this permitted them more flexibility and personal freedom from harassment. One did the job correctly, had room and board, access to other supplies and by and large could mind one's own business. Of course, quite a bit of smuggling took place, and a lot of people were carried when practical and possible, as nothing much was moving on the ground within Germany, apart from military transport. There was no postal service and no telephone communications for a long time, and the rationing of foodstuffs and clothing continued for quite a while.

By the autumn of 1945, about 27,000 former German naval men were employed, an astonishing number if one considers that the German Navy had fewer than 15,000 men and officers in service in 1932. This number was gradually reduced to 14,900 men and petty officers and 1,100 officers by the end of 1946. At the end of 1945 an astounding 575 German minesweeping vessels of all types were in constant operation, additionally supported by a further 180 converted fishing boats and auxiliary merchant ships. They were organized in eight M-boat minesweeping flotillas, six R-boat shallow-water and river mine-clearing flotillas, three flotillas of mine barrier detonator ships and three flotillas of auxiliaries and former fishing vessels.

At the end of 1947 the German Minesweeping Administration was officially closed. But in reality it was only reorganized and renamed, with a smaller number of ships and a reduced scale of personnel. The name of the British operations was changed to Frontier Inspection Service, and the American operations to US Labor Support Service. A small section of the British operations was composed of former German S-boats, PT or motor torpedo boats, equipped with special super-high-powered engines, commanded by Lieutenant Hans Helmut Klose, to land and infiltrate secret agents into Communist Poland and the Soviet-occupied Baltic countries, which were disguised as fishery protection vessels.

Additional naval judge advocates were brought into the German Minesweeping Administration, once they were released from prisoner-of-war camps, to give them a temporary position and some initial shelter. Most of them were gradually fed into the German civilian court system as openings occurred, while others were set up in private law offices with financial support and the referral of commercial legal work to get them rolling. Kai Nieschling was employed when he returned from America and ceased being a prisoner of war, completing the trio of wire pullers at the top, more and more now called the 'Hamburg Gang'.

Karl Heinrich Hagemann obtained a position in Kiel in July 1945, when he had been discharged as a prisoner of war. But Hagemann was fired by the British in March 1946, after many complaints were received about his arrogance. Hans Egon Breinig was hired in the summer of 1945, once he was discharged as a prisoner of war, and he worked mostly in Kiel and Flensburg. As far as the naval judge advocates were concerned, everything moved along smoothly and well.

In spring 1946, Heinz Kusch was contacted by two close friends of his son. They had just been discharged as prisoners of war, and wanted to find out what had happened to Oskar. These men had found jobs with the newly founded and growing press, one as a reporter, the other as junior editor, but on different papers. Heinz Kusch still lived in West Berlin, and was now the director of another insurance company. Both men were horrified when they were informed about Kusch's execution. They encouraged his father to have the facts checked and clarified to exonerate Oskar, at least posthumously. They felt the former naval judges and the denouncers ought to be found, sued and punished. They asked Kusch's father to post them copies of all papers received in 1944 from the Navy, and informed him they would publish this material in their newspapers with a strong commentary, hoping to generate additional information through responses from their readership.

On 8 July 1946, the first report appeared in the *Neue Zeitung*, a paper in Stuttgart, and shortly afterwards another in the *Aachener News*. Each article included a true copy of the official notification that Kusch's father had received from the Navy, and the form-letter regarding his burial. A flood of responses from people who had been treated in a similar way by the German Navy and other branches of the German forces during the Second World War reached the papers for weeks after the publication. Kusch's father was approached by several former naval officers who tried to persuade him to drop the matter as a lost cause, arguing it was best to let dead men rest, as nothing could bring them back to life. Heinz Kusch firmly and quickly brushed off these crude attempts to influence him. Living in the isolated city, surrounded by the Soviet zone of occupation, severely restricted travel and limited all types of communications. Even the postal service was only restored in several small geographical steps over a long period of time.

Kusch's father managed to get in touch with Oskar's defence counsel during the trial, Gerhard Meyer-Grieben, whose house had burnt down in Kiel, together with many of his records and papers. However, Meyer-Grieben nevertheless obtained two copies of the Kusch case court file and posted one of them to Kusch senior in West Berlin. Meyer-Grieben informed Heinz Kusch that he was only able to work on the case in Kiel. After some lengthy correspondence Kusch drew some incorrect conclusions from the court file, and accused Meyer-Grieben of mishandling the defence of his son in 1944. He complained that Meyer-Grieben had failed to obtain a reprieve or reversal of his son's death sentence, and get it changed to probation at the front, or a prison term. Meyer-Grieben pointed out to him that his son had refused to sign any application for reconsideration or an act of mercy on his behalf and that Oskar had repeatedly told him he would not sign such papers if submitted against his will. Meyer-Grieben felt wrongly accused by Heinz Kusch and declared that his post-war views were incorrect, based upon wartime conditions. Therefore he, Meyer-Grieben, could not work with him any longer, nor would he represent him in the future.

Therefore on 10 December 1946 Heinz Kusch wrote directly to the court director and the chief prosecutor of the higher court in Kiel, posting each a complete set of all the material he had collected since 1944, adding the list of names and addresses of surviving crew members of U-154 who had volunteered to testify for his son, and the whereabouts of all people involved with the Kusch trial in 1944. It was known that Druschel had drowned when U-154 had been sunk. Abel was still recorded as missing without definite information whether he was dead or alive. Fröhlich, Winter, Dittmers and Westphalen were British prisoners of war in England. The naval judge advocates Hagemann, Breinig and Meinert had recently been seen in Kiel, still wearing their naval 'Silberling' uniforms, now working for the German Minesweeping Administration. Janssen and Kirchammer reportedly lived in southern Germany, the American zone of occupation, but could not be located. Funke had survived the war, but could not be found anywhere.

It took some time before the court officials agreed to pass the Kusch case file on to the lower court in Kiel for a preliminary investigation to determine if a follow-up was warranted and possible. Once this was considered feasible, a full investigation was started on 3 February 1947. Five months later, the senior state attorney and principal prosecutor Dr jur. Thamm informed Heinz Kusch about the legal situation as seen by him.

At this time, he indicated, no indictment could be prepared against Hagemann that had any chance of being successful, nor against Breinig, as he had only requested a prison term for Oskar Kusch. And the military advisory judges Dittmers and Westphalen could not be punished for submitting to Hagemann's demand in chambers for the death penalty. Finally, Thamm wrote, he did not believe Karl Dönitz could be included in the list of those people who murdered Oskar Kusch, because Dönitz had refused reconsideration of the death penalty when reviewing the judgement. Moreover, Dönitz was now in Spandau prison and not accessible to German courts at this time.

In view of the time element, Thamm doubted that Abel had survived the loss of U-193, although his death could not be definitely ascertained. If new evidence were obtained or additional compromising material dug up, the case could be reopened in the future. However, at present there was no expectation that this might become the case or that supplementary information would be forthcoming from new sources, directly or indirectly.

Six months later, Dr Thamm was informed by Hans Pauckstadt, the original commander of U-193, that there was no possibility that Abel had survived the loss of the vessel and somehow become a prisoner of war. Furthermore, his family had recently petitioned the courts to have him declared legally dead. Therefore the claim of Abel denouncing another officer was deleted from the Kusch file.

Lastly, Dr Thamm was informed that Dittmers had just been discharged as a prisoner of war, and arranged for him to be questioned and a deposition to be prepared of his interrogation. But Westphalen would remain a prisoner of war longer and was not reachable until released by the British.

With this supplementary information to hand, Dr Thamm decided to reopen the Oskar Kusch case, and filed a broadened informational report with the appeal court in Kiel on 5 January 1948, stating that Hagemann, Dittmers and Westphalen had conspired in chambers to increase the prison term demanded by Breinig to the death penalty, without any legal justification for doing so. Therefore, all three men had connived secretly and jointly to condemn Oskar Kusch to death vengefully, on account of purely political motives. The three conspirators had purposely used the death penalty to eradicate a political opponent of the Nazi regime, an officer of outstanding ability, extraordinary professional competency and a clean military record, without any previous punishments whatsoever: Oskar Kusch.

The 'Hamburg Gang', Sieber, Kranzbühler and Nieschling, were informed that Westphalen was due to be discharged, and managed to visit him in the Neuengamme prisoner-of-war compound a few days before his release. The trio carefully prepared Westphalen and instructed him what to say and what to circumvent, when he was called for a deposition shortly after his discharge, both to protect himself legally in every possible respect, but also to shelter the professional standing of the naval judge advocates in every possible way.

When Westphalen was questioned by the Kiel court interrogator, he simply parroted faithfully the statement made by Dittmers earlier, a copy of which had been furnished to him by the 'Hamburg Gang' for his guidance, adding a few minor details to make it less obvious that he had been coached in advance.

It was unfortunate that the lawyer Meyer-Grieben had had a conflict of opinion with Kusch's father earlier. Meyer-Grieben's inside knowledge of the entire Kusch case, his complete information regarding the entire legal procedures and methods employed and his personal experience of the naval court system would have been invaluable. It could have helped to defeat the legal tactics and court manipulations planned and organized by the 'Hamburg Gang' to fight the retrial.

While he had severed all further connections with Heinz Kusch, Meyer-Grieben had advised the state attorney's office that he would be willing to testify as witness for the prosecution if the Kusch case were revived and went to trial, despite the intense attempts by the 'Hamburg Gang' to prevent this. There was no financial incentive or professional advantages for Meyer-Grieben to testify for the state – only vexation combined with political aggravation. But Meyer-Grieben had grown to respect Oskar Kusch and to admire his attitude during the 106 days of his incarceration in Kiel before he was executed by the Navy. Moreover, he had been forced in the line of duty to attend the shooting.

Early in February 1948, Dr Thamm filed an updated report with the higher court in Kiel and made a renewed application to bring the Kusch case on the docket for a trial, now stating:

> It may be questionable whether laws put into effect during the war within Germany still have enforcement power and if special intensified war court orders, including Paragraph 5, are valid, that were used to sentence Oskar Kusch do death. But even if that is the case, the judgement rendered was excessive, inhumane and criminal by any fair and reasonable consideration. Even during wartime, it was and is a crime against humanity to sentence a deserving officer to death because he criticized the criminal leadership of the regime in power, being concerned about the future of the German people and the country. This sentence was unjust and considerably harsher than the deeds involved could ever justify, even in the wartime situation as it existed in 1943/1944.
>
> This is evidenced and clearly confirmed by the prosecutor's request for a limited prison term as punishment. But these three men accused colluded in chambers to increase and raise the judgement to the death penalty without any legal need or justification, and for which no military necessity existed. It was done solely to exterminate a political opponent of the Nazi regime under false pretences. The three men accused acted inhumanely in doing so. This is quite clear from the lack in the court's final judgement of any legal and written explanation of the reasons for grossly increasing the penalty in chambers.
>
> Furthermore, the court's president, Admiral von Friedeburg, had expressly forbidden the judges from including any military points of consideration in the indictment, or having them mentioned in court, because military considerations were NOT applicable in this case. Therefore, ,such military requirements cannot be used now for the

justification of the death penalty under the then prevailing circumstances, much less retrospectively.

The depositions of Dittmers and Westphalen, on the contrary, now appear to attempt a total reversal of facts and events, and are trying to disregard entirely the instruction to the naval court in 1944.

But the state court's reviewing group totally rejected his effort on 16 February 1948, declaring that military necessity was the overwhelming point in the rejection of the state's plea and request. The depositions of Dittmers and Westphalen were very clear in that respect. It was the decisive factor for these *Beisitzer* judges in their support of Hagemann's request to change the sentence and their acceptance of that decision without objection. They voted for the death penalty on the basis of military disciplinary needs and patriotic conviction on their part to uphold the military order of the naval forces. These judges also declared that Hagemann had not bent the laws or twisted the naval regulations, because he had judged the Kusch case only on military grounds and had not considered any political aspects.

Nevertheless, the Minister of Justice of the state of Schleswig Holstein, Dr jur. Rudolf Katz, ordered on 23 March 1948 that the chief prosecutor in the state attorney's office should prepare a public indictment in the Hagemann case, owing to its importance and the possibility that it could become a cornerstone for future legal guidance.

On 14 March 1949, in the upper criminal court in Kiel, former naval judge advocate Hagemann was accused in writing by Dr Thamm, the head prosecutor for the state of Schleswig Holstein, of having exceeded his legal responsibilities by sentencing Oskar Kusch to death for purely political reasons.

Hagemann's defence was taken over, on Kranzbühler's recommendation, by the former naval judge advocate Bernard Leverenz, who had recently left the German Minesweeping Administration and gone into private law practice. Leverenz was from Rostock in the Soviet zone of occupation, and decided Kiel would be a better place for him to open his law office, with substantial financial and legal support by the 'Hamburg Gang' to get things going. Sieber, Nieschling and Kranzbühler had decided that they had to assist and support each and every court case coming up which in any way involved former naval judge advocates, whether accused, tried or merely investigated in a preliminary way. Consequently, they offered close and effective legal and financial support and assistance in court procedures to every defence counsel handling such a case, using their widespread legal and political connections to the utmost. The 'Hamburg Gang' also arranged for testimony by helpful witnesses obliged to Sieber, Kranzbühler and Nieschling, and covered their travel and legal expenses.

On 23 March 1949, Leverenz filed his contesting response of eleven pages, requesting that the court reject the state's indictment totally, and terminate once and for all the prosecution of his client, Hagemann, without any conditions. Leverenz stated that the naval judge advocates and the naval military court system were never influenced by orders from senior staff in any way. He claimed Hagemann could not have received those infamous, secret, criminal directives sent to the higher-placed naval judges from Berlin, as Hagemann's position was not high enough in the court hierarchy for that. This was a doubtful statement, if not an outright lie, as the secret 'Red Donkey' file was known to all naval judge advocates, and constantly consulted by them.

Leverenz then had the cheek to declare that to punish Hagemann retrospectively, when he had only done his duty and followed instructions to maintain law and order, would create a serious, even a dangerous, precedent for the future, which would frighten judges of independent mind from making determinations and decisions they considered necessary, and restrict their freedom to apply the punishment they viewed as essential.

On 2 May 1949, the preliminary court hearing started, and after extended arguments from both sides, twenty-two different legal points were reviewed, discussed and decided. However, one single fact remained unanswered and uncontested, that Hagemann had in chambers drastically increased the prison term requested by the prosecutor Breinig to the death penalty, although the naval prosecutor had not considered the Kusch case a capital one. Further clarification seemed necessary on that point to see if it could be decided later, either by discovering new documents or finding additional witnesses. It was suggested that witnesses who had attended the trial should be located, such as four officers from the staff of Admiral von Friedeburg delegated as observers, who sat in the visitors' gallery during the trial. Unquestionably, this would require a great deal of research and time-consuming investigation.

During this time considerable changes had taken place, and more were anticipated in the near future in the successor organizations of the former German Minesweeping Administration, which were due to the dramatic growth of the Cold War. This generated new policies and developments, which most folk would have believed impossible even a few months earlier. The rearming of Germany was on the cards, and many changes to make it possible were initiated. A new German Federal Navy became part of these plans, and step by step the organizational foundations were laid down and firmly established. Quite a few former German naval officers and petty officers were gradually checked out and selected for the new Federal Navy. Preference was given to those men who had served since 1945 or 1946 in the minesweeping flotillas, because they had gained a lot of additional seafaring experience. As a rule these men were reactivated with their last service grade in the former German Navy.

The selection process and the examination of candidates was handled in a fairly equitable and careful way. But some hitches occurred, and a certain amount of individual pull played a part in the hiring procedures. Several 'Old Boy' networks existed, and were often used to provide the correct answers to questions asked, or to furnish test questions in advance to favoured applicants.

Many of the former officers who were interested in rejoining the German *Bundesmarine* were viewed as too controversial or too old. Initially higher-grade positions were very limited and subject to political influence. Hans Meckel was turned down, though eminently qualified, as being too close to Dönitz. He became a translator in a publishing house instead. However, Gustav Adolf Janssen was rehired and eventually became a U-boat instructor, and later a U-boat commander again.

Yet there remained the super-ambitious Rösing, who had increasingly pulled back from all visible activities in the various German naval veterans' groups, and used his political connections to his personal advantage. His problem was his age and the scarcity of higher-grade openings. But Rösing could afford to wait until such positions were eventually created and became available. His patience paid off, and he was rehired as a full Navy captain.

But what made a lot of officers very furious was the immediate assignment of Rösing to the principal officers' selection team. Crafty as he had always been, he had once again worked his way into the inner circles of the new Federal Navy, and into the group of politicians assigned as watchdogs and supervisors of the Federal Navy's administration. Eventually, being a flexible and compliant yes-man, Rösing managed to become a rear admiral after all.

Thanks mostly to Joseph Stalin and his Communist regime in Soviet Russia, with its aggressive, intransigent and unpredictable policies, Germany had once again an Army, an Air Force and a new Federal Navy, with all the political and strategic consequences that this entailed, and the related actions which were required to keep these armed forces in full operation. One of the most undesirable factors was the reintroduction of the military draft, the obligatory military conscription of young men in great numbers.

However, another side effect of this development was the complete reha-bilitation of all former naval judge advocates, although very few of them could rejoin the Federal Navy administration because they were too old. But more important, almost all of them already occupied high-grade civil service jobs in the legal field or had opened private law offices somewhere and were doing so well financially that they simply could not afford to work for the Federal Navy, with its fixed pay scales, any more.

Naturally, none of these events had been intended or desired by the Soviet Union, yet the reality had become irreversible at this point, and the Communist functionaries were infuriated about a development that they had primarily caused themselves. Therefore, the Communists set up their own military forces in Eastern Germany, and in addition considerably increased the military presence of Russian troops, tanks, aeroplanes and ships.

In both Western Germany and Eastern Germany new mushrooming government bureaucracies quickly ordered limits on free speech, putting into effect quite rigid requirements of what their respective ruling power groups considered the obligatory 'correct political views', which were periodically subject to change. Unfortunately, these restrictions on free speech were retained, instead of being discontinued, when the Cold War ended in 1989, nor was the obligatory military draft of young men terminated after the reunification of Germany.

CHAPTER SIXTEEN

The Big Whitewash

Time was flying along rapidly, while the legal paperwork moved at its customary slow pace through the various bureaucratic channels. There were the usual delays caused by legal objections, disagreements over witnesses or technical experts, amended depositions, postponements, time extensions and difficulties in coordinating the availability of witnesses, counsel and judges on account of overlapping commitments.

In summer 1949, hearings had taken place and arbitration was suggested. However, neither side had been willing to accept that solution, and the trial became unavoidable. Nevertheless, agreement was reached that all non-controversial points, uncontested matters, amended depositions and recorded preliminary interrogations of witnesses and other parties were accepted as factual for the trial in order to obviate further wasteful efforts, non-essential costs and expenses, restricting repetition to the minimum possible. A stipulation was signed by all parties to that effect, unless new evidence was found or unexpected material changes occurred. Witnesses who had given depositions were excused from appearing in court if their testimony had not been contested or challenged on account of newly dis-covered facts.

When it seemed the case would go on trial, political problems developed, a lengthy election took place in the summer of 1950, and the former state government was voted out of office. But it took another two months before the victorious party was able to put a new state government and adminis-tration together. Many heads rolled and qualified replacements had to be brought into those positions, requiring time to get settled.

Finally, on 5 September the new party alliance took over and appointed Dr jur. Otto Wittenburg as minister of justice and court administration. The date of 18 September was set up as the starting date for the trial, which was expected to last a week or more.

The senior state prosecutor, Dr Thamm, was tied up with many things, and his first assistant, Dr jur. Albrecht, headed the prosecuting team and covered for Dr Thamm whenever necessary. Dr Albrecht had been working on the case since the beginning with Dr Thamm, and was fully familiar with the legal and technical details.

State Prosecutor Albrecht had become acquainted privately with several naval officers of Crew 37-A, former naval classmates of Oskar Kusch who were incensed about the handling of the case and wanted to help clear his reputation and name, at least retrospectively, to the greatest extent possible.

To circumvent nasty personal attacks on these men by old Nazis and some other former naval officers, they insisted on staying in the background or remaining completely anonymous. But they furnished Albrecht with information, clues, guidance or facts, ferreting out supportive evidence and documents for the prosecution.

Sieber, Kranzbühler and Nieschling had somehow found out about this support, and the 'Hamburg Gang' asked Meckel and Rösing to use their influence to suppress it, or at least make it ineffective by putting pressure on these men's employers, and threatening them economically with the loss of their jobs if they did not drop their assistance.

But Albrecht had kept his sources and their names secret and confidential, and only met these officers clandestinely, outside his office and away from the courthouse, since in several other cases such helpers had already been blackmailed, threatened, attacked or even beaten up.

Prosecutor Albrecht had found and contacted both Werner Winter and Gustav Adolf Janssen, in southern Germany. Winter readily agreed to become a court witness in Kiel, though Janssen was unable to travel, owing to an accident. But he had signed a Power of Attorney for Winter to represent him in court and to speak fully in his (Janssen's) name as witness. Albrecht had also located one of the four officers who had in 1944 worked under von Friedeburg and attended the Kusch trial as observers, who likewise agreed to testify in court.

Kranzbühler, Nieschling and Sieber became very nervous when they were informed about these new witnesses. The 'Hamburg Gang' immediately contacted all naval judge advocates and arranged for the strongest possible witness parade of them.

Leverenz had requested that the witnesses for the state should testify first, as suggested by the 'Hamburg Gang', which coordinated the defence in every respect. The witnesses of the defence were called towards the end, and it was hoped this would create a better impression and their words would stay more firmly and longer in the minds of the listeners.

Meyer-Grieben had volunteered as a state witness and was called at the beginning of the hearings, as it was expected that he might be able to raise some new facts and discover valuable connections with related matters, because he knew the entire Kusch naval and court file intimately. Leverenz did not wish to question him, as he was worried that Meyer-Grieben could introduce undesirable facts that would hinder Hagemann's defence.

Albrecht asked Meyer-Grieben how many naval court cases he had participated in as defence counsel between 1939 and 1945. Meyer-Grieben told the court that such cases numbered more than 200, starting in 1941. In addition to the Kusch case, eleven of those cases ended with the death penalty being levied. Meyer-Grieben related that he had filed for reconsideration and a review to get a reduction in those eleven cases, but the higher naval commands had refused each such plea, and all the men involved were shot.

In the Kusch case, no such petition had been filed, as Kusch had told Meyer-Grieben he would not request a reduction in his sentence, and if submitted against his will, Kusch would refuse to sign the application.

The only independence in decisions that Meyer-Grieben had been able to observe was the strong opposition by the naval courts and judges to any outside interference from Nazi Party functionaries, who liked to participate in such court martials. Otherwise, these judges were very tightly controlled and closely directed from Berlin.

Albrecht asked Meyer-Grieben what was done and how it was done in connection with the eleven death penalty cases that ended in executions. Meyer-Grieben stated that in all cases Dr Rudolphi turned up and became involved, both in person and as a counter-signer of the petitions. The name of Rudolphi was widely known and rather despised by all naval judge advocates and most defence counsel handling naval cases. The explanations given were that Dr Rudolphi wished things to be done his way. There would be difficulties with Dr Rudolphi unless things were processed precisely in the manner he wished. Dr Rudolphi was the decisive man in Berlin, who without fail checked, handled and processed all death penalty cases and examined the files repeatedly and minutely.

Kranzbühler almost choked when he had to listen to this testimony. But of course, to him and the other naval judge advocates, this was really an old story.

Albrecht asked Meyer-Grieben if he had had the impression that Kusch had become unwilling to do his duty commanding U-154 because he no longer believed in final victory for Germany. Or was Kusch depressive and hesitant to fight? Meyer-Grieben replied, no, Kusch continued to do his duty conscientiously, as he felt great responsibility for his petty officers and enlisted men. Meyer-Grieben said that while Kusch thought the war was lost, he would not shirk his obligations, leading his men to the best of his ability. Perhaps he did so without great enthusiasm. But with determination, grinding his teeth, Kusch would have fulfilled his task until the bitter end, and he had refused the opportunity for a transfer to become an instructor at one of the U-boat schools or training flotillas in the Baltic. This was a step taken by a number of U-boat commanders on their own initiative or on the direction of their superiors, as they could no longer handle the constantly greater operational pressure and strain. But Kusch had firmly refused such an alternative.

Like a great number of officers and men, Kusch made a very sharp distinction between Germany and her needs and requirements, and the demands and preferences of the Nazi Party and the Hitler regime, serving the needs and obligations of Germany, while hating the increasing demands of the Nazis. Yet he continued to do his duty and fulfilled the requirements of his job, even if doing so went more and more frequently against his conscience.

Prosecutor Albrecht then called a new witness, Lieutenant (Engineering) Rüdiger Burchards. He had served on the staff of Admiral von Friedeburg as detailer for technical and engineering personnel in 1944. Burchards had attended the Kusch trial as an observer, together with Lieutenant-Commander Harald Jeppener-Haltenhoff, Lieutenant Rolf Steinhaus and Lieutenant Wilhelm Franken, who had prepared the expert evaluation of Kusch's war patrol journals and records for the admirals and the naval court.

All four officers gained the strong impression that the Kusch case had been rushed unseemingly into court, without any military need to do so. While the defence counsel was allowed some leeway and enough time in court, this haste precluded any effective defence. Nor did it permit the defence to locate and bring into court additional witnesses for Kusch, who were familiar with U-154 and the U-boat operational problems in France and at sea, rather than only in the Baltic.

However, Burchards stated that he and the other three officers were jolted and greatly shocked when the prison term requested by Prosecutor Breinig had been increased to the death penalty by the judges in closed deliberation in chambers; especially because no reason or justification was given by Hagemann or anybody else. Nor had any additional or supplemental evidence been introduced or any new witnesses been heard. This was unprecedented, and was discussed at length by these four officers both in the visitors' gallery and afterwards.

Lieutenant Wilhelm Franken had approached Judge Advocate Hagemann as soon as the court's session was declared closed. He was very upset that Hagemann had completely ignored his expert evaluation and the instructions to the judges and the court by Admiral von Friedeburg. Hagemann first hemmed and hawed, then admitted he had been ordered to make an example of Kusch, as a warning to other political malcontents in the U-boat Command.

When questioned further by Albrecht, Burchards added that Hagemann had told Franken and the other three officers with him that Rösing, as the court's president, had interfered and insisted upon the death sentence to strengthen the discipline of U-boat Command officers and shake up other U-boat commanders with similar ideas or opinions.

Prosecutor Albrecht decided to remind the hearing judges and the witnesses that the military evaluation by Wilhelm Franken prepared for Admiral von Friedeburg and the naval court judges was still fully valid and pertinent, though it had been completely ignored since it had been issued, which was wrong as well as unfortunate. Consequently, Albrecht now read that report word for word, for the people in court: The trial would have to go forward and the judges as well as the pre-trial investigator, now prosecutor, had to be firmly instructed that all the military and fear aspects

were to be deleted completely from the indictment and only the entirely political complaints were to be retained and presented at the court martial.

The next witness Albrecht brought into court was Werner Winter, who
now worked as a college lecturer in Heidelberg. He was in frequent contact
with Gustav Adolf Janssen. Winter informed Albrecht and the court that
Janssen was hospitalized and unable to travel at present, but that they had
recently discussed the entire Kusch case and Janssen had executed a Power
of Attorney to permit Winter to speak fully in Janssen's name also.

When further interrogated on the trial procedures in 1944, Winter related
that several petty officers and enlisted men who had served on U-154 while
Kusch was her commander had offered both verbal and written testimony
about what had really transpired on U-154, but this was rejected by
Hagemann and Breinig as not necessary.

When Winter had questioned both of them after the trial, Breinig somewhat sheepishly conceded that Rösing had opposed the admission of such
witnesses, claiming this should remain a case only for officers. Breinig had
asked Rösing about the defence witnesses Winter and Janssen, whom he had
purposely not contacted, because Rösing had warned him that under no
circumstances would it be permitted to broaden the case or to increase the
number of witnesses and subjects presented in court. This would generate
more work for the court and require additional handling time. Breinig had
assumed that Meyer-Grieben had brought Winter and Janssen into court
nevertheless, but it had actually been Dieter Berger who contacted and
informed them, and requested their presence at short notice in the Kiel naval
court.

Winter pointed out that Abel had not handled this report in line with
prescribed naval rules and regulations. That, at the very least, would have
been to go through regular channels and to have initially informed the
superior officer, Captain Kals in Lorient, commanding the 2nd U-boat
Flotilla. Winter had never heard of a similar case, nor such a way of handling
any report. In fact, according to his knowledge and information, Abel's way
of doing it had never before happened in the Navy. Nor was there another
case when a U-boat commander had been stabbed in the back by his officers
in such an underhanded and irregular way, totally circumventing the established command structure and surprising the superior officers involved;
moreover, steamrollering the matter without any regard to normal naval
courtesy, thereby delivering an unblemished front officer to the killing
machinery of the naval court-martial system.

Furthermore, it had been impossible to select two military *Beisitzer* judges
who knew Kusch and were familiar with the situation in France and Lorient,
which had not been the case with the officers picked by the prosecutor in
Kiel. This turned out to be a tremendous disadvantage and an enormous legal
obstacle for Kusch, and would have been for any other officer, too.

Winter considered the entire Kusch case a disgrace, and a blot and stigma
on the honour of the German Navy. Gustav Adolf Janssen had the same

conviction, as his memory and view of the Kusch trial were identical.

Winter further stated that the Kusch case was discussed frequently and increasingly in detail, once more facts gradually became known, in his prisoner-of-war camp in England. It was there that most U-boat officers and commanders heard about this scandal for the first time, because it had been declared a secret command file, and those who attended the trial were ordered to keep silent and threatened with punishment if they did not.

Winter declared that it was high time that this court finally cleared Kusch's name and restored his honour as a person. At least retrospectively and posthumously they should remove this black stain on the shield of the U-boat arm.

Albrecht asked Winter why the Kusch file had been made a super-secret command matter and if this was customary or a frequent occurrence. Winter replied that he had not known of any other such case. To the contrary, most naval court cases were normally handled as an open matter, and visitors or spectators were ordered to attend the hearings. This had been considered a helpful attention-getting procedure, acting as an effective deterrent, especially for enlisted men. Winter said to the best of his memory and knowledge, Rösing, as the court's president, had been responsible for taking that step. But Winter did not know what the reason was, because no naval or military secrets of any kind had been brought up or discussed during the trial.

Albrecht therefore recalled Meyer-Grieben to the stand to answer the same question, as it was known that he had had full access to the Kusch file, papers and documents in 1944 and also after the war. Meyer-Grieben declared that no written or specific reason was ever given, but he had asked Breinig the same question in 1944, because it was so unusual, in fact exceptional. But Breinig thought some operational or technical secrecy matters might otherwise be spilled in court and become public knowledge that way, and so Rösing had arranged it.

When asked what he, Meyer-Grieben, personally had considered as the reason for this rare and uncustomary secrecy, he answered that it was probably to prevent the truth from becoming known to a wider circle of people. The Navy was often excessively secrecy minded, and sniffed treason, sabotage and violation of secrecy regulations behind every tree. But in the Kusch case, after hearing all the testimony and reading the depositions, there was only one possible explanation for Rösing's decision, to prevent knowledge of the truth about the real U-boat-front situation spreading and becoming known to more people on the home front.

Nothing was more feared by the Nazis than the spread of the truth and the passing on of the real military situation, which was seen as dangerous and had to be prevented at any cost. The Nazis, and in many respects the naval hierarchy, tried to preclude factual information from reaching the public, doped by constant waves of pure propaganda.

There was no doubt in Meyer-Grieben's mind that Oskar Kusch had been eliminated first and foremost as a political victim, and as an opponent of the

Hitler regime, because he was highly educated, smart and quite cosmopolitan in his experience. It was always obvious that the Nazis dreaded nothing more than the spread of the truth, just as the devil was scared of holy water. Consequently, telling the truth in Germany was a big crime that was punished by killing the person who insisted on it.

One unexpected witness was Miss Inge von Foris, Oskar Kusch's betrothed, whom he was unable to marry owing to documentary delays. Leverenz sensed immediately that she would be a dangerous witness, and repeatedly cut her short, telling her to stick only to the court case and the material submitted to the court.

Miss von Foris had been given one visitor's permit by Meinert, who refused a second one a few weeks later. Hagemann, the subject of the trial, she had met only briefly, as he passed her on to Meinert right away. She related the problems she had had with the Navy, and talked about the difficulties she and Oskar Kusch's parents were still having concerning moving the urn with his remains from Kiel to West Berlin's Waldfriedhof, a park-like cemetery. But Leverenz instantly objected, telling her this information was immaterial and had no bearing on the Hagemann court case at all, and was thus inadmissible as testimony.

When Inge von Foris lost her countenance and broke down crying bitterly, Dr Thamm called for a recess and a break in the hearings, and led her out of the hearing room to calm her down. Certainly, compassionate testimony was the very last thing Leverenz wanted to spoil his show in the court. The press had been excluded and the visitor's gallery emptied in advance of her being called, as it was expected that her highly emotional and personal testimony would be injurious to Hagemann. Leverenz did not even attempt to cross-examine her, swiftly realizing that a good-looking young lady in distress would hardly be an advantageous witness for Hagemann and his case.

The other witnesses for the state were either former crew members of U-154, who had been transferred off the U-boat before her loss, or were personal friends of Oskar Kusch, without direct knowledge of the matter. Leverenz cut the petty officers and enlisted men of U-154 short, constantly objecting to their views and observations as not having any direct bearing on the court case, because none of them had attended the 1944 Kusch trial. [As these witnesses did not contribute anything new or important, and were not cross-examined by either side, their testimony will be skipped here.]

Sieber, Kranzbühler and Nieschling had decided that Hagemann's defence had to accomplish two things. The first was to make Oskar Kusch the villain rather than the victim, and hammer away unceasingly on the assertion that Kusch's conviction was mandatory for purely military reasons and on the grounds of upholding discipline, order and the fighting fitness of the naval forces, claiming Hagemann only followed direct orders and did nothing but his duty. The second, a point that was especially important to Kranzbühler, the defence lawyer for Karl Dönitz, imprisoned in Spandau jail for ten years, was that under no circumstances should complications arise that could backfire on Dönitz in any way, because Dönitz had refused to convert the death penalty requested by Hagemann and strongly demanded by Rösing and Godt. The final responsibility had to be shifted onto Hermann Göring, who was dead. Kranzbühler, Sieber and Nieschling, together with Meckel, were firmly determined to block off even the slightest possibility of such complications.

For the 'Hamburg Gang', Hagemann was, in a sense, unimportant, and merely a vehicle to make absolutely sure of leaving no loopholes, legally or otherwise. The trio had not fully informed Leverenz, nor Hagemann himself, on this point regarding their priorities, as these were actually primarily long-term precautions.

Meyer-Grieben was a dangerous witness, with complete inside knowledge of the case on the naval side and substantial personal involvement. Therefore Leverenz tried to disallow any questions into the naval background of the 1944 situation. Thamm asked him only two short questions, as Leverenz constantly objected, but as these referred directly to Hagemann they could not be blocked. Meyer-Grieben related how he was first informed by Breinig, during the luncheon break, that Hagemann wanted to condemn Kusch to death, although Breinig felt a limited prison term would be sufficient. Breinig had added that if Hagemann insisted on his demand, he might have to agree, unless the two military *Beisitzer* judges objected and voted against it.

Leverenz tried to shorten his testimony, but Thamm called Breinig to ask him about the same point. Breinig had to confirm that this reflected the facts correctly. Then Thamm added a further question. Who had initially reviewed Hagemann's judgement, and why and by whom was a reduction in the sentence refused? Breinig was surprised, and took a minute to think matters over carefully. Breinig knew that Meyer-Grieben had studied the entire naval file and that he could not dodge the question or claim loss of memory.

He stated that after all papers and documents of the court case had been completed and the paperwork copied and finalized, the judgement was presented on 29 January 1944 to the official court president of the Western Regional U-boat Leader (FdU West), who confirmed it, without changes, as follows:

Angers-France, 5 February 1944
    The court's president has seen, read and approved the true copy of the final court protocol and report and advocates no reconsideration or any act of mercy in this instance.

A certified copy had been returned to Kiel, initialled and dated. However, there was no signature on it. So Thamm asked another question: 'Who was the president of the FdU Western regional court, and are these his initials?' Leverenz objected, stating the question was immaterial and had nothing to do with Hagemann at all. But he was overruled, and Breinig could do nothing but say, 'Naval Captain Hans Rudolf Rösing. The initials as put down, hrR, were written by me. They are not his initials. But were added after telephone reconfirmation that the certified copy was correct in every respect.'

Leverenz objected that such information was now irrelevant and unimportant, but got overruled again. Thamm pointed out that so far everybody had hidden behind regulations and orders, while the real culprit who had rejected any consideration of mercy for Kusch had never been determined. This was way overdue. It was RÖSING!

Kranzbühler, Sieber and Meckel telephoned Rösing when the next break occurred, to bring him up to date and warn him.

Senior state attorney Thamm announced that he had no further witnesses for the state.

From the thirty-eight defence witnesses, thirty-four were former naval judge advocates. Therefore, only the testimony of the other four defence witnesses will be covered in detail to obviate tiresome repetition.

The first one was the former Air Force legal director Christian von Hammerstein, who had occupied the same position in the German Air Force for Göring as Rudolphi did for Dönitz and the Navy. But Dr von Hammerstein exercised even more authority and had even greater influence than Rudolphi, because Göring was lazy and frequently absent from his office or command train. Dönitz was an avid reader of naval files and documents, no matter how busy he was otherwise, working long hours, trying to stay on top of things.

Von Hammerstein was a hostile witness, who appeared unwillingly, and only under subpoena. He was clearly unhelpful, and claimed his memory had become quite poor since 1944. But Prosecutor Dr Thamm neatly cornered him, asking him if the approval and confirmation of a death sentence were so routine in his position that he could not recall the details any more. How many naval officers were included in his reviews, particularly U-boat commanders? Von Hammerstein had to admit the number of such cases had been minute, because they were usually handled by the Navy alone, and processed between Rudolphi, Warzecha and Dönitz. The Kusch case had been a rare exception. But all the previous reviewers on the naval ladder had refused any reconsideration or conversion of Kusch's sentence into a milder judgement.

Thamm wondered why von Hammerstein had not remembered these details to start with, and automatically reported them. Von Hammerstein stated his declining health was responsible for that, as he was in a very precarious state of health, and suffering from several diseases. These quite often caused his memory to come and go in waves. Further questions seemed useless, and he was excused.

Generaladmiral Warzecha was the second witness. He now lived in nearby Malente, and sold insurance. Warzecha emphasized strongly that in the Kusch case only military considerations were taken into account when the judgement was rendered, and more so when Dr Rudolphi and he had reviewed that file. This had involved enquiries to Godt, von Friedeburg and

Rösing. All three had vigorously opposed any reconsideration of the judgement, and were determined that no act of mercy should be granted to Kusch. Rösing and Godt had in addition talked directly to Dönitz several times to voice their opposition to a retrial or any milder sentence than the death penalty. Therefore, Dönitz had eventually gone along with them.

Warzecha, the originator of the circular legal instruction letters and the main speaker during the meetings of the naval judge advocates in Berlin to inform the naval judges periodically about the prevailing naval policies and new legal rules and regulations, had the impudence to state that he or his assistants never ordered the naval judges to pass specific judgements and harsher sentences as the war dragged on longer and longer.

The next witness for the defence was the former FdU West, Rösing. Initially, he hemmed and hawed, claiming loss of memory or ignorance of details. He stated that he was constantly on the go with naval business, travelling over a wide area. He featured a poor memory whenever this suited him or helped to achieve his aims. However, in the Kusch case, the record and related documents hardly supported his claims.

Prosecutor Thamm had brought out this fact clearly when interrogating Breinig. Rösing first attempted to tell the court that he really had very little to do with the Kusch court case, personally and directly. But the documentary evidence presented earlier contradicted his claim very strongly. He immediately shifted his position, because Breinig had covered himself well. Now he reluctantly admitted that as the official court president he was only marginally involved – a brazen lie. He declared that senior staff had made most decisions and the final determination. Once the Kusch case was under way, it rolled along automatically, and von Friedeburg, who also was dead, became involved when it was moved to Kiel, while he, Rösing, was only informed periodically by telephone of what transpired. This was another outright lie by Rösing, who gave the directions and orders by telephone.

However, Warzecha had just testified earlier that Rösing had repeatedly urged Dönitz to reject any retrial, refuse any reconsideration and demand the execution of Kusch. Without batting an eye, Rösing changed gear again and talked about being too far away from Germany to get involved in details. This was his third obvious lie on the witness stand.

Suddenly, he remembered that the Kusch case had been filed and initially processed in a highly unusual and irregular way, outside prescribed naval channels. On that point, he was finally correct. Thamm asked him how well he had known Kusch, and if there had been any problems or complaints regarding his decisions as U-boat commander. Rösing admitted that he had not received any previous complaints. Kals, the commander of the 2nd U-boat Flotilla in Lorient, had viewed Kusch as a good officer and reliable commander. Rösing stated he had only met Kusch during inspections or briefly at social gatherings.

Although Rösing had read and studied the war patrol journals for Kusch's two war patrols as commander of U-154, and had signed them without objections or comments, now he declared that the desired operational success and the expected sinkings of enemy ships had not materialized. Therefore, he now considered Kusch's performance as unsatisfactory in retrospect. An outrageous statement!

Thamm wanted to know if there had been other U-boat commanders who returned without sinkings in the second half of 1943. Rösing had to admit that, yes, there had been other U-boat commanders who returned without sinkings, but he did not amplify his answer with details. Thamm then asked him whether, if Abel had filed his report through the customary naval channels and done so earlier in Lorient, this would have resulted in a different way of processing the case or brought about another court decision? Rösing hesitated a bit and replied that this was impossible for him to say.

He added that the fact that Kusch had repeated arguments with his officers over operational approaches and other shipboard matters indicated to him that the discipline aboard U-154 was not what it should have been. Under such circumstances, one would have to assume Kusch endangered the crew as well as U-154, and gambled with both. But he had to admit, when further questioned, that nobody had previously reported any disciplinary or operational problems, nor had any complaints come to the attention of any superior officer in Lorient or elsewhere. Finally, Rösing declared, he did not believe Kusch was either overcautious, cowardly or had tried to avoid combat operations while he commanded U-154.

Thamm switched his questions to more general matters. Rösing reluctantly confirmed that the education and training of all naval officers had been concentrated upon the fact that in 1917, and more so in 1918, the German fleet had revolted and hoisted red flags on most ships, and in all naval ports. Therefore, the leadership of the German Navy was strongly determined that such a mutiny should never again take place. Even the slightest possibility of any such occurrence would have to be extinguished instantly, with every type of means available and with the fullest force at hand. It was imperative to wipe out promptly, and without tolerance or patience, the tiniest chance of such a mutiny recurring.

Thamm replied that, even to his knowledge, only the battleships and other big ships, known as 'floating barracks', had been involved in these mutinies, not U-boats and other smaller surface ships like destroyers, torpedo boats or minesweepers. Rösing had to admit that this had been so in 1918. However, under no circumstances could the Naval High Command take any chances whatsoever, and had to maintain discipline and full military order firmly and without exception. Germany was fighting under enormous enemy pressure, with all her willpower and might, and all officers were expected to comply fully with all orders. Consequently, all officers had to carry on even more determinedly than ever.

Thamm asked Rösing to talk specifically about the actual operational situation at sea between May and December 1943, while Kusch had commanded U-154 on two long war patrols. Rösing replied that this was an extremely difficult time for all U-boat crews. Whether officers, petty officers or enlisted men, all lived under high stress, difficult operational conditions and enormous physical demands as U-boat crews. In fact, the conditions were almost superhuman and the nervous strain extraordinary. Several U-boat commanders had been unable to bear the pressure and committed suicide.

In 1943, the Allies had added a tremendous number of new aeroplanes with constantly increasing range and greater speed to their operations, over the entire Atlantic area. They also introduced new radar equipment and several other anti-submarine devices, which caused a growing loss of U-boats, month after month. Therefore, the naval leadership considered it their most important duty to uphold the fighting will and determination of the U-boat crews by any means available. Under these circumstances, the Kusch case simply could not be tolerated. Any loosening of the discipline aboard U-154 was unacceptable to the U-boat Command, and had to be extirpated ruthlessly.

At this point Dr Thamm excused Rösing, who had gradually grown paler and paler during his cross-examination, deciding that further questions would not bring to light new facts from him.

Finally, Eberhard Godt was sworn in and took the stand, the former chief of staff of the U-boat Command. Albrecht and Thamm had insisted that Godt must appear in person for questioning and direct cross-examination. The 'Hamburg Gang' had tried very hard to circumvent his personal appearance in court, and had attempted tenaciously to limit his questioning to a deposition, claiming falsely that Godt was in poor health.

He had been promoted to rear admiral on 1 March 1943, once Dönitz had become the supreme commander of the German Navy and they had moved from Paris to Berlin. Dönitz realized quickly that he would no longer have enough time to direct the day-to-day U-boat operations himself, owing to his growing involvement with other naval matters and, at his own choice, more and more political undertakings and assignments. Consequently, Godt handled the day-to-day U-boat operations, though Dönitz retained his former title, in addition to being the supreme naval commander.

Godt was a man who preferred to stay out of the limelight, unlike Dönitz, who was an eager public relations man. He liked to pull strings behind the scene and exercise his authority indirectly whenever possible. Furthermore, he was an officer who disliked making speeches, and simply detested it when he was forced to speak freely or spontaneously, without being prepared for the occasion. However, what he really hated was being grilled with sharp questions on details and specifics, without careful preparation on his part.

He was a hostile witness who would volunteer nothing. Whatever he said or was forced to comment upon had to be extracted from him by the prosecutors like teeth by a dentist. When replies were unavoidable, these were made grudgingly and slowly, with long pauses between words and phrases, limiting himself to as few words as possible. Thamm and Albrecht badgered Godt quite hard, and pressed him for details, but with little success.

Any admissions that he made were broad, general and unspecific. The prosecutors grew rather fed up with him. They seemed to be getting nowhere. Albrecht decided to ask Godt one last question, and asked him, without much hope of an answer, about the disciplinary situation within the U-boat Command, especially among the U-boats at the front, and if there was any difference between U-boat crews serving on school and training U-boats in the Baltic.

To the surprise of everybody, Godt breathed deeply and suddenly started to talk faster and more deliberately, forming complete sentences without breaks and pauses. Here is Godt's testimony on that question:

> There can't be any question nor any talk whatsoever in any way about the morale and discipline in the U-boat arm during 1943/4. It remained good, firm, stout and determined, in spite of constantly increasing anti-submarine countermeasures and steadily growing problems in both operational and physical ways. If anything, there was a small decrease in enthusiasm, combined with some fatalism, under mounting enemy pressure, while at the same time operational successes became fewer and fewer. However, U-boats departed on war patrols, nevertheless, right up to 3 May 1945, whenever U-boats were technically and operationally ready and ordered to depart on any type of war patrol or operational assignment of any kind.

Now that the prosecutors had finally pried a more than bare minimum comment out of Godt, they had no further questions for him. Much to his visible relief, he was excused from further testimony.

While Godt's observations and his statement were firm, clear and seemingly unmistakable, nevertheless, real naval insiders still had doubts. There had been naval stories and rumours for some time about particular occurrences that were automatically denied by the people in control. Later on, most historians accepted Godt's testimony as official, and did not question it in any way.

But the special naval investigators had looked into several situations and reached different conclusions. But these were unpopular with the senior staff in Berlin, and dismissed as short sighted and lacking complete information for seeing the 'whole picture'.

The interrogation of Eberhard Godt on 23 September 1950 was probably the highlight of the trial, the afternoon being taken up by the continuous parade performance of thirty-four former naval judge advocates. Kranzbühler and Nieschling had rehearsed them once more during the luncheon break to make absolutely sure that everything rolled off smoothly.

The naval judge advocates brought into court by the 'Hamburg Gang' appeared on the witness stand individually, one after the other. However, they talked like a flock of parakeets, being birds of the same feather and coached to sing their song in court, one that impressed the observers as firmly memorized, but very repetitious. Such a wave of colleagues and judge advocates the court judges simply could not resist, and they were pushed by them into the corner for final surrender.

As one of the reporters wrote: 'Just as one crow will not peck out the eye of another crow or one medical doctor dislikes, and if possible, will avoid testifying against another medical doctor, these judges were unable to condemn one of their profession, no matter how threadbare and faulty some of the explanations had been.'

The prosecution requested that Hagemann be sentenced to eighteen months in jail, because political influence and pressure had been obvious and Hagemann's servile cooperation with the demands from senior staff had been clearly demonstrated and confirmed in the Kusch case, even if the written record was incomplete, owing to precautions on the part of Rösing and others in the naval hierarchy.

Defence Counsel Leverenz demanded Hagemann's complete acquittal in every respect, and a judgement by the court that would unmistakably reflect this, that Hagemann should be fully rehabilitated so that he would be able to work again full time and without any restrictions or limitations in his profession as a lawyer.

In spite of the illuminating, new and additional testimony provided, the group of hearing judges nevertheless decided that Hagemann was NOT GUILTY!

A short and condensed report was issued by the Kiel court for the press and radio stations on 26 September 1950, to reduce publicity pressure and gain time to prepare the court's detailed and final verdict of forty-eight pages, which was issued two months later, on 25 November 1950.

The initial court judgement read like this: 'Kusch had been sentenced to death by Hagemann in 1944. Kusch had been sentenced in line with prevalent military requirements and needs to maintain naval discipline. While a more experienced judge than Hagemann might have reached another decision, it was not demonstrated that Hagemann was influenced by political pressure in reaching his judgement. Nevertheless, one could not be absolutely sure that Hagemann had not been influenced even slightly by Nazi Party doctrine. But no proof was submitted that he was. One must accept that naval judges reached their decisions by their own independent determination, instead of by means of instructions from above. Consequently, Hagemann had to be acquitted through lack of evidence, but not for his proved innocence.

Because the original 1944 judgement had obviously been reached on purely military grounds, it could not be reclassified retrospectively as a crime against humanity, based upon the Occupation Control Council Law 10 or any other law in effect in 1944, or for that matter later'.

Dr Thamm filed an appeal on 26 September 1950 for review and reconsideration to protect the interest of the prosecution, pending receipt of the written complete court determination.

Once this release became available, it was carefully studied by Thamm and Albrecht and their assistants. Both prosecutors then reported to the new minister of justice, Dr Wittenburg, and informed him of their conclusions and views.

Wittenburg decided, after this discussion with his prosecutors, to cancel the requested reconsideration and the appeal, and to accept the decision of the Kiel court as final, because it appeared hopeless to reach a different decision and there seemed to be no legal way to make an appeal successful.

Kranzbühler, Sieber and Nieschling with their assistants at the 'Hamburg Gang' offices perused the final decision release quite meticulously too. They wanted to make sure that no legal or other loopholes remained, not so much out of concern for Hagemann, as that would be the job of Leverenz, but to check how this final court decision could be used to influence favourably some pending court cases involving other judge advocates. However, Kranzbühler was already looking far ahead with respect to Karl Dönitz, then still held in Spandau prison.

The first of these cases involved Naval Judge Advocate Adolf Holzwig, who had been the senior judge of the naval court assigned to the German S-boat (PT/MTB) command in Norway. The case also included the Director/Leader of the S-boats (F.d.S.) Captain Rudolf Petersen (Crew 1925), who had been the president of that naval court and had reviewed as well as approved the judgement issued by Holzwig on 10 May 1945.

Holzwig had condemned three German sailors to death as deserters, as on 5 May 1945 they had celebrated the end of the war with many civilian Norwegians, and got pretty drunk doing so. Instead of handling the matter as a mere misdemeanour, Holzwig had grossly blown up the case and sentenced them to death, requesting an immediate review and quick execution to warn others. His decision was approved by Captain Petersen without any objection or request for a thorough investigation. Therefore, these three sailors were shot without delay on 10 May 1945, though the war had ended several days earlier.

After the war the case was brought before the higher court in Hamburg, and both men were sentenced by this court, Holzwig to five years in prison and Petersen to two years. An appeal was filed with the High Court of the British Zone of Occupation in Germany, but this court declined to handle the case, because only German citizens were involved, not Allied citizens. Therefore, the case was remanded to the Hamburg court for a further background investigation and a retrial.

In 1952 the Hamburg higher court reversed the initial judgement that these two men were responsible for killing three sailors after the war had terminated, and rendered a new decision, that Holzwig and Petersen had merely done their duty to uphold naval discipline and order during difficult times. Consequently, both men were now judged not guilty. The court ruled they had not acted in bad faith or with vengeful intentions. Both men were immediately freed and paid government compensation for the time they had spent in prison, and the state took over all legal, court and handling expenses.

Petersen retired to a farm belonging to his family near the Danish border. But Holzwig, born in Pasewalk, Pomerania, in the Soviet Zone of Occupation and the new Communist state of East Germany, had no desire to return there, and decided to set up a private law office with the assistance of the 'Hamburg Gang', Sieber, Kranzbühler and Nieschling. They provided financial help and referral assistance, as well as commercial business recommendations, so that Holzwig was able to rapidly build up his law practice.

The second case had also taken place in Norway. Naval Judge Advocate Curt Lüder, heading the Stavanger branch court under the Admiral Western Norway, had tried and sentenced four German sailors to death as deserters on 4 May 1945, because they had joined the crowds of civilian Norwegians and got mightily drunk in the process.

But Lüder added a fifth sailor to the case, sentencing him likewise to death, a man who was very intoxicated and refused to stop singing drinking songs. A medical officer/naval surgeon had attempted to give a calming injection to the sailor, who refused to pipe down, but he strongly objected to this tranquilizing shot, and defended himself against receiving it. Lüder interpreted his resistance as attacking a superior officer and refusing to take orders.

These five death sentences were promptly reviewed and confirmed by Admiral Otto von Schrader, the court's president. Consequently, all five sailors were executed on 8 May 1945, after the German capitulation and end of the war.

When the Lüder case came up in the higher court of Hamburg in 1951, von Schrader, a confirmed war criminal and old Nazi, had already committed suicide in 1945. Lüder was judged by this court as not guilty, although exhibiting poor legal judgement in his sentences and the court decision. The prosecution appealed against this verdict to the brand-new German Supreme Court in Karlsruhe. But after deliberation and long consideration, that court rejected the Lüder case and remanded it to the Hamburg court for further investigation and rechecking of both evidence and the testimony of several witnesses.

The 'Hamburg Gang' practically took over the case, and worked hand in glove with Lüder's defence lawyer, furnishing supplementary testimony by experts, additional documents, new witnesses and substantial support in every possible way. In that way several technical and legal border-line points could be eliminated, and were dropped.

In the 1953 retrial, Lüder was again declared not guilty and released from custody. The Hamburg high court stated: 'When Lüder sentenced these five sailors to death, he had only done his duty to uphold naval and military discipline firmly, during trying circumstances and in difficult times. However, it could not be proved, and no evidence was submitted, that Lüder had acted maliciously or in a vengeful way when sentencing the five men to death and pushing for their immediate execution'.

Lüder had been born in Leipzig, Saxony, in the Soviet Zone of

Occupation, which had recently been renamed the 'German Democratic Republic' by the East German Communist regime.

Because Lüder refused to move to East Germany, the 'Hamburg Gang' established him with a private law office, providing financial assistance, office equipment, legal work and commercial business recommendations, which enabled him to build up his legal business swiftly.

Kranzbühler, Nieschling and Sieber had introduced the Kusch case retrial decision into these two cases to tilt the determination in the same direction – a total change of the truth, or, in naval language, a turnaround change of course of 180 degrees. Sieber was now a judge in Essen, after an intermediate job as state attorney in Cologne. Kranzbühler had become a private lawyer, specializing in corporate legal cases, and Nieschling had taken over the law office of a retiring relative.

It turned out that all Kiel court hearing judges had been former Nazi Party members. However, all of them had been classified as '*Mitläufer*' only, of the inoffensive Category 3, and were cleared in that way for immediate re-employment as judges. That is to say that they were men who had just floated along with the crowd, and only joined the Nazi Party in order to keep their jobs, a mere paper formality, as some of them claimed afterwards.

Everybody had now, finally, been judged to be completely innocent, were scrubbed super-clean and again presented as lily-white. The old and incorrigible Nazis were jubilant!

CHAPTER SEVENTEEN

Unpredictable Uncertainties Pending

Within a year of the final Kiel court decision, the Criminal Investigation Service of the American Army once more opened enquiries to look into Dönitz's involvement in the Kusch case in 1944. It was the third time such an investigation was started, because secret sources reported that the East German Communist regime's propaganda ministry contemplated distributing a so-called brown book. The brown book was rumoured to include information about newly discovered war crimes in Poland, Russia and the Balkans, which had not been publicized before, including war crimes by German naval forces with direct connections to Karl Dönitz, who was supposed to have ordered them.

This was in response to the Western Powers' recently published white book, which had publicized the continued and uninterrupted use of former Nazi concentration camps in Eastern Germany, but now as internment camps for thousands of German opponents of the Communist regime, including people who were only suspected of being hostile to the intentions of the Soviet Union. Moreover, among these captives were people who were seen as possible future opponents, without any proof of their having so far done anything.

As this might involve Dönitz in a negative way, Kranzbühler could not disregard such a possibility, and had to be fully prepared. Eventually, the Soviet Union's political circles decided to cancel the brown book printing plan for internal reasons incomprehensible to people who were not Communist Party functionaries.

When this possibility was pending, Otto Kranzbühler had left the German Minesweeping Administration and its successor organizations. But he kept up all his former connections and never lost sight of particular possibilities and political changes related to them, especially when the wartime interests of the German Navy in general and of Karl Dönitz in particular were involved. After Kranzbühler had represented Dönitz so effectively during the Nuremberg war trials, a very close personal relationship had developed between the Admiral and his former defence counsel. Kranzbühler coordinated the family visits that Dönitz was allowed to have in Spandau, and he looked after his financial interests, including the family pension rights of Dönitz, his wife and his family.

Apparently, to be on the safe side in every respect and to preclude any kind of unpleasant surprise coming out of archives the Soviets had taken over in Eastern Germany, Kranzbühler discussed the Kusch case with Dönitz, during one of his periodic legal counsellor visits in Spandau prison. He suggested to Dönitz that he ought to try to remember whatever he still could of the Kusch case, and put it down in writing. Kranzbühler suggested Dönitz should do this in the form of a personal letter, which was to be turned over to Kranzbühler by one of the visiting Dönitz family members, after their next authorized visit in Spandau, thereby circumventing the prison's censor.

When one reads this undated letter, seemingly prepared in 1951, one must keep in mind that it was written more than six years after the war's end in the comparative isolation in which Dönitz was held in Spandau.

My memory is as follows: There was a complaint report that originated from the FdU West (Rösing) on the basis of several reports or statements from officers and crew members? Like the petty officer of the control room? of the U-boat in question.

Court-martial hearings followed and a process in the court of the commanding admiral U-boats (von Friedeburg) in Kiel. Death sentence, owing to sedition and constant undermining of the fighting ability of the Navy and damaging military discipline. Approval of the judgement by the court's president, Captain Rösing and also Admiral von Friedeburg. Out of the file it appeared that Kusch constantly criticized the *Führer*, as well as the plans and methods of the war's direction and any expectation that the war could still be won in the way we conducted it. On one (or also two?) very long war patrols.

This must have had a negative influence on his aggressiveness, military leadership and command of the U-boat in question. I had been extremely impressed by this case. How could this happen with one of my U-boat commanders? Why did things get this far? Why had neither other officer comrades nor the flotilla commander noticed anything at all, before the report was made and had Kusch educated and brought into line quietly? I had extensive discussions on this case with Godt and also Rösing several times. The file was sitting on my desk for an unusually long time. Because the Kusch case was painful to me personally. I would have liked to find a way to convert this maximum penalty into a more merciful one.

Another discussion followed with Godt and Rösing and thereafter with the legal experts at the Naval High Command, Admiral Warzecha and Admiral Judge Advocate Dr Rudolphi, to find a different solution.

The uniform and firm view of all of them was absolutely inflexible. Considering the severity of the case, actually a unique case in many respects, all of them opposed any reduction in the sentence and insisted that the death penalty was the only proper and fitting punishment. That any pardon or reprieve would be grossly unfair in comparison to the many cases when enlisted men or petty officers were involved. Therefore it would be out of the question to make an exception in the case of Lieutenant j.g. Oskar Kusch.

All of them were absolutely right in their views. The military interest in this hard, difficult and last year of the war demanded the execution of this judgement! Therefore, I also finally approved it. The *Führer* confirmed our decision and the judgement was subsequently carried out.

It is interesting that Dönitz does not mention Hermann Göring as the real final reviewer of the Kusch case, whom Dönitz disdained and for whom a great number of naval officers and millions of German citizens had a growing contempt – people who experienced the daily mass bombing attacks, which the German Air Force and Göring were unable to prevent, and, considering it impossible, had organized no effective air defence to counteract them. Göring had boasted frequently that this would be easy enough for him to arrange at any time.

Here originated Göring's latest nickname of '*Reichsmeier*' Göring. He had stated loudly, in his big-mouth way: 'If ever any hostile aircraft manage to get through our air defences and actually reach Germany, they will certainly never be able to return to their airfields again, or I shall immediately change my name to Meier!' Göring had kept his name, nevertheless, though the disaster of the German Air Force performance, or rather lack of it, was forcefully and painfully demonstrated every day and night to millions of German citizens.

Towards the end of May 1933, as interior minister of Prussia, Göring took a trip on that aged battle-wagon, the *Schlesien*. The Baltic turned a bit rough and Göring became seasick and threw up his luncheon. When, white as a sheet, he tried to recover in the officers' mess, a group of fun-loving, just-promoted ensigns promptly played a joke on him. The principal spirit and leader of this group advised Göring that a radio signal had just been received from Neptune, the god of the seas, awarding him the additional new title of '*Reichsfischfuttermeister*' (the Reich's Master Feeder of Fish) and the order of the net-type undershirt! This was in special recognition of Göring's firm sea legs and his manly behaviour aboard. Göring, however, was not amused by this humorous prank. Once back on land and in Berlin, he became increasingly furious, and filed an official complaint with Erich Raeder. The organizer of this caper had handed Göring a hand-painted certificate confirming the award, which he had signed. The ensign had been punished by the commander of the *Schlesien* with seven days' close arrest, for showing a gross lack of respect for Senior Officers.

Raeder at first refused to act on this complaint, as it was the normal and spontaneous sort of joke that young ensigns played on others in their customary high spirits. But Göring did not accept this explanation, and turned increasingly sour, eventually making it an official matter, going through channels. Raeder requested more information about the occurrence, but stalled Göring, who kept pestering him at every meeting and gathering about the impertinence of these naval snotty brats who did not act as officers should.

The complaint had to be acted upon, and it descended the naval chain of command until it reached the commander of the *Schlesien*, the then Captain Wilhelm Canaris, otherwise known as 'Uncle Willy'. Canaris informed Raeder that he had punished the ensign in question for lack of respect towards Göring as the Prussian Secretary of the Interior, but he refused to increase the penalty retrospectively, as demanded by Göring, and considered the case closed.

Raeder so informed Göring, much to the latter's chagrin, and he never forgot his personal humiliation by Raeder in general, and the German Navy in particular, for not overruling Canaris. In this connection, it is highly significant that Erich Raeder's last words directed to Hitler in January 1943 were: 'Please protect the German Navy and my successor Admiral Karl Dönitz against the constant intrigues and the slander of Hermann Göring!'

It is quite astounding that the Kusch case had not gone away after the final court decision in 1950. But Kranzbühler obviously considered it necessary to keep a close eye on the situation for many years. He did discuss the Kusch case several times with Dönitz, even some years after Dönitz had been released from Spandau and lived in retirement in Aumühle, near Hamburg. Here Kranzbühler visited Dönitz periodically. But owing to Kranzbühler's sickness, another exchange of letters on the Kusch case became necessary. He requested a complete update by Dönitz of his memory regarding the Kusch execution – evidently just in case new evidence might be found.

This time, the reply by Dönitz is dated, unlike the earlier letter from Spandau prison.

Aumühle, 30 November 1968

Regarding the death sentence of Kusch. No matter what has been said in the press or in the court hearings, here is my recollection of that case. When Kusch was executed, then it was my view and conviction at the time that it was my duty and military obligation to confirm this. I felt that I could not use two different measures to judge somebody who was an officer, but who had weakened the fighting determination of the U-boat Force, thereby bringing him into the safe protection of some jail, and yet to continue hard demands on U-boat crews and brave U-boat commanders, to continue fighting during the most difficult time in the war for U-boats, in order to bind and hold down enormous resources of the enemy that would otherwise become available to attack Germany directly. Particularly, hundreds of huge aircraft that would then attack our homeland instead of U-boats, and bomb civilians, women and children mainly in their homes, in Germany. All of those U-boat crews were still determined and willing to do their duty and fight on courageously until the very end.

Dear Kranzbühler, my question in that respect is now: Is there any possibility at all that the Kusch case will be reopened and could be reactivated by some persecuting juridical organization or court administration of the German government, after almost twenty-five years? Without a doubt, I did act lawfully if I actually confirmed the judgement. However, provided that was actually the case, I certainly did not do so with the intention of murdering Kusch.

I acted, as already mentioned, only because this was my heavy duty and necessary obligation that I had to comply with during that extraordinarily severe wartime of the U-boat arm, when it was imperative to maintain and uphold our fighting power fully. But I am absolutely sure that I also had the complete agreement and the concurrence of both Dr Rudolphi and Warzecha. If there had been any question or doubt about that point, I would know and remember this even now.

Kranzbühler did reassure Dönitz that there was at that time no legal trick that could be employed to reopen the Kusch case. A further follow-up prosecution would only be possible if a demonstrated bending of the laws in effect could be proved and documented.

It is significant that Dönitz still maintained that old excuse of the many hundreds, if not thousands, of additional aeroplanes, that would attack the German homeland if the U-boat operations were stopped. As had been shown again and again, all those very specialized anti-submarine-equipped aeroplanes were largely useless for attacks on ground targets or even cities or metropolitan areas, for a considerable number of technical reasons, apart from the time-consuming rebuilding of the various aircraft and re-equipping them for land warfare. The pilots and aircrews flying anti-submarine and over-water operations were more highly trained and had the best navigators with long experience aboard, because they usually operated alone or only in small groups. This was quite contrary to the mass-bombing attack groups, operating in dense, closed-up formations that were guided by special pathfinder target-selection units or otherwise directed visually and tightly via voice telephones by a few highly qualified attack leaders over the target area.

Most of the pilots in these mass-attack groups were incapable of individual aircraft attacks and operations, much less anti-submarine search operations. But it made a plausible excuse whenever civilians were involved, since they could not know better. However, this so-called binding of enemy forces by the U-boats at sea was really a fallacy, if not a total delusion of Dönitz and his yes-men. There did not exist any reasonable relationship, as was seen when U-boat successes and losses were tallied and compared in a realistic way. Actually, it was primarily a convenient propaganda slogan.

But what is most sobering and typical for Karl Dönitz, so many years after the war, is that he kept clinging firmly to his old prejudices and rigid ideas that he pushed relentlessly during the war. He fought common sense, logic and reason mercilessly. Until his death he firmly refused to accept the fact that Bletchley Park and Washington DC had decoded, read and utilized very effectively various radio signal circuits for many years, since an M-3 Enigma coding machine had been captured aboard U-110 on 9 May 1941, all because the commander, Fritz Julius Lemp, and his crew decided to jump into the ocean to get picked up by waiting British escorts, instead of making sure that U-110 did in fact SINK.

Again and again, U-boat commanders and other front-experienced signal analysts demonstrated that the German U-boat signals had been decoded and read by the Allies. However, the German communication experts refused to accept the truth, and insisted strongly that this was completely impossible. What must not be, simply can't be! Karl Dönitz, despite several extensive investigations, stubbornly accepted the views and decisions of these technicians and experts, as they evidently suited him more than having to bend and face facts. He refused to accept a truth that was so many times demonstrated and convincingly documented!

Many U-boats were sunk by direct Ultra operational instructions to find them, based almost entirely upon decoded German naval radio signals, which made it possible for the Allied ships and aeroplanes to track, locate and sink them.

The reading of the German radio signals became the most important factor in the defeat of the U-boat campaign after May 1941, followed by the centimetric radar/sonar search equipment complex. The High-Frequency Direction-Finding Equipment and its various models ('Huff Duff'), became the third most important U-boat destruction factor in the Battle of the Atlantic.

Yet all three of these possibilities were rejected outright by the German experts, and were refused acceptance by Dönitz, too. The truth was not of primary interest to them, unless it fitted their expectations and the prevailing and preferred convictions of the naval leadership.

The well-known British writer, BBC executive and programme director Ludovic Kennedy visited Dönitz in Aumühle in 1982 for an interview in connection with a BBC special programme on U-boats and the Battle of the Atlantic. Kennedy was astounded that Dönitz did not believe him, that Ultra had read and decoded all Enigma machine radio signals of nearly all circuits with little delay since 1941. Though this had been public knowledge since 1974, and much earlier for experts and investigators, it simply did not fit the ideas of Dönitz to accept the brutal truth.

Eberhard Godt's statement, that there were no disciplinary problems in the U-boat Command, was accepted by many people as factual. But to some insiders, who themselves had experienced the U-boat operational situation at sea, it appeared questionable, and it was doubted because Godt's allegation was not the full truth either. In reality, it was a strong effort by him to uphold the reputation of the U-boat crews, and even more, of the U-boat Command and its leaders, Dönitz, von Friedeburg and Godt.

However, over the past fifty or more years, some chinks have opened up in this official Navy picture, step by step. Clearly, most of these occurrences were not widely known in the German Navy in 1943, 1944 or 1945. But there can be little doubt that Dönitz, von Friedeburg, Godt, Rösing and a few other men were informed about them.

One of these cases was only recently discovered in Dublin. It involved U-260, a Type VII-C U-boat, commissioned on 14 March 1942 and built by the Vulkan shipyard in Vegesack, near Bremen. U-260 left Kiel on 10 September 1942 on her first war patrol, and transferred to the 6th U-boat Flotilla in Saint Nazaire. Her commander for five war patrols was Lieutenant Hubertus Przikling-Purkhold.

Early in April 1944, Purkhold was replaced as commander of U-260 by Lieutenant j.g. Klaus Becker (Crew 39-A), who had been her executive officer for four war patrols and afterwards passed through the qualification courses for prospective U-boat commanders. It was quite unusual for a former executive officer to later become the commander of a Type VII U-boat, although this was often the case with the more complicated U-boats of Type IX, because each one of them had some technical peculiarities of her own, particularly when diving and operating under water, which required time to master.

With her new commander, Becker, U-260 was involved in several short-term operations in the Bay of Biscay in connection with the Allied landings in France, mainly on a precautionary and protective basis. In August 1944, she was transferred to La Rochelle-La Pallice, because of special overhaul requirements that could no longer be done in Saint Nazaire.

On 3 September 1944, she left for a slow transfer war patrol to Norway, reaching Bergen on 17 October. But repair and overhaul facilities were insufficient in Norway, with many U-boats arriving from western France, and most of these U-boats, including U-260, had to continue to Germany. U-260 reached Flensburg on 25 October 1944 for an extended overhaul and the installation of the newest type of snorkel, requiring almost three months.

When this was finished, she proceeded to Kiel for final equipment adjustments, ammunitioning and getting fully supplied with all provisions needed for the next war patrol. She left Kiel on 9 February 1945 and journeyed to Horten, in Norway, for snorkel testing and training, which ended on 18

February. Now Becker continued with U-260 to Kristiansand, Norway, for last-minute supplies, and to top up her diesel fuel.

On 21 February she headed into the North Sea and the Atlantic. Becker had been assigned a tentative operational area by Godt in Koralle Bernau at the southern end of the Bristol Channel and St George's Channel in the Irish Sea, subject to change and redirection by radio signal, should this be operationally required.

U-260 proceeded on a course around the Shetland Islands and the north of Scotland, and then gradually turned south and travelled along the west coast of Ireland, mostly dived and using her snorkel equipment, which meant slow progress.

During the long stay in the shipyard, considerable changes had taken place in the composition of U-260's crew, including some of the officers. Directing engineer Lieutenant j.g. (Engineering) Karl Nagel remained aboard, though due for a reassignment. Just prior to departure from Kiel an additional engineering officer had embarked, whom Nagel was expected to train, so that the newcomer, without U-boat front-service experience could take over Nagel's position after this war patrol. This was Ensign (Engineering) of the Reserves Friedrich Bielecke, posted as watch engineer.

Ensign Siegfried Dreschel, who had previously been the second watch officer, remained aboard U-260 as executive officer. His replacement as second watch officer, Ensign Gottfried Kuntze, had arrived in Kiel on 8 February, and likewise had no U-boat front-service experience. Kuntze as second watch officer would be in charge of signals, all paperwork, the handling of all secret documents, operational manuals and the anti-aircraft guns. Becker took an instant dislike to Kuntze, after talking to him, and felt Kuntze was not only inexperienced but also not trustworthy. He discussed the situation with Nagel and Dreschel, asking them to keep a close eye on Kuntze. He was a repeater, who had been bumped from his original naval class into the next one following it, and had become an ensign only on 1 December 1944.

While proceeding along the Irish coast near Fastnet Rock in an easterly direction, dived at a depth of 80 m, about 20 m above the ocean bottom and within the three-mile border limit area of Ireland, U-260 moved quite slowly. The British had decoded and read the signals of the German U-boats and become aware of the routes they used within the Irish coastal area. Therefore, the Royal Navy had ordered the fast minelayer *Apollo* to put down a secret new minefield of more than 150 acoustic and pressure-type mines within the Irish coastal area, at a point where German U-boats had to transit going east or returning west. Becker had been told to stay as much as possible in the shallower coastal areas, within the so-called 200 m depth line, because U-boat Command assumed, incorrectly, that Allied anti-submarine search groups would not operate in areas so close to the coastline.

Suddenly, at 18.50 on 12 March, U-260 activated one of these recently placed mines, which was exploded by its proximity fuse detonator reacting to the approaching U-boat. The mine was not directly hit by U-260, which would have meant a total loss. But the explosion was powerful enough to rip off the covers of the bow torpedo tubes, bending them and causing a heavy seawater influx into the bow torpedo section and the battery areas. Becker and Nagel promptly ordered U-260 to the surface by blowing all tanks and using up their entire supply of pressurized air to overcome the weight of the seawater entering the vessel.

Becker was concerned that U-260 might activate or hit additional mines, as they were usually put down in groups, or fields. But when he was able to ascertain the damage while floating on the surface, Nagel doubted that U-260 could be repaired at sea and made secure for underwater operations. Becker immediately signalled the situation to Koralle Bernau, and received their answer with instructions within minutes. Godt suggested that U-260 should try to continue directly to Saint Nazaire, which was still in German hands, as well as Lorient and La Rochelle, provided she could be sufficiently repaired to dive safely, even if not deep.

Nagel decided that this was out of the question at sea, and the alternative option was selected: to scuttle U-260 unobserved in deep enough water, and take her crew on rubber floats and rubber boats to the Irish Republic for internment, without giving the Irish any details of the loss or the circumstances that caused it.

At 22.30 Becker signalled U-boat Command that he had to scuttle and was in the process of doing so after the destruction of all secret papers, documents and devices. Godt had ordered him to scuttle U-260 in deep enough water so that the Royal Navy could not easily raise and recover the wreck.

The crew boarded two large inflatable rubber floats, several smaller ones and a few one-man rubber dinghies. Becker, Nagel and two other men remained a bit longer on the sinking U-260, to make sure she actually got scuttled and sunk. When these four men left the U-boat, they had between them only their individual life vests and two one-man dinghies, and these soon leaked, so they ended up swimming.

Kuntze had taken over one of the floats with seven other men besides him on it, but there was room for a few more. However, when the swimming men, including Becker and Nagel, tried to hail this float and attempted to swim towards it to get taken aboard, Kuntze ordered the men to row away and put some distance between their float and the swimming men instead of pulling them out of the sea and taking them aboard.

The incoming tides and currents carried the floats to a smooth landing near Galley Head Point. Even the swimmers eventually made it, somehow. Local fishermen spotted them and called the police, who in turn mobilized the Irish Army, which organized truck transport and drove the group of stranded seafarers to Dublin. Becker, the officers and petty officers were immediately separated from the enlisted men. Once the Irish Army intelligence officer who interrogated them had determined they were sea-loss cases, and not deserters or voluntary arrivals, they were placed into four different internment camps.

A few days later, they were interrogated a lot more thoroughly. Becker had checked that all his men were alive, but had not seen Kuntze. Now he was suddenly in Dublin. The Irish had placed him in separate quarters when they noticed that he and the crew were hostile to Kuntze for refusing to take the swimming men aboard.

Kuntze had reported to Becker that all secret papers and documents, plus the secret equipment, had been destroyed. Kuntze had placed many papers rolled up into a long metal cylinder, especially the super-secret instructions and operational directions. He assumed the weight of the metal cylinder, once water had entered it and been soaked up by the various papers and documents, would be sufficient to make the metal container sink to the ocean's bottom.

However, it turned out that the cylinder was really watertight and it floated on the surface, instead. Drifting eventually towards the Irish coastline, it was later found on the beach by fishermen, who turned the metal container over to the police, and they in turn to the Irish Army.

About three months later, when the war had ended, the entire crew of U-260 was shipped in groups to Belgium and turned over to the British prisoner-of-war administration there, to be put into one of their prisoner-of-war holding camps for registration, classification and onward transport.

The super-secret documents, papers and directions which Kuntze had placed into that metal cylinder were immediately checked, perused and registered by the intelligence department of the Irish Army. Numerically recorded, classified and stamped Highly Confidential, every page of these secret documents was rubber-stamped MILITARY ARCHIVES, CATHAL BRUGHA BARRACKS, RATHMINES, DUBLIN-6, by a framed stamp 7.5 cm by 2.8 cm. These barracks are named after Cathal Brugha, the first Irish war/defence minister in the Michael Collins government that in 1921 negotiated the 'Free State' Agreement to end the military occupation of Southern Ireland by Great Britain.

For reasons that are difficult to understand, Ireland is still unwilling, more than fifty years after the end of the war, to declassify these documents, and the Irish are cagey about the entire matter, rejecting most applications by historians and investigators to either obtain copies or to study these documents and papers on the premises in Dublin.

So how did I manage to peruse and copy these secret papers? A few years ago, Colin Barnes, an Irish scuba diver, located the wreck of U-260 lying at a depth of 70 m on the ocean bottom, about 7 km south of Glandore, in County Cork. Barnes checked out the wreck, which was still in fairly good shape, and took some very good pictures of her. He had already searched for U-260 for quite some time, based upon the signalled naval grid square of AM-8883 and the U-boat's signalled scuttling position, 51° 50' N, 9° 28' W,

Barnes repeated his dives and visits to U-260, and accumulated more pictures and some other material.

It was decided to develop his discovery into a television film running for fifty-five minutes, teaming up with Glyn and Pamela Carragher and Mark Byrne, a professional photographer. For historical background research they brought naval Commander Peter Young into the project, to publicize the U-260 story. Finders and salvage rights are now owned by David Casswell and his firm, Avoca Arklow County Company of Wicklow, Ireland.

The developers sought financial support for their film project, and looked for potential buyers/users of their TV film in Europe. I was asked by such prospective buyers to evaluate the Dublin material, double-check the authenticity of the secret papers and judge them for genuineness. Consequently, I studied these papers in the Dublin archives and looked at the various documents by special arrangements through the Irish diver-developer group. There were two main-groups, the first of which was so-called informational signals regarding particular operational experiences of several U-boats, with recommendations, if not orders, by Dönitz, that were issued in numerical sequence as Super-secret Command Matters.

First was a signal report with secret command registration Number 171, issued on 5 November 1944, by Karl Dönitz.

One U-boat, ordered to operate off the North Channel departing from Norway, selected a route through naval grid squares AF-12, AE-35 and AF-99, but did not approach the operational area any closer than grid square AM-5736, because the commander was far too impressed by sound detection recordings of ships. Naturally, if a commander does not approach his operational area any closer than that, he is unable to be successful.

The experiences of many commanders prove clearly: the snorkel permits a route into the operational area without course deviations. The snorkel allows us to remain in shallow coastal waters, in spite of the most intense anti-submarine operations in that area, and, nevertheless, to achieve success. Directions and actual reports about operational experiences are being signalled constantly and also information about the enemy's defences.

I demand from all commanders that they take advantage of the great possibilities that the snorkel equipment offers them to the maximum extent feasible to overcome the defence of the enemy, with all their energy and strength to defeat that defence completely. That they proceed directly and close enough to the point of origin of the ship traffic and attack targets at that point without hesitation. The prevalence of hostile defensive forces is normal, logical and must be expected, while the extent of their circumvention, regardless of whether these are ships or aeroplanes, actually depends upon the cleverness and ability of the U-boat commander, and shows his competency and willingness to attack the very centre of enemy shipping routes.

I shall demand and insist upon total accountability from all commanders for their actions, if the same were not undertaken with that old responsibility and reckless daredevil approach of our U-boat arm and the weapons available.

U-boat Headquarters Secret Command Matter 231.

Signed: Dönitz

On 6 October 1944 the Secret Command Matter 165 was radioed to all U-boats at sea and handed to those getting ready for operations, also issued by Karl Dönitz:

In the last few days we have received messages from four U-boats, operating either in the North Channel or the Bristol Channel, that they have not located any ship traffic nor seen any targets whatsoever. But we know for certain that during the periods these U-boats were in these operational areas a considerable number of escorted convoys have transited those specific sea areas. Inability to find traffic on such particular and narrow convoy routes can only be possible if these U-boats either did not really search in the operational areas reported but elsewhere, or otherwise did not approach the real concentration points of convoy traffic, having remained and operated much too far away from the actual convoy routes. Therefore, we must emphasize herewith:

1. It has to be the unconditional ambition of every U-boat commander to be able to get into an effective attack position. This calls for daring boldness and approaching as closely as possible to the target. But also clever and tenacious persistence to be combined with patience to stay in positions that promise success, regardless of how strong the enemy's defence concentration may be.

2. U-boats that operate directly in front of those traffic concentration points off the British coast must approach as closely as required to the coastline at such narrow points where traffic reaches maximum concentration, and must pass through without chance of deviation.

We have received reports that the enemy has arranged defensive catching zones about 150 miles off his coastline by aeroplanes and surface ships in order to catch all approaching U-boats before they reach the coast itself. The forces of these defensive zones are equally strong on the outer side and on the inner side. But experience shows the inside positions are often less alert and aggressive. It stands to

reason one finds ship traffic easier and surer on that inside sector with less interference by defensive activity, which is always more closely directed towards the outside area. On the outside, chances of finding targets are smaller, the further out to sea one is positioned.
3.   Shallow-water coastal areas with less than 200 m water depth have been found to be the most favourable attack positions, and are much more auspicious for U-boat operations in general. (See also our previous Experience Report 160.)

U-boat Headquarters Secret Command Matter 242.

Signed: Dönitz

There were several other similar signals and messages from Dönitz to the U-boat commanders, which were issued between August 1944 and January 1945, but are not very different in their content.

To round off the picture, there was a two-page exhortation that originated from Admiral Hans Georg von Friedeburg, the commanding admiral U-boats. It was issued and distributed to all U-boats departing from German ports, usually Kiel, and a few others that left from southern Norwegian ports. Because the content of this special release contradicts Eberhard Godt's rigid statement in court of no disciplinary problems, it is featured in full.

This document had been handed to Klaus Becker as commander of U-260 just before he left Kiel, and was recorded by the second watch officer, Siegfried Kuntze, under Secret Command Matter Registration 213 in the secret paper register of U-260.

SECRET – PERSONAL:
* *
A WORD TO ALL U-BOAT COMMANDERS!

Brains and smartness are a two-edged sword out of hard steel and with a shiny edge. But character is actually the handle for it, as without that handle the sword is worthless!

The appointment of an officer to the position of U-boat commander signifies an extraordinary amount of trust and is clear evidence by the leadership not just of the officer's competency and professional ability, but of his personal quality as far as his character is concerned and thus a very special honour.

All of you know that slogan, which was featured during the Middle Ages and posted above all offices of the Hansa commercial group, that read:

HONOUR IS DUTY AND FORCE ENOUGH!

The high responsibility and dutiful obligation that this demands from the selected officer has only recently been made clear again for everyone in the extremely impressive special decree by the Navy's chief in command [Karl Dönitz], entitled: Why U-boat war?

In this report it was stated that the engagement to the fullest of each and every naval soldier is of the same importance in the forthcoming new U-boat operations that are going to start soon, if in fact not even more so, than the fighting employment of our best tank destroyers or people grenadiers on our widely spread fronts anywhere. One is therefore quite correct to consider a U-boat commander a first-line fighter, even as an example of a first-line CHAMPION on this crucial battlefront at sea, of decisive war importance and influence.

For the front-line champion it is a self-evident obligation and a dutiful expectation that he utilizes each and every means for combat that has been entrusted to him, to demonstrate the absolutely most aggressive attacking spirit and carry the same forward, right to the very point of origin, and also concentration, of the enemy's sea traffic points.

All U-boat commanders who possess this overwhelming and extra-ordinary willingness to attack recklessly confirm enthusiastically that our new snorkel equipment offers us unique possibilities of succeeding. The brand new U-boats coming to the front soon [the Types XXI and XXIII electro boats] will offer even greater possibilities for these determined, brave and courageous commanders.

By contrast, there exist a small number of overcareful officers who depend in their decisions to an excessive degree upon the thought of negative ideas, which makes them almost sick and indecisive. This includes all those officers who rely almost entirely upon their ears and listening devices and give them much too much influence in their thinking, instead of wanting to take a direct look at what is going on. For such commanders, the enemy has invented and uses the noise-making sound buoy. For those commanders the enemy arranges for aeroplanes and search groups in all sea areas, dropping depth-charges at random and as a mere precaution, because the enemy knows that some commanders will assume such indiscriminately dropped depth-charges are destined for them.

We all remember that old story by Günther Prien, who interpreted a heavy attack by hostile aircraft upon German surface ships many miles away as a depth-charge pursuit of his own U-boat U-47. After this experience, Prien never again made such erroneous assumptions, and only considered depth-charges to be directed against his U-boat if they were actually dropped in the very close area around him, never again at a considerable distance and directed against other units.

At that time [April 1940] we lacked experience, and had first to gain it gradually in combat. Courageous commanders collected this type of actual front experience, and it was made available afterwards through extracts from KTBs [war patrol journals] or special informative messages signalling such actual experiences and through constant and continued advice, messages or instructions from shore provided to all officers.

Those who are guided by the slogan and view, 'Fear is no acceptable philosophy for life', to that group also belong those commanders who postpone their contemplated attack first from the daytime to the darker night, and then once more from the night to the daytime for better observations, and who justify these postponements with a great number of intellectual considerations and endless deliberations retrospectively, unfortunately only after any and all possibilities for a successful attack are long since gone and have been completely lost.

In addition, there are a very small number of officers, Thank God for that!, who, let's say this quite clearly, candidly and openly, have sometimes a great fear of doing their duty as required.

It is not the fright as such that one has to reprimand or to rebuke, as I should like to meet the soldier whose heart has never trembled in hard-fighting combat situations. I maintain that there are simply no such soldiers anywhere! He who refuses to accept this fact has either never really been involved and engaged in any truly decisive and tough fighting situation or otherwise the man simply lies!

That, my comrades, is not the important point. The officer in question, as the front fighter and leader of the soldiers who have been entrusted to his command, must take his heart into both hands firmly, or, as I have always stated in my speeches to you, he must acquire an iron heart!

If a U-boat commander who now has to take responsibility in front of a naval court martial for his actions [Lieutenant Walter Köhntopp of U-995] tells his officers that it is now senseless and hopeless to operate against a convoy, refrains from doing so and refuses to pursue and follow it tenaciously with the highest speed possible in order to attack it; when a U-boat commander, after observing an aircraft very far away, which does not even drop any bombs on him, does not rise again quickly to periscope depth to check the situation, when he does not rise to the surface again once a careful look around through the periscope confirms that the area is clear and nothing can be seen, but decides instead to remain dived without any reason at all, while other U-boat commanders, his comrades, track and chase that convoy in hot pursuit instead, if he states after getting a clear report from his sound-detection operators concerning a broad band of shipping noises that the directing engineer and both watch officers identify as a convoy with enemy ships, based upon their experience; when such a commander disputes these facts and insists the noises are really caused by another German U-boat instead, and are typical diesel noises – nothing else; it really does not require a military court martial to confirm and determine that such a commander is simply a coward!

If another U-boat commander, out of fear of the enemy, simply does not proceed with his U-boat into the designated operational area to which he has been ordered to proceed, but thereafter deceives the U-boat Command with an untrue signal that he actually did reach and stay in the operational area that he had been ordered to, he will be exterminated without consideration, and with every right and justification possible, because he has besmirched the honour of our U-boat arm and has contravened the unconditional requirements and demands of his position, he lacks moral fibre and the decisiveness that is essential: namely that one has to first take strong action oneself before one is able and successful in killing opponents.

For weaklings and cowards, there is simply no room in the U-boat Command, nor anywhere in the German Navy.

The U-boat combat arm is a sworn group of men who are experienced in using their weapons, and utilize their weapons with joy and pride. Men who have learned in the past to obey orders implicitly and are led and directed by men who have learned to command and give orders without hesitation.

We are extremely proud that since that unfortunate setback that we have suffered on the Western Front [after the Allied landings in France] the German Navy has turned into the defensive backbone of all those coastal fortresses that have been encircled and become the principal force of resistance in France, delaying and holding off the efforts of our enemies long enough to allow the formation of a new line of resistance and a new defensive front, in that way gaining the time required to accomplish this.

We are extremely proud that the total uprising of the German people, fighting at each and every road crossing and in each and every house, has brought about the grimmest resistance and most dogged fighting against our enemies everywhere. This has generated tremendous consternation in the camp of our opponents and has defeated and knocked down all of the enemy's plans for a swift victory, and completely invalidated their predictions of a victorious campaign within a short time, which they had loudly forecast.

Because we shall continue to fight resolutely and with the firmest determination required, being willing to pay any price necessary to win the war still! We know that any people will be eliminated who no longer produce men who are first of all fighters. That the history of any people is really a history of their past fights for existence.

Our German people have experienced their complete rebirth. Our *Führer* stands firmly, like a huge rock in the raging surf of the wild seas against all violent dangers and the toughest forces that are attacking us; he has never been more strongly convinced that we shall overcome and will achieve final victory for our just cause than now!

Out of this situation grows for all of us, but particularly for the U-boat commander at the front facing the enemy, and for all officers who have been appointed to that proud and responsible position and demanding task to lead their soldiers to success and victory the

HOLY DUTY

to be leader and first-line champion in the front-lines for their men in the truest sense of the word, the hardest fighter of his group of soldiers, surpassing each and every one of his men somehow, completing any and all tasks or assignments that he may receive in the line of duty and in accordance with our old U-boat arm watchword:

ATTACK! APPROACH CLOSELY! SINK THEM!

in total militarily reckless daredevil ways, using any means available to accomplish the success of any order given without fail.

Only in this way can the U-boat commander show his appreciation and demonstrate that he merits the great trust and the enormous honour involved in getting the appointment for his responsible position.

For his decisions and his actions in this struggle TO ACHIEVE FINAL VICTORY REGARDLESS OF THE PRICE REQUIRED and the toughness needed to make this possible, there can only be one guideline and direction:
'HONOUR IS OBLIGATION ENOUGH!'

Kiel, October 1944　　　　　[signature　v. Friedeburg
　　Aboard U-boat Tender　　facsimile]　Admiral
　　　　　　　　　　　　　　　　　　　Otto Wünsche
　　　　　　　　　　　　　　　　　　Commanding Admiral
　　　　　　　　　　　　　　　　　　　　of U-boats

Evidently, those assurances on the witness stand of the Kiel court by Eberhard Godt: 'There were no disciplinary problems in the U-boat command during the war' were too broad and an overstatement of the facts, as they actually existed between 1943 and 1945 at sea.

While von Friedeburg did not provide the names of the U-boat commanders cited in his exhortation edict, one of them was Lieutenant Walter Köhntopp (Crew 1936), as already mentioned. Köhntopp was removed as commander of U-995 operating out of Narvik-Norway with the Barents Sea command. The medical examiner of that command testified that Köhntopp had severe medical and psychological problems, which the court martial accepted as mitigating circumstances. Köhntopp was transferred to Trontheim and the 13th U-boat flotilla, but the war's end precluded a retrial and he also retained his commission.

Another of these officers was Lieutenant Commander Johann Reckhoff (Crew 1928), who had commissioned U-398 and commanded her for one war patrol in August of 1944 out of Norway. Von Friedeburg removed Reckhoff as commander of U-398 for disregard of orders, reporting false positions and entering faked information in his operational records. Dönitz rejected the death penalty for him and transfered Reckhoff to the sailingship Albert Leo Schlageter as commander. This training ship was awarded to

Soviet Russia as war booty in 1945. Reckhoff delivered her to a Soviet Russian base in the Baltic. There he accepted a long-term naval instructor's contract and remained in Soviet Russia. When the East German communist regime started up the 'people's navy' several years later, Reckhoff transfered to that force and retired as rear admiral in 1976.

However, those other two or even three U-boat commanders cited by von Friedeburg in his decree could so far not be reliably identified.

CHAPTER EIGHTEEN

Fanatics During the Finale

On 3 March 1941, the first major landing operation by British commando troops on the coast of Europe started, named Operation Claymore, but more often called the Lofoten Raid. British destroyers, the *Somali*, *Bedouin*, *Eskimo*, *Legion* and *Tartar*, escorted the assault ships *Princess Beatrix* and *Queen Emma* with 500 selected soldiers of the newly created commando task force, and arrived off the Norwegian coast.The troops landed and conquered the fishing villages of Stamsund, Brettesnes, Henningsvaer and Svolvaer.

The attackers destroyed the fish-oil and canning factories of these villages. They sank seven German merchant ships of 14,929 tons waiting to take on loads. They also sank the Norwegian fishing vessel *Maryland* of 321 tons and the German auxiliary harbour patrol boat *Krebs* (*Crawfish*) Number 59-NN04. From the sinking *Krebs*, the commandos recovered several new Enigma M-3 machine coding wheels, which were taken back to England. This permitted the codebreakers in Bletchley Park to crack and read the German naval messages sent on the Homewaters circuit a few days later. A total of 213 German prisoners of war were taken, and also twelve Norwegians of the Quisling government administration. But 314 other Norwegians spontaneously joined the British troops and returned to England with them, volunteering to enlist in the Free Norwegian Forces in Great Britain.

Hitler became almost apoplectic when he was informed about the Lofoten Raid, and shouted: 'Why can't we Germans arrange this sort of successful landing operation in Great Britain?'

On 3 March 1942, another daring commando landing took place, which became known as the Bruneval Raid. British parachutists and landing troops arrived in a coordinated operation on Cape d'Antifer, about thirteen miles north of the French port of Le Havre, capturing the German Freya and Würzburg Giant radar observation equipment that the Experimental and Test Regiment of the *Luftwaffe* had installed in the Bruneval ravine.Technical specialists removed the super-secret parts and the operational instruction books, and were picked up by fast landing ships that took them back to England.

Hitler severely berated the fat Hermann Göring, the commander of the *Luftwaffe*, and held him responsible for the ineffective defence of these radar installations, which had permitted such a formidable success by the British commandos.

On 27 March 1942, not even a month later, British ships with commandos managed to get ashore in Saint Nazaire. The destroyer *Campbelltown* succeeded in ramming the gate of the huge dry dock in the port. Then 353 crewmen of these ships, together with 268 selected commando landing troopers, stormed into Saint Nazaire and started a night of hard and close fighting in the port area. The destruction of this big dry dock was the main object of the Saint Nazaire Raid, also known as Operation Chariot, because the Royal Navy knew that this was the only dry dock large enough to accept the German battleship *Tirpitz*, a sister ship of the ill-fated *Bismarck*, which had been sunk in the Atlantic on 27 May 1941. The German Navy wrongly assumed that the purpose of this attack was to put the U-boat base out of commission and to blow up U-boats being serviced and overhauled in the concrete U-boat pens of the inner harbour. However, the joke was that the German Navy could not even contemplate operating the *Tirpitz* in the Atlantic because the constant and rapid improvements of the British radar equipment, which had finally been recognized, made such operations extremely hazardous. In addition, unknown to the Royal Navy, there already existed at that time a severe shortage of fuel oil for German surface ships, which precluded further long-distance operations, although the diesel fuel that was used by U-boats was fairly readily available.

Vice-Admiral Dönitz had visited Saint Nazaire that very day, to inspect the crews of several U-boats that had returned from war patrols. He had also arranged that a special officers' meeting would take place after these inspections. U-boat commanders and officers, not only from Saint Nazaire, but also from other French U-boat bases, had been ordered to come to Saint Nazaire to attend this exhortatory session.

Although Dönitz and his staff had returned to his headquarters in Kerneval, near Lorient, when the attack started, the U-boat officers had remained in town for parties and to visit the gambling casino. All had been lodged in commercial hotels in the nearby seaside resort of La Baule. Once the combat in Saint Nazaire had ended, the *Campbelltown* was checked out by German security experts and cleared for visitors and curious sightseers, who boarded her to look her over. However, these inspectors had failed to discover that her entire forecastle was filled with tightly packed containers of high explosives and delayed timing fuses, to blow up the lock-gate of the dry dock after the British crew had managed to get off the ship to join the night-fighting on shore.

As soon as the *Campbelltown* was cleared for vistors, she became so crowded with U-boat officers and technicians that the field police had to limit and restrict the boarding of the destroyer, making moving around almost impossible. But at 11.45 whistles were blown and warning signals were sounded to get all U-boat officers off the destroyer without further delay, in order to get them into the waiting cars and motorcoaches for a prompt return to the officers' mess hall in La Baule, as the mess officer had informed everybody that the doors of the mess hall would close at 12.05 sharp; no latecomers would be admitted for luncheon, and no exceptions would be permitted.

This loudly cursed order saved the U-boat officers from being blown up in pieces, because at 12.08 the *Campbelltown* blew up with a chain of enormous explosions, killing more than a hundred visitors who had got aboard the ship once the U-boat officers had vacated her. By a mere whisker and a narrow margin of luck, the U-boat Command had avoided losing a substantial number of the most experienced front officers – a disaster that would have almost paralyzed U-boat operations for a long time.

When Dönitz was informed about the situation, he reportedly blanched, and was so stunned that for several minutes he did not make any remark at all. But Hitler really hit the ceiling when the Saint Nazaire Raid was reported to him. Dönitz was ordered to move his headquarters from Kerneval back to Paris, away from the French coast, as rapidly as possible. Hitler feared that Lorient might be the next landing target for these British commando operations and that they might capture and kidnap Dönitz and his staff in the process.

On 18 October 1942, one of Hitler's many super-secret special orders was issued, called the '*Nacht und Nebel Erlass*', meaning a decree for secret actions during the night and in fog during the day. This was in response to, and directed against, British commando raids, where specially trained soldiers landed in the dark to capture new secret German equipment or to destroy German facilities, blowing up bridges, docks, harbours, ships, the Norsk Hydro AB heavy-water factory at Ryukan, in Norway, and other important installations.

This decree by Hitler read as follows: 'From now on I order that all enemy soldiers participating in these so-called commando raids and operations in Europe and Africa who are caught or are encountered by German units shall be eradicated without any trace and killed to the last man, regardless of whether they are uniformed soldiers, agents in civilian clothing or special-action or special-operations troops. It makes no difference whatsoever whether they are armed or unarmed, if they wish to surrender or have already been taken prisoner.' In other words, such men would literally disappear, and no record of any kind would be kept of their names, serial numbers, service grades or other personal identification. They were to be killed, butchered and massacred, and then buried in unmarked graves or otherwise eliminated in such a way that no traces would remain of them. Furthermore, no information whatsoever would be furnished in response to enquiries, nor any notification to any authority made. To summarize, these men would just disappear, 'lost in the night and in the fog', without evidence as to their end.

Erich Raeder had passed this illegal order onwards to many, but not all, naval commands. There was a provision dispatched with these orders: 'The junior officers, petty officers and enlisted men should only be informed and instructed about this secret order *verbally*, in a suitable way.'

In most commands this super-secret decree was filed away quietly or placed in a safe and ignored. However, there were some exceptions. For the U-boat Command, Dönitz claimed that he had not passed on this decree and order, because he considered it counter-productive for U-boat crews.

But there was one area where this edict of Hitler was implemented, and the information spread widely: this was in western and southern Norway. Here Admiral Otto von Schrader had ruled since 1940 – a fanatical, un-reasonable and vociferous Nazi Party supporter and admirer of Adolf Hitler since 1923. He was a typical Nazi loud-mouth, something of an exception among the senior naval officers in Germany, a totally political admiral.

By his imbecilic, harsh decisions he had become an object of hate for many Norwegians, and was one of the men largely responsible for the German occupation forces being hated more fiercely in Norway than in most Nazi-occupied countries, generating a stronger hostility to Germany than elsewhere in Western Europe. This was unlike France, where there was practically no open hostility until the spring of 1944 and the Allied landings seemed imminent, which created a sudden growth of the so-called French Resistance, a negligible factor until that time, apart from a few radical Communist groups. The French had largely accommodated themselves to the German occupation as well as they could, to continue living.

Eventually, there were only two known cases where this Hitler decree was followed and fully observed by the German Navy, both in Norway. In November 1942, in the Narvik area, a British two man mini-submarine, called a 'Chariot' had tried unsuccessfully to attack the battleship *Tirpitz* at anchor. One man of the crew did survive and managed to get away, attempting to escape overland to the nearby Swedish border. But he was caught there by SS/SD border guards, who promptly arrested him. Upon the request of the German fleet command in northern Norway, the captive was turned over to a group of naval interrogators and investigators of the attack, to clarify the circumstances of this operation, related technical matters and planning details. However, the proviso was that this prisoner of war had to be returned forthwith to the SS/SD after the naval interrogation had been finished. He was consequently returned, and was shot by the SS/SD without further ado, and his body was made to disappear.

However, the really big case occurred on 27 July 1943, when a British motor torpedo boat, MTB-345, with a mixed English and Norwegian crew, approached the extremely tricky Norwegian coastline for a contemplated minelaying operation, but ran aground at Aspoy, near Bergen. MTB-345 was blown up, but the noise and commotion brought a German patrol boat, the V-5301, to the scene. The crew were captured, made prisoners of war and taken to Bergen for interrogation by German naval intelligence officers. During these lengthy proceedings the naval intelligence specialists determined that the captives were entitled to become prisoners of war, though some of them were in uniform, while others no longer had any uniforms because of the sinking of MTB-345. All should be shipped to Germany, to be placed in a *Marlag* naval prisoner-of-war camp.

But Admiral von Schrader, the regional commander, rejected this conclusion by the intelligence specialists, and overruled their decision. Then he ordered that they must be turned over forthwith to SS/SD special units, in accordance with the Hitler anti-commando order of Night and Fog, because in his view these men were nothing but pirates. And in spite of strong objections by the junior intelligence officers, this was done. The next morning they were shot by Gestapo police forces. The bodies were tossed on a truck and driven to the coastline. Here they were placed in wooden military coffins with detonation charges attached, and taken out to sea after dark. The coffins were dropped into the sea and the charges exploded at a pre-set depth, according to the usual SS/SD and Gestapo practice in all such cases, so as to remove all traces.

After the German capitulation in May 1945, when the Norwegian Resistance movement retook power, supported by the British Navy and English command troops, this case was solved, because some of the SS/SD and Gestapo men involved had survived, and the search for MTB-345 could finally be documented, confirmed by these captives. But when it became clear that the real villain responsible for this atrocity was von Schrader, the Royal Navy ordered his removal from a prisoner-of-war camp where he had been placed, and wanted to arrest him for this war crime. He committed suicide just before the arrival of the British military police. This was a disgraceful blot on the history of the German Navy.

Several other brutal murder cases occurred in Norway. Some took place at the end of the war, or even afterwards. However, only two of them were later brought to court, and the people responsible indicted for their actions and behaviour. Yet there were quite a few others where the culprits were not even accused, much less punished, after the war, as nobody filed a complaint!

The first of the two cases in question involved Naval Judge Advocate Adolf Holzwig and Navy Captain Rudolf Petersen, and the other one concerned Naval Judge Advocate Curt Lilder and Admiral Otto von Schrader. There were retrials of both these cases, which are covered in full in Chapter Sixteen.

However, two other cases involving naval judge advocates and the naval court system were eventually documented and publicized, though only some years later, and without any legal consequences for the originators of these verified heinous cases.

The first one involved the commander of the 15th U-boat Flotilla in Kristiansand, Norway. This flotilla was only established on 15 April 1945, at a time when many German submarines were expected to operate from southern Norway, because there remained hardly any German ports in German hands any more. The man was Lieutenant-Commander Ernst Mengersen (Crew 1933), one of a minority of convinced and vociferous Nazis among front-service U-boat officers. He had commanded several U-boats, and had been awarded the Knight's Cross of the Iron Cross, when he was relieved as U-boat commander in spring 1943 and shifted to a shore position in the Baltic Training Command.

On 4 and 5 May 1945, a string of radio signals was received from Dönitz, who had moved with his staff to Flensburg after taking over as Adolf Hitler's successor on 1 May 1945, that Germany had capitulated, that an armistice had been arranged and that the war had terminated. The Rainbow scuttling order for U-boats was rescinded by Dönitz. All U-boats and any other ships on operations were ordered to cease combat operations and terminate all hostilities at once. U-boats at sea were instructed to return to their bases or to Germany. Should this be impossible for fuel or supply reasons, they were to surrender at the closest Allied port, having hauled down their flag and hoisted a black surrender flag, instead.

Dönitz and the U-boat Command staff had vacated Camp Koralle in Bernau, near Berlin, on the morning of 20 April 1945, a mere thirty minutes ahead of the arriving Russian tanks and troops. They had then driven to Berlin to participate in the birthday congratulation ceremonies for Hitler that afternoon, and subsequently continued to Plön, in Holstein, to the naval Camp 'Forelle', or 'Trout'. When British forces conquered Hamburg and approached Plön, Dönitz moved on to the naval academy in Flensburg-Mürwik, next to the Danish border.

All German ships, commands, units and naval bases still in operation, particularly in Norway, had received these radio signals from Dönitz, and were aware that all German military forces had capitulated without conditions. The Kristiansand U-boat base was still in the process of being established, but communication connections were already fully operational. Mengersen was very unhappy over these signals, and disliked the developments they created. He fantasized about continuing the fight from the Norwegian mountains and to resist Germany's enemies virtually to the final bullet and the very last man. While practically all German sailors, soldiers and officers were relieved and happy that these final months of pure butchering of men had now ended, Mengersen did not share these feelings and the general gladness in any way. To the contrary, he fumed and cursed, seemingly still hoping for that miracle, which Hitler and his yes-men, now suicides in the ruins of Berlin, had promised. He turned quite morose and unwilling to accept the orders to cease hostilities, one of the few officers who refused finally to face facts and accept the full truth.

Several sailors and other naval soldiers had left the fenced-in compound of the U-boat base area at the port, to walk into the town of Kristiansand. Many of them carried a good supply of booze with them, because the Norwegians had none and were always very keen to get hold of hard liquor in any form, no matter how or from whom. On 8 May 1945, these celebrations hotted up even more, and in the afternoon several of the sailors were so drunk that they could hardly walk any more. Loud singing and rather erratic behaviour had become prevalent, and some petty officers and sailors were forced to sit down in the grass on the roadside, because their feet no longer obeyed them very well. So they rested, taking a break in a meadow, on their way back to the naval base.

With the sun shining and the world seemingly at ease and content, Mengersen, his adjutant and another one of the base personnel of the 15th U-boat Flotilla drove into town to see what was going on. He had the car turned around when he spotted several of the drunken sailors relaxing in the grass, and instructed his adjutant to go over, check their identities, obtain their names and tell them to return to the base and their command without further delay.

When this group of sailors reached the naval enclosure, at about 15.00, they were immediately arrested on Mengersen's orders by the guards on duty, and placed in the basement of the 15th U-boat Flotilla's administration building, where they were shackled and chained to the wall, as directed by Mengersen. At about 18.00, all U-boat crews, all men of the other naval commands in the general area and the crews manning a few small surface-ships in port were advised that they must assemble in front of the U-boat Flotilla's base building, if possible in blue dress uniforms, for a general military assembly and participation in an emergency express court martial for several deserters at 21.00.

As the men arrived in large and small groups, they were formed into a huge U-shaped horseshoe, which took some time before it was arranged properly. A single table had been set up at the open end of this horseshoe formation, draped with a red tablecloth and the naval war flag, and decorated with a naval dagger and sabre. On the table a ship's lantern had been fastened, and Adolf Hitler's book, *Mein Kampf* ('My Struggle'), was placed below it. By now it was slowly getting dark.

The waiting soldiers grew unhappy at having to wait, just standing there without any purpose, killing time. As the men were gradually able to see better, they noticed three wooden gallows with some sort of stand below and three nooses hanging down, that swayed periodically in the evening breeze. This made the men even more concerned and nervous. The whole set-up was rather unexpected, creating a threatening atmosphere, just as it must have done in the Middle Ages during the public trials of witches, heretics or major criminals.

Suddenly, Mengersen and his adjutant stepped out of the dark background, moved to the front of the horseshoe formation and called the assembled soldiers to order. Mengersen set off on a loud declaratory speech, or sermon, somewhat to the bafflement of the assembled men: 'Soldiers! I have called you together to demonstrate to you how we shall avoid another 1918! I have already discussed the case of these undisciplined deserters with the leading judge of this area in Bergen, and now await his decision, confirmation and approval by telephone. Because I am going to make an example of these three deserters here and now! An example that will strike fear into the hearts of any man with revolutionary tendencies! We shall protect those ideals installed in us by our martyred, unforgettable *Fuhrer*! Guards! Bring these men to justice without further delay!'

The three inebriated captives were dragged into the lighted area. They had been brought from the basement with their hands tied behind their backs. The light confused and dazzled them for a minute, after coming out of the dark basement. Each soldier was led by two guards. However, they had sobered up considerably in those hours since they had been arrested. Suddenly they caught sight of the gallows against the night sky. In deathly fear, combined with furious determination to save themselves, they tore loose from their guards and tried to escape, by running towards the nearby woods, to reach the cover of the pine trees. The surprised guards let them get away. Mengersen and his adjutant immediately drew their pistols and fired the entire magazines, without any warning calls or admonitions to halt. The fleeing petty officer was hit hard and dropped to the ground instantly, while the two enlisted men seemed to be hit less severely and fell to the ground bleeding profusely, short of the tree line. Mengersen yelled, 'These deserters must be hanged as they are, without any further delay or waiting for legal clearance!' However, this turned out to be impossible. The guards, while trying to make the wounded men stand up, found it was no longer feasible. In this disgusting, confusing and chaotic situation, with Mengersen shouting and others screaming and yelling, a runner appeared out of the dark from the office building of the 15th U-boat Flotilla, stopped in front of Mengersen, and reported, 'The confirmation to hang these deserters has just come through from Admiral von Schrader in Bergen and his senior judge and legal adviser: to do so forthwith!' This judge advocate was also the legal adviser of the regional leader of U-boats in the Western area, Captain Rösing.

Mengersen, though elated, realized that these men could no longer be hanged, as they were already half-dead after attempting to tear loose twice more, trying to escape into the woods. Therefore, he ordered a standby platoon of marine riflemen to shoot the helpless men at once, as they cringed on the ground, like mad or wild dogs in the road somewhere in the deepest Middle East or darkest Africa. The bodies, once they had finally expired, were just left lying in the dirt. The volley of rifleshots had finished this deplorable, disgusting 'Spectacle of Justice'. Mengersen and his staff did not even bother to arrange for the removal and burial of the dead soldiers lying on the ground, now completely ignored. After this sordid and horrifying presentation, the assembled men were curtly dismissed. All the naval soldiers were deeply shocked, and just walked silently away. The presence of the armed marine platoon had prevented any assistance or interference to help the murdered men. Mengersen's dramatic demonstration had achieved its purpose – to warn the naval soldiers to watch their step carefully, even though the war had ended and Germany had surrendered unconditionally. Mengersen was never prosecuted, nor were the naval judge advocates nor any of the officers who were involved in this outrageous crime, and authorized it.

Just before midnight, Lieutenant j.g. Herbert A. Werner (Crew 39-B), who was forced to attend this emergency court martial and legal travesty, got together with two petty officers, who were likewise present during this despicable demonstration. They were shocked and dismayed about Mengersen's 'Horror Show', and arranged for a sea burial of the dead men's remains, left unattended in the dirt. Werner had served as a midshipman on U-557, and was subsequently the executive officer of U-612 and U-230 before he finally commanded U-415 and U-953, all of them Type VII U-boats.

With U-953, Werner had returned to Trondheim on 9 April 1945 from his last war patrol. U-953 was in need of lengthy repairs after severe damage at sea, before she could depart again. Rösing, visiting Trondheim, decreed that Werner was just too experienced a U-boat commander to be permitted to wait around for these repairs to be made, and so ordered him to travel by train via Bergen to Kristiansand as a courier, in order to take over as commander one of the new electro U-boats that were to arrive shortly from Germany, because there was a lack of front-experienced U-boat commanders for them. Werner had arrived on the morning of 4 May 1945 at the Kristiansand U-boat base, and was forced to join the U-boat men in port ordered to attend this travesty of justice. In the meantime the war had ended and no further U-boats could or would arrive from Germany any more. The improvised burial group felt that this burial was the least they could do for these men, whose families were never informed about the vile termination of their lives. Twenty years later, Herbert A. Werner became the author of that extraordinarily personal and touching book, *Iron Coffins*, which should have been named *The Dönitz Coffins*, as the U-boat men themselves had called their U-boats since that Black May of 1943.

However, there occurred another documented case of multiple murders, where German naval soldiers were killed as late as 20 May 1945 in the Greater Oslo area of Norway, along the Oslo fjord. Naval Judge Advocate Hans Filbinger was the man responsible for that, being the senior judge of the Oslo fjord sea-frontier area command. His travelling court rotated through the region as needed, and he continued to sentence naval soldiers to death as late as two weeks after the war's end.

Most of the cases processed by Filbinger were blown up and grossly inflated or exaggerated in the most incredible way by him, in order to expedite decisions and reduce handling time for himself. He made major events out of the smallest misdemeanours, so that he could sentence to death naval soldiers who had the misfortune to fall into the hands of his court. Naturally, in each and every case, he only intended to uphold naval discipline, order and the fighting strength of the naval commands that his court visited.

Eventually, he became a prisoner of war and was shipped to northern Germany. Here he managed to arrange a quick discharge, and for a short period was employed by the legal assistance group of Kranzbüler, Siebert and Niesehling, the 'Hamburg Gang'.

Filbinger originated from Mannheim and was in touch with family members. He managed to get discharged into the American Zone of Occupation after a few months, and then proceeded to Stuttgart. Here, after his arrival, he opened a private law office, with financial support by the Sieber group in Hamburg, who also furnished recommendations and commercial law work for him, in addition to substantial legal help and financial support. Soon he entered politics and joined the newly founded Christian Democratic Party, rapidly turning into a full-time politician. He rose in several stages, finally becoming the *Ministerpresident* (Governor) of the large state of Baden-Württemberg. He held that influential position for many years, growing more arrogant and conceited as time passed.

At last, the playwright Rolf Hochhuth was informed about Filbinger's past as a naval judge advocate, and with the help of the German and Swiss press he exposed this awful man. He illuminated the sordid, buried naval past that Filbinger fervently denied, until the evidence grew so overwhelming that his stubborn and brazen lies were useless, and he was forced to resign his high position, claiming, of course, that he had only done his duty to uphold naval discipline, and law and order, during very trying and difficult times.

CHAPTER NINETEEN

Better Late Than Never

In 1992, almost fifty years after the execution of Oskar Kusch, the monthly publication of the Association of German Naval Officers, active and retired, called the *Marine Forum*, decided to publish an article by a post-war historian of maritime matters regarding the Kusch case and the various investigations and court hearings connected with it. The senior editor introduced this contribution with a strong editorial leader containing several sharp remarks and observations, rather typical for a post-war person who had not himself experienced the Second World War.

Many of the subscribers and readers heard about the Kusch case in this way for the first time. Some had limited information, though usually only bits and pieces rather than the whole story, much less the actual facts; or else the twisted and considerably changed court versions of 1950, which had greatly pleased the concrete blockheads and the dyed-in-the-wool Nazis.

Obviously, the publication had underestimated the interest of the members and subscribers. They were overwhelmed by a storm of readers' responses that caught the editors totally unprepared. Swiftly the waves of excitement rose very high, and many of the readers' comments generated yet more letters, to respond to those published, bringing new details to the fore. An extensive and acerbic debate developed, which kept growing with each monthly issue of the publication.

The editorial staff had seemingly become too busy with these responses and the replies to previous letters, which in turn triggered yet further comments. Therefore the editorial board decided arbitrarily in 1993 to close the subject and stop printing letters regarding the Oskar Kusch execution. Clearly this was a premature decision, as many angry readers told the editors. Quite a few subscribers considered this as unreasonable and totally uncalled-for censorship.

There were the usual number of letters from the people who had learned nothing and remained the wartime hate-mongers of old, or those blockheads who rejected even the slightest criticism of Dönitz as sacrilegious and wrong. But there were numerous interesting responses covering a broad field of views and experiences. Quite a few letters illuminated particular facts not generally known before. Many of the responses originated from far away places like Canada, South Africa, Venezuela, Japan, Australia and the USA, making valuable information available to a broader readership.

Space does not allow me to quote more than a small selection of these responses and comments. I have picked out three letters from the mailbag that made the most sense to me and reflect quite well the wartime '*Zeitgeist*' instead of the hindsight of post-war folk who had not been around themselves.

Two of these writers were outstanding engineering officers on U-boats, while the third one was a watch officer. Two of the three men had known Oskar Kusch well. All three participated in the sea war personally to a considerable extent.

The first letter was written by Professor Dr Tech. Ulrich Gabler, who had been handpicked by the irrepressible Reinhard 'Teddy' Suhren, as his directing engineer, once Suhren had reached his 25th birthday and Dönitz permitted him to become a U-boat commander. Suhren had earned the Knight's Cross of the Iron Cross as watch officer on U-48 on 3 November 1940. When he commissioned U-564, a Type VII U-boat, on 3 April 1941, Gabler had already been in the shipyard for a while, to familiarize himself with the new vessel.

Gabler served as directing engineer on seven war patrols under 'Teddy' Suhren. U-564 was based in Brest, but for technical reasons she was also overhauled in Lorient and La Pallice-La Rochelle.

When returning to Brest after his last and longest war patrol on 18 September 1942 from the Caribbean Sea, Suhren spotted his naval classmate Horst Uphoff, commander of U-84, in the welcoming crowd lining up at the entrance to the U-boat pens. Suhren was so happy to see his friend that he grabbed a loud-hailer and, disregarding the higher brass and all the waiting people, shouted loudly, 'Hein, are the Nazis still in power?' Uphoff was stunned, but yelled right back, 'Yes indeed, Teddy!' Whereupon Suhren, standing on the conning tower of U-564 shouted even more loudly, 'Both engines full speed in reverse!' The waiting crowd instantly fell silent, then laughed like mad. The flotilla commander blanched and told Suhren afterwards: 'Man, that kind of practical joke in front of several hundred spectators could hit you in your eye.' Teddy Suhren then called: 'Stop engines – slow speed forward. I just have to get a drink after this long war patrol!'

Gabler, who was still in the control room, was uncertain what was taking place on the bridge. He assumed navigational problems with the strong cross-currents in Brest harbour connected with the considerable tide changes, or Suhren was trying not to hit a pier or another ship.

Here is his reader's response letter:

That famous exclamation by Teddy Suhren was meant as a practical joke, but several hundred people heard it, and within a few days virtually everybody in the U-boat Command everywhere had likewise been told about it. Suhren, at times somewhat brash, aired his frustrations candidly and clearly, as was his habit. As directing engineer of U-564 on all war patrols commanded by Teddy Suhren, I was well aware of his frank and outspoken ways. On our U-boat, the same as on any other U-boat, there were invariably many conversations, at times quite controversial ones too, in the officers' mess area. They were of similar, if not identical, content, to those discussions aboard U-154 that caused the death of Oskar Kusch. However, there was one big difference: There were no denouncers aboard U-564!

Sincerely Yours, Dr Ulrich Gabler

The second letter was written by Lieutenant (Engineering) Gerhard Bielig, who had been the directing engineer on U-103 until summer 1942, when he had been replaced by the Lieutenant j.g. (Engineering) Otto Strelow, a naval classmate of Oskar Kusch. Both officers had become close friends of Kusch, who served as watch officer at the same time aboard U-103. Bielig was transferred to U-177, a Type IX-D-2 U-cruiser as directing engineer, and had been awarded the Knight's Cross of the Iron Cross on 10 February 1943 for his outstanding record as directing engineer of both U-103 and U-177. Finally, he was assigned to the testing department for the brand-new Type XXI electro U-boats to train other engineering officers, and became the directing engineer of the Type XXI U-2513, once these U-boats were actually built.

Here is the letter by Gerhard Bielig:

In Germany, only every tenth man actually served on the very front. The other nine men were in supporting, administrative or supply positions only, while in Soviet Russia the percentage of those actually serving in the front lines was substantially higher. Oskar Kusch belonged to that élite group of men who fought at the actual front, in stark contrast to the naval judge advocates, who performed far away from the front, in cushy office positions.

Kusch's life had been at stake where the real action took place. As I served with Kusch on U-103 for a long time, we became good friends, Kusch as watch officer and I as directing engineer. For numerous hours and sometimes the entire night we talked about every imaginable subject. While I myself was at that time still a convinced Nazi, Oskar Kusch already had a far wider horizon, and was frequently able to see the 'cloven hoof' hidden in so many situations and things. However, he always remained a reliable, steadfast and determined soldier doing his duty. He did not look for or grab any possibility for being transferred to a shore command as instructor, which always existed or could be applied for.

It would have been simply inconceivable to denounce somebody for his political views! Even more incredible that another officer should do so.

However, it is totally unbelievable that Karl Dönitz would not protect one of his U-boat commanders and shield him completely against any such injustice, rather than turning such a commander over to the Navy's hated judge advocates, who did not belong to that élite. We would all fight tooth and nail to snatch each and every real U-boat man out of their bloody claws, who had the misfortune to clash with these naval judge advocates, regardless of the reason they had got into their infernal paws. I admit, when I finally found out about the actual ending of the Oskar Kusch case, long afterwards, executed for purely political reasons, my entire view and pride in the German Navy in general and Admiral Karl Dönitz in particular, collapsed with a shocking and sobering crash!

Sincerely Yours, Gerhard Bielig

The third letter was written by Hellmuth Kirchammer, who had become a radio commentator and arranger of stage shows and theatre performances, and the director of a well-known film company in Munich after the war.

Kirchammer had thoroughly discussed his response with his naval classmate Horst Fröhlich, living in Hannover, with whom he had served as a midshipman aboard U-154 in the spring of 1943, because he wanted to include Fröhlich's views, comments and observations in his letter, too, which follows now:

I should very much like to tell you about Lieutenant j.g. Oskar Kusch, with whom I had the privilege of participating in a war patrol as midshipman, together with my naval classmate Horst Fröhlich, aboard U-154 from March to July 1943. This was the first war patrol with Lieutenant Kusch as commander of that U-boat. During the almost four-month duration of this operation, Oskar Kusch became for both of us midshipmen the true example of an outstanding naval officer, courageous, clever, sovereign and highly educated, constantly concerned about both his U-boat and his crew. During combat situations and in battle he kept quiet, cool, alert and secure in his orders and actions. Under extreme operational conditions he always radiated confidence and calmness, invariably demonstrating full control of the situation.

My classmate and I are of the same opinion in the way we viewed and considered our 'old man'. He certainly was one of the best naval officers whom we had known or got to know later. He was a man who placed his own evaluation and conscience above blind obedience and ideology. We had that firm opinion in 1943 and did not acquire it after years of re-education or after gaining more maturity, considering that we were then very young and impressionable.

Consequently, we were filled with consternation when we were ordered to appear at a court martial of our so highly admired commander, as witnesses. A court-martial trial that had been set in motion by a malicious and spiteful denouncer! This had created strong indignation and furious opposition in a wide circle of U-boat Command officers, as Lieutenant Gustav Adolf Janssen told me in January 1945, when he commanded U-3037 and I was a watch officer on U-3517.

My classmate Horst Fröhlich became a prisoner of war, the same as Commander Werner Winter and many other U-boat men. There he also heard many critical comments, and with a few exceptions, only disgust and contempt regarding the judgement in the Kusch case, as it gradually became known to more officers and other U-boat men after the war. Both of the military *Beisitzer* judges [Dittmers and Westphalen], were in his prisoner-of-war camp, too, and were greatly disdained by most of the other naval officers there.

We both certainly hope that it will finally become possible to clear Oskar Kusch's name, reputation and record, to permit him to occupy an honoured place in the records of the U-boat Command, the German Navy and future sea history, which he deserves.

Most sincerely yours,

Hellmuth Kirchammer

In the aforementioned article in the *Marine Forum* publication, the following question was raised and replies requested:

Had Oskar Kusch been connected in any way, form or kind, directly or indirectly with the German Military Opposition to the Hitler regime. Perhaps, through personal or informational connections with military or civilian opposition groups by means of some of his former Bündische Boy Scout friends and comrades?

While this was a somewhat academic question, it was no doubt both legitimate as well as logical for younger post-war historians and their research assistants, who had not been personally involved in war operations, as they were either too young or had not been around as yet!

However, the question was asked and the issue raised. Therefore, it is important to cover the subject thoroughly. Both with respect to Oskar Kusch as individual and the German navy as organization and system, before facts get turned around and twisted once again, some time in the future.

The military and civilian opposition was primarily represented by Colonel Claus Schenk Count von Stauffenberg as coordinator. Who himself placed the bomb, that was to kill Hitler in his headquarters on the 20 of July 1944, as leader of the army military opposition, which, unfortunately, did not succeed.

The German military and civilian opposition was based nearly entirely upon inside support from several groups within the German Army. Most of the plotters were army reserve officers who had influential positions. Army reserve officers constituted 59% of all serving officers during the war and they were extremely influential, because many of them had a better education, a broader professional experience and, a wider international and business background than most regular, active army officers. Moreover, any practical, much less effective, opposition to an entrenched police system as the Nazis had instituted, was impossible from any other source.

The civilian opposition groups were composed of a wide variety of people with very differing personal and professional background, from political to religious groups. In some of these various groupings former Bündische Youth group leaders were involved, but as second or third rank participants, although most of them had been buried in Russia. However, there were none of them amongst the front line opposition activists.

What concerned the naval side of things, where reserve officers constituted only 37% of the officers serving during the war, things were slightly different and greatly influenced by a broad geographical spread and service on ships that were often away from ports for long periods of time with a strictly limited flow of information. Therefore, the army plotters had decided, naval officers were not very suitable to be brought into the active opposition groups.

Berthold Count von Stauffenberg, the older brother of the army colonel, was a full time, pre-war naval judge advocate, and one of the 30 peacetime naval judge advocates of the navy.

But , he had been transferred shortly after the war started to the special prize court, a branch of the German Supreme Court (Reichsgericht), as senior judge. However, since 1942 there were for practical purposes no futher prize ships to be processed and judged. Thus, Berthold von Stauffenberg had lots of free time and very little legal court work. Consequently, he supported the activities of his brother in any way possible, acting as the legal counsel for the conspirators.

Yet, there were two active naval officers, who participated in the military oppositions activities in the very front line. One of them is today virtually unknown, except to real insiders. Lieutenant Commander Alfred Kranzfelder(Crew 1927), who served as admirality staff officer and international relations specialist at the OKM, the Naval High Command in Berlin. He handled matters and subjects of international or foreign interest for the navy. This included looking after prisoners of war and dealing with the different organizations and diplomatic representatives of both the German prisoners of war in Allied hands and their respective protective powers and those of the various Allied prisoners of war in German hands and their respective protective powers. Although, primarily involved with naval prisoners of war, held in the navy's Marlag PoW camps, at times also other PoWs too. Kranzfelder was recognized for the clarity of his reports and orders and his remarkably keen judgement of both people and subjects at hand.

Kranzfelder had become acquainted with and was gradually absorbed into the army circles in Berlin, who increasingly opposed the Nazi regime in general and Hitler, Himmler and Göring in particular. Over the years, Kranzfelder had grown into a full confidant of the leaders of the army plotters and was respected by them for his firm, reliable and serious support of their plans, aims and undertakings. Kranzfelder was one of the first officers, who had become convinced, that a complete elimination of not only Hitler, but also of Himmler, Göring and Goebbels would be imperative for a successful overthrow of the Nazi regime, to end the terrible war as soon as possible. Otherwise the power and control of the SS/SD, the general S.S., the Gestapo and police forces could not be overcome swiftly. Something opposed by the civilian religious and Christian groups for a long time, for humanitarian reasons as well as legal ones. These people still dreamed of putting Hitler and his henchmen up for a trial by the German Supreme court. A rather unrealistic idea under the circumstances, that prevailed in Germany during the war.

Karl Dönitz had pushed the German navy steadily closer towards the Hitler regime and the interests, intentions and ideas of the Nazis as his admiration for Adolf Hitler was almost total, though Dönitz disliked some of the full time Nazi party functionaries, for their incompetence and borderline moral behaviour. Consequently, the army conspirators had concluded correctly, that they would never be able to count on any support from Dönitz and the German navy directly. Therefore, Alfred Kranzfelder was instructed to keep a close eye on Dönitz and his whereabouts, whenever possible. To isolate Dönitz and his batch of Yes men, once the overthrow of the Nazi regime was attempted finally. Obviously, it was impossible for one man to do this in every respect and still handle his customary workload too. But Kranzfelder tried to be informed as much as possible regarding the movements of Dönitz.

Thus, in the end, Alfred Kranzfelder was the only active naval officer, who participated fully in the attempt on the 20 of July 1944 to eliminate Hitler in his headquarters. When it failed, Kranzfelder's activities could no longer be protected and covered successfully.

Alfred Kranzfelder was immediately arrested and included in the first group of army field marshals and army generals, who were dragged before that infamous 'People's Court' in Berlin to be condemned to death by Roland Freisler, the prosecutor of that pure Nazi party court and hanged. Alfred Kranzfelder being both the sole naval officer and the only lower ranking officer in that first show process, copied from Stalin's political court system. Only his importance in the military opposition movement can really account for Kranzfelder's inclusion in the first proceedings with the much higher-ranking army officers.

In order to please Hitler, Dönitz had arranged to kick Alfred Kranzfelder out of the German navy. Once he was removed from the naval ranking list he was then considered a civilian which made it possible for the People's Court to hang him without trial or investigation. As a naval officer, Kranzfelder would have been entitled to be judged by a naval military court.

However, this would have made little factual difference in the end, Kranzfelder would have been shot like Oskar Kusch, instead of hanged.

Though for the dead man it would make little difference, for his family there still prevailed some legal distinction. Kranzfelder was amongst the first officers who paid the price of their conviction. Reflecting the importance that the Nazis attached to Kranzfelder was his selection by Gestapo Müller and Himmler personally and jointly, for inclusion in the first trial with the higher ranking and more senior army generals and field marshals.

Nonetheless, for practical purposes, Alfred Kranzfelder is today an unknown man in Germany! More so for the German Federal Navy, the Bundesmarine, where traditional connections with the past are strongly discouraged, widely disdained and even entirely rejected, whenever past history enters the picture. Primarily, for presently prevalent ideas and political considerations of 'political correctness', which are at times almost incomprehensible to others on the outside!

Nevertheless, but in no way contrary to what has just been said, there was admiral Wilhelm F. (Franz) Canaris (Crew 1905). He was one of the first German officers, who grew to understand the essential evilness of Hitler, Himmler, Göring and Goebbels and the entire Nazi system!

Canaris had become the head of the *Abwehr* (the combined German intelligence and counter intelligence organization) at the beginning of 1935 almost accidentally. Erich Raeder had already prepared retirement papers for naval captain Canaris, sidelined as harbour and fortress commander of Swinemünde in the Baltic.

His predecessor in that position, naval captain Conrad Patzig (Crew 1907) had constantly fought the growing influence of the SS/SD directed by Himmler and Heydrich. This was aggravating enough, but Patzig had also disregarded orders and instructions from the war minister, Field Marshal Werner von Blomberg, known in the army as the 'rubber lion'. Eventually, von Blomberg grew so mad at Patzig, that he asked Raeder to take Patzig back into the navy and replace him with somebody less stubborn and disobedient. Patzig was appointed commander of the pocket battleship Graf von Spee, still outfitting at the shipyard. While Raeder did not like Canaris very much, and von Blomberg considered Canaris as unfathomable, there simply was no other qualified officer in the navy for the job.

So Raeder agreed reluctantly to his appointment, otherwise, an army officer would again take over that post. Canaris was soon promoted to rear admiral and moved rapidly from the dead end of Swinemünde back into the power centre of Berlin. Contrary to many officers, Canaris was a good listener and let others talk instead. This was greatly liked by Hitler, who talked for hours without interruptions.

Starting in 1937, Canaris turned gradually against the Nazis, due to the rapidly growing influence of Himmler and Heydrich and Hitler's mounting determination to solve political or geographical problems by force, rather than honest negotiations. Therefore, Hitler looked for more pliable leaders of the army, whom he could easily influence. In 1938, von Blomberg, a widower, married a young woman of questionable background and was forced to resign forthwith. Hitler simply took over his position, in addition to his many others and no successor was needed that way, while Hitler was now able to direct the armed forces himself.

Shortly thereafter, Heydrich and the SS/SD engineered the dismissal of army commander general Werner von Fritsch, with perjured and faked papers, depositions and a phony witness stating: Von Fritsch was homosexual, where the witness had been blackmailed by the Gestapo to testify falsely. Canaris and the *Abwehr* discovered this doctored plot and exposed it, but a few days too late.

Von Fritsch was retired against his wishes and Hitler brought in a replacement, obligated to the Nazis financially and a compliant Yes man, while reorganizing the command structure of the armed forces to fit his needs better. During these investigations and manipulations, Canaris had become acquainted with the chief of the army's general staff, general Ludwig Beck. Beck was another one of the more intellectual type of officers, as was Canaris, highly revered by the army's officer corps. Beck was utterly bewildered by the devious, sneaky and fraught-filled actions of the SS/SD directed by Heydrich, which Canaris had unravelled.

Both officers quickly became close friends and mutual confidants. In reality, both were still imperial officers in many ways and in their thinking, ideas and approaches to most things. They had served as subaltern young officers in the First World War under the Emperor and had not changed much since, despite the political adjustments that had taken place over the years.

From 1938 onward, these two officers had turned into the brains of the growing military opposition to the Hitler regime and many Nazi policies. However, by 1944 both of them were a lot older and had become gradually the wirepullers behind the scenes primarily, instead of the acting front men.

Overthrowing the Hitler government and the Nazi organizations in control of it, required determined, aggressive men of action now, the can-do types, forceful and with tough as well as new ideas. But Canaris was 57 years old, yet feeling and looking older than that! His demanding job had worn him out. The weight on his mind of the awful information he received was great and almost unbearable, for such a sensitive and humane person like admiral Canaris .

The growing clashes and fights for turf with the SS/SD and especially, Reinhard Heydrich, who grew more powerful constantly, were a wearing problem on Canaris. The continued fights with Göring and Hitler and the endless sermons by Hitler, were mighty hard to bear. But Heydrich, who wanted to merge the *Abwehr* into the SS/SD and become the new joint boss, was all the time looking for ways and means to accomplish this, no matter how opposed the army leadership was to his plans!

Heydrich, was a cashiered former naval Lieutenant j. g. (Crew 1922), who had been kicked out of the navy in 1931 by Reader after an officers' honour court checked a claim made against Heydrich by one of the big Kiel shipyard directors: 'That Heydrich had got his daughter "compromised" but refused to marry her!' During this investigation, Reinhard Heydrich declared calmly: "I have for some time another girlfriend, to whom I consider myself engaged and she is the one I shall marry!" Erich Raeder was so shocked, that he discharged Heydrich from the navy immediately.

Thus, in the deepest economic depression, Heydrich found himself out in the street, unemployed and without any job prospects. But his girlfriend, a strong Nazi type who knew Himmler well, introduced Heydrich to him. Though the Nazis were still far from gaining power, Himmler already planned a huge expansion of his S.S. organization. Heydrich drew up an organizational outline of how to manage this, including a new S.S. security and intelligence service, to be called the S.D., which was to be developed and headed by Heydrich within weeks.

Now Heydrich's influence, overt and covert, grew by leaps and bounds. However, because Heydrich seemed to aim directly for Himmler's job, if not Hitler's position eventually, Himmler got extremely worried about wider and wider influence, Heydrich's intrigues and underhanded manipulations. Yet, the British Secret Service took care of that problem for Himmler in 1942, when Heydrich was killed by two parachuted Czech expatriates from England, who gunned Heydrich down in the street and finished Heydrich off with a hand grenade, so that he died from an infection, caused by this attack in Prague.

By 1943 the influence of Canaris had waned considerably. Mainly because Canaris was unable to deliver any desired news or the type of information demanded by Hitler and his Yes men camarilla. Furthermore, Canaris shied away from personal appearances in Hitler's headquarters because Canaris simply could not stomach Hitler's monologues any more; they had become so tiresome and unrealistic.

Germany had made a deal with Sweden in 1940, when it looked like Germany might have a chance to win the war, to permit German military transports across Sweden to and from Norway and Finland. Using the Swedish ferry steamers and Swedish railroads, with the use paid by Germany and installing teletype, telephone and other military communication lines to these countries through Sweden.

By the summer of 1943, the military situation had changed dramatically. The Swedish socialist prime minister Per Albin Hansson, the foreign minister Östen Undén and the trade minister Gunnar Myrdal moved even further to the left politically. Germany had been the largest trading partner of Sweden. Now it looked more and more like the Soviet-Russian regime of Joseph Stalin, would grow into the most powerful country in Europe soon.

These Swedish socialist politicians were now convinced Sweden would be able to replace Germany as Russia's largest trading partner in the future. Replacing the destroyed German market with an even bigger Soviet-Russian one eventually. It dictated that Sweden had to reduce all relations with Germany to a point short of a complete diplomatic break. Germany was still the main purchaser of Sweden's iron ore. Yet these politicians did not wish to close down the Gellivara area iron mines, making their union supporters jobless. Furthermore, Sweden badly needed the German coal shipments provided in exchange. This required an economic and diplomatic balancing act, as done by jugglers in the circus. But Hansson and Undén were confident that they could manage this speculative political gamble successfully.

On the 29 of July 1943, their socialistic government announced, that they would terminate and cancel the 1940 Transit Travel Treaty for German military forces and their supplies and no further German military units would be permitted upon its expiration to cross Swedish territory and to travel on Swedish trains and steamers. The communist party members in Sweden were elated and lead their Danish union friends on, to demonstrate their joyous support of this measure somehow.

Danish shipyard and dockworkers in Odense—Funen and Copenhagen went on strike and refused to repair German ships. The strike grew like wildfire and riots as well as demonstrations flared up all over Denmark within days. On the 9 of August 1943, the still acting Danish government under emergency national unity prime minister Erik Scavenius resigned, but was forced to stay in office until the 28 of August 1943, by the newly arrived SS/SD director Werner Best, the former legal advisor of Heydrich.

The peacetime German ambassador, Count Cecil von Renthe-Fink, had retained his former position, which had been raised to German Plenipotentiary in Denmark. Renthe-Fink was now replaced by Karl Werner Best and recalled to Germany.

Himmler demanded immediately, to set up the Final Solution plans for Denmark, without further delay. The Danish King Christian X declared he would himself put the Yellow Jewish star badge on his breast, if such legislation was forcefully adopted in Denmark. A general strike was called by all unions and government employees in Denmark. Best got scared and suggested to Himmler to pull back somewhat and to remove only Jews from Danish civil service government positions and to register all known Jewish communists and left-wing socialists, who had escaped from Germany and some other European countries to Denmark.

Himmler threatened to place the names of all known Danish underground resistance leaders on this list, thereby labelling them as communists who would be liable to be arrested and deported to Germany without lengthy investigations, unless this unrest stopped immediately.

By now, Best realized that the Danish situation was extremely explosive and tried to postpone such action, because this would increase popular resistance and opposition greatly. Best told Himmler, that amongst the Jews registered officially in Denmark, 6,500 roughly, there were no more than 31 civil service employees and a further 60 who owned small business enterprises, but all of them had signed up for German government work contracts.

While there were 1,351 German Jews registered in Denmark as refugees, the majority of them had their German citizenship taken away by the Nazis in 1938. Additionally, the Gestapo estimated there were about 5,000 Jews living in Denmark underground, as unregistered refugees.

Best attempted to work out some cooperative arrangement with the Danish Scavenius government, which had resigned in strong protest over these German measures, to keep the government running with the help of a group of technical and experienced men temporarily. Yet, there was not a single such civil service type, who agreed and accepted any such assignment.

To break the general countrywide strike, general Hermann von Hannecken, the commander of the German army of occupation, was ordered to declare martial law throughout Denmark, with a very strictly enforced curfew. Himmler ordered that the entire Danish military forces, the Danish police and even the Danish customs service officials must be arrested and deported into concentration camps in Germany. The small Danish navy either scuttled their ships or they escaped to Sweden.

By now virtually everything had come to a total standstill in Denmark generally and in Copenhagen in particular. Himmler then ordered Best to seize and arrest all Danish Jews, including those living underground, immediately and under cover of the army- announced curfew. In the first week of September 1943 resistance by the general population had grown to boiling point and opposition to any attempted measures increased swiftly, as these arrests and deportations became known to the public in Denmark.

Canaris was blamed by Himmler, Göring and Hitler, for the *Abwehr* not advising them in advance about these potentially explosive problems in Denmark, so that could be prevented, reduced or even entirely circumvented and avoided. Canaris was called on the carpet, but submitted proof, that the excessive actions of the SS/SD were really responsible for expanding some small local blazes into a wild fire all over Denmark.

However, Canaris really hit the ceiling when he was informed about Best's deportation plans and arresting orders. Best had requested the assistance of the *Abwehr* and the German field police in Denmark, to round up the various Jewish groups quickly and without any warning. As the SS/SD and the Gestapo did not have enough manpower and experienced linguists to do this job themselves. Nor the ships to transport these prisoners to Germany.

Georg F. Duckwitz, the Copenhagen shipping representative of the *Abwehr* and several other *Abwehr* officials in Denmark, had warned the Jewish elders and the known leaders of the Danish resistance movement right away about these demands, to make the deportations impossible and the seizure of the Jews a failure. Canaris ordered three highly trusted Danish speaking naval *Abwehr* officers, including Frank Petersen, from France to proceed immediately to Denmark and Sweden on '*Abwehr* business'. This was done to make doubly sure that the Danish resistance movement would unhesitatingly support the escape of these Jewish groups to Sweden, and to obtain the full assistance of the Swedish authorities and their police and that of the Swedish Red Cross.

These *Abwehr* officers contacted the various German naval commands, port and coastal defence and harbour patrol units, practically all of them commanded and directed by older reserve officers, to gain their agreement and concurrence that the German navy was NOT a police force, nor part of the Gestapo or a supporting organization of the SS/SD and Werner Best. Neither were they to be forced to become informers, stool pigeons or helpers of any kind for the SS/SD commands in Denmark with respect to these refugees.

Soon small boats, even sailing boats, row boats and fishing boats of all sizes started a nightly exodus of Jewish refugees from many Danish ports to nearby Sweden, crossing the Sound or Kattegat at night within two to seven hours. Depending upon the Danish place of departure, the type of vessels involved, the power of their engines and the weather. Within days, an effective support organization had gone into action in Denmark collecting, sheltering and feeding these Jewish refugees and transporting them to pre-selected points of departure for Sweden. Here the Swedish Red Cross coordinated the reception and care for these people, many of them women with children and older people.

Thousands of Danish citizens supported these clandestine movements in any way they could.

The German naval shore patrols and harbour protection commands turned a blind eye to these nightly refugee transports. Instead of searching for them and arresting the Jewish escapers and their Danish helpers, as demanded by Best, who was furious over the naval disregard of his requests and orders. Himmler grew livid when he was informed of the situation and he immediately reported the situation to Hitler, who ousted Canaris for the first time, for his refusal to help with the Jewish deportations in Denmark, when eventually over 12,000 Jewish people were ferried over to Sweden.

This happened in spite of diligent searches and constant identity checks by the SS/SD, the Gestapo and their local criminal informers and helpers at all hotels, hospitals, museums, cinemas, churches, theatres, restaurants, rail-stations, bus terminals, ports and all other places where people congregated or were forced to pass through somehow.

The majority of the Jews that the Gestapo managed to arrest and catch somewhere, were either quite elderly or even no longer able or willing to flee. The great majority who were still physically able to escape had disappeared and evaporated into the underground swiftly and got away sucessfully.

Best then requested army assistance and demanded that the German field police forces in Denmark should help the SS/SD and the Gestapo with these deportations. But general von Hannecken, the army commander in Denmark, refused this request for military security and safety reasons. Consequently, Best could only obtain 50 field policemen directly from Keitel at Hitler's headquarters and Best was only able to requisition one steamer for the transport of the captured Jews to Germany, the *Wartheland*, moored in Copenhagen. Best had to use these 50 field policemen to guard the steamer *Wartheland* against sabotage and being set on fire by the Danish underground resistance.

But, for the roundup of the Jews outside Copenhagen, in the countryside in Jutland or on the various islands, such as Funen, the SS/SD and Gestapo lacked the necessary manpower to do this rapidly. The German army refused to provide additional helpers, in spite of heavy political pressure to do so by Best and Himmler.

Therefore, the Gestapo and SS/SD only managed to arrest 360 Jewish refugees in and around Copenhagen, who were put on the steamer *Wartheland* to be shipped to Swinemünde, for onward transport to concentration camps. Another 478 Jewish prisoners were captured elsewhere and transported to Germany in smaller groups by trucks. But slightly more than 12,000 Jewish refugees were carried safely to Sweden, within five weeks of the start of the Gestapo deportation actions.

Best advised Himmler, that further harsh measures and mass arrests would unquestionably lead to widespread sabotage and the eventual the loss of the Danish agricultural, food and fish production for Germany.

The Danish policemen, soldiers and other officials arrested were largely shipped to the concentration camps of Neuengamme and Flossenbürg. Most of the Danish Jews were placed into the Theresienstadt concentration camp, a so-called 'show camp' for the Swiss and the International Red Cross and other type of inspections or visitors.

All those deported to Germany, the Danish men and the Jewish refugees, were looked after eventually by the Swedish Red Cross directly and supported with food parcels and medical assistance, thus most of them survived.

Canaris was quietly returned to his former position, because Himmler and Kaltenbrunner, the successor of Heydrich, had to admit that they lacked the experienced men and linguists to handle the military aspects of the *Abwehr*'s work and could barely manage to follow through on the political assignments swiftly. Moreover, they just did not have the experienced investigators necessary to cope with sabotage and related military-damage cases, which required professionals with long training and extensive experience.

Yet, this was only a temporary reprieve. Early in 1944 Canaris was deposed once more and moved to a dead-track position under close watch and tight personal observation, but with virtually no responsibility any more, where all his calls and communications were recorded.

Things had grown so bad by now, that experience or competency were becoming unimportant to Himmler, Schellenberg and Kaltenbrunner. While to Hitler such traits had always been secondary to begin with. The *Abwehr* was taken over in several steps by them, except for the purely military intelligence, particularly on the Eastern front, which was reorganized within the various army commands.

Naturally, this type of change could not produce favourable or more desirable information and news by itself, unless pure lies were presented by the new set of *Abwehr* officers. Pretty soon Hitler grew as angry with them as he had towards Canaris and his representatives. During one of his more and more frequent outbursts of fury, Hitler screamed in disgust: "That these nitwits just did not know what they were doing! That the entire flock belonged in an insane asylum where they should be locked up! The asylum to be headed by major general Reinhard Gehlen of the army's Russian/Eastern front section!"

Shortly after the 20 of July bombing attempt to kill Hitler, which, unfortunately, was not successful, Canaris was taken in protective custody by Schellenberg, who offered Canaris the chance to shoot himself, as had been given to Ludwig Beck, but Canaris refused this offer by Schellenberg outright. Dönitz had retired Canaris already on the 30 of June 1944, rejecting any further use of him by the navy. Arrested on the 25 of July 1944, Canaris was placed into the Gestapo jail in the Prince Albrecht Street in Berlin, where the SS/SD and the Gestapo held people for investigations or to blackmail them. Canaris was interrogated longer and more frequently than any other Gestapo prisoners before him. Nonetheless, he was so clever and unfathomable that they could not obtain any information from him that had not already been printed in the Nazi party papers. Canaris was grossly mistreated at first, finally tortured, but, Canaris did not give away one single name which had not been published earlier in the Völkischer Beobachter, the worst Nazi mouthpiece. Canaris knew, of course, each and every one of the conspirators since 1938. Thus, when he mentioned anybody, they had already appeared before the bloody People's Court judge Freisler and most had been hanged.

While Canaris had been largely isolated and neutralized in that summer of 1944 he had, nonetheless, arranged that the plotters were furnished with a supply of semtex, mouldable explosive and special time clock detonators that the *Abwehr* had confiscated in the Netherlands from captured British Secret Service representatives and Dutch parachutists dropped by the British Secret Services, usually SOE. In Germany at that time, mouldable semtex explosives and acid contact timers were neither produced nor could they be manufactured.

A part of these semtex supplies and detonators were used to build the bomb to kill Hitler, when Colonel Claus Schenk Count von Stauffenberg undertook that job at Hitler's headquarters, the 'Wolf's Lair' near Rastenburg-East Prussia, on 20 of July 1944.

Yet, for practical purposes, Canaris was totally isolated, closely watched and without any direct influence, during that summer of 1944. When Colonel von Stauffenberg telephoned Canaris, to inform him about his attempt to blow up Hitler, the quick-witted Canaris, always instantly alert, asked the caller, whose voice he recognized immediately: "Who did it? The Russians?" Because Canaris knew his phone was tapped and the Gestapo recorded, taped and monitored all his calls.

Incidentally, according to the Gestapo records, this had been the 39th attempt to kill Hitler since he had assumed power in Germany!

However, through a chain of misunderstandings and the perfidy of an army driver, a part of the Canaris diaries were finally tracked down and found in the supersecret Belinda section of the German army headquarters compound at Zossen, where they had been deposited into the largest and strongest safe available. The Gestapo cut it open with blow torches, burning a part of the contents in the process. But the Canaris diaries were not burnt and they furnished Himmler and Hitler with the proof they had looked everywhere for. To Himmler's stupefaction, the diaries revealed that opposition to Hitler had started as early as 1938. Consequently, the interrogations of Canaris were sharpened even more.

Early in February of 1945, the Gestapo Prince Albrecht Street jail and headquarters building was hit by American bombs, damaged and set partially on fire. A few lucky prisoners were able to escape in the resulting chaos and confusion, including Fabian von Schlabrendorff, the adjutant of major general Henning von Tresckow, the army opposition coordinator on the Russian front. Von Schlabrendorff, a reserve officer, later became instrumental, as one of the few survivors, in reporting many details of Gestapo operations. Gestapo-Müller ordered immediately that all prominent prisoners should be evacuated to Southern Germany and the *Abwehr* group was to be split up between several concentration camps.

Canaris, together with five other *Abwehr* prisoners, was shipped to Flossenbürg concentration camp, near Weiden in the Franconia section of Bavaria. The group of *Abwehr* prisoners arrived there on the 5 of February 1945 accompanied by special SS/SD guards furnished by Kaltenbrunner and with specific instructions by Gestapo-Müller as to their treatment in transit and at the destination. The small group was put into the special concrete fortified cell block for prominent prisoners separated from the general camp area, fenced off with barbed wire, especially secured in other ways and closely watched.

Canaris was placed in cell # 22, shackled and chained to the wall. The other five *Abwehr* prisoners were: Pastor Dietrich Bonhoeffer, army chief justice Karl Sack, *Abwehr* army captain Ludwig Gehre, *Abwehr* major general Hans Oster and *Abwehr* army reserve captain Josef Müller, a catholic Bavarian lawyer, who had often represented the *Abwehr* in the Vatican and in Italy. Better known as 'Ochsensepp', that is 'Joe the Ox', as he came from the small town of Ochsenfurt in Bavaria. Müller became the sole survivor, due to some file confusion with his very common last name. After the war, Müller got into politics and eventually became the minister of justice for Bavaria. Every captive was placed into one of these isolation cells in the bunker area.

Canaris soon established contact with his next-door cell neighbour by means of a morse knocking code. This man in cell # 21 happened to be the Danish army colonel Hans Mathiesen-Lunding, who had been the director of Danish army intelligence in Jutland and Copenhagen. Shortly before the strikes and demonstrations, Lunding had been arrested by the Gestapo. Then Lunding had been shipped to the Flossenbürg concentration camp, instead of a prisoner of war camp, arriving on the 6 of July 1944. Lunding was, therefore, quite familiar with the set-up in Flossenbürg.

Just before this time, this concentration camp had held many Danish army, police, customs service and navy men, who had been arrested wholesale by the Gestapo, during the 1943 general strike and the escape of the Jewish refugees to Sweden. They had just been picked up and collected by the Swedish Red Cross, in a convoy of vehicles and taken to Sweden. A deal had been brokered by Count Folke Bernadotte, the president of the Swedish Red Cross, with Himmler, to free and transport to Sweden 95% of all Danish and Norwegian SS/SD prisoners and captives.

Lunding had been one of the leaders of the Danish underground resistance movement, whom Canaris had known for many years. Canaris informed Lunding what had transpired in Berlin and how he had been treated by the Gestapo and SS/SD in the last couple of months. In one word: 'Beastly!'

The world owes it to Colonel Lunding, that this information was obtained and preserved for history because the Nazis eliminated all traces and burnt all records promptly. The British SIS army captain S. Payne Best, who was likewise held in the special cell block in Flossenbürg and had been captured by the SS/SD during the fall of Holland in 1939, during the so-called Venlo Incident and had escaped previously from less strict facilities, asked the S.S. guards, when he saw the mishandled Canaris: 'Is this how you treat German officers?' But the guards just yelled that he ought to watch himself, instead of getting involved with others or else he would be likewise exterminated shortly!

Himmler and Gestapo-Müller had been *told by Hitler, that these Abwehr prisoners must not survive under any circumstances.* A special flying S.S. court was organized, directed by S.S. official Walter Huppenkothen, who was instructed to process the *Abwehr* men and sentence them to death by hanging and arrange the executions immediately! The Huppenkothen death express command took care of the *Abwehr* prisoners in the concentration camps of Oranienburg and Buchenwald first and reached Flossenbürg on the 8 of April 1945.

After making the needed local arrangements through the camp administration, the *Abwehr* prisoners were called individually and condemned to death by Huppenkothen and his two killer assistants, reading a short formula to each of them. But they bypassed Josef Müller because his file had disappeared in the general confusion.

Canaris transmitted the information to Lunding when he returned. He was badly beaten up by the Gestapo bullies and barely able to drag himself back into his cell. Somebody had whispered to Canaris, while he was waiting his turn, that the Russians were almost at the Elbe and the Americans had reached Nuremberg already, only 100 miles South of Flossenbürg. Thus, even a short delay might be helpful for the prisoners. But, this remained a lost hope for most of them.

On the early morning of the 9 of April 1945, when it was still totally dark outside, Canaris and the four other *Abwehr* men were called, asked to strip themselves of all clothing and be ready totally naked within five minutes for the gallows.

They were led one after the other to the scaffold and then hanged singly with thin piano-wire, to lengthen their agony. These proceedings were filmed, to confirm to both Himmler and Hitler, that these gruesome murders had indeed taken place as ordered and the S.S. guards had complied with their instructions!

The naked bodies of the hanged men were tossed on a pile of other bodies, to be burnt later by a different bunch of S.S. guards, who did not even know who these dead men were, nor did they care in the least about it, doing their daily routine work as ordered!

Josef 'Oxen Sepp' Müller only realized what had taken place when shreds of burnt skin were blown into his cell by the wind. Müller fainted and collapsed, once this realization penetrated his mind.

When, only a few days later, American tanks and troops arrived in the area and reached the Flossenbürg concentration camp, sadly, very few of these 'important prisoners' were still alive to experience their liberation.

If it had not been for colonel Lunding and the incredibly lucky Josef 'Oxen Sepp' Müller, nobody would have been able to report these facts and to clarify the real events as they took place. The SS and the Nazis tried very hard to cover them up . . . even during the last weeks of this insane war and tried to eliminate all traces and any evidence of their murders.

Apart from these two officers, there were no others in the German navy directly or indirectly involved with the active and organized military or civilian opposition to the evil Hitler regime and its power structure.

While there was a small number of naval officers who had some marginal knowledge or limited information of some aspects of the military conspiracy they were not active participants. Geographic distances and operational assignments precluded it. Especially when they served aboard ships at sea or outside, Germany.

But, there exists no reliable evidence that Oskar Kusch had been one of these naval officers. Although, Kusch would have joined the conspirators I believe, if he had known of their efforts. Nevertheless, to face up to the brutal power of the firmly entrenched Nazi government and the military killing machine which was part of it, as a mere individual human being, is certainly highly admirable and required a tremendous amount of personal courage, a strong conviction and an enormous determination, combined with a personal belief that the truth must eventually win and come out on top regardless of the circumstances that prevailed at that time.

After some drawn-out struggles and extended arguments, it was finally possible to correct certain U-boat records where Oskar Kusch had simply been left out as the third commander of U-154.

On 27 September 1970 it was possible to reopen the U-boat Memorial in Möltenort-Heikendorf on the shore of the Kiel Fjord, which had been grossly run down during and after the war. The original set of bronze plates, featuring the numbers of lost U-boats and the names of their crew members who did not return with them, at that time still incomplete, listed 27,491 men.

In June 1978 records had been updated enough to permit the erection of additional bronze plates with 1,247 further individual names of U-boat men who died while their respective U-boats were not lost at sea, many from aircraft machine-gun attacks on surfaced U-boats. A revised total of 28,728 names were listed of U-boat men killed in the Second World War, although even that number was still deficient with respect to the actual number of those killed. After an awful lot of pressure, the name of Oskar Heinz Kusch was finally included among these individual additions, and it is now displayed on Plate 83.

A separate section of the U-boat Memorial is dedicated to the dead U-boat men of the First World War who remained at sea aboard the 199 U-boats lost between 1914 and 1918, on which another 4,744 U-boat men are listed.

I should like to point out that the U-boat Memorial was visited and studied by Maya Lin, the architect who later designed the remarkable Vietnam Memorial in Washington DC. Its layout was partially copied, with the full names and service grades of 58,193 dead American soldiers who did not return from Vietnam etched individually on those black marble plates. Naturally, the overall layout is somewhat different because of the much larger size of the Vietnam Memorial grounds in Washington, which calls for another kind of landscaping.

Just before Christmas 1990, after the complete collapse of the former Communist Eastern Germany, the so-called German Democratic Republic, and the reunification with Western Germany, I attended a convention with various seminars regarding future business possibilities in that region and in other former Communist Warsaw Pact countries.

Another participant in these meetings was Frank W. Petersen, who had become an international airline executive. We had previously met at other international business conferences in Asia, and became well acquainted over the years. There was always some free time after the official functions, and we ended up spending some of it together. Usually economic matters, business management problems and political outlooks were the subject of our conversations.

But now Petersen brought up the subject of Oskar Kusch's execution and the various investigations and court hearings resulting from it. He had received a tip that some type of report had been put together by a historical research group, headed by an officer of the Federal German Navy, who had been able to obtain a financial grant from some foundation for this undertaking. Eventually, the report was offered to the *Marine Forum* for publication, as already described at the beginning of this chapter.

As the subject interested me, Petersen furnished a whole batch of naval documents, copies of many legal and other related papers, and loaned me his own personal wartime diary, which provided a lot of additional information and quite a few supplementary facts, because Petersen had known Oskar Kusch in Lorient quite well.

Here was the starting point of this book, requiring years of time-consuming research, many visits to archives and quite a bit of travel to interview numerous sources in various countries. As it turned out, I had considerably underestimated the length of time necessary to turn this project into a readable book.

What sustained my curiosity and determination were the facts I discovered and ferreted out over the years, and my conviction that the truth must prevail, eventually, no matter how long and hard the fight happened to be to bring it to the surface.

As that raving reporter, Egon Erwin Kisch, said so rightly, 'Nothing is more exciting than the truth!' Unfortunately, it is often very deeply hidden. While Kurt Tucholsky observed, 'The truth is frequently so adventurous that it is at times not believed or accepted as either fact or the truth.' And yet, as stated by Morris West, 'You can't drive a stake through the heart of the truth, because it will just lie there waiting, even if buried, for the day of revelation and judgement.'

Epilogue

It turned out to be one of those great December mornings when the weather in Florida is simply at its best, pleasantly warm, a light breeze from the ocean and low air humidity. Moreover, the high winter-season rates would only start on 16 December, when the crowds of snowbirds and tourists arrived for the holidays. We had been out fishing in the Gulf Stream off Jupiter Inlet, and the catch had been worthwhile. Humming birds were fluttering along the blooming hibiscus hedges, while red cardinals, robins and finches looked for their breakfast on the lawn. The world seemed to be so incredibly peaceful that one could only wish that it would always be like this. But, as the saying goes, always is not for ever.

Being an early riser, I sipped my freshly squeezed orange juice before breakfast, waiting for my visiting friends, who were packing their suitcases. Twenty minutes later my contemplation of nature suddenly came to an end when they came bouncing onto the balcony, hungry for breakfast and eager to talk.

Tom started the conversation by stating, 'I remember a competent and successful intelligence service director who proceeded whenever possible this way: "The best camouflage and the most reliable cover is always the truth. Because nobody really believes it or accepts it as being true." '

Harry then told us that Eberhardt Godt had only recently passed away, after his 95th birthday, adding that he had also seen Hans Rudolf Rösing in Kiel a few weeks previously, still alive at 99.

And so, in no time at all, we were back on the Oskar Kusch execution with all its ramifications, which had been the subject of my research for more than ten years. Hopefully, the end was finally in sight. Nevertheless, a few minor details were still somewhat unclear, concerning the personal motives of certain principal players, because they had tried very hard to hide them with a blanket of secrecy and to cover themselves by the distortion of facts.

Then Tom raised a new but very interesting point of view, which certainly seemed to have a lot of merit and appeared logical as well as plausible, reporting this:

On 22 December 1894, the French Army Captain Alfred Dreyfus was sentenced by an army court martial to loss of his commission, reduction in rank to common soldier and exile for the rest of his life on Devil's Island, off the coast from French Guiana [Cayenne]. The military court of seven judges had followed the instruction of the French generals and complied with their demand to condemn Alfred Dreyfus as a traitor and spy for Germany.

But Dreyfus was completely innocent and had never been a traitor or spy for Germany. However, he was both an Alsatian and a Jew, which made him the patsy and target of certain cliques in the French Army. Dreyfus was convicted by means of bogus evidence and false statements under oath by people who personally hated him or wanted to get even and protect their own rear ends at the same time.

The sole evidence was a letter that had been sneaked out of the German embassy in Paris by the cleaning woman Marie Bastian, who was in the pay of the French secret service and, among other work, emptied the wastepaper baskets in the German embassy. Two officers stated that none other than the disliked Alfred Dreyfus could have been the originator of that letter offering information to the Germans. To add insult to injury, one of them hated Dreyfus because he had taken away his girl-friend. The other, Major Charles Walsin-Esterházy, was the actual writer of this letter and the man who sold military information to the Germans to pay off his gambling debts and cover his losses for speculating on the stock market.

When proof was later obtained that Walsin was the traitor, the French general staff organized another court martial to clear him and reaffirm the lies about Dreyfus. The military hierarchy could not tolerate being found to be wrong, making a mistake that almost killed an innocent man and did totally ruin him. Years later Dreyfus was pardoned by the civilian political circles, but he returned as a mental and bodily wreck from Devil's Island.

On 13 January 1898, the Dreyfus scandal became an enormous controversy when Emile Zola, already a well-known writer and holder of the French Légion d'honneur, heated up the situation with a rousing front-page editorial in the form of an open letter to the French president, Félix Faure, in the Parisian newspaper L'Aurore headlined 'J'accuse . . .', which publicized the Alfred Dreyfus scandal.

The French generals were furious and considered this accusation dangerous and traitorous. Zola had to flee to England during the night. He was condemned *in absentia* by a French military court to a prison term for his courage. However, Zola's passionate public appeal caused the terrible truth to become widely known. The French politicians later suspended Zolas's jail sentence and pardoned him, so that he could return to France. On 29 September 1902, Zola suffocated owing to the 'accidental' failure of his heating system. This was never cleared up, but everybody knew that the French Secret Service had arranged Zola's death on orders from the generals.

The French military rulers never acknowledged, much less rectified, this horrible injustice they had committed. The French civilian authorities pardoned Dreyfus in 1906, after a lot of political pressure, but the French military hierarchy have not admitted their criminal misjudgement to this very day. This remains a painful sore for many Frenchmen, but is typical of false French military pride and the French generals' stubborn refusal to face the truth.

Could it be that the German admirals in 1944 intended to imitate the Dreyfus decision and procedures? Might it be possible that they needed to demonstrate their own personal feelings of power and glory? Is it conceivable they wanted to compensate their inferiority complexes and insecurity with the Oskar Kusch naval court decision? Could his execution have been a cover-up for their own errors?

The dominating German Army establishment had never forgotten that the German Navy mutinied and revolted in 1918, and 'stabbed the German Army in the back'. The German Army blamed the German admirals for their failure to suppress the 'Red Mutiny' without mercy. Unquestionably, a strong motivation existed not only to emulate the French generals, but to go even a big step further than the French had, by executing Oskar Kusch.

Naturally, proving it now after all these years would be practically impossible, irrespective of how right this conclusion appeared to be. Tom agreed that that was the case, but the strong possibility ought to be seriously considered.

Harry then recalled the sailing of the Type IX-D-2 U-cruiser U-200, commanded by Lieutenant-Commander Heinrich 'Hein' Schonder, which departed from Kiel on 12 June 1943. U-200 had a special *Abwehr* sabotage team aboard, which was scheduled to land in South Africa and foment unrest, working with the *Brandvagt* anti-British Boer underground organization, and starting their activities by blowing up the naval dry dock in Durban, upon the direct orders of Karl Dönitz. 'Hein' Schonder had earned the Knight's Cross as commander of the Type VII-C U-77 in the North Atlantic and the Mediterranean. When the lines were pulled in, he shouted through his loud-hailer to his many waving friends on the pier: 'Fellows, never forget! There are only three kinds of people on this globe: the Living, the Dead, and the folk sailing the Seven Seas . . . eternally.' U-200 was sunk with all hands twelve days later, south-west of Iceland. But 'Hein' Schonder will never be forgotten by his friends as long as they live.

Tom raised the subject of the Nuremberg War Criminal Trials and the ten-year prison term in Spandau received by Karl Dönitz. Clearly, some sort of political compromise deal was largely responsible for his sentence. Evidently the Russians demanded the death penalty for him, while the American and British judges viewed the case somewhat differently, although certain political circles in England intended to punish Dönitz for the U-boat campaign, as a matter of principle.

For a long time, Dönitz was of no concern to the Russians, who regarded the sea war in the Atlantic as fairly unimportant to them. However, when he strongly opposed the evacuation of the German armies from the Baltic countries, Courland and East Prussia to protect the U-boat training areas in the Baltic, the Russians grew quite angry. And once he ordered the surviving German surface warships to employ their guns in extensive shore and coastal bombardments in the Baltic, they became furious, because these operations caused heavy Russian casualties and considerably delayed the forward movements of the Soviet armies.

Harry stated that Dönitz was made an example without much regard to the facts, on account of mainly political considerations. Harry felt strongly that Dönitz should have been sentenced and judged by a German court, instead, for his pitiless conduct of the U-boat war, causing useless sacrifices of the German U-boat crews, considering that the Admiral had firmly insisted upon the continuation of these hopeless operations that could not accomplish anything any more, but permitted the Nazi leadership to stay in power longer, pushing the resistance to the last man and the final bullet, leaving Germany wasted and in total collapse.

Tom pointed out the great contrast of the war's end in comparison with the First World War in 1918, when the leadership of Hindenburg and Ludendorff had forced Kaiser Wilhelm II out of power and arranged the Armistice in a responsible way, organizing the brilliant and orderly military retreat operation by the German armies from France and Belgium without any loss of men and material, to the amazement of the Allied Powers. However, they also preserved a German government, preventing any of the fighting within Germany and the complete chaos left behind by the Nazis in 1945, because of their fanatical idiocy, which Dönitz accepted and had strongly assisted to the very end.

I had to observe that no German court existed at that time that could have judged and sentenced Dönitz. Furthermore, the post-war events culminating in the Oskar Kusch retrial confirmed this, demonstrating that Dönitz would never have been condemned by any German court nor by any group of German judges, for his irresponsible orders, which needlessly sacrificed thousands of German U-boat men.

Then I emphasized that in times of political confusion and intentional political deception, with computerization and generalized record keeping, by far too many and frequently rather obscure government agencies, of everybody and almost everything, it is becoming even more important to remember that famous bumper sticker stating:

QUESTION AUTHORITY!

Moreover, there hardly prevailed any real difference between the Nazis and the Communists, it being a well-known fact that even more people were butchered, killed and starved to death by the Soviets under Lenin and Stalin than by the Nazis under Hitler; although the Nazis, because of Himmler, handled killings even more effectively.

There existed an influential 'socialistic' wing among the Nazis, with pure Communistic ideas and expectations. Furthermore, many former Communists joined the Nazi Party and in 1933 became the dominating group in the SA, the Storm Troopers. Later, many Nazis turned into Communists after 1945 and were very influential in the East German Communist regime.

In addition, many Communists cleverly camouflage themselves and use a variety of helpful covers, from acting as pure peace lovers to claiming that they suffer from persecution for their anti-fascistic activities, beliefs and schemes, while relentlessly pushing their ideas and plans, in spite of loud claims to the contrary by most left-wingers and many so-called intellectuals everywhere.

Both these types of political organization, movement and their followers were directed by fanatics and brutal, remorseless groups of functionaries, who were only interested in gaining absolute power over the general population to the exclusive advantage of their own party members. The main difference is that Russia is immensely huge and Germany is by comparison really quite small, though extremely over-organized by far too many government bureaucracies that are overstaffed and fight one another for more authority, territory, influence or turf.

Therefore, many things could be done in Russia that were practically impossible in Europe, in Germany, or in the USA, because of the geographical vastness, the customary Russian super-secretiveness, a considerable degree of illiteracy among the multi-ethnic and subdued population, a general lack of higher education, combined with limited communications, travel restrictions and the almost complete lack of a free, independent and critical press as political watchdog.

It is an unrealistic expectation, if not a total illusion, to think and believe that events in Russia have run their course and will turn into democratic developments. No matter what these new or reformed Communists state and promise, the situation remains quite dangerous and unpredictable; although at present it appears that the Chinese Communists are in the long run even more perilous, apart from the various Islamic sects and the religious fanatics of those types of group.

The morning had flown by as if it consisted only of minutes rather than hours. It was now time to take my visitors to Panama Hattie's for a leisurely luncheon before driving them to West Palm Beach airport for their return flights, and allow them a better meal than that served by the airlines these days. We managed to get a table overlooking the busy Inland Waterway, watching the continuous stream of different boats and yachts going by in both directions. After the delicious fresh grouper fillets had been served, our conversation resumed, as if it had never been interrupted.

Now we talked about what lessons the U-boat war could teach us; what we can learn from the experience gained at high cost and with tremendous effort during the Battle of the Atlantic. I pointed out that there was hardly any possibility that similar sea-war operations would repeat themselves, with such large numbers of ships and men engaged in them, because of the enormous expense of building atomic-driven submarines, which no country could afford to construct in the large numbers that Germany had done during the Second World War. Moreover, atomic-propelled submarines are generally a lot larger than those diesel-powered U-boats had been. Furthermore, they need a great deal of sea room to be able to operate, compared to those obsolete U-boats, and so they are unsuitable for pack or group operations in tightly positioned patrol lines.

Nevertheless, one should be able to learn something worthwhile from the 1939–45 U-boat war and some of the men involved in it, including those not covered by past reports and published books. Clearly there was a need for younger, more intelligent and more flexible admirals, and a far less rigid way of thinking and acting on their part. Many of these admirals were positioned too far away from the front lines, and most of them were too strongly influenced by bureaucratic directions and at times political interference. The majority preferred a traditional and conservative approach to naval operations, frequently out-moded by events and technical progress, and they often displayed hesitation toward untried solutions or new challenges, except under duress and as a last resort.

Besides, most reports, articles and books published in the past have been based on operations and men featured in official government releases. In my opinion, they are far too much centred on, and concentrated upon, such government sources, and the authors and writers usually emphasized what these sources liked to publicize for different reasons. In addition, a very heavy stress was placed on the excitement of combat operations, and the heroic firefight activities were often over-glamourized by all sides.

However, I think it is essential to cover regular and repetitive operations and unspectacular activities, which really constitute the great majority of organized undertakings in all military services in general and in sea-war operations in particular, especially when the normal human element became involved in them.

Therefore, I have tried to bring some of those types of so far unpublicized events and unknown men to light in a truthful way, although they might have been viewed as unimportant in the past, for a variety of reasons. I have done this because I feel it is essential and important to tell you about such events and men before the last participants and witnesses with personal experience of them depart on their final voyage.

Now it was time to drive my visitors to the airport to drop them off at the curb check-in of Delta Airlines. But the different problems and matters that we discussed kept churning around in my head for many hours afterwards, and I was unable to go to sleep, staying awake until late in the night thinking about the subjects and events we had talked about.

Lastly, I must tell you about a rather frequent experience I had in Germany while doing the extensive research for this book. Because this happened quite often, I decided to investigate the matter thoroughly, as I was constantly confronted with strong reservations, great reluctance and considerable hesitation on the part of many government officials and local politicians with respect to permitting me prompt access to historical records and old files. This happened with both men and women, most of them belonging to the so-called 1968 full-time demonstrator and protester generation of then quite young Germans, who never suffered in any way, form or fashion from the Second World War.

Many of them are involved in weird political activity groups, are very opinionated and have rather unrealistic ideas or slanted views of historic actuality and the truth. A lot of them are imbued with left-wing political leanings or peculiar socialistic equalization daydreams of wishful thinking. These people take great delight in throwing dirt on Germany's history, not limited to the gruesome Nazi period, and they even disdain their own fathers, grandfathers and other relatives, or, for that matter, any man who served in the German military forces, usually with little choice in the matter. They state that their own forefathers, who were soldiers in any capacity, were really murderers and nothing but common criminals. This is an attitude and belief quite incomprehensible and amazing to Americans, the British and other nationalities, who are quite puzzled or confused by it. To have to deal with and get any cooperation from these types of people is quite trying, and requires an extraordinary amount of patience.

But as the ancient Greeks realized, everybody has to find some way to be happy and content, no matter how peculiar it may appear to others.

Comparative Naval Ranks, 1939–1945

AMERICAN (US) NAVY	BRITISH ROYAL NAVY	GERMAN NAVY
FLEET ADMIRAL	ADMIRAL OF THE FLEET	GROSSADMIRAL
no equivalent	no equivalent	GENERALADMIRAL
ADMIRAL	ADMIRAL	ADMIRAL
VICE-ADMIRAL	VICE-ADMIRAL	VIZEADMIRAL
REAR ADMIRAL	REAR ADMIRAL	KONTERADMIRAL
COMMODORE	COMMODORE	KOMMODORE
Courtesy title only for a captain occupying a flag rank position:		
CAPTAIN	CAPTAIN	KAPITÄN zur See
COMMANDER	COMMANDER	FREGATTENKAPITÄN
LIEUTENANT-COMMANDER	LIEUTENANT-COMMANDER	KORVETTENKAPITÄN
LIEUTENANT	LIEUTENANT	KAPITÄNLEUTNANT
LIEUTENANT Junior Grade	SUBLIEUTENANT	OBERLEUTNANT zur SEE
ENSIGN	Junior SUBLIEUTENANT	LEUTNANT zur SEE
SENIOR MIDSHIPMAN	SENIOR MIDSHIPMAN	OBERFÄHNRICH zur SEE
MIDSHIPMAN	MIDSHIPMAN	FÄHNRICH zur SEE

Glossary of Naval Terms

To minimize repetition of information, irritating footnotes, tiresome explanations of similar or identical names and boring notes concerning equipment and technical matters, this glossary is provided for general reference purposes.

AAL (Eel) Naval slang or pet name for any type of torpedo.

AGRU-FRONT The technical training and testing group for U-boats. Also responsible for simulated emergency and combat exercises.

ASDIC British name for the original underwater sonar equipment already developed in 1917, but which was originally overrated because it was insufficiently tested. However, later substantially improved, and growing increasingly more effective during the Second World War.

ABWEHR The German intelligence-gathering and counter-intelligence service. While the name was assigned originally to a small military defence unit that protected military installations and objects against spying and sabotage by other countries, it grew into a large information-gathering organization that kept branching out into numerous activities, as the German armed forces increased by leaps and bounds. It also engaged eventually in active espionage undertakings and anything connected with communications and decoding work.

B-DIENST B-Service, the naval *Beobachtungsdienst*, meaning Observation Service. Actually the equivalent of the

British Y-Service. Watching radio signal waves to listen and record them carefully. Then interpreting same and, if possible, decoding and reading the intercepted messages and signals.

BdU

The commander (*Befehlshaber*) of U-boats, equivalent to Flag Officer of Submarine Forces. However, often colloquially used for the complete U-boat Command organization and structure.

CREW

German naval designation for a particular intake of naval officer candidates and cadets, entering naval service at the same time.

ENIGMA

The designation of the German signal coding and decoding machine used by all German military forces and later other organizations too. A mechanical-electrical cipher type of machine with various models. During the war, the German Navy used mainly the M-3 and M-4 versions of the Enigma machine.

FAT

A new type of torpedo (*Feder Apparat Torpedo*) that had special directional gear, which could be programmed to run on various courses, not only straight, but also in curves, circles or even in zigzag lines in order to find targets when fired blindly towards ships or into a convoy.

FdU

Leader-Director (*Führer*), the officer commanding U-boats until changed to BdU. Thereafter used for the regional commanders of combat U-boats: FdU Nordmeer (Barents Sea U-boat Commander), FdU Italy commander of U-boats in the Mediterranean Sea, FdU West, regional coordinator of U-boats in western France originally, later on in southern Norway, FdU Ost, commander of war service U-boats in the Baltic Sea not connected with school and training operations.

FuMB

The radio wave search detector or radar detection device. Frequently called Metox-Schwarzkopf observation equipment.

HF/DF

High-Frequency Direction-Finding equipment, colloquially called 'Huff-Duff'. An electronic device and apparatus to locate U-boats or any other radio signal originator by fixing such radio transmissions and obtaining their point of origination thereby, either automatically or manually by turning observation devices.

HSO A former merchant marine officer or captain holding such patents, a *Handels Schiffs Offizier*, accepted by the Navy as an officer candidate with accelerated promotion initially, based on age and experience.

IWO First (Senior) Watch Officer, the equivalent of an Executive Officer in the US Navy. In charge of torpedo firings and the non-technical crew members.

IIWO The Second (Junior) Watch Officer. While usually more junior and with less operational experience than the First Watch Officer, sometimes previous U-boat experience or combat experience was also taken into consideration. Thus, occasionally, the First Watch Officer would have less seniority but more U-boat combat experience than the Second Watch Officer.

IIIWO Third Watch Officer. Usually this position was filled by a senior petty officer/warrant officer who at the same time was the navigator of the U-boat and leading the third watch on the bridge. From 1944 onwards, sometimes a third officer was assigned to this position as additional (Z for *Zusatz*) watch officer because navigation became more difficult and time-consuming once U-boats operated mostly dived and using the snorkel. Likewise, on the long and demanding voyages to the East Asian bases, an extra officer was appointed for rotation and in case of sickness problems.

KdK The super-secret command of small battle forces (*Kommando der Kleinkampfverbände*). This was a command where mainly young volunteers were trained in the use of new weapons such as one-man torpedoes; various types of frogman and their equipment; explosive-loaded, close-approach motorboats; and various types of mini-submarine. The best of them was the Seal (*Seehund*), operating with two men, rather than one man only, as the various one-man submarines were technically and operationally unsatisfactory when tested. Sometimes referred to as Kamikaze Operational Command.

KONFIRMAND An understudy commander, i.e. a commander in training, without previous U-boat experience, expected to learn from the actual commander in charge. This often applied in the case of comparatively senior officers transferred into the U-boat Command from other naval commands, or officers who had previously served in naval aviation.

KTB

War Patrol Journal (*Kriegs Tagebuch*). The operational diary.

LI

Chief Engineering Officer or Directing Engineer (*Leitender Ingenieur*) in charge of both the technical people and the entire machinery and equipment concerning maintenance and operational readiness.

LORDS

Colloquial name for the enlisted men. Sometimes called People, instead.

LUT

A supplementary piece of equipment that would be attached to the electrical torpedoes in order to allow firing from any angle and without having to aim directly at any target or having to work out and calculate a firing approach solution. Could be programmed for a variety of figures to cover all possibilities. An improved development of the FAT.

MARINE HJ

Naval Hitler Youth. A section of the general Hitler Youth, taking in boys from 14 to 18 years of age. They worked with different types of boat, including sailing boats, and engaged in water sport activities. Used for pre-military training.

NID

British Naval Intelligence Division

OKM

German Naval Supreme or High Command in Berlin (*Oberkommando [der] [Kriegs] Marine*). Also included the entire naval ministry administration.

ONI

American Office of Naval Intelligence in Washington DC, with branches elsewhere as required.

Op-16-Z

Sub-department within ONI of the Special Activity Branch of the American Navy, handling the interrogation and evaluation of both prisoners of war and also captured equipment. Not informed about, or in receipt of, Ultra decoded material and specifics. Therefore, considerable duplication of effort was often involved.

PK Mann

Propaganda Company Man assigned to special units, working mostly in the field as war reporters, recorders and photographers. Most men drafted for these companies were reservists and in peacetime were employed by newspapers, magazines or the governmental radio station network. There were also photographers, painters, sculptors and advertising men. They were assigned by naval specialists in Berlin and by Nazi-directed regional managers to make sure that the output fitted the expectations of the Naval High Command.

PoW   Prisoner of War

RAF   Britain's Royal Air Force. Divided into several sub-commands, such as Coastal Command, Fighter Command, Bomber Command, Training Command, etc.

RITTERKREUZ   The higher Knight's Cross version of the Iron Cross, the latter being awarded only as Second and First Class, while for the Knight's Cross three superior steps existed: the Oakleaves Cluster, the Crossed Swords to the Knight's Cross and the Diamond Clasp.

S-BOATS   (*Schnellboote*) The German equivalent to PT Boats or MTB Boats. Literally 'Very Fast Boats', used primarily as torpedo-attack boats, but they could carry a number of mines if torpedoes were removed and spare torpedoes were left in port. They had special equipment to create artificial fog to hide themselves and permit a closer approach to targets.

SNORKEL   An elevated tube (*Schnorchel*) that could be raised and lowered in the later versions, and extended from U-boats above the water's surface when they moved under water, in order to pull in fresh air and expel the exhaust of the diesel engines, which could then be used for underwater travel, in place of the electric motors. Running the diesel engines under water recharged the batteries and kept them fully charged. Exhaust problems, smoke and smelly air inside the submarine often caused breathing difficulties and health complications when the snorkel equipment was used for extended periods of time.

U-BOOT WAFFE   The entire U-boat combat force, including the support, schooling, training and operating units and forces. Usually used to refer in general terms to anything connected with the U-boat Command structure.

ULTRA   The British, and later also the American, codename for all information obtained by decoding, reading and interpreting the German Enigma machine radio signals of all circuits. Used both for furnishing such secret information to specific key people or commands and to transmit decoded information to particular units or commands for tactical or operational instructions, directions and attack orders.

UZO   *Überwasser Ziel Optik*, the aiming device and torpedo-firing equipment for surface torpedo attacks handled by the Executive Officer, with automatic transmission of ascertained or estimated target calculations into the torpedoes, before firing them.

WABO (S)   Usual name for depth-charges dropped by ships or aeroplanes on U-boats or dropped by German ships or aeroplanes in anti-submarine attacks on submarines. A contraction of *Wasserbomben*, literally water-bombs, but actually underwater bombs.

WI   *Wach Ingenieur*. A second or third engineering officer, a watch officer of the engineering branch who was assigned as training subject to the directing engineer, to take over his position later or to be appointed as directing engineer on another U-boat or ship, once he had acquired sufficient practical and operational experience. On the very long U-cruiser or supply-boat operations to and from the ports in south-east Asia, WIs were additionally assigned because of the length of such patrols and the tremendous demands upon the LI, when competent assistance was essential, or as sickness replacements.

WINTERGARTEN   The rear section of the U-boat's bridge or tower, where the anti-aircraft guns were mounted. Starting in 1943, there was a second aft section added to place further anti-aircraft guns there, while the regular guns were removed in turn as a weight-saving measure, because artillery attacks had become almost impossible to make by that time.

ZAUNKÖNIG   The camouflage name for the T-5 acoustic torpedo, meaning 'Wren', the tiny bird. They were first used in September 1943, and were a faster and improved version of the original T-4, known as *Falke* (Falcon), for camouflage. The T-4 was too slow and unsatisfactory in the heavy seas of the Atlantic. The T-5 was insufficiently tested, had technical bugs and responded to the U-boat's own engine noises. Consequently observation of results was impossible, which often led to overestimation of successes. The effective use of these acoustic torpedoes was countered by noisemakers dragged behind ships, like the Foxer. The final improved version was called T-11.

ZENTRALE	The Central control-room section of the U-boat where the control boards, valves and all measuring devices were concentrated. The battle station of the LI, the Directing Engineer, the Navigator and the most experienced men aboard.

Select Bibliography

Abbazia, Patrick, *Mr Roosevelt's War*, Naval Institute Press, Annapolis, Maryland, 1975

Beesly, Patrick, *Very Special Intelligence*, Hamish Hamilton, London, 1977

Beesly, Patrick, *Room 40, British Naval Intelligence*, Hamish Hamilton, London, 1982

Buchheim, Lothar G., *The Boat*, Alfred A. Knopf, New York, 1975

Buchheim, Lothar G., *U-Boat War, a unique picture report*, Alfred A. Knopf, New York, 1978

Cremer, Peter E., *U-Boat Commander U-333*, Naval Institute Press, Annapolis, Maryland, 1984

Dorian, James G., *Storming Saint Nazaire, The 1942 Commando Raid*, Naval Institute Press, Annapolis, Maryland, 1998

Gannon, Michael, *Black May (1943)*, HarperCollins, New York, 1998

James, Sir William, *The Eyes of the Navy*, Methuen & Co., London, 1955

James, Sir William, *The Most Formidable Thing*, Hart-Davies, London, 1965

Kahn, David, *Seizing the Enigma*, Houghton Mifflin Co., Boston, Mass., 1991

McLachlan, Donald, *Room 39, Naval Intelligence in Action During the Second World War*, Weidenfeld & Nicolson, London, 1968

Martienssen, Anthony, *Hitler and His Admirals*, Secker & Warburg, London, 1948

Martienssen, Anthony, *Fuehrer Conferences on Naval Affairs, 1939–1945*, Greenhill Books, London, 1990 (updated reprint)

Mulligan, Timothy P., *Lone Wolf, The Life and Death of U-Boat Ace Werner Henke*, University of Oklahoma Press, Norman, Oklahoma, 1992

Padfield, Peter, *Doenitz, the Last Fuehrer*, Victor Gollancz, London, 1984

Padfield, Peter, *War Beneath the Sea*, John Wiley, New York, 1995

Rohwer, Jürgen, *Axis Submarine Successes, 1939–1945*, Naval Institute Press, Annapolis, Maryland, 1999

Rohwer, Jürgen and Hümmelchen, Gerhard, *Chronology of the War at Sea 1939–1945*, Naval Institute Press, Annapolis, Maryland, 1999

Roskill, Stephen W., *Churchill and the Admirals*, William Collins & Sons, London, 1977

Scalia, Joseph M., *Germany's Last Mission to Japan, U-234*, Naval Institute Press, Annapolis, Maryland, 2000

Tarrant, V. E., *The U-Boat Offensive, 1914–1945*, Naval Institute Press, Annapolis, Maryland, 1989

Terraine, John, *The U-Boat Wars, 1914–1945, Business in Great Waters*, G. P. Putnam's Sons, New York, 1989

Tuchman, Barbara W., *The March of Folly*, Alfred A. Knopf, New York, 1984

Van Der Vat, Dan, *The Atlantic Campaign, 1939–1945*, Harper & Row, New York, 1988

Vause, Jordan A., *Wolf, U-Boat Commander Portraits*, Naval Institute Press, Annapolis, Maryland, 1997

Werner, Herbert A., *Iron Coffins*, Holt, Rinehart & Winston, New York, 1969

Witthingham, Richard, *Martial Justice on Prisoners of War, the last mass execution in the United States*, Naval Institute Press, Annapolis, Maryland, 1997

Winterbotham, Frederick W., *The Ultra Secret*, Weidenfeld & Nicolson, London, 1974

Wouk, Herman, *The Caine Mutiny*, Little, Brown and Company (Time Warner Inc.), Boston, Mass. and New York, 1968

Y'blood, William T., *Hunter-Killer, Escort carrier group operations in the Atlantic*, Naval Institute Press, Annapolis, Maryland, 1988

Index